Lu Xun and World Literature

Lu Xun and World Literature

Edited by Xiaolu Ma and Carlos Rojas

Hong Kong University Press
The University of Hong Kong
Pok Fu Lam Road
Hong Kong
https://hkupress.hku.hk

© 2025 Hong Kong University Press

ISBN 978-988-8876-80-8 (*Hardback*)

All rights reserved. No portion of this publication may be reproduced or transmitted in any form or by any means, electronic or mechanical, including photocopying, recording, or any information storage or retrieval system, without prior permission in writing from the publisher.

British Library Cataloguing-in-Publication Data
A catalogue record for this book is available from the British Library.

Digitally printed

Contents

List of Figures and Table	vii
Note on Sources	viii
List of Contributors	ix
Preface	xiii
Carlos Rojas	
Introduction: Lu Xun, China, and the World	1
Xiaolu Ma	

Part 1: Lu Xun and the World

1. Lu Xun, World Poetry, and Poetic Worlding: From Mara Poetry to Revolutionary Literature   19
   Pu Wang

2. The Young Lu Xun and *Weltliteratur*: The Making of *Anthology of Short Stories from beyond the Border*   33
   Wendong Cui

3. Lu Xun's Russian Intertexts and the Dialectics of Optimism and Pessimism   49
   Keru Cai

4. What Happens after a Text Leaves Home? Lu Xun, Ibsen, and Ichiyō   65
   Satoru Hashimoto

5. Guarded Pages, Borderless Books: Lu Xun and the Revolution of the Book in Modern China   83
   Xiaoyu Xia

Part 2: Lu Xun into the World

6. (Geo)politics of Aesthetics: Transculturation of Lu Xun in Korea   101
   Shijung Kim

7. Belated Reception and Residual Influence: Lu Xun and Spain   117
   Carles Prado-Fonts

vi   Contents

8. Penitence, Mercy, and Conversion: Lu Xun as a Topos of World
    Literature   131
    Xiaolu Ma

9. Ghostwriting the Subalterns: Rereading Ah Q through Wong Bik-wan's
    Lielaozhuan   146
    Wayne C. F. Yeung

10. "Each of Them Is a Lu Xun": Lu Xun's Virtual Children in Southeast Asia   163
    Carlos Rojas

Part 3: Lu Xun and Worlding

11. Structure of Suspicion: Body, Time, and the Worlding of
    Nontranscendence in Lu Xun's and Guo Moruo's Fiction on Laozi   179
    Kun Qian

12. Beyond Oneself: Writing and Effacement in *Wild Grass* and *Morning
    Blossoms Gathered at Dusk*   195
    Eileen J. Cheng

13. The Severe Style: Law, Irony, and the Absolute in Lu Xun   210
    Roy Chan

14. Lu Xun, Nonhumans, and the Critique of Domination   226
    Christopher K. Tong

Postface   239
    Carlos Rojas

Appendix: Chinese Characters of Lu Xun's Names, Pen Names, and
Work Titles Cited in This Volume   243

Bibliography   249

Index   279

List of Figures and Table

Figures

Figure 0.1: Detail from Lu Xun's Chinese translation of Gogol's *Dead Souls*   xviii

Figure 2.1: Cover of *Aus fremden Zungen*'s special volume, on "Novellen, Erzählungen, Skizzen des Auslands"   41

Figure 2.2: Cover of Lu Xun's *Anthology of Fiction from beyond the Border*   41

Figure 2.3: Image from 1905 volume of *Aus fremden Zungen*   41

Figure 5.1: Cover of Natsume Sōseki's *I Am a Cat*   86

Figure 5.2: Cover of Lu Xun's *Anthology of Fiction from beyond the Border*   89

Figure 12.1: *Morning Blossoms Gathered at Dusk (1928)*. Cover Design by Tao Yuanqing (1893–1929).   198

Figure 12.2: *Wild Grass* (1927). Cover design by Lu Xun.   201

Figure 12.3: Illustration by Lu Xun, from the essay collection *Graves* (1929)   202

Figure 15.1: Death mask of Lu Xun, cast in plaster by Okuda Koka   240

Table

Table 2.1: The titles translated or selected by Lu Xun and their German sources   44

Note on Sources

In this volume, we use an abbreviated citation format (author, abbreviated title, page numbers) with full bibliographic information appearing in the bibliography. We also provide Chinese characters for Chinese authors and titles when they are cited in a chapter's main text, with exception of works by Lu Xun himself. Instead, all of Lu Xun's works are cited simply in English translation. Readers desiring more information about specific works may consult the appendix, which contains a list of all of Lu Xun's works cited in this volume, arranged chronologically, and another list of the same works, arranged alphabetically by the work's English title. Readers can consult the first list to confirm a work's original publication date and the title and date of the volume in which the work was first anthologized, and they can consult the second list to confirm the correspondence between the English and Chinese titles of those same works.

Contributors

Keru Cai is lecturer in Chinese studies in the School of Modern Languages at the University of St Andrews. She works on modern Chinese appropriations from Russian, English, and French literatures. Her first book project, *From Russia, with Squalor: Poverty in Modern Chinese Realism*, will show how Chinese intellectuals drew on Russian literature to write about poverty in a bid to enrich Chinese culture by creating a syncretic new realism. She has articles published or forthcoming in journals such as *Modern Language Quarterly, Comparative Literature, Modern Chinese Literature and Culture, Prism: Theory and Modern Chinese Literature,* and *Chinese Literature: Essays, Articles, and Reviews.* Prior to joining St Andrews, she was assistant professor at Penn State University and Fellow by Examination at Magdalen College, University of Oxford.

Roy Chan is associate professor of Chinese at the University of Oregon. His research interests are modern Chinese and Russian literatures. His recent work engages Chinese and Russian/Soviet aesthetics and their relationship to modern philosophy. His book, *The Edge of Knowing: Dreams, History, and Realism in Modern Chinese Literature,* was published in 2017.

Eileen J. Cheng is professor of Chinese in the Department Asian Languages and Literatures and faculty director of the Oldenborg Center for Modern Languages and International Relations at Pomona College. She has published extensively on Lu Xun. Her publications include a translation of Lu Xun's experimental essays and memoir *Wild Grass & Morning Blossoms Gathered at Dusk* (Harvard University Press, 2022), a coedited volume of translations of his polemical essays, *Jottings under Lamplight* (Harvard University Press, 2017), and the monograph *Literary Remains: Death, Trauma, and Lu Xun's Refusal to Mourn* (University of Hawai'i Press, 2013).

Wendong Cui serves as an assistant professor in the Department of Chinese Language and Literature at the Chinese University of Hong Kong. Specializing in modern Chinese literature, he has a specific focus on notable writers such as Liang

x   Contributors

Qichao and Lu Xun. Wendong earned his PhD from the Chinese University of Hong Kong and subsequently served as a visiting fellow at the Harvard-Yenching Institute. His research articles have been published in journals such as *Literary Review, Journal of Chinese Studies*, and *Bulletin of the Institute of Chinese Literature and Philosophy*. Wendong is honored to have received the Stephen C. Soong Translation Studies Memorial Awards on two occasions.

Satoru Hashimoto is assistant professor of comparative thought and literature at the Johns Hopkins University. His research explores interplays between East Asian and Western literatures and intellectual histories at the intersections of aesthetics, ethics, and politics. He is the author of *Afterlives of Letters: The Transnational Origins of Modern Literature in China, Japan, and Korea* (Columbia University Press, 2023). He serves as a series co-editor of Brill's East Asian Comparative Literature and Culture.

Shijung Kim is a PhD candidate in the Department of Comparative Literature at Harvard University and the Sorbonne Nouvelle (Paris 3). Her research mainly focuses on Franco-Chinese and Franco-Korean encounters in arts and letters during the twentieth and twenty-first centuries, but she also maintains an interest in Korean-Chinese encounters in arts and letters during the twentieth century. Her dissertation project, tentatively titled "Becoming-China: A Sinography of Twentieth-Century French Letters," examines moments of significant change in meanings of Chineseness mostly in the sphere of French literature during the eponymous period, and she recently published a blog post titled *Finding "Small Health" in Lu Xun's Translation Practices*.

Xiaolu Ma is assistant professor in the Division of Humanities at Hong Kong University of Science and Technology. She engages in research in the interrelationship of trans-Eurasian literature and culture in the nineteenth and twentieth centuries. She is the author of *Transpatial Modernity: Chinese Cultural Encounters with Russia via Japan (1880–1930)* (Harvard University Asia Center, 2024). Her research articles have been published or are forthcoming in peer-reviewed journals, including *JAS, PMLA, Comparative Literature Studies, Modern Chinese Literature and Culture*, and *Twentieth-Century China*, among others.

Carles Prado-Fonts is professor in the Department of Arts and Humanities at the Universitat Oberta de Catalunya. He works on comparative studies with a particular focus on Chinese and sinophone literatures and cultures. He is the author of *Regresar a China* (Trotta, 2019; winner of the 2021 International Convention of Asian Scholars Book Prize) and *Secondhand China: Spain, the East, and the Politics of Translation* (Northwestern University Press, 2022). He has also translated into

Catalan and Spanish language Chinese authors and intellectuals such as Lu Xun, Lin Huiyin, Mo Yan, Dai Jinhua, and Wang Hui.

Kun Qian is associate professor of Chinese literature and film at the University of Pittsburgh. She is the author of *Imperial-Time-Order: Literature, Intellectual History, and China's Road to Empire* (2016) and assistant director of the oral history–based documentary *The Revolution They Remember* (2020), a film on the Chinese Cultural Revolution. Her publications have covered a variety of topics ranging from traumatic memory, representation of empire, time image, to ecocinema. Her current research deals with the discourse of economics and the portrayal of desire in modern China. She is also working on a collaborative project on artificial intelligence and digital privacy.

Carlos Rojas is professor of Chinese cultural studies at Duke University. He works on modern and contemporary cultural production from China and the global Chinese diaspora. He is the author, editor, and translator of many books, including *Homesickness: Culture, Contagion, and National Transformation in Modern China.*

Christopher K. Tong is a tenured professor specializing in Asian studies at the University of Maryland in Baltimore County near Washington, DC. He was educated at Stanford University and the University of California, Davis and completed a postdoctoral fellowship at Washington University in St. Louis. His upcoming book from Oxford University Press analyzes the emergence of modern science and ecological consciousness in Chinese and Western societies. He has been recognized as a Fulbright Scholar, a China Studies Fellow by the American Council of Learned Societies, a William S. Willis Jr. Fellow by the American Philosophical Society, and a Marjorie Harding Memorial Fellow by the Thoreau Society.

Pu Wang, poet, translator, and scholar, is currently associate professor of Chinese literature and chair of Comparative Literature at Brandeis University. His monograph, *The Translatability of Revolution: Guo Moruo and Twentieth-Century Chinese Culture*, was published in 2018. His collection of critical essays on modern poetry is forthcoming in Chinese.

Xiaoyu Xia will be joining the Department of East Asian Studies at Princeton as assistant professor of modern Chinese literature in Fall 2025. She is currently a Costen Postdoctoral Fellow at Princeton University. Her research spans modern Chinese literature, cinema, and media, translation studies, and book history. Her academic work has appeared in venues including *Modern Chinese Literature and Culture* and *Chinese Literature: Essays, Articles, Reviews.*

xii   Contributors

Wayne C. F. Yeung is an assistant professor at the University of Denver. His research interests include modern to contemporary sinophone and francophone literature, as well as the culture of social movements. His publications include "Poetics of the People: The Politics of Debating Local Identity in Hong Kong's Umbrella Movement and Its Literature (2014–16)" (*Modern Asian Studies*, 2021), "The Concept of the Cantophone: Memorandum for a Stateless Literary History" (*Sino-Platonic Papers*, 2023), and "Deep Imperial Time in Sinophone Poetics of History" (*Journal of Asian Studies*, 2024).

Preface

Carlos Rojas

Two of the earliest publications by the author now known as Lu Xun were produced in 1903, shortly after the twenty-two-year-old arrived in Japan with the intent to study medicine. Evidently taking inspiration from Chen Shoupeng and Xue Shaohui's Chinese translation of Jules Verne's *Around the World in Eighty Days*, the aspiring medical student tackled two of Verne's earlier science fiction works: *From the Earth to the Moon* and two chapters of *Voyage to the Center of the Earth*.[1] Although Chen and Xue had retranslated *Around the World in Eighty Days* from an English version of Verne's novel, Lu Xun, who did not read English, instead relied on Inoue Tsutomu's Japanese retranslations of English translations of Verne's original French texts. The resulting Chinese texts diverged significantly from the originals, not only because of inevitable slippages resulting from this process of multiply mediated relay translation but also because Lu Xun took considerable liberties in adapting the novels for a local Chinese audience. Speaking of one of the texts, Lu Xun later remarked, "Even though I called this a translation, it was actually a transformation" (雖說譯，其實乃是改作).

The 1903 translation of *From the Earth to the Moon* was published under the pen name Zhou Chuo, while the first two chapters of the translation of *Voyage to the Center of the Earth* were published under the pen name Zhijiangsuozi (though when a more complete translation of the novel was released three years later, it was instead published under the pen name to Zhijiangsuoshi). Zhou Chuo, Zhijiangsuozi, and Zhijiangsuoshi are just three of the hundred-plus pen names Lu Xun used over the course of his lifetime. The author's birth name was Zhou Zhangshou, and his courtesy names were Yushan and Yuting, which he later changed to Yucai. In 1898, he adopted the name Zhou Shuren, which is now commonly identified as his real name,

---

1. Lu Xun published translations of *From the Earth to the Moon* and the first two chapters of *Voyage to the Center of the Earth* in 1903, and he released a more complete translation of the latter work in 1906. Curiously, however, he misidentified the original author of both novels, claiming that *From the Earth to the Moon* had been written by an American author while *Journey to the Center of the Earth* had been written by a British author.

xiv Preface

and he did not use the pen name Lu Xun until the 1918 publication of "Diary of a Madman." To the extent that Lu Xun's persona is currently the author's public face, accordingly, his early translations of Verne's novels and other works could be viewed as part of his "pre-face"—part of the literary work that he produced before becoming the iconic figure that he has now become. Even during this early prefatory period of his literary career, however, we can find an anticipation of some of the characteristics that would come to define his overall oeuvre and particularly his interest in processes of translation and textual transformation.

To begin with, although Lu Xun is currently best known as an author and essayist, translation is a practice to which he remained committed throughout his adult life. While his approach ranged from a process of loose translation (a "domesticating" approach that creatively transforms the source text for the benefit of the target audience) to his later emphasis on what he called "hard translation" (a "foreignizing" approach that attempts to preserve as much of the syntax of the source text as possible), his interest in translation reflects his commitment to introducing foreign literary works into the Chinese literary sphere. Although Lu Xun translated literary works from many different nations, with approximately half of his total translations being of works originally written in Russian, he frequently had to rely on intermediary translations of the original works when producing his own Chinese versions, given that Japanese and German were the only foreign languages he knew well.

Even as Lu Xun remained actively involved in translating foreign literature into Chinese, translations of his own Chinese-language works into foreign languages began to appear as early as the mid-1920s, only a few years after Lu Xun began publishing original fiction. For instance, the first English rendering of one of Lu Xun's fictional works was George Kin Leung's 1926 translation of Lu Xun's 1921 story "The True Story of Ah Q," and Jing Yinyu completed a French translation of the story that same year. The 1915 Nobel laureate Romain Rolland wrote a letter in support of the latter translation, in which he observed that "at first glance this story is an unremarkable work of realism. However, then you discover the sharp humor contained in it. After reading it, you surprisingly feel that this tragic and comic fellow won't leave you. You can't bear to part with him." Rolland's original text was later found in his posthumous manuscripts, but his comments initially circulated primarily through a series of mediated translations and paraphrases, such as when the French translator Jin Yinyu himself claimed that Jing had proclaimed that "the story of Ah Q is a superb work of art, the proof being that I felt it was even better on the second reading." This sort of loose translation of Rolland's original assessment that may have contributed to Lu Xun being considered for the Nobel Prize in literature in 1927—although when fellow author Liu Bannong and Swedish Academy member Sven Hedin reached out to Lu Xun to inform him that he was being considered for the prize, Lu Xun reportedly responded that he felt that "China still really has no person who should receive the Nobel Prize," and consequently declined to be considered for the award.[2]

In her study *The World Republic of Letters*, Pascale Casanova argues that works' inclusion into the category of world literature is predicated on a process of vetting and validation by prestigious literary institutions based primarily in the West, which thereby grant literary works the symbolic capital necessary to be recognized a transnational sphere.[3] Lu Xun's consideration for the Nobel Prize may be viewed an early example of this process of institutional validation, a similarly symbolic moment in Lu Xun's entry into the world literature pantheon occurred in 2009, when he became the first modern author to be included in the Penguin Classics series with the publication of Julia Lovell's retranslation of Lu Xun's complete fiction in *The Real Story of Ah-Q and Other Tales of China: The Complete Fiction of Lu Xun*.[4] Before the publication of the Penguin Classics volume, the most influential English-language versions of Lu Xun's works were the ones completed in the 1950s by the husband-and-wife team Yang Xianyi and Gladys Yang. Whereas the Yangs' mid-century translation was part of a China-driven project to introduce Chinese literature to a global audience, the Penguin Classics project instead reflects an inverse process wherein Lu Xun's work has increasingly come to be embraced by literary institutions based in the West.

Discussions of world literature are informed by considerations not only of works' global circulation and reception but also of how the world itself is perceived and imagined. Unlike Verne's *Around the World in Eighty Days*, which describes a realistic voyage through the contemporary world, both *From the Earth to the Moon* and *Voyage to the Center of the Earth* featured journeys to sites far removed from the planet's surface. In adopting this sort of otherworldly perspective, both works offer a fresh perspective on issues relating to the world at that time. In this respect, Lu Xun's decision to translate these two works of science fiction reflects his early interest in processes of worldmaking and worlding, whereby literary works permit readers to view and imagine the world otherwise.

---

2. The preceding three quotes are all cited in Paul Foster, "The Ironic Inflation of Chinese National Character."

3. Pascale Casanova, *The World Republic of Letters*.

4. Although Lu Xun was the first modern Chinese author to be included in the Penguin "Black Classics" subseries (the name alludes to the fact that all the volumes in the series have black covers), which includes "works written up to the beginning of the 20th century"), the subseries does contain several premodern Chinese works such as the *Daodejing* and *Dream of the Red Chamber*. The press's parallel "Modern Classics" subseries, which includes "an ever-evolving list of books from the 20th- and 21st centuries that have achieved classic status," features several works by two other Chinese-language authors (Eileen Chang and Qian Zhongshu), https://www.penguin.co.uk/company/publishers/penguin-press/penguin-classics.

In addition to his translations of foreign literary works into Chinese, Lu Xun also produced many "virtual" translations in which he incorporated elements from other literary works into his own. This practice is perhaps most obvious in his 1935 story collection, *Old Tales Retold*, which consists of eight works that each retells different Chinese myth or legend, but even his first work of fiction, the 1918 story "Diary of a Madman," draws on Nikolai Gogol's homonymous 1835 story, which Lu Xun had read in Japanese and which his brother Zhou Zuoren translated into Chinese five years later. One of Lu Xun's best-known and most influential works, "Diary of a Madman," follows the lead of Gogol's earlier story in adopting the first-person perspective of a narrator who has apparently gone insane, but Lu Xun adds an external frame in the form of a preface that describes how a friend of the madman had found the (fictional) diary and decided to preserve it for medical research. In this way, Lu Xun's work affirms its indebtedness to Gogol's precedent, while simultaneously illustrating the way that texts can be reappropriated for divergent purposes.

Like Lu Xun, Gogol specialized in writing short stories, but in 1835, the same year he published his original "Diary of a Madman," Gogol began working on his first full-length novel, *Dead Souls*. The work's protagonist, Pavel Ivanovich Chichikov, travels through Russia visiting the estates of Russian landowners to purchase administrative responsibility for the serfs who have died since the last census but who remained on the tax ledgers—with the idea being that he would then cover the residual tax liability resulting from the deceased serfs while simultaneously mortgaging the (virtual) peasants to raise funds to purchase his own estate. Gogol had originally planned to write the novel as a trilogy, but after publishing the first volume in 1842, he never managed to complete the other two. Shortly before his death in 1852, Gogol burned most of what he had completed of volume 2, and only portions of the first four chapters of volume 2 ended up being preserved for posterity.

Meanwhile, in 1935, precisely a century after Gogol began working on his novel, Lu Xun began translating the novel into Chinese. At the time Lu Xun began his project, there was already a Chinese translation based on an English version of the work, but Lu Xun had read a German-language version and noticed many discrepancies between the two translations. He therefore resolved to retranslate the novel into Chinese, based on German and Japanese translations of the Russian-language work. Lu Xun serialized the translation of the first volume of the novel in two different literary magazines but was eventually forced to discontinue the serialization, and when he passed away in October 1936, his own translation of Gogol's incomplete novel was itself still incomplete.

Throughout most of his career, Lu Xun did not grant much importance to his original manuscripts, and consequently many of those texts are no longer extant. In 1936, however, as he was reviewing the proofs for his translation of volume 1 of *Dead Souls*, he noticed numerous typographical errors and asked that the press return his handwritten manuscript so that he could double-check it against the printed version. The five-hundred-plus-page manuscript—which includes Lu Xun's translation of volume 1 and the first three chapters of volume 2 and is filled with his own handwritten emendations and corrections—was still in the author's possession when he passed away and has subsequently been published in manuscript form. Like Gogol's original text, the final chapter of Lu Xun's manuscript literally ends on an ellipsis, and it is immediately followed by a brief translator's note on the original text. The first line of the note specifies that Gogol began writing the novel in 1835, but in the manuscript version of the text Lu Xun accidentally miswrote the year 1835 as 1935—inadvertently substituting the year that Gogol began working on the original text with the year, a century later, that Lu Xun himself began working on the translation, perhaps suggesting that Lu Xun was unconsciously conflating his process of translation with Gogol's original process of literary creation (Figure 0.1).[5]

The happenstance that Lu Xun was completing a translation of *Dead Souls* when he died is fitting, not only because the novel itself is literally about death but also because the entire premise of Gogol's novel offers a compelling metaphor for Lu Xun's own postmortem legacy. That is to say, Chichikov's attempts to purchase the administrative rights to dead serfs in order to derive a speculative value from those same "dead souls" directly mirrors the ways in which generations of scholars, publishers, politicians, and general readers have attempted to lay claim to different portions of Lu Xun's legacy for the sake of a resulting set of symbolic benefits. Lu Xun's postmortem legacy, in other words, can be viewed as a continual process of translation and transformation, of translation *as* transformation. In this way, the focus on translation that dominated his initial pre-face has come to characterize the public face of his entire literary oeuvre and its legacy.

5.　Beijing, *Lu Xun yi* Si Hunling, vol. 5, 513.

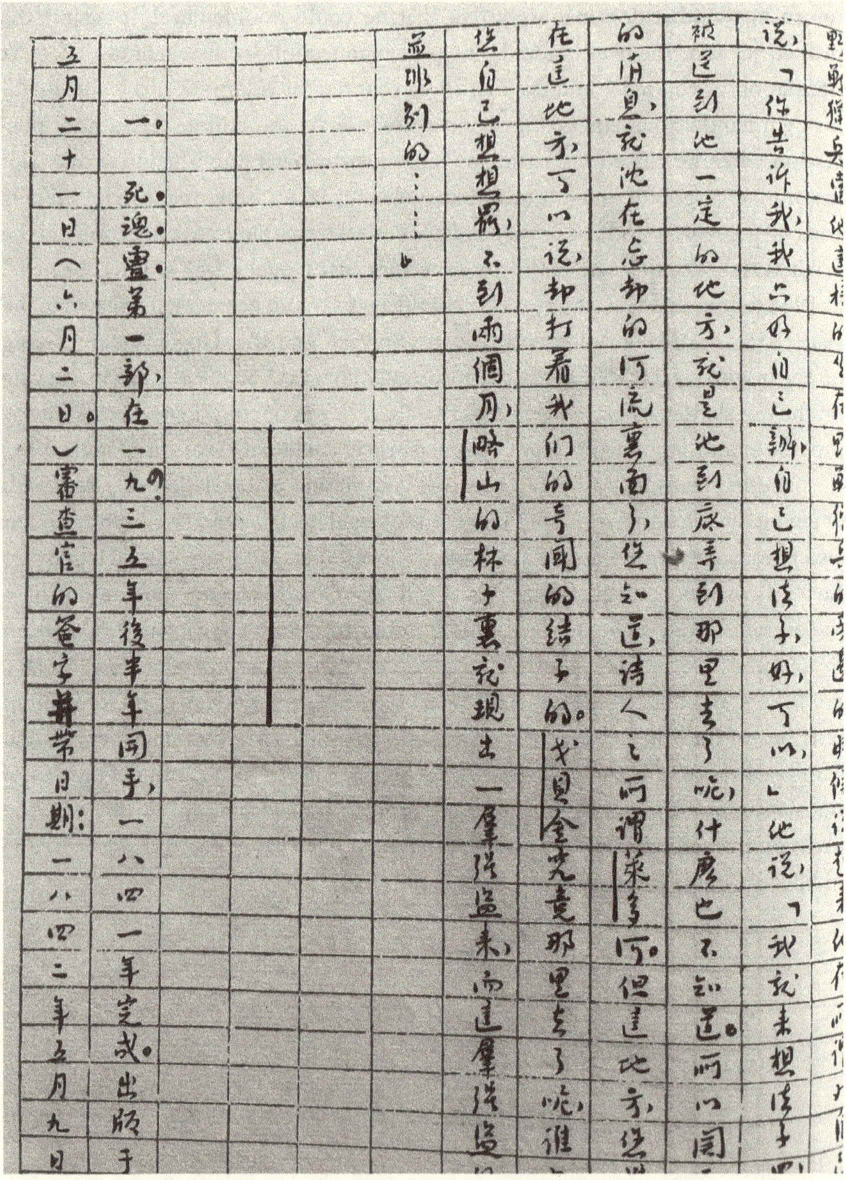

一。死。魂。靈。第一部，在一九三五年後半年開手，一八四一年完成。出版于

五月二十一日（六月二日）審查官的簽字并带日期：一八四二年五月九日

Figure 0.1: Detail from Lu Xun's Chinese translation of Gogol's *Dead Souls*

Introduction

Lu Xun, China, and the World

Xiaolu Ma

Lu Xun is one of the most widely read Chinese writers of the twentieth century. In China, he has been revered as the voice of the nation's conscience, while outside of China he is frequently compared to authors such as Gogol, Chekhov, Gorky, and Orwell. Similarly, he has inspired numerous disciples abroad, who have earned epithets such as Taiwan's Lu Xun and Malaysia's Lu Xun.[1] Gloria Davies praises Lu Xun as a "founder of discursivity"—someone who, through his stories helped create "a possibility for something other than [his] discourse, yet something belonging to what [he] founded."[2] It is not only literary tropes and rhetorical devices that establish Lu Xun's stature but ultimately the circulation and appropriation of his ideas and themes both inside and outside of the Sinophone world. Lu Xun's spirit that continues to inspire admirers of modern Chinese literature should not simply be reducible to a single type of humanism popularized by China's current government but rather as a spirit of inquiry flexible enough to accommodate the historically situated concerns of generations to come.

In 1827, Johann Wolfgang von Goethe (1749 –1832) welcomed the era of world literature (*Weltliteratur*) in his conversation with Johann Peter Eckermann (1792–1854), remarking that "national literature is now rather an unmeaning term; the epoch of World-literature is at hand."[3] As David Damrosch has highlighted, Goethe envisioned "an era of international exchange and mutual refinement, a cosmopolitan process in which Germany would assume a central role as a translator and mediator among cultures, leading an international elite to champion lasting literary

---

1. Zhang Kangwen, "'Mahua Lu Xun' yu 'Dongya Lu Xun'—duihua de keneng yu bukeneng."
2. Gloria Davies, *Lu Xun's Revolution*, 10–11.
3. Johann Wolfgang von Goethe, *Conversations with Eckermann*, 133.

values against the vanities of narrow nationalism and the vagaries of popular taste."[4] But Goethe's Weltliteratur is not a stable term, and in the modern period many scholars have proposed various conceptual models that can be applied to world literature. For instance, inspired by Walter Benjamin, Theodor W. Adorno endorsed a heterogenous constellation to address the possibility of a literary epistemology.[5] Even-Zohar describes the networking of world literature as a polysystem,[6] whereas Franco Moretti illustrated the evolution of world literature as either a tree or a wave.[7] Pascale Casanova, meanwhile, borrows an economic and sociological paradigm to assign value to different works according to their distance from the center of world literary capital.[8] These various models suggest that the conceptualization of world literature may be a utopian project, yet they offer a critique of the contemporary system of aesthetic value and a reminder of the importance of cultural otherness and transfusion. Instead of attempting to propose a better model of world literature, this volume asks a simpler question: What is the relationship between Lu Xun, world literature, and underlying processes of worlding?

By situating Lu Xun as being always already an indispensable part of world literature, this collection seeks to clarify Lu Xun's relationship to world literature and vice versa. Scholars have long acknowledged the importance of the connection Lu Xun established with foreign literature to the understanding of his literary contributions. For this purpose, this project can be viewed as an addition to the study of Lu Xun (or "Luxunology"), which has become a substantial subdiscipline within the study of modern Chinese literature. We move beyond hagiographic treatments of Lu Xun and instead consider the ways in which the ripples, refractions, and differences generated by the author shed new light on our understanding of world literature more broadly.

What makes Lu Xun an essential component of world literature? How has he been canonized in different cultural contexts? To what extent is his literary influence a result of geopolitical, economic, and intercultural negotiations? If Lu Xun's works provide a literary paradigm in East Asia and the Sinophone world, how has this paradigm been reinterpreted and transformed over time? In what ways does Lu Xun contribute to the establishment of a new order or hierarchy of world literature? These are the questions we address as we explore Lu Xun's worldliness.

---

4. David Damrosch, "Introduction," 1.
5. Walter Benjamin, *The Origin of German Tragic Drama*; Theodor W. Adorno, *Negative Dialectics*.
6. Itamar Even-Zohar, "Polysystem Studies."
7. Franco Moretti, "Conjectures on World Literature."
8. Pascale Casanova, *The World Republic of Letters*.

Lu Xun Reading World Literature

Lu Xun would not have become who he was without his lifelong reading of and engagement with world literature. Although he is mostly known outside China as a fiction writer, it is no exaggeration to say that his literary career began and ended with the practice of translation. As an avid reader of foreign literature, he had already immersed himself in the translation of foreign literature long before he began writing fiction;[9] at the end of his life, he was still working on translating the second part of Nikolai Gogol's (1809–1852) *Dead Souls* (*Mertvye dushi*). In all, Lu Xun translated the works of over a hundred writers from Russia, Japan, the United Kingdom, France, Germany, Austria, the Netherlands, Spain, Finland, Poland, and several other Eastern European countries.[10] These translated works, which included fiction, poetry, drama, fairy tales, and literary criticism, totaled over three million Chinese characters.

Lu Xun's early translations involved both canonical writers such as Victor Hugo (1802–1885) and popular writers such as Jules Verne (1828–1905), but he soon turned to less known writers as the scope of his reading expanded. A snapshot of Lu Xun's correspondence with his brother Zhou Zuoren from the summer of 1921, during the period of their mutual interest in literature of injured nations, suggests the scope of Lu Xun's vision of world literature. Writers mentioned by Lu Xun in these letters include the Polish poet Adam Asnyk (1838–1897), the Finnish author Juhani Aho (originally Johannes Brofeldt 1861–1921), the Romanian poet Luca Ion Caragiale (1893–1921), the Croatian writer Ksaver Šandor Gjalski (1854–1935), and the Bulgarian writer Ivan Vazov (1850–1921).[11] Lu Xun was not only translating and introducing these writers to the Chinese audience but also was encouraging his brother to collaborate on this project. It has been calculated that, in his writing, Lu Xun mentions 571 writers from 27 different countries.[12] This is particularly noteworthy given that, in contrast to someone like Goethe, Lu Xun's access to world literature was constrained by the smaller number of languages he could read fluently, which meant that instead of reading foreign works in the original, he often had to rely on Japanese and German translations.

It was also not always easy for Lu Xun to obtain foreign books. Zhou Zuoren described how, while in Tokyo, Lu Xun studied German mostly on his own,

---

9. Lu Xun claims that initially he was not overly enthusiastic about literary creation and instead paid more attention to the introduction and translation of foreign literature (Lu Xun, "Wo zenme zuoqi xiaoshuo lai," 525).

10. Ge Baoquan, "Lu Xun zai shijie wenxue shi shang de diwei," 415; Wang Jiaping, "Lu Xun fanyi wenxue yanjiu de xiangdu yu chuangxin."

11. Lu Xun, "210713 Zhi Zhou Zuoren," 11:392; Lu Xun, "210731 Zhi Zhou Zuoren," 11:401; Lu Xun, "210806 Zhi Zhou Zuoren," 11:404.

12. Wang Xirong, "Lu Xun de 'shijieren' gainian he shijie de 'ren' gainian."

4   Introduction: Lu Xun, China, and the World

scavenged old bookstalls for German translations of and introductions to foreign literature, and often waited for months for books to be delivered from Europe.[13] When it became more difficult for Lu Xun to access German books after he returned to China, Japanese publications became his main source of information. This shift in reading practice is reflected in the references included in his translations in which the proportion of Japanese titles increased significantly in his later career. In particular, his translation of Soviet literary theory and proletarian literature relied mainly on Japanese sources. Furthermore, of the books that Lu Xun did manage to acquire, one genre predominates: multilingual dictionaries, including German-Japanese, English-Japanese, and Russian-Japanese ones.[14] The preponderance of multilingual Japanese dictionaries suggests that Japanese was a key route by which Lu Xun accessed global literature, though in some cases he was forced to rely on a combination of both Japanese and German as intermediary languages, such as when he used a German-Japanese dictionary to translate Gogol's *Dead Souls* into Chinese from Otto Buek's (1873–1966) German translation of the original Russian.

As an exchange student from a declining traditional Chinese literati family who hoped his education abroad would prepare him for a career in medicine, Lu Xun eventually decided to turn to literature because he considered it a better remedy for what he perceived to be the paralysis of Chinese people's spirit and the deadening of their hearts. Lu Xun's pragmatism ultimately led him to advocate a practice of "grabbism" (*nalaizhuyi* 拿來主義), which is described by Eileen J. Cheng as "the selective appropriation of the foreign as a means to self-strengthening,"[15] on the assumption that "new voices from alien lands" (別求新聲於異邦)[16] could help revitalize elements of indigenous culture—a vision that surpasses the national and colonial discourses enforced by superficial adoption of foreign/Western culture.[17] Lu Xun was convinced that "all great works of world literature can open one to the wonder of life and allow one to intuit the facts and laws of life, something science is unable to do."[18] Lu Xun's grabbism also motivated him to advocate for a practice of "hard translation" that prioritized word-for-word correspondence between source

---

13. Zhou Zuoren, "Zai shi Dongjing (Lu Xun de qingnian shidai shi'er)," 614–15.
14. Xu Guangping in an interview recalled at least fourteen dictionaries that Lu Xun constantly used for his work (Deng Xiaolin, "Zui yaojin de shi you yibu hao zidian—zaitan Lu Xun xiansheng he cidian," 97). The titles of some of the dictionaries Lu Xun used are included in the catalog of Lu Xun's book collection (Beijing Lu Xun bowuguan, *Lu Xun shouji he cangshu mulu*, 3). Although Lu Xun never gained the sufficient ability to read Russian and English fluently, his collection contained a significant number of multilingual dictionaries in addition to the books in Russian and English languages, suggesting that Lu Xun never gave up his hope of reading Russian and English originals.
15. Eileen J. Cheng, "'In Search of New Voices from Alien Lands,'" 589.
16. Lu Xun, "Moluo shili shuo," 1:68.
17. Eileen J. Cheng, "'In Search of New Voices from Alien Lands,'" 589–90.
18. Lu Xun, "On the Power of Mara Poetry," 106; Lu Xun, "Moluo shili shuo," 1:74.

and target text—an approach, he believed, that better rendered the foreignness of the translated text.[19]

Even as Lu Xun relied mainly on German and Japanese sources for his access to world literature, he paid special attention to Slavic and Eastern European literatures.[20] His literary preferences are also reflected in his literary creation. As Julia Lovell, a translator of Lu Xun's stories, points out, "the traces of Lu Xun's cosmopolitan reading habits (in Chinese, Japanese and German translations) are in evidence throughout [his narratives]."[21] Indeed, in his writing, Lu Xun frequently incorporated elements from his reading of foreign literature, but rather than reflecting a passive acceptance of colonial influence, Lu Xun's grabbism instead resonates with his simultaneous aspiration to and resistance against Western modernity.[22]

Lu Xun's search for the "new voices from alien lands" demands a careful listening to the "voice of the heart" (*xinsheng* 心聲) of the foreign poets, as a crucial means for cultivating the Chinese people and revitalizing Chinese culture. For him, the reading of such literature sets the path to the "nation of human beings" (*renguo* 人國)—a nation that cherishes self-esteem and respects individual value.[23] This nation is the ultimate goal of his eclectic, cosmopolitan selection of world literature, and the intimate tie between world literature and nation building constitutes one of the important reasons for Lu Xun's global popularity.

Lu Xun in the World

David Damrosch defines world literature as "all literary works that circulate beyond their culture of origin, either in translation or in the original."[24] By this definition, an indispensable factor in the entry of Lu Xun's works into the domain of world literature is their circulation outside of China. By the 1980s, Lu Xun's works had been translated into more than seventy languages in over fifty countries.[25] These works' strong national character made them easily legible for international readers. In the meantime, they stimulated different interpretations. In Japan, there even appeared

---

19. Lu Xun, "*Tuo'ersitai zhi si yu shaonian Ouluoba* yi hou ji," 10:338.
20. Thanks to the efforts of scholars from Japan, China, and elsewhere, there is rich scholarship on Lu Xun's reliance on the Japanese sources. Recently, scholarship has also begun to focus on his German influence. See Cui Wendong, "Qingnian Lu Xun yu deyu 'shijie wenxue'"; Xiong Ying, "Lu Xun dewen cangshu zhong de 'shijie wenxue' kongjian"; Zhang Huiwen, "Lu Xun contra Georg Brandes."
21. Julia Lovell, "Introduction," xxi.
22. Haiyan Xie, "'Grabbism' and Untranslatability," 126.
23. Lu Xun, "Wenhua pian zhi lun," 1:57.
24. David Damrosch, *What Is World Literature?* 4.
25. Wang Xirong, "Lu Xun de 'shijieren' gainian he shijie de 'ren' gainian."

6   Introduction: Lu Xun, China, and the World

titles such as "Takeuchi's Lu Xun" and "Maruyama's Lu Xun," highlighting the diversity of scholars interpreting his oeuvre.

It is worth noting that Lu Xun hoped his works would "perish soon" (*suxiu* 速朽),[26] and he resisted recognition from outside China. He declined a nomination for the Nobel Prize for literature, on the grounds that he did not consider the quality of his work to match the standards of the prize, nor did he want the publicity of being recognized as a Chinese or Asian Nobel Prize winner: "If I want to win this prize, I need to make a bigger effort."[27] Even though the Nobel Prize is, accordingly to Pascale Casanova, "one of the few truly international literary consecrations" that represented "the designation and definition of what is universal in literature,"[28] canonization and consecration were not Lu Xun's goal. He refused to defer to "the politics of recognition," a phenomenon observed by Shu-mei Shih when criticizing what she perceives to be the Western puffery of Gao Xingjian.[29] Instead, given his "obsession with China"—which C. T. Hsia has argued was a common feature of Chinese intellectuals of his time[30]—Lu Xun used his literature to tackle specific national crises.

Nonetheless, the transience and perishability that Lu Xun aimed to achieve in his works became part of their charm: The temporal tension contributes a sense of intensity for digesting and consuming Lu Xun's works, which can be integrated into the geopolitical and transnational frictions that helped shape Lu Xun's readership outside China. In regions where people can read Lu Xun's works in the original, such as Sinophone Southeast Asia, Lu Xun has been celebrated as an embodiment of a revolutionary spirit, and he is particularly close to the heart of the leftists due to his political views. Many readers confronted their colonial experiences with his anti-imperialist spirit and even took inspiration from him in their resistance to political, social, and racial oppression. The Taiwanese poet Loa Ho 賴和 (1894–1943), for instance, was known as Taiwan's Lu Xun for his appropriation of Lu Xun's works in his depiction of the suffering and depression in colonial Taiwan. Authors in Singapore, Malaysia, and Indonesia reworked and parodied Lu Xun's novellas and short stories to reflect on local issues. In this way, the issue of "national character" that fascinated Lu Xun was translated into the Sinophone world's inquiry into Chineseness, a search for their national and ethnic identity.[31]

---

26. Lu Xun, "A Q zhengzhuan," 1:512.
27. Lu Xun, "270925 Zhi Tai Jingnong," 12:73.
28. Pascale Casanova, "Literature as a World," 74.
29. Shu-Mei Shih, "Global Literature and the Technologies of Recognition," 25.
30. C. T. Hsia, *A History of Modern Chinese Fiction*, 533–54.
31. Ma Feng, "Lu Xun zai Yinni de chuanbo yu yingxiang"; Zhang Songjian, *Wenxin de yitong*, 3–53; Zhuang Huaxing, "Lu Xun zai lengzhan qianqi de Malaiya yu Xinjiapo."

Beyond the Sinophone world, foreign readers' acquaintance with Lu Xun can be dated back to 1909 when the journal *Japan and Japanese People* (*Nihon oyobi nihonjin* 日本及日本人) published an article on Lu Xun and Zhou Zuoren, introducing their *Anthology of Fiction from beyond the Border*.[32] Zhou Zuoren was the first to translate Lu Xun's work into another language, having published his Japanese translation of "Kong Yiji" in *Beijing Weekly* (*Beijing zhoubao* 北京週報) in 1922, five years earlier than Japanese translators published their own translations.[33] Many of the other early translators of Lu Xun—including Soviet sinologist Boris Vasil'ev (1899–1937), Czech sinologist Jaroslav Prŭšek (1906–1980), and Japanese scholar Masuda Wataru 増田渉 (1903–1977)—either met Lu Xun in person or exchanged letters with him.

There are two more groups who contributed to the initial dissemination of Lu Xun's works. The first included exchange students and immigrants with Chinese backgrounds. For instance, the first translator of Lu Xun's work into English, George Kin Leung 梁社乾 (1899–1977), was a Chinese American who grew up in Atlantic City, New Jersey, before returning to China in the early 1920s, and translated "The True Story of Ah Q" in 1926.[34] In France, Jean Baptiste Yn-Yu Kyn 敬隱漁 (1901–1931) and Sung-nien Hsu 徐仲年 (also known as Xu Songnian 徐頌年, 1904–1981) contributed to the initial dissemination of Lu Xun's works.[35] Kyn enrolled in the Institut Franco-Chinois de Lyon (IFCL) in 1925 and is best known for connecting the two great literary figures of France and China: Romain Rolland (1866–1944) and Lu Xun.[36] He was the first to translate Lu Xun's story *The True Story of Ah Q* into French in 1926, followed by "Kong Yiji" and "My Old Hometown" in 1929. Sung-nien Hsu enrolled in the IFCL under a work-study program in 1921 and joined the Université de Lyon in 1926. In 1931, he published his introduction to a collection of Lu Xun's short stories, *Outcry*, in *La Nouvelle Revue Française* (The new French review), and his 1933 *Anthologie de la Littérature Chinoise des origines à nos jours* (Anthology of Chinese literature from the origins to the present) also included his translation of Lu Xun's "Kong Yiji."[37]

The second group that contributed to Lu Xun's global dissemination were missionaries. In *Histoire de la Littérature Chinoise Modern* (History of modern Chinese literature), Henri van Boven (1911–2003) of the Congregatio Immaculati Cordis Mariae devoted a chapter on Lu Xun's literary contribution and his pro-Communist

---

32. Fujii Shōzō, "Lu Xun yu Riben ji shijie wenxue," 006.
33. Fujii, "Lu Xun yu Riben ji shijie wenxue," 006.
34. Baorong Wang, "George Kin Leung's English Translation of Lu Xun's *A Q Zhengzhuan*."
35. Paolo Magagnin, "Agents of May Fourth."
36. Paul B. Foster, "The Ironic Inflation of Chinese National Character."
37. Liang Haijun, "Lu Xun zai Fayu shijie de chuanbo yu yanjiu," 30–31.

8   Introduction: Lu Xun, China, and the World

political stance.[38] Designed as a textbook, this volume attempted to remain as neutral and nonideological as possible. However, given the author's stationing in Beijing, the book succeeded in capturing precious moments unknown to readers outside China. Octave Brière (1907–1978), a member of the Society of Jesus who resided in China for from 1934 to 1953, is another example of a missionary with considerable interest in modern Chinese literature. Brière considered reading Chinese contemporary literature to be the most effective way to learn Chinese culture and its people, and in a series of essays he published on modern Chinese writers between 1942 and 1949, he wrote an article in which he commented on Lu Xun's fiction and essays, while also reflecting on why Lu Xun never wrote full-length novels.[39] Others, including Joseph Schyns (1899–1979) and Jean Monsterleet (1912–2001), resided in China around the same time and published essays and book chapters on Lu Xun.

These early interpreters and translators of Lu Xun's works shaped the initial reception of Lu Xun by global audiences. In the early stage of dissemination, when resources were limited for the translators, relay translation was a common phenomenon. Ida Bastman's Finnish translation of Lu Xun's works in *Nykyaikaisia kiinalaisia kertomuksia* (Modern Chinese stories) in 1929 was based on Yn-Yu Kyn's French translation. This relay translation was earlier than the English relay translation also based on Kyn's translation by E. H. F. Mills in 1930. In India, many readers first learned about Lu Xun's work through Edgar Snow's (1905–1972) English translation in *Living China: Modern Chinese Short Stories* (1936), and it was not until the 1940s that Lu Xun's works were translated from English into Urdu.[40]

Politics in Dissemination

Lu Xun's literary activity is deeply entangled with politics. His works' dissemination in the global book market also reflects geopolitical realities and sometimes constitutes an apologetics.[41] These political entanglements were particularly obvious during the Cold War period, and as Irene Eber notes, "the reception accorded Lu Xun's works often reflects the thaws and freezes in international relations."[42] One salient example is the different treatment Lu Xun received in East and West Germany after World War II. In contrast to East Germany, where Lu Xun was celebrated as the most important figure and a revolutionary hero in modern Chinese literature, in West Germany enthusiasm for him emerged much later and was motivated by

---

38. Henri van Boven, *Histoire de la littérature Chinoise moderne.*
39. Octave Brière, "Un écrivain populaire."
40. Jia Yan and Jiang Jingkui, "Yijie yu chuanbo: Lu Xun de Yindu 'laisheng,'" 28.
41. Daniel M. Dooghan, "Old Tales, Untold," 31.
42. Irene Eber, "The Reception of Lu Xun in Europe and America," 242.

the global leftist movement in the 1960s and 1970s.[43] Interestingly, it was precisely as interest in Lu Xun was waning in East Germany due to the Sino-Soviet split in the late 1950s that West German scholars such as Hans Christoph Buch (1944–) not only began paying attention to Lu Xun's revolutionary literary legacy but also noticed the dark side of his work.[44] Even in the Soviet Union, despite the reduction of translations and critical studies resulting from the Sino-Soviet conflict, the relief of guidance from Mao allowed Soviet sinologists space for more thorough and sophisticated analysis.[45]

Meanwhile, some in the West regarded Lu Xun with suspicion due to his socialist inclinations. Chi-chen Wang (1899–2001), a professor of Chinese literature at Columbia University who translated many of Lu Xun's short stories, even resigned from Harriet Mills's (1920–2016) dissertation committee out of fear of McCarthyite reprisal because her dissertation mainly addressed Lu Xun's leftist activities.[46] However, when the third world independence struggles won enthusiasm for Maoism and the Chinese Cultural Revolution in Western Europe that gave birth to the cult of Mao, Lu Xun attracted Western theorists' attention as a widely recognized leftist writer. In 1957, for example, Simone de Beauvoir (1908–1986) published *La longue marche: Essai sur la Chine* (The Long March: An essay on China), which reports her trip to mainland China in 1955 with her partner Jean-Paul Sartre (1929–1980). In the chapter on Chinese culture, Beauvoir records how Chinese readers viewed Lu Xun as China's Gorky, forging modern Chinese literature and utilizing it on behalf of the revolutionary cause. She describes how Lu Xun's portrait hung in the place of honor at all writers' meetings and congresses and how his house in Shanghai had become a site of pilgrimage.[47] Yet, she considers Lu Xun to be more closely related to Chekhov because of a certain spirit of obscurity and dubiousness that resists the label of socialist realism.[48]

Like Beauvoir, Elvi Sinervo (1912–1986)—one of the driving forces of the cultural association Kiila, which was founded in 1936 by Finnish left-wing writers to combat the fascist currents—also visited China in 1956 and became interested in Lu Xun. She translated several of Lu Xun's works, including *The True Story of Ah Q*. Her book *Uudenvuoden uhri ja muita kertomuksia* (New Year's Eve and other stories) was published by Kansankulttuuri, a Finnish publishing house that marketed primarily to radical leftists and which published socialist and Marxist works. Similarly, the introduction and translation of Lu Xun's works in the Netherlands in the 1950s and

---

43. Fan Jin, "Lu Xun yanjiu zai Deguo," 65–66.
44. Fan Jin, "Lu Xun yanjiu zai Deguo," 69.
45. Irene Eber, "The Reception of Lu Xun in Europe and America," 244.
46. Jon Eugene von Kowallis, "On Translating Lu Xun's Fiction," 196.
47. Simone de Beauvoir, *The Long March*, 294.
48. Beauvoir, *The Long March*, 296–97.

10   Introduction: Lu Xun, China, and the World

1960s mostly relied on Dutch leftist writers Theun de Vries (1907–2005) and Jef Last (1898–1972). This global leftist fever was also prominent in the English world as a radicalism of the late 1960s and early 1970s, which led to an overwhelming enthusiasm for China's Cultural Revolution and growing fervor over Lu Xun.[49]

In conjunction with the international leftists' enthusiasm, we should not forget Chinese government-sponsored translation activities that assisted the promotion of Lu Xun in the West. Yang Xianyi 楊憲益 (1915–2009) and Gladys Yang (1919–1999) were well known for their co-translations of Chinese literature into English. The couple worked for the Foreign Languages Press, a state-owned enterprise in China whose responsibilities included the dissemination of Chinese literature in foreign languages. Not only have the Yangs' translations of Lu Xun's works been included in many anthologies, but they were also used as the basis for relay translations into other languages, such as Hans Christoph Buch's (1944–) German translation of Lu Xun's work *Der Einsturz der Lei-feng-Pagode: Essays über Literatur und Revolution in China* (The collapse of the Lei Feng pagoda: Essays on literature and revolution in China), were also based on the Yangs' translations. The Foreign Languages Press also translated Lu Xun's works into French, German, Spanish, Korean, Japanese, Arabic, Hindi, Urdu, Bengali, Esperanto, and other languages, and many of these translations were widely read.[50] This government-sponsored activity reflects China's attempt to ensure a properly guided interpretation and a stable coverage of readership.

Thus, Lu Xun became a canonized writer due to the joint efforts of sinologists, exchange students, missionaries, and fans of Chinese literature. Some played the role of cultural ambassador voluntarily, while others were sponsored by the Chinese government or by international institutions. The variability of media also resulted in disparate treatments of Lu Xun's literary legacy. Nonetheless, these assorted engagements prove the versatility and variability of Lu Xun that made him a writer of world literature. Conversely, these diverse and divergent readings of Lu Xun also manifest the specificity of distinctive cultural spaces, while also reflecting an image of the world back to itself.

Worlding Lu Xun

The discussion of how Lu Xun read world literature and how Lu Xun was read as part of world literature inevitably raises the question of how we understand world literature itself. The two components of the German term *Weltliteratur*—world and literature—are both fluid and capacious, encompassing the variegated social world

---

49. Irene Eber, "The Reception of Lu Xun in Europe and America," 244.
50. Ge Baoquan, "Lu Xun zai shijie weixue shi shang de diwei," 417.

in which literature is produced and read. Although the German term *Welt* (world), as Ben Etherington and Jarad Zimbler point out, carries etymological connotations of "the material world; humanity's present, temporal state of existence; earthly things, or temporal possessions; an age; a person's conditions of life; the course of human affairs,"[51] our modern understanding of the world also includes notions of globalization and transnationalism. Therefore, the study of world literature necessarily involves what Etherington and Zimbler call "planetary expansion of capitalism" and "its attendant forms of communication, market exchange, and statecraft."[52] In the twentieth century, the field of world literature departed from its Eurocentric vision to incorporate a broader scope of transculturation across different regions of the world. Recently, many scholars have attempted to resist anthropocentric assumptions inherent in earlier concepts of the world, adding more weight to the environment and its depiction in literature.[53]

In what ways would a broadened scope of world literature enhance the study of Lu Xun? Does the examination of Lu Xun provide us with theoretical and methodological implications for the study of world literature? Emily Apter has cautioned against approaching world literature through a simple "endorsement of equivalence and substitutability" or a "celebration of nationally and ethnically branded 'differences,'"[54] and our volume similarly underscores the temporal and spatial vicissitudes that underlie the category of world literature itself. Moreover, as Pheng Cheah reminds us, *world* is not only a spatial category but is also—and even more importantly—a temporal one because "before the world can appear as an object, it must first *be*,"[55] and our volume examines not only the processes by which the category of world literature is constituted but also the ways in which Lu Xun engagement with world literature contributes to normative processes of worlding in its own right.

As an indispensable part of Chinese literature, Lu Xun's works invite us to delve into the mission Yingjin Zhang envisions when he specifies that the process of "exploring how and where China is mapped in world literature reveals various positions of view and modes of engagement open to readers and scholars.[56] Furthermore, invoking Martin Heidegger's (1889–1976) concept of worlding, David Der-wei Wang explores the possibility of studying modern Chinese literature as "a flux of

---

51. Ben Etherington and Jarad Zimbler, "Introduction," 2–3.
52. Etherington and Zimbler, "Introduction," 3.
53. See Bryan L. Moore, *Ecological Literature and the Critique of Anthropocentrism*; Sten Pultz Moslund, Marlene Karlsson Marcussen, and Martin Karlsson Pedersen, *How Literature Comes to Matter*; Sabine Lenore Müller and Tina-Karen Pusse, *From Ego to Eco*; Barbara Braid and Hanan Muzaffar, *Bodies in Flux*.
54. Emily S. Apter, *Against World Literature*, 2–3.
55. Pheng Cheah, *What Is a World?*, 2.
56. Yingjin Zhang, "Mapping Chinese Literature as World Literature," 9.

12   Introduction: Lu Xun, China, and the World

unfolding experience" and examining Chinese literature as a necessity to "bringing China to the world and the world into China."[57] In this volume, we treat Lu Xun as a focal point for examining modern Chinese literature and interrogate how he has been an active agency in the ongoing configuration of the world. We reflect on how the reading and appropriation of Lu Xun have enriched the imagination of world literature in China and around the globe, while also considering how our inquiry might help advance a better understanding of the world and worlding, especially as it is manifested in the making of world literature.

To this end, this volume approaches the topic of Lu Xun and world literature from three interrelated perspectives. In Part 1, we consider ways in which Lu Xun engaged with foreign literature and with the concept of world literature. Via attention to his literary translations, we consider the ways in which he drew on literary motifs, models, syntax, and even design elements from other literary traditions in developing his own distinctive style. In Part 2, we turn to the question of how Lu Xun's works have circulated beyond China's borders, considering processes of both translation as well as of transculturation. Finally, in Part 3, we consider how Lu Xun's works themselves reflect on the notions of world and worlding that are complicated by his own conflicted relationship with world literature.

Part 1 opens with a chapter by Pu Wang that examines Lu Xun's engagement with world poetry. Despite being a prolific and complex author, Lu Xun was recognized outside of China mainly as a fiction writer, although his fiction comprised only a small portion of his publications. Beginning with Lu Xun's essay on Mara poetry that he wrote in 1908 while still in Japan, Wang reflects on Lu Xun's lifelong interest in foreign poetry. The figure of Lu Xun that emerges is a Promethean poet, grappling with the crisis of worlding inflicted by the revolutionary urgency of poetry. By tracing three poetic moments in Lu Xun's life, including his poetic composition and translation, Wang underscores the poetico-political dynamic in modern Chinese literature and questions the possibility of constructing an anti-imperialist and anti-hegemonic poetic world space.

In chapter 2, Wendong Cui turns to *Anthology of Fiction from beyond the Border*, the collection of translations of foreign-language fiction that Lu Xun and Zhou Zuoren published in 1909. Although Zhou Zuoren was responsible for most of the volume's actual translations, Cui argues that Lu Xun appears to have played a crucial role in helping shape the collection's literary vision. To develop his argument, Cui considers a range of sources, including information about Lu Xun's private book collection as well as German-language publications to which Lu Xun had access when he and Zhou Zuoren were preparing their volume, arguing that these German-language

---

57. David Der-wei Wang, "Introduction: Worlding Literary China," 13.

resources played an important role in helping shape the distinct Eastern European focus that characterizes the resulting translation collection.

In chapter 3, Keru Cai examines Lu Xun's engagement with modern Russian literature, but rather than focusing on his translational work, she instead considers some of the ways that Lu Xun incorporated Russian literary elements in his short stories "Diary of a Madman," "Medicine," and "The Lamp of Eternity." Cai inspects how Lu Xun drew on the works of Gogol, Leonid Andreev, and Vsevolod Garshin to unfold the impasse of Chinese intellectuals incapable of overcoming the distance to reach out to the masses. As Cai argues, Lu Xun's appropriations from Russian literature enabled him to explore the reformer's problem of communicating with the social other, evoked the dialectics of pessimism and optimism therein, and attempted to revitalize Chinese culture by borrowing elements from abroad.

In chapter 4, Xiaoyu Xia analyzes the role of the materiality of books in constructing Lu Xun's conceptualization of world literature and specifically the related phenomena of uncut or deckle-edged volumes and of unopened or fused volumes in which each pair of pages are connected on the side opposite the spine and need to be cut open before the book can be read. In the early twentieth century, these practices were still relatively novel in China, and Lu Xun enthusiastically entered a local debate over the merits of uncut or unopened volumes—a publishing practice that he viewed as an opportunity to "retrain the Chinese reader and to reform the Chinese mind." Xia's analysis serves as a reminder of the relevance of material culture studies to the study of world literature.

In chapter 5, Satoru Hashimoto examines the ways in which Henrik Ibsen's *A Doll's House* was received and transculturated by Lu Xun in China and by Higuchi Ichiyō in Japan, as both writers refused the normalization of Ibsen's play as a social and literary practice. The textual relationship constructed in this transcultural environment is not based on the mere reading of Ibsen's *A Doll's House* as a pure literary work. Lu Xun's and Ichiyō's appropriation of issues of female independence and gender conflicts, both of which are central themes in Ibsen's work, contributed to the construction of a network of world literature that constantly challenges the boundaries of literature itself. Thus, Hashimoto underscores the importance of understanding world literature beyond the model of textual circulation. Even when a literature is read in its cultural point of origin, it is already open to a world beyond itself.

In Part 2, we flip the lens to consider the reception of Lu Xun's work around the world, focusing on various regions in Asia and Europe. These chapters consider foreign translations of Lu Xun's works, how his works have been received internationally, and how they have impacted local literary traditions.

In chapter 6, Shijung Kim considers the reception and translation of Lu Xun's works in Korea, which began as early as the 1920s. Kim divides Korea's reception of

Lu Xun into five phases, underlining the geopolitical dimension of literary exchange in each of the corresponding historical periods, together with the ways Korean writers interlaced elements from Lu Xun's works based on their own cultural and literary experiences.

In chapter 7, Carles Prado-Fonts similarly considers the reception of Lu Xun's works in Spain and their translation into the country's various languages. Whereas Korean readers began engaging with Lu Xun's work as early as the 1920s, during his own lifetime, in Spain the corresponding response was rather belated, not beginning until the 1970s. After considering some of the possible reasons for this lengthy delay, Prado-Fonts discusses some of the characteristics of Spain's eventual reception of Lu Xun, with a particular attention to why, even then, Lu Xun's influence in Spain remained comparatively modest.

In chapter 8, Xiaolu Ma examines Lu Xun's self-portrayal and his refiguration in Dazai Osamu's and Inoue Hisashi's works. Ma proposes that the concept of world literature should not only concern the circulation of literary texts but also the transfiguration of authors themselves. This emphasis is in line with Lu Xun's own understanding of world literature, which values equally the influence of poets on the shaping of national literature and the construction of a common world of human beings. Ma focuses on two incidents recounted in Lu Xun's autobiographical writing and in two Japanese writers' narration—the accusatory letter and the lantern slide incidents. By detailing how they approach these two key moments of Lu Xun's life, she reveals how Lu Xun is transformed from a person who abhors evils as deadly foes into a Tolstoyan figure who advocates kindheartedness and mercy.

In chapter 9, Wayne C. F. Yeung uses Hong Kong writer Wong Bik-wan's 2012 award-winning novel *Lielaozhuan* to reread Lu Xun's "The True Story of Ah Q." Yeung's approach challenges the traditional conceptualization of world literature that emphasizes either tributary indebtedness to the cultural center or insurgent appropriation by the political periphery, outlining a unidirectional pattern of the diffusion of world literature. As Yeung reveals, the Hong Kong writer's extraterritorial displacement of the canonical text toward its repressed margin is indicative of the complex negotiation of Sinophone writers with the Chinese canon. Wong's acknowledgment of subaltern heroism and resilience informs an alternative episteme and enables a back-reading of Ah Q for the character's unacknowledged survivalist ethos vis-à-vis the Confucian ideology as the imperial unconscious of national allegory.

In the final chapter of Part 2, Carlos Rojas uses the contemporary Malaysian Chinese author Ng Kim Chew as a prism through which to consider some of the issues involved in Southeast Asia's reception not only of Lu Xun's works but also of the broader category of modern Chinese literature. In particular, Rojas considers how Ng uses May Fourth fiction in general, and Lu Xun's work in particular, to reflect on the way in which the Southeast Asian Sinosphere remains haunted by the lingering influence of Chinese literary canons, even as it simultaneously attempts to differentiate itself from those same literary legacies.

Part 3 considers some of the ways Lu Xun's works engage with processes of world making, including his engagement with biopolitical, existential, postcolonial, and posthuman visions of the world. From his early interest in foreign science and Nietzschean transvaluation to his later engagement with leftist politics, Lu Xun maintained an enduring commitment to imagine the world otherwise. This last section probes the conceptualization of the world and worlding, using the concept of *world* not simply as a modifier of *literature* but more fully as a key to our understanding of world literature.

First, Kun Qian's chapter offers a comparative analysis of two stories by Lu Xun and fellow May Fourth author Guo Moruo, both of which reimagine the legend of Laozi's departure (and return) through the Hangu Pass, which ultimately led to his composition of the Daoist classic the *Daodejing*. Qian argues that Lu Xun and Guo Moruo—in these two stories and other writings—exhibit a deeply ingrained self-doubt that, Qian argues, is alien to the Daoist tradition but is consonant with what literary critic Paul Ricoeur, in his discussion of the legacy of Nietzsche, Freud, and Marx, famously calls a hermeneutics of suspicion. Qian notes that Lu Xun and Guo Moruo both expressed interest in the writings of these three paradigm-shifting Western thinkers, but Qian also notes that—ironically yet fittingly—Lu Xun and Guo Moruo appear to have approached these three Western thinkers with the same suspicious attitude that Ricoeur argues those thinkers helped to promote in the first place.

In chapter 12, Eileen Cheng considers Lu Xun's prose poem collection *Wild Grass* (1927) and his collection of autobiographical essays *Morning Blossoms* (1928), arguing that both volumes use a strategy of self-effacement to explore a set of worlds located beyond the real world, including the world of memories, dreams, the fantastic, and the imaginary. By examining how these various "beyond" worlds are constituted in Lu Xun's writings, Cheng simultaneously reflects on how worlds themselves are understood and imagined in Lu Xun's literary universe.

In chapter 13, Roy Chan interrogates the vision of universality often demanded by world literature. He reminds us of the difficulty of applying universality transcendentally, as a given norm lying outside time and space. Reading Lu Xun's engagement with the ironies of law and norm alongside British philosopher Gillian Rose's lifelong project of the "retrieval of speculative experience," Chan details Lu Xun's comments on law, norms, and fair play in semicolonial Shanghai. Specifically, Chan details the ways in which Lu Xun sought to ironically expose the groundlessness of universal propositions that betray their own premises in the complicated context of power and domination. While Lu Xun rejected simplistic desires for transcendence,

16   Introduction: Lu Xun, China, and the World

his work nevertheless proposes the necessary horizon of the absolute, one from whose vantage point the contradictions of actuality could come into view. Lu Xun's descent into irony and the negative provided the soil for a tenuous and difficult form of secular faith.

In chapter 14, Christopher K. Tong turns to the issue of domination across species and national and ideological boundaries. Noting that Lu Xun's work includes references to more than two hundred types of nonhuman animals, ranging from farm animals to wild animals, from terrestrial creatures to marine creatures, and from fowl to critters, Tong considers the philosophical and political implications of this extensive engagement with animality in Lu Xun's works. By scrutinizing Lu Xun's treatment of animals, Tong presents a multispecies approach to world literature.

The contributors of this volume draw on diverse analytical approaches including translation studies, book history, and sociology of literature. Just as Stefan Helgesson and Pieter Vermeulen conclude that "world literature is made, not found,"[58] this volume similarly contends that the question of Lu Xun's relationship to world literature necessarily involves a reflection on the processes by which the category of world literature is constantly being reconstructed and reimagined. The volume does not attempt to cover all possible grounds about Lu Xun and world literature; instead, it offers readers new resources for grappling with Lu Xun's work and the paradigm of world literature itself.

---

58. Stefan Helgesson and Pieter Vermeulen, "World Literature in the Making," 1.

Part 1: Lu Xun and the World

1

Lu Xun, World Poetry, and Poetic Worlding

From Mara Poetry to Revolutionary Literature

Pu Wang

"I let the past drop here and seek new voices from foreign countries. . . . I cannot detail each varied voice, but none has such power to inspire and language as gripping as Mara poetry. . . . Now I look to all the poets whose theme was always revolt and whose purpose was action, and yet who were little loved by their age . . . and include them in [Mara poetry]; and I introduce their words, deeds, ideas, and the impact of their circles, from the sovereign Byron to a Magyar (Hungarian) man of letters."[1] Thus, a twenty-six-year-old Lu Xun, using the pen name Ling Fei, wrote in 1908, interpreting pan-European Romanticism into a kind of "Mara poetry" heralded by Lord Byron and fulfilled in such revolutionary patriotic writers of Eastern Europe as Sándor Petőfi. Near the end of his life, Lu Xun mourned a martyred Chinese poet on a spring night of 1936 and commented on poetry for the last time, describing a kind of revolutionary poetry that "is a glimmer in the east, an arrow whistling through the forest, a bud at the end of winter, the first step in the army's advance, a banner of love for the pioneers, a monument of hate for the despoilers."[2]

In this chapter, I situate Lu Xun's evolving lifework—that is, a trajectory from a champion of Mara poetry to a hero of cultural leftism—in the emerging constellation of modern world poetry. I do not attempt to offer a full mapping of the influences Lu Xun received from a variety of foreign poets, nor am I primarily preoccupied with his role as a poet, even though I will scrutinize one of his prose poems. Rather, this chapter demonstrates how his literary development embodied an ongoing configuration of modern world poetry. Not only do I define world poetry as a modern global network of writing, reading, translation, interpretation, and appropriation,

---

1. Lu Xun, "Moluo shili shuo," 68; Lu Xun, "On the Power of Mara Poetry," 99, translation modified.
2. Lu Xun, "A Preface to Bai Mang's *The Children's Pagoda*," 262.

20 Lu Xun, World Poetry, and Poetic Worlding

but I also propose to see it as an opening of poetic-political modernity, a dynamic of poetic worlding.

Therefore, I first turn to the young Lu Xun's vision of Mara poetry and propose a new understanding of world poetry. And then I move to his prose poem "Hope" in which the Hungarian poet Petőfi continues to figure prominently. This prose poem serves as a bridge toward his final years on the left, which he describes as a decisionist act of "grappling" with the "emptiness" and resisting both "hope" and "despair."[3] Moreover, I explore his encounter with Alexander Blok's poem *The Twelve* and Trotsky's reading of it. This chapter thus ends with Lu Xun's translation as a trial of working through the foreign revolutionary theory in which foreign poetry continues to glimmer and illuminates a self-critical metaphorical production. In seeing Lu Xun's work as an opening of world poetry, I attempt to argue for a poetic-political world making or worlding that is not a force of the dominating world system but a dynamic of seeking truly different—and revolutionary—possibilities.

Mara Poetry as Modern World Poetry

In early 1908, Lu Xun published "On the Power of Mara Poetry" (hereafter "Mara"). Described by Jon Eugene von Kowallis as "an early manifesto for [Lu Xun's] entire literary career,"[4] "Mara" lays open a radical poetics by introducing Byronic Romanticism as a pan-European phenomenon into China on the eve of the 1911 Revolution. Lu Xun's depiction of pan-European Romanticism as the satanic school of poetry embodies a poetico-political dynamic in which literary modernity and radical politics share one and the same structure of origin.[5] Meanwhile, Lu Xun's idea of the power of Mara poetry, based on a creative interpretation of Byronic individualism and Romantic nationalism, seems to confirm the "mode" of "world literature" as "circulation and reading"[6] and especially its ripple effects from European literary modernity to non-Western modernizing projects. Thanks to Kitaoka Masako's 北岡正子 outstanding studies on the sources of the "Mara" essay, we can readily trace the young Lu Xun's consultation of Japanese biographies of Byron and Shelley, German translations of Slavic and Hungarian poets, various literary histories written in English, and Georg Brandes's books on Russia and Poland.[7] As is well known, the Danish literary scholar Georg Brandes (1842–1927) represented an early European conception of modern world literature as a growing network of rising national literatures.[8]

---

3. Lu Xun, "Hope," 34–37.
4. Jon Eugene von Kowallis, "Lu Xun and Terrorism," 85.
5. Pu Wang, "Poetics, Politics, and Ursprung/Yuan," 39.
6. David Damrosch, "What Is World Literature?" 200.
7. See Kitaoka Masako, *Moluo shili shuo cai yuan kao.*
8. See Georg Brandes, "World Literature."

At first glance, Lu Xun's "Mara" essay seems embedded in this model and serves as yet another example of the expansion of Europe-centered world literature in parallel to that of the modern world system. However, precisely as far as the exemplar existence of Lu Xun's early essay in world literature is concerned, several points must be added here to show that Lu Xun's case actually lends itself to a more provocative reflection on the modern world and its poetic making.

First, we may observe that the "Mara" essay, as an engagement in global literary modernity, is preoccupied with poetry, a genre that is not usually representative of universalizing force of world literature. In contrast, the novel, a truly globally traveling genre, has served as a central locus of world literature and global literary modernity. The focus on the travels of the novel can be seen in Franco Moretti's treatment of world literature as a "problem," and his reading of the literary system that is "one and unequal" is inseparable from the critical cartography of the ever-expanding capitalist "world system" that is "one and unequal."[9] Nor can we characterize the early Lu Xun's selections of European-Romantic poetic works—including those by Shelley, Byron, Pushkin, Lermotov, Michiewicz, Slowacki, Krasinski, and Petőfi—as examples of the world text that, according to Moretti's definition, engages the world system in totality and speaks to world history that is modernity.[10] Rather, the young Lu Xun's insight points to modern poetry's vibrancy at the heart of a revolutionary sequence—that is, the sequence starting with British Romantic poetry as a response to the French Revolution and culminating in the poetic-political spirit of the national revolutions across Europe in 1848. Then what is the position of an early twentieth-century Chinese reading of nineteenth-century European "Mara poetry" within world history and vis-à-vis the world system? This question leads to the next few points I want to make.

Second, Lu Xun's vision of Mara poetry demarcates a literary world space whose logic is anti-imperialist and anti-hegemonic. In her theory of world literature, Pascale Casanova offers the idea of a literary world space as an alternative to the echo chamber of world-system, and proposes to see this globalizing space as "another world . . . with its own laws, its own history, its specific revolts and revolutions."[11] Indeed, as Eric Hayot observes, "the 'world' of 'world literature' is not the same as the 'world' of 'world-systems.'"[12] Moreover, the literary world space is also a key force field in which the struggle against the domination of capitalist world system plays out. In particular, the law of such a literary world space is for Lu Xun nothing but "revolt."[13] The formation of this Mara poetic world is clearly part of the

---

9. Franco Moretti, "Conjectures on World Literature," 55.
10. See Franco Moretti, *Modern Epic*.
11. Pascale Casanova, "Literature as a World," 276.
12. Eric Hayot, *On Literary Worlds*, 33.
13. Lu Xun "Moluo shili shuo," 68; Lu Xun, "On the Power of Mara Poetry," 99.

historical process that, according to Casanova, gave birth to a modern literary world.[14] And yet at the same time, it is a radical response to a global system of imperialist domination to which the old Chinese civilization fell prey. In other words, Lu Xun's Mara world is in resistance to the imperialist world system and its hegemony. At the center of this Mara worldview is an ideal poet of revolt, resistance, and struggle: a revolt against oppressive domination, as Byron exemplifies, a resistance to the imperialist rule, as the Polish "poets of revenge" demonstrate, and a struggle for individual and national liberation, as the Hungarian poet Sándor Petőfi shows. Kitaoka Masako has convincingly stated that this ideal poet of resistance represents a foundation of Lu Xun's search for not only a "national salvation" but also a new "humanity" and human world.[15] And in this sense, the ideal of the Mara poet offers an underpinning logic that helps guide China's embrace of a literary world space in the revolutionary twentieth century. It is within this logic that Lu Xun is able to link together a wide variety of European poets and their radically different national situations. Byron was a champion of rebellious individualism, but out of the same passion for human dignity, he participated in—and died for—the Greek struggle for national independence. On the other hand, as Kitaoka Masako shows, Lu Xun draws on Brandes's works on Russia and Poland and arrives at an implicit preference of the Polish patriotic poets over Pushkin because Pushkin is a "patriot of brutality" and surrenders to the imperial power of the czar.[16] And Petőfi, as a poet of the 1848 revolutions, figures prominently in Lu Xun's later modernist work.

Third, if Brandes was among the first to lay out the dialectical tension between the national and the international in world literature, then Lu Xun heralded the poetic-political vision of the international solidarity of national struggles in a Chinese and non-West world making. Writing in 1899, Brandes described "bellicose nationalism" in Europe,[17] which was a result of imperialist competition in the late nineteenth century and eventually contributed to the outbreak and bloodbath of the World War I. Brandes also pointed out the disadvantageous position of writers from Europe's "small lands" in their "struggle for world renown," lamenting the difficulty of translating lyrical poetry for a universal readership.[18] But delving into literary biographies and histories about those small lands, Lu Xun teased out, and solidarized with, a revolutionary genealogy of poetic voices of the oppressed and wretched countries. Rebecca Karl, among others, has demonstrated that at the turn of the nineteenth century and twentieth century, the Chinese intellectuals were preoccupied with how to "stage" the world both diachronically and synchronically:

---

14. Pascale Casanova, "Literature as a World," 277.

15. Kitaoka Masako, *Lu Xun Jiu wang zhi meng de qu xiang*, 80–81.

16. Kitaoka, *Lu Xun Jiu wang zhi meng de qu xiang*, 61.

17. Georg Brandes, "World Literature," 27.

18. Brandes, "World Literature," 24–25.

on the one hand, the Euro-American-Japanese power at the center of the social Darwinian global stage and, on the other hand, the tragic fate of China and others and their immanent opportunity to fight against this global unevenness.[19] Writing on the eve of the 1911 Republican Revolution that would put an end to dynastic rule in China, Lu Xun negated the imperialist-based bellicose nationalism that surrounded his own historical moment and pervaded the prologue of the twentieth century. Instead, he decisively turned to a bygone European revolutionary romanticism and the early nineteenth-century struggles for national liberation in the small lands far from China.

Fourth, with Lu Xun's search for the Mara voices of foreign lands from an earlier era, with this (new) international solidarity with (failed) national revolutions, we arrive at the superimposition of the long nineteenth century and China's short revolutionary twentieth century in Lu Xun's poetic world making. The long nineteenth century was a bourgeois, Western-centered, capitalist century, starting with the French Revolution and ending with the global accumulation of capital and imperialist domination of the earth. Wang Hui, a Lu Xun scholar and Chinese intellectual historian, then periodizes China's twentieth century as a short revolutionary century: "China's whole 'revolutionary century' [was] the era stretching from the Republican Revolution in 1911 to around 1976. The century's prologue was the period running from the failure of the Hundred-Day Reform in 1898 to the 1911 Wuchang uprising."[20] According to Wang Hui, the birth of China's revolutionary century was accompanied by "global comparison": the new Chinese consciousness of world relations was conditioned by constant references to the nineteenth century and its modernity as a "prehistory" and continuous comparisons to other national experiences.[21] This revolutionary century was both an acceptance and a critique of nineteenth-century modernity, both an effort to incorporate the West and a fight to overcome the mode of Western domination and oppression, both a modernizing project and a search for truly different alternatives. The particularity of the Chinese Revolution as a singular-plural world-historical event lies in the fact that it encompassed the bourgeois revolution, national revolution, and socialist revolution all at once, embodying a utopian critique of capitalistic modernity and pointing toward a new humanity.[22]

Fifth, Lu Xun's formulation of Mara poetry is fundamental to this world making in the transition from the long nineteenth century to China's revolutionary century. In his theory of worlding, Pheng Cheah argues for the normative force of world

19. Rebecca Karl, *Staging the World*, 16.
20. Wang Hui, "Depoliticized Politics, from East to West," 29.
21. Wang Hui, *Shiji de dansheng*, 111.
22. Wang Hui, *Shiji de dansheng*, 171.

literature, explaining that *normativity* "refers to what ought to be."[23] Based on a critical reading of Heideggerian philosophy, Cheah suggests that "temporalization worlds a world" and indicates that such a worlding—especially for non-Western literature—can be a resistance to the "cartographical approach" of capitalist globalization and world system.[24] Lu Xun's "Mara" may be seen, in this light, as a case of non-West worlding of poetry, resisting an essay mapping of political-economic power and incorporating a revolutionary-romanticist "normative force"—that is, "Mara power"—of poetry originated in European modernity. And yet, along the line of temporalization, my reading is intended to go beyond even the idea of "normativity." Lu Xun's act of "seeking new voices from foreign lands"[25] is also part and parcel of a "desire to leave for a foreign place, to take a different path, and to seek a different kind of people,"[26] a desire represented in his own contributions to China's literary, cultural, and intellectual revolution. "Mara poetry" as modern world poetry shows not only a normative force but also a search for revolutionary alternatives to the modern world system—that is, for truly different possibilities of a transformative literary world and human world. In this sense, Lu Xun's world making is indeed "temporalization": what Cheah sees in non-Western literature as "revolutionary time"[27] is both an incorporation of the rebellious spirit of European poetry and a periodization of new possibilities—that is, a new revolutionary sequence in world history and against a capitalist-imperialist world domination. With this poetic-political note of "worlding/temporalization," we now turn to the crisis of the revolutionary world making and periodization in Lu Xun's prose poem, a poem in which he invokes once again Petőfi.

"Hope": The Crisis of the Present and Poetic Worlding

Written on New Year's Day 1925, "Hope" was a prose poem that marked Lu Xun's new spiritual wandering amid the uncertainty of the waning May Fourth New Culture (loosely 1917–1925) and the burgeoning National Revolution (1925–1927). This prose poem was subsequently included in Lu Xun's collection of prose poems, *Wild Grass*, one of the most obscure and magnificent works of modern Chinese poetry.[28] A lot of ink has been spilled about this book's remote resemblance to Charles Baudelaire's reinvention of prose poetry in *Le spleen de Paris* and its direct

---

23. Pheng Cheah, *What Is a World?* 6.
24. Cheah, *What Is a World?* 8, 5.
25. Lu Xun, "Moluo shili shuo," 68 ; Lu Xun, "On the Power of Mara Poetry," 99, translation modified.
26. Lu Xun, "Preface to *Cheering from the Sideline*," 22, translation modified.
27. Pheng Cheah, *What Is a World?* 13.
28. On the inclusion of this book of prose poetry into the modernist tradition of China's New Poetry, see Hong Zicheng et al., eds., *Shijian he qi*, 1. For the first comprehensive study of *Wild Grass* in English, see Nicholas Kaldis, *The Chinese Prose Poem*.

relationship with Kuriyagawa Hakuson's 廚川白村 *Symbols of Angst*, thereby situating Lu Xun's prose poems in a broader travel of modernism in world literature. In this essay, I will limit my discussion to "Hope" as a key text, focusing on the crisis of periodization/worlding and the figuration of the Hungarian poet Petőfi in this prose poem.

"But now there are neither stars nor moonlight, no vagueness of laughter, no dance of love. The young are peaceful, and before there is not even a real dark night."[29] Near the end of "Hope," Lu Xun seems faced with a historical void of "now" in which all figurative signifiers fall into an absence of signification. As I will show, this poem also conceals a topological preview of how Lu Xun reperiodized this vain present ("now") into a radical political possibility of his final years as a leftist. The turbulent years from the dissolution of the May Fourth intellectual movement in the 1920s to the founding of the Leftist Writers' League in the wake of the massacre of Communists by the Guomindang (GMD) regime have long been considered as a period of crisis in Lu Xun's lifework. The question that commonly follows is how to define and understand the so-called late Lu Xun. I believe that a more interesting question is how the very textuality of Lu Xun's transition exemplifies the periodizing/worlding force within China's revolutionary century. This chapter thus sees "Hope" as a site of the crisis of periodization and world making. The prose poem should not merely be read as an exemplar of the poetics of Lu Xun's historical anguish; it also twists Lu Xun's vain present into a "throwing" (一擲) of his "old age."[30] If this action of writing as throwing opens up the "real" as "hazard" in historical necessity,[31] then one may say that the outcome of this "throwing" was manifested in Lu Xun's eventual identification with a new historical dynamic of the Chinese Revolution in the 1920s and 1930s. That is where this chapter will end with a glimpse of the traces of world poetry in Lu Xun's contentious engagement in revolutionary literature.

Nowhere in Lu Xun's work is the theme of temporalization/worlding more obvious than in "Hope." The prose poem takes on the repetition of variation between youth/revolution and loneliness/nothingness. Opening this text with the return of the pervasive feeling of loneliness ("My heart is extraordinarily lonely"), Lu Xun traces the concept back to the "withering away" of "youth," first the "my youth" and then the poet's "outer youth."[32] As Kiyama Hideo 木山英雄 has indicated, the two types of youth represent two temporalities and two concrete historical situations, the former being "the pre-Republican youth in the revolutionary trend" and the latter being "a symbol of the youth of the Republic."[33]

---

29. Lu Xun, "Hope," 35.
30. Lu Xun, "Hope," 36, 37, translation modified.
31. Alain Badiou, *Théorie du sujet*, 111.
32. Lu Xun, "Hope," 33, translation modified.
33. Kiyama Hideo, *Wenxue fugu yu wenxue geming*, 32.

First of all, the poet's youth is characterized by "sanguinary songs, blood and iron, fire and poison, resurgence and revenge"[34] and refers implicitly to the 1911 Revolution, the first Chinese Revolution. This revolution as an event, Maruyama Noboru 丸山昇 argues, was interiorized into a subjective process for Lu Xun.[35] Eventually the incompletion of this revolution left Lu Xun in a state of "loneliness" (寂寞) and "nothingness" (空虚).[36] In other words, the subjectivity is infused and then emptied by a revolution and its failure. Still, this event initiates the primal symbolic order in the temporality of the withering youth inside the subject. For Lu Xun, it takes the form of the "shield of hope" (希望的盾):[37] although on both sides of the resisting shield is nothingness (which is to say, the hope is vain), this structure of tension decides the initial order of signification. To put it in Alain Badiou's language, in the disappearance of the truth event, the poet's subject turns into a fidelity to the syntax of the revolutionary temporality ("youth"), which assumes "sanguinary songs," and yet this fidelity itself is bound to be consumed by the "invasion" of nothingness.[38] In this sense, the hope means nothing but the belated fidelity to the event, the loneliness nothing but the political "anguish of void" or "the lack of lack."[39] The "shield of hope" is then a meaning-giving trope of periodization and worlding: it gives to the void meaning "revolutionary time" and the worldedness;[40] it gives a dynamic of struggle to an empty history.

Then the hope placed on "the outer youth" amounts to Lu Xun's insistence of this fidelity in the historical situation of the May Fourth New Culture movement. His engagement in New Culture was at least partly based on his "faith" on a new generation or what Lu Xun calls "the outer youth." The belief that "the youth outside me still existed"[41] provides the content that fills the lateness of his fidelity to the withering "inner youth." Or, to use Kiyama's language again, the "outer youth" fulfills a "symbol"[42] of the substitute revolutionary temporality: "stars and moonlight, limp fallen butterflies, flowers in the darkness, the funereal omens of the owl, the weeping with blood of the nightingale, the vagueness of laughter, the dance of love"[43]— these are the democratic bourgeois imprints of the May Fourth youth. While such "a youth of sadness"[44] defines the social reference of Lu Xun's cultural-political

---

34. Lu Xun, "Hope," 33.
35. Maruyama Noboru, *Lu Xun, geming, lishi*, 29–37.
36. Lu Xun, "Hope," 32, 33.
37. Lu Xun, "Hope."
38. Lu Xun, "Hope."
39. Alan Badiou, *Théorie du sujet*, 98.
40. Pheng Cheah, *What Is a World?* 13.
41. Lu Xun, "Hope," 32, 33.
42. Kiyama Hideo, *Wenxue fugu yu wenxue geming*, 32.
43. Lu Xun, "Hope," 33–35.
44. Lu Xin, "Hope," 35.

practice, in this poem it is withering away, too. Historically, this withering away of the outer youth led to a further disillusionment that Lu Xun was experiencing at the moment of writing.

Therefore, on the one hand, a metonymical shift from "my youth" to "outer youth" and, on the other hand, a metaphorical correspondence between youth and the historical references. Together they form Lu Xun's syntax of subjective process as a topology of revolutionary temporality. We may then follow the example of Badiou's poetic-philosophical reading and name the two temporalities of youth as two "vanishing terms"[45] of this prose poem while adding a historical dimension to this terminology. This then invites a reformulation of Badiou's question—"why there have to be two vanishing terms in a poem"[46]—into a more concrete historical context: why is there a repetition of the withering away for the Chinese prose poet writing in the mid-1920s?

If we read Lu Xun as a poet of repetition and repeated hope and disillusionment, then we must read "Hope" as the second coming of Petőfi in Lu Xun's lifework. At an end point of what Badiou would call the poem's "metaphorical network" and "metonymical corrosion,"[47] when it reaches the ultimate crisis of the withering away of both the inner and outer youth, Petőfi is invoked and cited:

> But why is it now so lonely? Is it because even the youth outside me has departed, or the young people of the world have all grown old?
> I have to grapple alone with the dark night in the emptiness. I put down the shield of hope, hearing the Song of Hope by Petőfi Sandor (1823–49):
> "What is hope? A prostitute!
> Alluring to all, she gives herself to all,
> Until you have sacrificed a priceless treasure—
> Your youth—then she forsakes you."
> It is already seventy-five years since the great lyric poet and Hungarian patriot died for his father land on the spears of the Cossacks. Sad though his death, it is even sadder that his poetry has not yet died.[48]

We know the title of Lu Xun's text comes from Petőfi's poem. Whereas the young Lu Xun's introduction of Petőfi's lifework and the Hungarian Revolution in the "Mara" essay relies heavily on Frederick Riedl's 1906 book *A History of Hungarian Literature*—a book included in the series of *Short History of the Literatures of the World*[49]—Lu Xun reads and translates Petőfi's "Hope" from a Reclam edition of

---

45. Alan Badiou, *Théorie du sujet*, 98.
46. Badiou, *Théorie du sujet*, 98.
47. Badiou, *Théorie du sujet*, 113.
48. Lu Xun, "Hope," 35.
49. For a discussion of poetry and the Hungarian Revolution, see Frederick Riedl, *A History of Hungarian Literature*.

Petőfi's poems in German translation. As Kitaoka emphasizes, this Hungarian poem expresses the patriotic poet's existential crisis "combining despair with expectation" in the days of European national revolutions.[50] Lu Xun then seizes on another reference of "hope" in Petőfi and carries another quote of Petőfi into the prosaic-poetic repetition of hope and despair, meaning and emptiness, worlding and void:

> But—so wretched is life—even a man as daring and resolute as Petőfi had in the end to halt before the dark night and gaze back toward the distant Orient.
>
> "Despair, like hope," he said, "is but vanity."
>
> If I must still live in this vanity which is neither light nor darkness, then I would seek the youth of sadness and uncertainty which has departed, even though it is outside me. For once the youth outside me vanishes, my own old age will also wither away.
>
> But now there are neither stars nor moonlight, no limp fallen butterflies, no vagueness of laughter, no dance of love. The young people are very peaceful.
>
> So I have to grapple alone with the dark night in the emptiness. Even if I cannot find the youth outside me, I would at least have a last flight in my own old age. But where is the dark night? Now there are neither stars nor moonlight, no vagueness of laughter, no dance of love. The young people are very peaceful, and before me there is not even a real dark night.
>
> Despair, like hope, is but vanity.[51]

The crisis of periodization/worlding is culminated in an ending of no resolution, an ending that is the repetition of a Petőfi line. According to Kitaoka Masako's investigation, this line is not from a poem but a travel journal. Petőfi's original signifies the "deceptive" nature of both despair and hope, whereas in Lu Xun's rendering, they are both "vain."[52] Kitaoka Masako also emphasizes the broader influence of Petőfi in Lu Xun's prose poem. Petőfi's lamentation of "Europe's calming"[53] obviously reminds us of Lu Xun's observation that "the young people are very peaceful."[54] Notably, the ideal of the Mara poet is the very opposite of being peaceful.[55]

In this void where even the metaphorical phrase "dark night" ceases to be "real," in this vanity of both historical hope and existential despair, the prose poet's final effort of periodization and worlding is an act of "throwing" his "old age" into the sheer void and "grappling" with this emptiness.[56] On the one hand, this poetic move itself manifests the intensity of the subjective crisis of periodization and bears testi-

---

50. Kitaoka Masako, *Moluo shili shuo cai yuan kao*, 208.
51. Lu Xun, "Hope," 35, 37.
52. Kitaoka, *Moluo shili shuo cai yuan kao*, 218–19.
53. Kitaoka, *Moluo shili shuo cai yuan kao*, 227–28.
54. Lu Xun, "Hope," 37.
55. Lu Xun, "Moluo shili shuo," 69.
56. Lu Xun, "Hope," 35–37, translation modified.

mony to the fathomless anguish of void. On the other hand, the obverse side of Lu Xun's anguish is precisely what Badiou calls "the poet's courage,"[57] and the "throwing" aims to open up a new periodizing and worlding process. Such an act is against causal necessity or historical determination; in Kiyama Hideo's words, it is again Lu Xun's "non-logic" of poetic action arising from the collapse of metaphorical-metonymical signification.[58] With this act, Lu Xun submits his lateness (the "old age") to the historical contingency that a subjective process, as a matter of fact, can never avoid. This historical impulse shows Lu Xun's political "courage" to risk yet a new internal scission of the present void and the void present. The temporalizing torsion of "throwing" the "old age" into the void, then, turns into a dialectic of void and worlding in a moment of crisis, a dialectic of the poet's anguish and courage, based on Lu Xun's creative reading of Petőfi. We then move on to the difficulty and more poetic layers of this decisionist act of worlding within the historical void.

Poetry and Revolution: Relay Translation, Relay Reading

Lu Xun's later work on the left in 1930s Chinese cultural politics, as is well known, was prepared and preconditioned in his engagement in the issue of literature and revolution in the second half of the 1920s. One year after the writing of "Hope," in 1926 Lu Xun translated into Chinese the Russian-Soviet revolutionary Leon Trotsky's "Alexander Blok" via a Japanese translation, and this relay translation marked Lu Xun's involvement in the leftist controversy of what is a "revolutionary poem." His response to China's "revolutionary literature debates" (革命文學論爭, 1928–1930) concluded in his "hard translation" (硬譯) of Lunacharsky, Plekhanov, and other Marxists.[59] Lu Xun's "hard translations" are often relay translations via Japanese sources, where the poet flings himself into translation, revolutionary theory, and intellectual reorientation.[60] Here, I am particularly interested in the poetic dimension of his relay translations and intellectual-theoretical flinging. I want to stress that in this case, relay translations are also relay readings of poetry, such as Lu Xun's reading Trotsky reading Blok's long poem *The Twelve*.

Lu Xun translated Trotsky's essay on Blok from Shigemori Tadashi's 茂森唯士 Japanese rendering of *Literature and Revolution*. He included this essay in the book of Hu Xiao's 胡斅 Chinese translation of Blok's *The Twelve* and wrote an afterword. In this famous essay, Trotsky sees Blok as a great poet of mysticism and decadence belonging to prerevolutionary Russia, and appraises *The Twelve* as "Blok's highest

---

57. Alan Badiou, *Théorie du sujet*, 124.
58. Kiyama Hideo, *Wenxue fugu yu wenxue geming*, 22.
59. See Lu Xun, "Yingyi yu wenxue de jiejixing."
60. For a discussion of Lu Xun's practice of relay translation, see Pu Wang, "The Promethean Translator and Cannibalistic Pains."

30 Lu Xun, World Poetry, and Poetic Worlding

achievement," then specifies that "'The Twelve' is not a poem of the Revolution."[61] Trotsky continues and repeats this critical judgment throughout the rest of the essay, even though Blok's polemical masterpiece is about the revolution. For Trotsky, "Blok's anxious state of chaos gravitated into two main directions, the mystic and the revolutionary. . . . Blok, who . . . translated [the period] into his own inner language, had to choose, and he chose by writing 'The Twelve.'"[62] But on the other hand, "the inner meaning of the Revolution remains somewhere outside the poem. . . . That is why Blok crowns his poem with Christ. But Christ belongs in no way to the Revolution."[63] Trotsky's highly dialectical approach to Blok's work arrives at a key passage for Lu Xun: "The poet seems to want to say that he feels the Revolution in this also, that he feels its sweep, the terrible commotion in the heart, the awakening, the bravery, the risk , and that even in these disgusting, senseless, and bloody manifestations is reflected the spirit of the Revolution."[64]

Lu Xun accepts Trotsky's powerful conclusion: "Blok is not one of ours, but he reached toward us. And in doing so, he broke down. But the result of his impulse is the most significant work of our epoch. His poem, 'The Twelve,' will remain forever."[65] Lu Xun's own "Postface to *The Twelve*" echoes this critical discourse. He admires Blok as a rare poet who "sees poetry in an oscillating revolution":

> The old poets have fallen silent, have found themselves clueless, or have fled. The new ones haven't touched on the totally new lyre. In Revolutionary Russia, Blok alone listened to the '. . . music of destruction.' He heard the wind of the dark night and white snow, the whining of the old lady, the wandering of the priests, millionaires and madams, the negotiation of the price for prostitution in the conference hall, the song and gunshots of revenge, the blood of Katka. And yet he also heard the old world like a mangy dog: he reached toward the Revolution.[66]

This highly sympathetic view of Blok reinforces the self-contradictory yet sincere existence of the poet in a historical moment of revolution. As a result, even though his poem is "not a poem of the Revolution," it is "not empty."[67] It is interesting to note that Lu Xun's appraisal of such a poet's existence at the storm center of history reverts to the figurative language that we have seen in both the "Mara" essay and the prose poem "Hope." More and more scholars have turned to the question as to whether Trotsky's influence determined Lu Xun's conception of the "revolutionary human" and whether Trotsky's idea of literary fellow traveler gave rise to Lu Xun's

---

61. Leon Trotsky, *Literature and Revolution*, 107–8.
62. Trotsky, *Literature and Revolution*, 107.
63. Trotsky, *Literature and Revolution*, 109.
64. Lu Xun, "Shi'er ge hou ji," 110.
65. Trotsky, *Literature and Revolution*, 111.
66. Lu Xun, "Shi'er ge hou ji," 221–22.
67. Lu Xun, "Shi'er ge hou ji," 222.

self-positioning as a fellow traveler of the Communist revolution. More specifically, in his study of Lu Xun's acceptance of Trotsky's theory of revolutionary literature, Nagahori states that "through Trotsky's depiction of Blok, Lu Xun superimposes himself on the image of the poet Blok."[68] I would add that Lu Xun's conception of the revolutionary human and the revolutionary fellow traveler is an extension of the Mara poet ideal and the existential struggle in the emptiness. The poet's grappling is self-contradictory and yet real—real also in the sense that it is a poetic opening of the real human struggle. From this perspective, we can better understand his later conclusion: revolutionary literature must be the output of the revolutionary human in the historical activity—that is to say, revolutionary literature is the world making, the periodizing force and the poetic opening, of active revolutionary existence.[69]

If "Mara" represented Lu Xun's initial search for the new voices from the foreign, then Lu Xun's hard translation of Marxist aesthetic theories concluded his second phase of "seeking a different path." Like his translation of Trotsky, Lu Xun's hard translation is also relay translation primarily via Japanese sources. This new round of relay translation contains again a relay reading of poetry. In his 1930 essay "'Hard Translation' and the 'Class Nature of Literature,'" Lu Xun invokes the figure of a suffering Promethean translator in his famous defense of his engagement in Marxism:

> Then I feel that such theory [of the proletarian revolution that has been translated into Chinese] is too little to provide a frame of reference, and as a result everyone's mind is more or less confused. To chew and anatomize the enemy now seems inevitable, but if we have a book of anatomy and a book of cuisine to guide our practice, then the structure [for anatomy] and the taste [for chewing] can be clearer and better. People like to compare Prometheus, the legendary figure in the Greek mythology, to revolutionaries, believing that the magnanimity and forbearance, which Prometheus showed when he was punished by Zeus but remained unrepentant for stealing fire for man, are the same [as that of a revolutionary]. But I stole fire from foreign countries only with the intention of cooking my own flesh, in the hope that if I find the taste agreeable, it would benefit more to those who chew [my flesh], and the consumption of my body would not prove in vain.[70]

This rewriting of the Prometheus myth has long been considered as the ultimate allegory of Lu Xun's self-understanding within revolutionary cultural politics.[71] Lu Xun's Promethean myth refers back to Lunacharsky's work, and it is worth mentioning that according to Lunacharsky's theory, a tragedy transforms horror and

---

68. Nagahori Yuzo, *Lu Xun yu Tuoluociji*, 21.
69. See Nagahori, *Lu Xun yu Tuoluociji*.
70. Lu Xun, "Yingyi yu wenxue de jiejixing," 213–14; Lu Xun, "Hard Translation and the Class Character of Literature," 82, translation modified.
71. See Leo Ou-fan Lee, *Voices from the Iron House*, 189.

suffering into an aesthetic experience.[72] In fact, in "Art and Life," an essay included in *On Art*, Lunacharsky has a long quote from Goethe's poem "Prometheus," including the following lines:

> Who helped me
> Against the Titans' arrogance?
> Who rescued me from death,
> From slavery?
> Did not my holy and glowing heart,
> Unaided, accomplish all? And did it not, young and good,
> Cheated, glow thankfulness
> For its safety to him, to the sleeper above? . . .
>
> Here I sit, forming men
> In my image,
> A race to resemble me: To suffer, to weep,
> To enjoy, to be glad—
> And never to heed you,
> Like me![73]

Corresponding to the modern revival of the Prometheus myth, Lunacharsky cites this poem to repudiate the religious transcendental world and to reinforce an aspiration for human dignity.

Lu Xun reads Lunacharsky reading Goethe and a Promethean tradition in modern European poetry. The image of the fire-stealing and tormented Prometheus serves—for Goethe as much as for Shelley (who appears as another key poet in "Mara")—as a self-image of the modern poet. In line with the Marxist incorporation of the Prometheus myth, the Promethean poet becomes the Promethean translator in the later Lu Xun, and one must add that this rebellious figure of struggle and self-struggle, based on a relay translation/reading, is also a second coming of the Mara poet and an outcome of his grappling with the void and throwing of the old age in the sheer crisis of worldedness.

To summarize, I have demonstrated how several of Lu Xun's poetic engagements help constitute an alternative world poetry rather than simply mapping them onto a cartographical route within a literary world system. Simply put, world poetry in Lu Xun's case means a poetic worlding and its crisis. Through such a revolutionary urgency of poetry, a search for truly different possibilities—namely, truly different human worlds—becomes a decisive imperative or, to return to the theoretical language of the world literature debates, a radical normativity.

---

72. See Anatoly Lunacharsky, *Yishu lun*, 231.
73. Johann Wolfgang von Goethe, "Prometheus," 29, 31; see also Lunacharsky, *Marukusu Shugi Geijutsuron*, 181–83; Lunacharsky, *Yishu lun*, 267–69.

2

The Young Lu Xun and *Weltliteratur*

The Making of *Anthology of Fiction from beyond the Border*[1]

Wendong Cui

The concept of world literature has been a subject of debate since its inception.[2] Consequently, the resurgence of studies on world literature in the last two decades has exhibited a variety of perspectives. Scholars have viewed world literature as a system of genre dissemination, as a republic in which authors from various countries compete for recognition, or as a mode of reading literary classics in their original languages or translations. In the historical context, however, readers were more likely to engage with world literature through its material circulation than through theoretical debates, as demonstrated by Venkat Mani's timely research on the trajectory of *Weltliteratur* (world literature) in Germany.[3] In other words, world literature/ Weltliteratur was not only constructed by scholarly conceptualizations but also, perhaps more frequently, by the physical circulation of translated foreign literary works, mediated by a variety of publications such as literary magazines and book series. Expanding his perspective beyond Germany to encompass the entire world, Mani's insights allow us to explore further questions: How did the material circulation of world literature spread beyond German-speaking countries? What types of entanglements occurred when German sources of world literature such as books and

---

1. I would like to express my gratitude to Professor Leo Ou-fan Lee for his inquiry and encouragement in guiding me toward the research topic of this essay. I am also thankful to Professor Lucie Merhautová and Mr. Richard Davies for providing valuable research materials. I would like to express my appreciation to Professor Jon von Kowallis for his detailed comments on the early version of this essay, as well as to thank the editors of this volume for their insightful suggestions and unwavering support during the revision process. Last, I appreciate the support of the Research Grant Council of Hong Kong (Project No. 21601021) which made my overseas research trips possible.

2. John Pizer, *The Idea of World Literature*; Zhang Longxi, *From Comparison to World Literature*, chap. 10; Thomas Oliver Beebee, "Introduction," 5–16.

3. Venkat Mani, *Recoding World Literature*.

34 The Young Lu Xun and *Weltliteratur*

magazines encountered other cultures? How have new cultural contexts spawned innovative ideas and practices in world literature? Using Lu Xun's *Anthology of Fiction from beyond the Border* as a case study, this chapter addresses these questions.

Anthology of Fiction has generally been recognized as a two-volume collection of foreign stories collaboratively translated and compiled by Lu Xun and his brother Zhou Zuoren when they studied in Japan.[4] Whereas Zhou Zuoren handled the majority of the sixteen stories from English, Lu Xun took charge of just three stories from German. This approach has long posed a conundrum for scholars.[5] On the one hand, they often credited Lu Xun with the collection's distinctive character, which includes a preference for lesser-known Eastern European works of literature, a keen fondness for short stories, and an innovative approach that involved faithful renderings in an archaic *wenyan* style. On the other hand, it was challenging for these scholars to elaborate on Lu Xun's contributions due to his seemingly modest involvement.

This chapter reinterprets *Anthology of Fiction* as a publication initiative primarily launched by Lu Xun under the influence of German world literature sources (Zhou Zuoren had no knowledge of German). In contrast to previous research that concentrated solely on the sixteen published short stories, I trace Lu Xun's overall plan, which includes at least thirty-one stories (with fifteen remaining untranslated and unpublished), mediated by a unique material form.[6] Through comparative examination of German magazines and book series alongside *Anthology of Fiction*, I argue that German materials empowered Lu Xun to develop his distinctive concept of world literature and an innovative practice of displaying world literary works by compiling an anthology, both of which contributed to generating a dialectic between cosmopolitanism and nationalism in a Chinese context. The first section investigates how Lu Xun adopted the material form of *Aus fremden Zungen* (From foreign tongues, 1891–1910), a long-forgotten German literary monthly dedicated to presenting world literature. The second section examines how Lu Xun selected titles from a vast corpus of several book series, such as Reclam's Universal-Bibliothek (Universal Library). These series, known for their affordability and inclusiveness, gave young Lu Xun access to literary works that aligned with his objectives. Whereas scholars have long focused on his link to Japanese literature and culture,[7] my research directs

---

4. For recent examples, see Mark Gamsa, *The Chinese Translation of Russian Literature*.
5. Lawrence Wang-chi Wong, "The Beginning of the Importation of New Literature from Exotic Countries into China," 175–91. Wong solved this dilemma by demonstrating that the dominant role was played by Zhou Zuoren, which is different from my approach.
6. In the chapter, I use the first edition published in 1909. Kuaiji Zhoushi xiongdi, *Yuwai xiaoshuo ji*.
7. For earlier Japanese scholarship, see Itō Toramaru, *Ro Jin to Nihonjin n*; Fujii Shōzō, *Roshia no kage*; Kitaoka Masako, *Ro Jin bungaku no engen wo saguru*. For recent English scholarship, see Eileen J. Cheng, "Performing the Revolutionary"; Xiaolu Ma, "The Missing Link."

scholarly attention to Lu Xun's long-standing engagement with German sources, dating back to his early years.

From the Magazine of World Literature to *Anthology of Fiction*

As Mani suggests, magazines played a pivotal role in promoting world literature in Germany.[8] However, most of these periodicals, once popular among German readers, have faded into obscurity, even among academics. Notably, *Aus fremden Zungen*, a bimonthly publication that significantly influenced Lu Xun, met a similar fate and garnered little scholarly attention except for Lucie Merhautová's study.[9] This section begins by examining the magazine's purpose, content, and material form, combining Merhautová's analysis with my investigation of the publication. A reading of *Anthology of Fiction* alongside a reference to the magazine reveals how Lu Xun conceived the idea of compiling it and where he drew inspiration for its material form.

Aus fremden Zungen was established in 1891 by the Deutsche Verlags-Anstalt (German Publishing House), one of the largest publishing houses in Germany at the time. It was born out of a cultural climate in which world literature was seen as a key component of middle-class education and nationalism was on the rise. Consequently, the periodical inevitably incorporates a dialectic of cosmopolitanism and nationalism. On the one hand, Goethe's ideals have a profound influence. In his editor's note, the magazine's founding editor, Joseph Kürschner, stresses the publication's commitment by quoting Goethe: "The time has come for the epoch of world literature, and everyone must work to bring it on."[10] On the other hand, he highlights its nationalistic mission: "But one of the most beautiful qualities of the German spirit is its ability to always take for itself in a noble way the literature created by foreign nations. Even those who think that this tendency is somewhat excessive will not deny that it makes our literature universal, in addition to national. This is something that no country can match."[11] Thus, the more foreign literary works Germans introduce, the stronger the German national spirit grows. German culture is exceptional on a global scale because of its unrivaled capacity to introduce and appreciate world literature.

To compete with other magazines debating world literary concepts, Joseph Kürschner and succeeding editors characterized *Aus fremden Zungen* as the first of

---

8. Venkat Mani, *Recoding World Literature*, 124–28.
9. Lucie Merhautová, "Česká literární moderna v časopise Aus fremden Zungen," 93–125.
10. Joseph Kürschner, "Was wir wollen."
11. Kürschner, "Was wir wollen."

36   The Young Lu Xun and *Weltliteratur*

its kind devoted solely to the translation of contemporary foreign fiction. This singular focus was maintained for an impressive twenty-year period. The journal typically released twenty-four issues per year, which could be divided into two volumes. Each issue featured serialized novels as the primary content, complemented by short stories and reviews of contemporary authors and their works. Form-related modifications were also implemented sometimes. For instance, in 1904 and 1905, the journal underwent a redesign, adopting a smaller size and a revised layout. This new arrangement divided each issue into three sections: "Romane des Auslandes" (Novels of foreign countries), "Novellen, Erzählungen, Skizzen des Auslands/ Novellen, Erzählungen, Skizzen, Lyrik des Auslands" (Novellas, narratives, sketches of foreign countries/novellas, narratives, sketches, lyrics of foreign countries), and "Illustrierte Rundschau" (Illustrated review). As each section is paginated consecutively, readers and the publisher have the option of rebinding the entire year's issues into two volumes of novels, two volumes of short stories, and one volume of reviews. *Aus fremden Zungen* thus constituted a major editorial innovation for the first time in Germany as "a magazine and book at the same time."[12]

Meanwhile, *Aus fremden Zungen* established a new method of presenting world literature by juxtaposing works from a broad range of languages and national literature. Editors have increasingly broadened their horizons by introducing literary works from as many languages and nations as possible. For instance, the magazine covered works translated from French, English (British, American), Russian, Icelandic, Italian, Swedish, Hungarian, Polish, Croatian, Catalan, Danish, and Serbian in the first year and Norwegian, Ukrainian, Dutch, Flemish, and Czech works in the second year. In general, French literature has attracted the most attention for over the course of its twenty-year existence, followed by Russian and Scandinavian literature.[13] The table of contents of the bound volumes often reorders these titles by language/nation to display the national literature represented more clearly, showcasing the magazine's exceptional command of world literature and its superb contribution to the advancement of the German national spirit.

Aligned with their preferences for French and Russian literature, the editors' literary tastes strongly emphasized naturalism and realism. The magazine was among the first in Germany to promote these works at a time when critics and readers found these new endeavors controversial: "A large portion of foreign literature, especially French and Russian literature, breaks with tradition, establishes new ideals, picks up the exploratory impulse of the time for beautiful literature as well, and, in the pursuit of truth and knowledge, reveals what has hitherto remained hidden in darkness."[14]

---

12. Anonymous, "An unsere Leser."
13. Merhautová, "Česká literární moderna v časopise Aus fremden Zungen," 93–125.
14. Kürschner, "Was wir wollen."

The author who has received the most recognition was Émile Zola. Since its first year, the magazine has serialized his works, including almost all his notable novels. Leo Tolstoy, Thomas Hardy, and Alphonse Daudet are among the other authors on this list of favors. While using the terms "naturalism" and "realism," the editor often referred to these movements as having a "fin-de-siècle" style, stating that they "broke with many old views and directions, but also in the sense of a conscious reaction against literary untruthfulness."[15]

In response to the magazine's affinity for a fin-de-siècle literary style, it integrated fin-de-siècle art into its design and layout. From 1899 to 1905, the cover page featured a "Jugendstil" (youth style)—the German counterpart of art nouveau—painting by Johann Vincenz Cissarz, depicting a poet laureate dressed in ancient Greek robe transcribing a text, surrounded by his peers (see Figure 2.1). As in the nineteenth century, Germans considered themselves as the sole inheritors of Greek culture among humankind, the illustration likely serves as a self-reference to the role played by the magazine: the German translators, akin to the Greek poet laureate, enrich and glorify their own cultural tradition by introducing world literature. Since 1904, each column has been adorned with a multitude of illustrations sharing a similar style and featuring diverse subjects, thereby transforming the journal into a semi-pictorial publication.

Lu Xun's encounter with *Aus fremden Zungen* and other German publications was influenced by historical circumstances. As a medical student, he became proficient in German; during his time in Japan, he exhibited a profound enthusiasm for German culture. In his later years, Lu Xun revealed how he discovered German literary periodicals such as *Das literarische Echo* (The literary echo) in a Tokyo secondhand bookstore.[16] *Aus fremden Zungen* was also on Lu Xun's list of collections, as Zhou Zuoren later recalled that his brother had been impressed by a review of the Dutch author Frederik Willem van Eeden that was published in the journal. This review can be found in the 1905 volumes of *Aus fremden Zungen*, suggesting that Lu Xun must have acquired at least that particular issue from that year. Furthermore, Zhou Zuoren emphasized the high cost of the magazine, suggesting that Lu Xun may have purchased the bound volumes rather than individual issues (one volume cost 7 marks while one issue cost only 50 pfennig).[17]

Lu Xun was driven to purchase these journals based on his desire to construct Chinese national literature by learning from world literature. His musings on the dialectics of nationalism and cosmopolitanism, which diverge significantly from Kürschner's perspective, revealed themselves completely in his 1907 article "On the

---

15. Joseph Kürschner, "Zum dritten Jahrgang."
16. Lu Xun, "*Xiao yuehan* yinyan," 280.
17. Zhou Zuoren, "Guanyu Lu Xun zhi'er," 165–66.

38   The Young Lu Xun and *Weltliteratur*

Power of Mara Poetry." Lu Xun claims that the objective of literature is, on the one hand, to make the authentic voice of the heart and imagination audible and, on the other hand, to express the national spirit and inspire patriotism. His belief is that "the development of the national spirit is linked to the breadth of world knowledge"; thus, when traditional culture collapses due to arrogance and conservativeness, the only feasible approach of reviving national literature is to "search abroad for new voices."[18] To this end, he illustrates the transcultural flow of Byronism, which played a significant role in the revival of national literature in Poland, Russia, and Hungary. Since these nations, which Zhou Zuoren later referred to as "oppressed nations,"[19] endured similar suffering and repression as the Chinese, their literary works embodying brilliant voices and extraordinary imaginations serve as the best source of inspiration for the Chinese to create their own.

Although Lu Xun primarily delved into poetry in his theoretical discussion, his greatest fascination lay in fiction; thus, *Aus fremden Zungen* provided him with a specific reference of how to "seek abroad for new voices." According to Zhou Zuoren, Lu Xun originally planned to publish a literary journal named *Xinsheng* (New life, Chinese translation of Dante's *Vita nuova*) to promote foreign fiction. However, as the project faltered, he compiled short stories originally intended for the magazine into *Anthology of Fiction*.[20] The dual nature of the 1904 and 1905 volumes of *Aus fremden Zungen* as both magazines and books likely facilitated Lu Xun's transition from his initial plan of creating the first Chinese magazine of foreign short stories to instead compiling the first Chinese anthology of world literature. Among these volumes, Lu Xun was particularly impressed by "Novellen, Erzählungen, Skizzen des Auslands," and the title *Anthology of Fiction from beyond the Border* is almost a literal translation of the German one. Although Lu Xun used the broad term *xiaoshuo* (fiction) in the title of his book, likely because there were no precise Chinese equivalents for each word at that time, the anthology covered various types of short stories, such as *Novelle*, *Erzählung*, and *Skizze*, in a German sense.

It is worth noting that *Anthology of Fiction*, while appropriating the framework of *Aus fremden Zungen*, modified its vision of the "world," more akin to "Mara poetry." Lu Xun specifies in his editor's note that "my collection pays unbalanced emphasis to works from northern European countries because those are the regions where literature has recently flourished the greatest. The collection will eventually include works from southern Europe and the Orient as I plan to publish multiple volumes, making it a comprehensive presentation of foreign literature."[21] Two versions of

---

18. Lu Xun, "Moluo shili shuo," 67.
19. Zhou Zuoren, "Guanyu Lu Xun zhi'er," 166.
20. Zhou Zuoren, *Lu Xun de gujia*, 307.
21. Lu Xun, "*Yuwai xiaoshuo ji* lüeli," 170.

the world literature were identified. In the long term, Lu Xun expects *Anthology of Fiction* to generate a "comprehensive presentation" encompassing northern Europe, southern Europe, and the Orient, which is consistent with the vision of *Aus fremden Zungen*. However, in the short term, *Anthology of Fiction* prioritizes an unbalanced version, aligning with what Lu Xun identifies northern European literature.

Using this concept of northern European literature, Lu Xun appears to have been drawing on the North-South literary divide that European literary academics have been developing since the nineteenth century. For instance, the French literary critic Germaine de Staël classified European literatures into southern and northern. The former was classical and joyous, as represented by Greek, Roman, Italian, Spanish, and Louis XIV-era French literature, while Romantic literature, as represented by English, German, and Scandinavian literature, was emotional, philosophical, and imaginative, foreshowing the direction of literary development.[22] Madame de Staël's writing was presumably unknown to Lu Xun, but he was aware of this group of ideas because they frequently featured in the various writings of literary histories with which he was familiar.

The two versions of world literature correspond to the titles Lu Xun selected for *Anthology of Fiction*. The two published volumes featured sixteen short stories and sketches from six nations: Russia (seven), Poland (three), Bosnia (two), England (one), America (one), France (one), and Finland (one). Lu Xun offered two lists of works to be translated on the back pages of two published volumes: Russian (seven), Finnish (three), Hungarian (two), Norwegian (two), Danish (two), English (one), and Polish literature (one). Most of these works can be classified as northern European literature, giving readers a clear impression of an unbalanced version. However, it is noticeable that French literature was translated, and Lu Xun indicated in the back pages that the works from "southern Europe countries" and new Greece would also be selected in the near future, illustrating his endeavor to achieve a "comprehensive presentation." Why did Lu Xun prioritize literature from the North? One probable explanation is that these works are more imaginative and emotive and thus more capable of moving Chinese readers if we adhere to the original definition. Moreover, these nations more or less overlap with the "oppressed nations" highlighted in "Mara poetry," and their writings are more likely to stir the Chinese's national spirit.

The dialectic between cosmopolitanism and nationalism also manifests in the cover design of *Anthology of Fiction*. Lu Xun was inspired by the cover of *Aus fremden Zungen*'s bound volumes from 1904 and 1905, particularly the special volume on "Novellen, Erzählungen, Skizzen des Auslands": The title of the periodical is positioned at the top, the title of the special volume in the middle, and a "Jugendstil"

---

22. René Wellek, *A History of Modern Criticism 1750–1950*, 2:221.

40   The Young Lu Xun and *Weltliteratur*

illustration of the poet laureate at the bottom (Figure 2.1). The cover of *Anthology of Fiction* features a similar design: at the top is a rectangular illustration depicting a Greek maiden or a Muse playing the lyre in the forest by the sea, with white doves flying in the haze, and below is the book title in the small seal script written by Lu Xun's calligrapher friend Chen Shizeng (Figure 2.2). Lu Xun substituted the image of the poet with that of the maiden, another Jugendstil illustration from the 1905 volume of *Aus fremden Zungen* (Figure 2.3), most likely because it better encapsulates the purpose of the anthology: the lyre and the maiden/goddess can be interpreted as embodiments of literature as a new voice of heart and as symbols of what Lu Xun referred to in his preface as the "new style of exotic literature."[23] Therefore, the combination of German artwork and the title written in small seal writing may also be seen as a visual representation of young Lu Xun's vision for a new literary movement that integrates cosmopolitanism and nationalism.

From Book Series of World Literature to Anthology of Fiction

Whereas the concept of exhibiting an unbalanced version of world literature in a magazine and eventually a book was inspired by the material form of *Aus fremden Zungen*, a closer examination of the sources of titles translated and selected for *Anthology of Fiction* reveals that Lu Xun heavily relied on the German book series, such as the Universal-Bibliothek, which remains popular to this day. One might wonder why Lu Xun, an avid reader of periodicals, completely ignored their translated content when compiling this anthology. Therefore, it is essential to summarize the qualities of these book series to offer possible clues.[24]

The world literature book series was primarily distinguished by its vast scope and extensive inclusion, offering readers such as Lu Xun a significantly larger corpus of texts from which to explore a wide array of literary works.[25] The Universal-Bibliothek, regarded as the most prominent of these series, was founded in 1867 by the Leipzig-based publishing house Reclam Verlag (Reclam Publisher). The series initially devoted to reprint German classics by authors such as Goethe, Lessing, Schiller, and Jean Paul. With the inclusion of an increasing number of foreign literary classics over time, the Universal-Bibliothek has evolved into a series showcasing

---

23. Lu Xun, "*Yuwai xiaoshuo ji* xuyan," 170.
24. Prior research has examined how Lu Xun appropriated these German works but has neglected to address the *Anthology of Fiction*. Beijing Lu Xun bowuguan Lu Xun yanjiushi, ed., *Lu Xun cangshu yanjiu*; Xiong Ying, "Lu Xun dewen cangshu zhong de 'shijie wenxue' kongjian," 38–46. The editions of German books cited in this chapter are based on the record in Beijing Lu Xun bowuguan, ed., "Xiwen shu muci."
25. Venkat Mani, *Recording World Literature*, 121–24, 139–40.

Figure 2.1: Cover of *Aus fremden Zungen*'s special volume, on "Novellen, Erzählungen, Skizzen des Auslands"

Figure 2.2: Cover of Lu Xun's *Anthology of Fiction from beyond the Border*

Figure 2.3: Image from 1905 volume of *Aus fremden Zungen*

42   The Young Lu Xun and *Weltliteratur*

world literature. Since the 1870s, the series has been engaged in rendering contemporary foreign literature into German, mostly Russian and Scandinavian, by prominent authors such as Turgenev, Gogol, Tolstoy, Chekhov, Gorky, Ibsen, and Strindberg. Similar to *Aus fremden Zungen*, the Universal-Bibliothek encompassed a diverse range of works translated from minor European and Asian languages but on a much grander scale and with a considerably broader spectrum of literary styles. In the late nineteenth century, rival publishers such as Verlag von Otto Hendel (Otto Hendel Publisher) and Meyers were inspired by Reclam's success and launched ventures such as the Bibliothek der Gesamt-Literatur des In-und Auslands (Library of the Total Literature of the Country and Abroad) and Volksbücher (Folkbooks), both of which garnered a substantial audience.

At the same time, these book series gained an edge over other types of publications due to their compact format and affordable price.[26] Anton Philipp, the creator of Reclam, firmly believed in the educational ideal of the classics and aimed the series at educating not just the middle classes but the working classes as well. The publisher implemented significant changes to make the series more accessible to a broader audience. First, in a notable departure from previous marketing, which required consumers to purchase an entire series of books, the Universal-Bibliothek published each copy in pocket-size paperbacks and sold all works independently, allowing buyers to assemble their own collections based on individual preferences and needs. Second, because the publisher did not have to pay for publishing rights, it could offer an astonishingly low price of 20 pfennigs. That is, one may purchase one item of the Universal-Bibliothek at 40 percent of an issue of *Aus fremden Zungen*. Third, the publisher cooperated with overseas partners to expand its market. For instance, as Japan in the late Meiji period was an enthusiastic admirer of German culture, Japanese dealers such as the Maruzen bookstore worked with Reclam and introduced the German book series to readers in Japan; it was in such a milieu that Lu Xun was exposed to these book series.

Zhou Zuoren's vivid recollection of young Lu Xun's days in Tokyo demonstrates the advantages of these book series. According to him, the brothers shared a keen interest in literary works from "bizarre" nations, such as Russia, Poland, Czechia, Serbia, Bulgaria, Finland, Hungary, Romania, and modern Greece. Additionally, they focused on Denmark, Norway, Sweden, and the Netherlands, while France, Spain, and Italy received comparatively less consideration. Since these works from minor languages were translated into Japanese and English less frequently than they were into German, Lu Xun regarded book series such as the Universal-Bibliothek as particularly valuable. Because the book series was sold at a low cost, Lu Xun was able

---

26. Georg Jäger, "Reclams Universal-Bibliothek bis zum Ersten Weltkrieg," 25–49; Lunda J. King, "Reclam's Universal-Bibliothek," 1–6.

to acquire them in large quantities by placing orders with the Sagamiya bookstore, which would then obtain volumes from the Maruzen bookstore. [27] In contrast, *Aus fremden Zungen* was not only more expensive but also inaccessible and could only be obtained in secondhand bookstores. Furthermore, the magazine's affinity for French naturalism and Russian realism limited the range of literary styles that Lu Xun could be exposed to.

Zhou Zuoren's assertions can be verified by examining the inventory of Lu Xun's German book collection held at the Beijing Lu Xun Museum. Notable European literature, such as German (including Austrian, forty-seven items), French (thirty-one), and English (three), is represented, but these were not Lu Xun's primary interests. In line with Zhou Zuoren's claim, the majority of the collection demonstrates Lu Xun's strong penchant for works from the so called bizarre countries such as Russian literature (over one hundred), Hungarian (thirty-five), Polish (twenty), Czech (ten), Greek (nine), Finnish (four), Romanian (four), Bulgarian (one), Croatian (one), and Serbian (one).[28] Other European literature had a complementary role, including Norwegian (eighteen), Danish (seventeen), Swedish (eight), American (six), Spanish (six), Italian (six), Icelandic (five), Dutch (four), Belgian (four), and Portuguese (one). Oriental literature not addressed by Zhou Zuoren, such as Turkish (one) and Indian (one), was included in the collection as well. Suffice it to say that Lu Xun's collection of German books closely mirrored the unbalanced version of world literature or northern European literature that he suggested while witnessing his desire for a "comprehensive presentation."

Given this, the titles chosen by Lu Xun for the anthology can be viewed as miniature representations of his extensive collection of German works. Although he personally translated only three works—specifically, "Man (Lie)" and "Mo (Silence)" by Andreev, and "Siri (Four Days)" by Garshin—in the two published volumes, his role in the compilation process was more significant than previously believed. Among the sixteen titles published, we can trace the German sources of three more works by Garshin, Chekhov, and Aho back to book series. It is plausible to assume that Lu Xun first discovered them and subsequently entrusted Zhou Zuoren with the translation task. Additionally, the back pages of the two published volumes list fifteen titles slated for translation. By examining Lu Xun's collection, we can further identify the sources of nine short story titles in various German versions. Thus, almost half of the content of *Anthology of Fiction* can be attributed to Lu Xun. To clearly showcase the fifteen titles selected or translated by Lu Xun and their German origins, I present table 2.1.

---

27. Zhou Zuoren, "Guanyu Lu Xun zhi'er," 165–66.
28. Beijing Lu Xun bowuguan, "Xiwen shu muci," 27–28.

44 The Young Lu Xun and *Weltliteratur*

Table 2.1: The titles translated or selected by Lu Xun and their German sources

Nation	Author	Title in Chinese Translation	German Sources	Publisher
Russia	Andreev	Man 謾	Die Lüge (Lie)	Otto Hendel, Deutsche, Reclam
Russia	Andreev	Mo 默	Das Schweigen (Silence)	Otto Hendel, Deutsche, Reclam
Russia	Chekhov	Saiwai 塞外	In der Verbannung (In exile)	Reclam
Russia	Garshin	Xiehou 邂逅	Eine Begebenheit (An incident)	Reclam, Insel Verlag
Russia	Garshin	Siri 四日	Vier Tage (Four days)	Reclam, Insel Verlag
Russia	Garshin	Jianghua 絳華	Die rote blume (A red flower)	Reclam
Russia	Korolenko	Hai 海	Das Meer (The sea)	Reclam
Russia	Korolenko	Linlai 林籟	Der Wald rauscht (The forest rustled)	Reclam; Insel Verlag
Finland	Juhani Aho	Xianqu 先驅	Die Ansiedlung (The pioneers)	Otto Hendel, Reclam
Finland	Päivärinta	Huangdi 荒地	In der Einöde (In the wilderness)	Reclam
Finland	Päivärinta	Shuren 術人	Der Zauberer (The wizard)	Reclam
Denmark	Andersen	Liaotian sheng-hui 寥天聲繪	Bilderbuch ohne Bilder (A picture book without pictures)	Reclam
Denmark	Andersen	Hemeiluori longshang zhihua 和美洛斯壟上之華	Eine Rose von Homers Grab (A rose from Homer's grave)	Reclam
Norway	Bjørnson	Fu 父	Der Vater (The father)	Reclam; Meyers
Norway	Bjørnson	Rensheng mishi 人生闚事	Ein Lebensrätsel (A mystery of life)	Reclam

It is evident that the works chosen to fit within the framework all originate from book series published by Insel Verlag, Otto Hendel, and Reclam, with some content overlapping. The largest proportion consists of works by Russian writers such as Andreev, Chekhov, Garshin, and Korolenko. These are complemented by Finnish writers like Päivärinta and Aho, the Norwegian writer Bjørnson, and the Danish writer Anderson. Different types of short stories, including novellas, narratives, and fairy tales, captivated Lu Xun's attention in terms of literary genres. Existing research has often underscored the young Lu Xun's profound attraction to Russian literature, suggesting his fascination with romantic and symbolic styles.[29] As Patrick Hanan observes, "Lu Xun rejected the European Realists and Naturalists, as well as the Japanese Naturalists, not because of Flaubert's objectivity or Zola's social determinism . . . but because he was simply not interested in the techniques of Realism. His taste for Andreev, who flirted with Symbolism, and for Gogol, . . . who specialized in satire and even irony, are indications of a search for a basically different method."[30] My previous research has further substantiated that Lu Xun's choices among the works listed in the table from other national literatures were similarly rooted in his fascination with various symbolic or romantic elements.[31] In stark contrast to the naturalistic and realistic content found in *Aus fremden Zungen*, all of these titles resonate with the style of northern European literature as understood by Lu Xun and can effectively convey authentic emotional expression.

In addition to the aesthetic aspect of Lu Xun's selection, it is noticeable that these titles exemplify, to varying degrees, the dialectic between cosmopolitanism and nationalism, which must have also influenced his decision. Finnish literary works are particularly illustrative in this regard. As a typical "oppressed nation," Finland did not gain independence from Russia until 1917. However, its flourishing literature, corresponding with Lu Xun's definition of northern European literature, provides a remarkable reference for Lu Xun on how literature succeeded in expressing the national spirit and inspiring patriotism even before achieving national freedom. As new burgeoning Finnish literature quickly transcended its own territory through German book series, it successfully integrated into the realm of world literature, providing Lu Xun the opportunity to "explore new voices from abroad."

Among the Finnish writers, Pietari Päivärinta particularly drew Lu Xun's attention, probably because he was widely recognized as a pioneer of Finnish national literature and a significant contributor to world literature. According to Gustav Lichtensein, the translator of Lu Xun's source text, the two-volume *Finnische novellen* (Finnish novellas, 1890, 1892) from the Reclam edition, Päivärinta's work, noted for

---

29. Douwe W. Fokkema, "Lu Xun," 63–83; Leo Ou-fan Lee, *Voices from the Iron House*, 19–21.
30. Patrick Hanan, "The Technique of Lu Hsün's Fiction," 53–96.
31. Cui Wendong, "Qingnian Lu Xun yu deyu 'shijie wenxue.'"

its "psychological observation, warm and profound depiction of life, and its simple yet moving portrayal," should be labeled as "the best accounts of the lives of rural people in world literature."[32] Lichtensein further asserts that Päivärinta's novellas are "among the most astonishing masterpieces in contemporary Finnish literature,"[33] especially considering that he was the first author to write in the Finnish language.

The dialectic between cosmopolitanism and nationalism is also distinctly apparent in the two German translations of Päivärinta's works—namely, "The Wizard" and "In the Wilderness." In "The Wizard," the author emphasizes universal values while setting the story in a remote Finnish village. The narrative revolves around a farmer who practices sorcery to make a living, while the younger generations lose faith in his abilities. One night, as the sorcerer sneaks into cattle barns to cut off their ears, a group of young men discover him and teach him a lesson. They punch him, fling him into the lake, expose him to the villagers, and finally dress him as a demon to reveal his wizardry as a sham. As the author states at the beginning, the story depicts a time when some individuals "still adhered to the old notions, and therefore a war between the forces of darkness and light remained." In the end, the author concludes, "it was the responsibility of the expanding Enlightenment to destroy this idea [superstition], and this could not be accomplished using gentle means. That demanded strong blows."[34] In so doing, the narrative effectively illustrates the inevitable triumph of the Enlightenment over superstitions.

In contrast, "In Wilderness" places greater emphasis on the national spirit of the Finnish people while depicting the shared human experience of rural life. After trespassing into a desolate wilderness, the first-person narrator encounters a severe storm and seeks shelter in a modest cabin inhabited by a family of settlers. Through conversations and observations, the narrator comes to understand that despite their prolonged and strenuous efforts, the family struggled to make ends meet, and both generations suffered significant losses among their children due to the harsh environmental conditions. The author explicitly connects the plight of the settlers to the progress of Finnish civilization at the end of "In the Wilderness" when the narrator exclaimed that "when countries and empires are captured via battle, it costs an immeasurable quantity of human blood and innumerable lives. How many cultural and spiritual lives did Finland's triumph cost?"[35] This connection is reinforced by the inclusion of a stanza from the Finnish national poet Johan Ludvig Runeberg's verse "Our Land," which is commonly regarded as the unofficial Finnish national anthem.

---

32. Gustav Lichtensein, "Vorwort," 1.
33. Lichtensein, "Vorwort," 1.
34. Pietari Päivärinta, Finnische novellen, 1:87.
35. Pietari Päivärinta, Finnische novellen, 2:65.

Through these elements, "In the Wilderness" serves as a poignant national allegory, illustrating the resilience and sacrifices of the Finnish people.

It is unclear why Lu Xun was unable to translate these two stories. Instead, another work, "Xianqu," was included in volume 2 of *Anthology of Fiction* as a substitute. This story was translated by Zhou Zuoren from the English version "Pioneers," originally written by an equally renowned Finnish author Juhani Aho. The selection should have been made by Lu Xun, as he had collected two German renditions of Aho's short stories, both of which covered "Die Ansiedlung," the German version of "Pioneers." Although Aho, known for his lyrical style, was not typically considered a national writer like Päivärinta, this story shares a similar theme with "The Wizard" and "In the Wilderness," reflecting the dialectic between cosmopolitanism and nationalism that Lu Xun advocated.

The narrative follows the life journey of an anonymous young Finnish couple who leave the comfort of the priest's house to venture into the wilderness of Finland. They encounter illness, suffering, and disaster, ultimately meeting their demise. Yet, their endeavors lay the foundation for future settlers, turning the rugged terrain into arable land. Aho's work overtly pays homage to those nameless pioneers who sacrifice their youth and vitality for the progress of civilization, a sentiment emphasized in the story's conclusion: "When the rye blooms and the ears of corn ripen in our fields, let us call to mind these first martyrs of the settlement. We cannot raise monuments upon their graves, for their number is many thousands, and their names we know not."[36] Much like "The Wizard," the narrative vividly portrays the universal experiences of rural life in the face of adversity. Similarly, as with "In the Wilderness," it serves as a tribute to pioneers who have left an indelible mark on Finnish civilization and functions as an allegory of the Finnish national spirit characterized by unwavering persistence and resilience.

Conclusion

Goethe's concept of Weltliteratur had a profound and enduring influence on German-speaking nations. Motivated by this ideal, nineteenth-century German intellectuals published numerous works promoting world literature. As a result, German culture excelled in the translation of foreign literatures, surpassing all other nations. These German sources of Weltliteratur, including magazines and book series, transcended geographical boundaries, eventually reaching Japan through their material circulation. As a Chinese student studying in Japan with a profound interest in literature from diverse cultures, Lu Xun stumbled upon these sources. Inspired by them, he initiated a creative endeavor that culminated in the creation of *Anthology of Fiction*.

---

36. Juhani Aho, *Novellen*, 8; Juhani Aho, *Junggesellenliebe und andere Novellen*, 98.

48 The Young Lu Xun and *Weltliteratur*

Drawing on the physical format of *Aus fremden Zungen* and selecting texts from book series such as Universal-Bibliothek, Lu Xun's anthology showcased his unique perspective on world literature—an "unbalanced version" particularly relevant to Chinese readers—and established a dialect between cosmopolitanism and nationalism within a Chinese context. On further exploring Lu Xun's later literary career, it becomes evident that these sources of Weltliteratur exerted a consistent and substantial influence on his literary compositions, translations, and compilations. Most previous research has focused on Lu Xun's and other Chinese writers' practices of assimilating other foreign literary sources, such as English, French, and Japanese, while ignoring the substantial contribution of German sources to the development of modern Chinese literature. By highlighting the impact of Weltliteratur's material circulation on the formation of *Anthology of Fiction*, this chapter indicates how the fusion of world literature and modern Chinese literature studies will offer new insights.

3
Lu Xun's Russian Intertexts and the Dialectics of Optimism and Pessimism

Keru Cai

This chapter forms a bridge between two important bodies of criticism about Lu Xun's writing: on the one hand, scholarship about Lu Xun's reading of world literature in general and of Russian literature in particular;[1] and on the other hand, scholarship about Lu Xun's ambivalent attitude toward the relationship between the intellectual and the masses thought to be in need of reform.[2] These two sets of concerns are intertwined in his fiction because they are both about overcoming otherness. Lu Xun's appropriations from the foreign cultural other enable him to explore the problem of whether a would-be reformer can successfully communicate with the social other. The implication in his fiction is that if elements of the cultural other can be incorporated into Chinese literature, thereby rejuvenating and transforming it, then this radical aesthetic practice can potentially facilitate communication with the social other within China.

The first body of criticism discusses how Lu Xun's writings synthesize elements from a number of foreign intertexts, from Gogol to Soseki to Nietzsche,[3] often exhibiting caution toward the project of importing ideas.[4] In 1934, Lu Xun famously proclaimed the necessity of "grabbism," appropriating from abroad in order to

---

1. See, for instance, Sun Yu, *Lu Xun yu Eguo*; Mark Gamsa, *The Chinese Translation of Russian Literature*, 141–89; and Xiaolu Ma, "The Missing Link" and "Transculturation of Madness."
2. See Marston Anderson, *Limits of Realism*, 90; and Theodore Huters, "Blossoms in the Snow," 68–69. Roy Chan has explored how Lu Xun's prose poetry presents the limitations of identification, as well as the transcendence thereof, between a first-person narrator and the characters he observes. See *The Edge of Knowing*, 39–73. See also Leo Ou-fan Lee, *Voices from the Iron House*, 69–88.
3. See, for instance, Jon Eugene von Kowallis, "Lu Xun and Gogol"; Eileen J. Cheng, "'In Search of New Voices from Alien Lands'"; J. D. Chinnery "The Influence of Western Literature," 319; and Marián Gálik, *Milestones in Sino-Western Literary Confrontation*, 26; and Lee, *Voices from the Iron House*, 56.
4. See, for instance, Cheng, "'In Search of New Voices from Alien Lands.'"

breathe new life into Chinese culture.[5] Above all, he maintained a keen interest in Russian culture, beginning from his student days in Japan, when he and his brother Zhou Zuoren read many translations of Russian literature, briefly studied Russian, and published several translations of Russian texts. Throughout his life, Lu Xun translated prolifically from Russian literature by means of mediating languages (particularly Japanese and German),[6] and he acknowledged the imprint of Russian texts on his own writing.[7]

The second body of criticism interrogates Lu Xun's perennial skepticism toward his project of writing to save the nation by bringing about reform. Lu Xun's profession of writing was, according to his account in the preface to *Outcry*, motivated by the desire to save his countrymen from benightedness and numbness (*mamu* 麻木).[8] Yet the preface goes on to recount his initial failed foray into literary production and subsequent descent into loneliness and hopelessness. Can the intellectual in fact communicate meaningfully with the countrymen whose purported state of benightedness and numbness he wishes to reform? In the end, he claims that he only reluctantly takes up his pen to write in case trying to awaken the slumbering prisoners of the iron house might be better than doing nothing.[9] Lu Xun explains that his stories are not relentlessly suffused with pessimism only because he had to obey his *jiangling* 將令 (general's orders) and avoid infecting readers with his sense of loneliness.[10] This ambivalence about the attainability of his ambitions in writing is reflected in his fiction.[11]

In several of Lu Xun's stories, we find forerunners of "native soil" literature,[12] where the intellectual who left the native soil to become educated is now an outsider when he returns and reencounters the native residents of his hometown. There is an unresolved tension between outsider and insider, between what is extrinsic and what is intrinsic to the native place. A parallel tension is at play formally in the stories as well: Lu Xun the Chinese writer has intellectually departed the precincts of his home culture, reaching outside of the native soil to appropriate literary elements

---

5. See "Nalai zhuyi," in *LXQJ* 6:38–40.
6. See Wang Yougui, *Fanyijia Lu Xun*, 14–22, for an account of Lu Xun's knowledge of foreign languages.
7. "I have found more in Russia than in any foreign culture," Lu Xun reportedly said in 1926. Jon Eugene von Kowallis, "Lu Xun's Early Essays," 13. Lu Xun stressed the humanism of Russian literature and its championing of the "insulted and the injured." See Lu Xun, *Lu Xun lun waiguo wenxue*, 24–25.
8. *LXQJ* 1:438.
9. *LXQJ* 1:441.
10. *LXQJ* 1:441.
11. See Marston Anderson, *Limits of Realism*, 92. As Wang and Hashimoto discuss in their chapters in this volume, Lu Xun explores this preoccupation with the problem of hope elsewhere in his writings as well.
12. See David Der-wei Wang, *Fictional Realism*, 249.

extrinsic to the Chinese tradition, and by doing so attempts to reinvent Chinese literature. The intellectual characters in his stories may fail to change the lives of the people they encounter in their native soil, but Lu Xun has irrevocably changed the trajectory of his native Chinese literature in the composition of these stories.

To demonstrate the impotence of the intellectual outsider in saving the Chinese people, Lu Xun uses narrative techniques he, the educated intellectual, gleaned from beyond Chinese culture. Yet it is from these foreign materials that Lu Xun simultaneously adapts ways of implying that an outsider's intervention may be efficacious to some degree in breaking down the walls of the iron house. As Lu Xun writes in his preface, the stories imply both pessimism and optimism, and it is often by means of *qubi* (distortions) that he manages to inject some semblance of optimism into their endings.[13] I wang to suggest that some examples of these distortions derive from Lu Xun's intertextual engagement with Russian literature.

Below, I examine three stories that appropriate techniques from Russian texts to illustrate the chasm between the would-be savior and those whom he hopes to save, while also adapting Russian elements to offer a glimmer of hope in the would-be savior's aspirations. The first story is Lu Xun's 1918 "Diary of a Madman," which redeploys structural properties of Nikolai Gogol's (1809–1852) *Zapiski sumasshedshego* (Diary of a madman, 1835). The second work is the 1919 story "Medicine," which adapts the narrative of Leonid Andreev's "Ben-Tovit" (1905) and employs elements gained in the process of translation of Andreev's (1871–1919) *Molchanie* (Silence, 1900) as well as his *Krasny smekh* (Red laugh, 1904). The third work is the 1925 story "The Lamp of Eternity," which revises thematic and formal elements of Vsevolod Garshin's (1855–1888) *Krasnyi tzvetok* (Red flower, 1883). Lu Xun's intertextual engagements with Russian texts evoke the dialectics of hope and hopelessness in his ever self-deprecating aspiration to revitalize Chinese culture by grabbing elements from abroad.

The Diaries of Madmen

How hopeful is the ending of "Diary of a Madman"? The story's preface, written in a classical Chinese that the diary entries notably eschew, tells us that the madman has recovered from his mental illness and is waiting to join the state bureaucracy.[14] Does this mean that he has relinquished his hopes of reform as well as his exhortation to "save the children"?[15] Have his critiques fallen on entirely deaf ears? As David Der-wei Wang remarks, the story exposes "the predicament of speaking

---

13. See *LXQJ* 1:441.
14. *LXQJ* 1:444.
15. *LXQJ* 1:455.

out in a society which refuses to listen."[16] Certainly, the validity of the madman's convictions—about the cannibalistic immorality inherent in millennia of Chinese tradition—have been undermined from the beginning by his labeling as a madman, within both the *fabula* (by the people around him) and the *siuzhet* (in the story's title). This is the result of borrowing the form of the madman's diary from Gogol, whose entries are as garbled as the diarist's paratextual notation of dates—for both stories make it clear that the madmen lack a clear grasp of both temporality and reality, such that no one lends credence to their passionate denunciations of social structures or cultural histories.[17] So on the most basic level, Lu Xun's appropriation from Gogol's story undermines hope that the protagonist will be taken seriously, either intradiagetically by the madman's interlocuters or extradiegetically by Lu Xun's readers. Choosing the title "Diary of a Madman" signals that Lu Xun does not hold out hope that audiences are ready to accept the story's radical critiques of Chinese society.

Yet in subtler ways, Lu Xun adopts elements from Gogol's story that inject glimmers of hopefulness that the madman's critiques are not doomed to be entirely stifled in the iron house. Commenting on the *qubi* in Lu Xun's fiction, Marston Anderson cites the ending of "Diary of a Madman," with the exhortation to "save the children," as one of these interventions that mitigate the pessimism of the *siuzhet*.[18] This famous injunction has roots in the parting cry of Gogol's madman, Poprishchin, who is a civil servant crushed under the dehumanizing social hierarchy of the Petrine table of ranks. Poprishchin's diary ends with a cry of help for a child, but in this case the child is himself: "Dear mother, save your poor son!"[19] He makes this plea after suffering beatings in the asylum, where he has been dragged after announcing that he is the new king of Spain. Poprishchin is here above all calling out to Mother Russia. The diary entries leading up to this final one are littered with references to Western European politics and personages. But at the moment when he can take the abuse no longer, the madman casts himself no longer as the king of Spain but as a child of Mother Russia: "Save me! take me! give me a troika of steeds swift as the wind! . . . A forest races by with dark trees and a crescent moon; blue mist spreads under my feet; a string twangs in the mist; on one side the sea, on the other Italy; and there I see some Russian huts. Is that my house blue in the distance?

---

16. David Der-wei Wang, *Fictional Realism*, 6.

17. Critics have noted the resonances between the two stories. See, for instance, Song Binghui, "Cong Zhong'E wenxue jiaowang kan Lu Xun 'Kuangren riji' de xiandai yiyi—jian yu Guogeli tongming xiaoshuo bijiao, "135; Sun Yu, *Lu Xun yu Eguo*, 125–27; Chinnery, "The Influence of Western Literature," 310; and Ma, "The Missing Link" and "Transculturation of Madness."

18. Marston Anderson, *The Limits of Realism*, 87.

19. Lu Xun, "Diary of a Madman," 293. Theodore Huters has noted the imagery of the pietà evoked by this passage (*Bringing the World Home*, 273).

Is that my mother sitting at the window?"[20] He spots European Italy in this vision, but it is toward the motherland that he finally turns. For Poprishchin to fantasize that a quintessentially Russian mode of transport (the troika) has taken him to see traditional Russian peasant dwellings where his mother(land) could save him is a desperate turn back to the non-urban, pre-Westernized, premodernized forms of temporality outside of St. Petersburg.

If the child and parent function as components in a national allegory for Gogol, this is no less true for Lu Xun, whose madman hopes to save the next generation of Chinese youths from millennia of cannibalistic, mercenary social relationships and textual legacies.[21] But unlike Poprishchin, Lu Xun's madman eschews national tradition in his search for salvation. Whereas Gogol's madman turns homeward and inward, focusing on himself and his native land, Lu Xun's madman instead looks outward beyond his own troubles and beyond the precincts of Chinese tradition. He wants to move forward in time, thinking about China's future, unlike Poprishchin, who wants to turn back the clock from Westernized urbanism to the agrarian Russian countryside.

Lu Xun's "Diary of a Madman" appropriates the final cry for help in Gogol's story, altering it to open up the possibility that there is a way out of the cycles of rapacity inherent in Chinese history: there is hope for China's future in spite of the millennia of alleged cannibalism, because future generations have not yet been inculcated in violence. Yet the story's preface seems to undermine this hope, as it implies that this would-be savior of China's future generations has already relinquished his crusade. However, there is one final element of the narrative frame that preserves the possibility of hope: the story is not bookended by a postface at the end of the diary entries. We begin with an unnamed narrator who tells us to consider this diary only as a psychiatric specimen, but because this "sane" voice does not reappear at the end of the entries to remind us of the madman's insanity, the story leaves us with only the madman's resounding cry to save the children. It is this injunction that is the story's final word, not an undercutting thereof.

This preservation of the power of the madman's final exhortation is something that Lu Xun notably changes from Gogol's story. Throughout his diary entries,

---

20. Nikolai Gogol, "Diary of a Madman," 293.
21. Of note is the difference in how Gogol and Lu Xun perceive of kinship. For Poprishchin, whose oppression arises from an impersonal social order, the fantasy of salvation lies in contemplation of his next of kin, however impossible this salvation may be. For Lu Xun, by contrast, it is the nearest of kin who are themselves the most terrifying threat, as elders not only eat their younger siblings and children, but go on to teach the surviving children to eat others in turn. Perhaps Lu Xun's madman has not recovered from his insanity, as the story's preface informs us, but has in fact been eaten by his elder brother, who then perpetrates the conspiracy of labeling his victim a madman, thereby undermining the radical threat of his epiphanies. Family is dangerously powerful precisely because of the intimate access provided by close kinship.

Poprishchin is consistently portrayed as delusive, absurd, and pretentious. Yet in the final entries, he becomes increasingly sympathetic when he seems to gain clarity and realize that he is not in fact being ordained as the next monarch of Spain but in reality suffering from torture in the asylum. As we have seen, his last diary entry leaves the realm of the ridiculous for that of the sublime (vast landscapes with mist, water, wind, and celestial bodies). Huters and Holquist have both noted the sudden moment of sanity, clarity, and even divinity at the end of Poprishchin's story, but I want to point out that there is a final bathetic jolt: "Dear mother! pity your sick child! . . . And do you know that the Dey of Algiers has a bump (*shishka*) just under his nose?"[22] Gogol does not allow the tale to end with Poprishchin's lingering cry for mercy, but instead undercuts his hero one last time. Poprishchin resumes his comedically crazed ramblings. So it is all the more telling that Lu Xun does not deploy this final undermining maneuver at the end of his story: he allows the madman's desperate, solemn plea to resound, without cutting it off or rendering it ludicrous. Indeed, Lu Xun's story ends with a series of ellipses, which David Wang has interpreted as a silence expressive of the futility of interlocution and of the madman's "subjective truth."[23] But if we contrast Lu Xun's ellipses with the question mark that ends Gogol's "Diary of a Madman," then the former's ending seems to leave open a space for hope: there remains uncertainty, but the plea to save the children lingers on.

"Medicine" and the Andreev Trifecta

The would-be savior of Lu Xun's "Medicine" is even more decisively silenced than that of "Diary of a Madman," for he ends the story in his grave. His message of reform has been capitally punished, yet Lu Xun concludes the story with another *qubi*, leaving a clue that perhaps somebody has heeded the revolutionary call. Just as Lu Xun's intertextual engagement with Gogol provided the narrative techniques that facilitated his dual presentation of pessimism and (tenuous) optimism in "Diary of a Madman," in "Medicine" Lu Xun's appropriates from Andreev the elements that demonstrate both the failure to communicate the necessity of change as well as the (ambiguous) potential that the voice in the iron house has not fallen on deaf ears. "Medicine" adapts the plot structure of Andreev's story "Ben-Tovit" to underscore the psychological distance between the would-be savior and those whom he hopes to save in "Medicine." And from Andreev's "Silence" and *Red Laugh* comes, via a set of (mis)translations, a ray of hope at the end of Lu Xun's story.

---

22. Gogol, "Diary of a Madman," 293.
23. David Der-wei Wang, *Fictional Realism*, 6.

The medicine in the title refers to a white steamed bun that, dipped in the blood of an executed young revolutionary, is meant to save the life of a young villager, Xiao Shuan, who is dying of tuberculosis. The treatment fails, however, and in the story's final scene, the mother of the deceased consumptive youth encounters the mother of the executed revolutionary at the cemetery, where both women are visiting the gravesites of their respective sons. The mother of the young revolutionary finds a wreath of red and white flowers, left anonymously on her son's grave. Convinced that her son's spirit is reaching out to her, she exhorts him to make a crow perched on a nearby tree fly onto his grave. There is no response. In the story's closing line, the crow flies off toward the horizon like an arrow.

Lu Xun himself observed that "Medicine" echoes certain stylistic elements of Andreev's fiction, in particular its "somber chill" (*yinleng* 陰冷).[24] The journalist and editor Sun Fuyuan 孫伏園, a fellow native of Shaoxing, wrote, "Mr. Lu Xun once told me that in Western literature there are works similar to 'Medicine.' For example, Russia's Andreev has a story called 'Ben-Tovit,' which describes that when Jesus was crucified on Golgotha, near Golgotha there was a merchant with a toothache. He is like Lao Shuan and Xiao Shuan in thinking that their own ailment is much more important than the unjust death of a revolutionary."[25] Zhou Zuoren's 1919 translation of "Ben-Tovit" is titled *Chitong* 齒痛 (Toothache),[26] which emphasizes bodily experience, just as Lu Xun's story largely elides the revolutionary's execution (and its world-historical implications) in order to focus on the bodily illness of the Hua family's boy, as well as the white bun dipped in blood, the stand-in for the cannibalized revolutionary's body. Both Andreev's "Ben-Tovit" and Lu Xun's "Medicine" satirize the all-consuming nature of personal monetary and bodily preoccupations to the exclusion of loftier ideals.

I would add that the stories also share a similar temporal structure. In both texts, as the time of world-historical events marches forward, both the protagonists and the narratives themselves hardly register these cataclysmic executions, for they are distracted by the individual's affective present of bodily pain. For instance, whereas in Andreev's text the crucifixion of Christ, "the great crime of earth" has ramifications for the arc of human history,[27] Ben-Tovit can only experience time by means of tiny increments, moments that stretch out and dilate in sensations of pain:

---

24. See "Qie jie ting zawen er ji" and a letter to Xiao Jun 蕭軍 and Xiao Hong 蕭紅, both written in 1935, in Lu Xun, *Lu Xun lun waiguo wenxue*, 116–17. Marián Gálik has alleged that "*Medicine* would probably never have been written (at least not in the form known to us) without Andreev's short stories *Ben-Tovit* and *The Silence*" (*Milestones*, 33). See also Wang Furen, *Lu Xun qianqi xiaoshuo yu Eluosi wenxue*, 98–99.

25. Sun Fuyuan, *Lu Xun xiansheng er san shi*, 20; translation mine.

26. It is likely he translated via Mori Ogai's Japanese translation; see Mark Gamsa, *The Chinese Translation of Russian Literature*, 239.

27. Leonid Andreev, "Ben-Tovit," 1:1362, translated as "On the Day of the Crucifixion," 48.

"Ben-Tovit sat up in his bed and swayed back and forth like a pendulum [*maiatnik*]. His face wrinkled and seemed to have shrunk, and a drop of cold perspiration was hanging on his nose, which had turned pale from his suffering. Thus, swaying back and forth [*pokachivaias'*] and groaning for pain, he met the first rays of the sun, which was destined to see Golgotha and the three crosses, and grow dim from horror and sorrow."[28] The sun, the marker of world-historical time, shines down upon the scene on Golgotha that day; Ben-Tovit, transformed figuratively into a pendulum, has a completely different solipsistic experience of time. Similarly, in "Medicine," the sun gradually rises upon the throng that gathers to watch the execution of Xia Yu, but the narrative elides direct description of the execution itself, mimicking the Hua family's fixation on Xiao Shuan's interminable coughing.

Lu Xun thus redeploys the tactics of focalization and temporality from "Ben-Tovit" to emphasize the insurmountable difference in perspective between the revolutionary and those around him, who have neither time nor attention for his message. Tempering this bleakness in "Medicine" are elements with roots in Andreev's "Molchanie" (Silence, 1900). The protagonist of this story, Father Ignatii, alienates his daughter Vera with his stern and sanctimonious demeanor. Vera has recently returned from St. Petersburg harboring a secret that eventually drives her to suicide. The title refers to the resounding, reverberating silence that deafens Father Ignatii after Vera's death, as his belated attempts to communicate with the deceased Vera and his paralyzed wife meet with no response. Andreev's story is thus about the foreclosed possibility of communication and mutual understanding. Lu Xun takes this thematic premise, as well as the plot point of a parent attempting to reach a deceased child, and gives it national repercussions, along with a tenuous possibility of hope.

Andreev's "Silence" was translated twice into Chinese in the first decades of the twentieth century. Lu Xun first translated it in 1909, relying on a prior German translation. Liu Bannong 劉半農 translated it into Chinese again in 1914, relying on a prior English translation.[29] Whereas Lu Xun's version, "Mo" 默, remains close to the original in terms of plot, detail, and description, Liu Bannong's version, "Moran" 默然, departs significantly from Andreev's original. Indeed, in Liu's version, which only includes the latter half of Andreev's original story, Vera appears to have died of illness rather than by suicide. Zhang Lihua argues that Lu Xun incorporated elements of Liu Bannong's translation into his "Medicine." For instance, the final scene of "Medicine" features precisely the red and white flowers and the figure of a bird

---

28. Andreev, "On the Day of the Crucifixion," 44.
29. Zhang Lihua, "'Yiwen,'" 68.

that, though missing in Andreev's original story and in Lu Xun's translation, appear in Liu Bannong's loose translation.[30]

This wreath is one of the distortions (*qubi*) that Lu Xun claims he added to his stories in a forced attempt to relieve their unremitting gloom: its presence on the grave of the deceased revolutionary may signify that somebody has paid homage to his message of reform. Perhaps, in spite of the portrayal of perspectival disconnect between the revolutionist and the townsfolk, he has managed to communicate successfully with somebody after all. Anderson considers the crow in this scene to be another of Lu Xun's *qubi*. This crow, which the mother of the revolutionary would like to endow with superstitious symbolism, fails to satisfy her hopes, but as it flies toward the horizon it serves as an ambiguous signifier of a future untethered to traditional superstitions.[31] I hypothesize that this imagery of the crow may have been lifted from Andreev's *Red Laugh*, a novella about a soldier whose experiences of atrocity in the Russo-Japanese war triggers his descent into madness. Lu Xun translated parts of this novella in 1909, and it informed the writing of his "Diary of a Madman" as well.[32]

In the penultimate section of *Red Laugh*, the narrator remembers a mother "who kept receiving letters from her son for a whole month after she had read of his terrible death in the papers . . . each letter was full of endearing and encouraging words and youthful, naïve hopes of happiness [*naivnoi nadezhdy na kakoe-to schast'e*]."[33] This mother, like the one in Lu Xun's "Medicine," seeks hope in the posthumous communications of her son. But as in "Medicine," messages from the dead are not heartening. The soldier's letter details the bloodshed of war: "To drink the

---

30. Zhang Lihua, "'Yiwen,'" 72. Critics have described this wreath of flowers as a distinctly Western object, such that there forms a contrast "between the naturally grown, 'homemade' emblem [on the other graves] and the human-made, imported symbol (the wreath was introduced to China)" (Gang Yue, *The Mouth that Begs*, 95; see also Ann Huss, "The Madman that Was Ah Q," 139). The wreath was not present in Andreev's original story "Silence" but appears out of nowhere in Liu Bannong's translation and Lu Xun's story, just as intradigetically the wreath of flowers springs out of nowhere onto the grave of the executed revolutionary. According to Lu Xun, the wreath is a surplus detail that he added only to satisfy the editors and readers of his story; it is an extrinsic intervention, not something that arose intrinsically and organically in his original conception of the story. The wreath is a Western object, but is written into being by a Chinese pen. We can read this wreath, then, as a sign of the textual surplus or residue that arises out of the encounter (involving translation, mistranslation, appropriation) with Western texts. It is not a Barthesian reality effect, signifying that "this is real" since its appearance on the grave is not at all realistic according to the logic of the story; rather, it is an "intertextuality effect," signifying that this story is the product of intertextuality.

31. See also Milena Doleželová-Velingerová for a dual interpretation of the crow, culminating in the "affirmation of a frightening, but cathartic symbol of revolution" ("Lu Xun's 'Medicine,'" 231). Ming Dong Gu argues that the message of the crow remains indeterminate ("Lu Xun, Jameson, and Multiple Polysemia," 441–42).

32. See Patrick Hanan, "The Technique of Lu Hsün's Fiction," 65–68.

33. Leonid Andreev, *The Red Laugh*, 100.

blood of one's enemy is not at all such a stupid custom as we think," he writes. "The crows are cawing. Do you hear, the crows are cawing. From whence have they all gathered? The sky is black with them." This nexus of details in Andreev's text weaves into the fabric of Lu Xun's "Medicine": the mother's hope to hear from her murdered son, the drinking of blood, and the message from the dead featuring the ambiguous symbolism of the crow. Andreev's deceased soldier continues to describe the cannibalistic carnage and repeats this refrain, "The crows are cawing [*voron'e krichit*]. Do you hear, friend, the crows are cawing. What do they want?" Here, as in Lu Xun's story, they are associated with the grim death of a national struggle gone awry, and they leave open more questions than they can resolve. In "Medicine," however, the imagery of the crow is perhaps not quite as grim as Andreev's portrayal. A symbol of death, and yet it does not just caw inscrutably but instead takes wing, flying away into the distant future, ending the story with a forward-moving vector of velocity and perhaps of change—albeit with indeterminate and equivocal optimism.

The Flower and the Flame

The revolutionary's fundamental perspectival disconnect from the villagers who execute him and the tenuous symbols of hope and communication embedded in the *qubi* at the end of "Medicine"—these are the elements of pessimism and optimism at tension in Lu Xun's story that arise from his intertextual engagement with Andreev's works. The madman of "The Lamp of Eternity" bears resemblance to both the revolutionary in "Medicine" and the madman of "Diary" in that he is unable to persuade anyone of the validity of his convictions. Lu Xun here adapts Garshin's basic plot structure in "Red Flower" and makes alterations in content and form that emphasize the hopelessness of saving China, with perhaps one beacon of hope at the end: the lamp has not been extinguished, but neither has the madman's voice.

Although Garshin was not otherwise influential in China, Lu Xun and Zhou Zuoren admired him greatly and translated some of his stories. Lu Xun was able to read Garshin's stories in Japanese and German translation,[34] and for the 1909 collection *Anthology of Fiction from beyond the Border* he translated Garshin's *Chetyre dnia* (Four days, 1877). As Cui points out in her chapter in this volume, a few other stories by Garshin were assigned to Zhou Zuoren to translate for their anthology. Zhou Zuoren remarked upon the resemblance between Garshin's "Red Flower" and Lu Xun's 1925 story "Lamp of Eternity."[35] In a biographical blurb on Garshin in the 1909 edition of *Anthology of Fiction*, Lu Xun describes how "Red Flower" draws on

---

34. See Xiaolu Ma, "Missing Link," 333–35.
35. Zhou Zuoren, "Lu Xun xiaoshuo li de renwu," 179. There are clear resonances with "Diary of a Madman" as well.

Garshin's own experience with mental illness,[36] and in a 1921 preface to a translation of Garshin's *Ochen' koroten'kii roman* (A very short novel, 1878), he mentions "Red Flower" as a famous work.[37] A second preface to this same translation, written in 1929, summarizes the plot of "Red Flower" and describes the possibly semiautobiographical protagonist as being "half-mad" (*bankuang* 半狂).[38] Lu Xun also notes that Garshin's "Red Flower" had already been introduced to Chinese readers "five or six years ago."[39] So by the time Lu Xun wrote "Lamp of Eternity," he had already encountered Garshin's "Red Flower." In this story, Garshin's madman is fixated upon the eponymous poppy flowers which, in his mind, represent the distillation of all evil in the world, and which he therefore feels duty bound to extirpate. Sacrificing his remaining strength in this endeavor, the madman escapes the restraints placed upon him and finally destroys the last red flower in the asylum's garden, dying in his triumph.

"The Lamp of Eternity" is set not in a mental institution but rather in a community called Jiguang tun 吉光屯 (Luckylight Village), so called because according to local legend, the lamp in the temple has never been extinguished since it was first lit by Emperor Wu of Liang. Having purportedly protected the village for centuries, the lamp is now endangered because the scion of a local scholar-gentry family has, in a state of supposed madness, resolved to put out the light because he is convinced that it is the locus of all ill fortune: once it is extinguished, he tells his fellow villagers, all plagues and disasters will come to an end. However, everyone else is equally convinced that putting out the light will bring calamity upon the village, so the battle lines are drawn: the villagers attempt to foil the alleged madman's attempts, and the latter decides that the best way to put out the light would be to set fire to the entire temple. Finally, the villagers lock up the madman in an empty room within the temple itself. The story ends with children playing outside who, overhearing the madman's continued threats to set the place on fire, alter their games to incorporate the madman's exhortations into the nonsense of their riddles.[40]

The thematic similarities between Lu Xun's and Garshin's stories are clear: both madmen struggle against the guardians of their objects of fixation because they are convinced that they alone are shouldering the weight of their fellow humans' salvation. Both madmen are described as having a fiery light in their eyes, matching the fiery glow of the objects they wish to destroy, the red flowers and the red flame. In the eyes of Garshin's protagonist "burned a motionless hot glow" (*goreli*

---

36. See Lu Xun, *Lu Xun lun waiguo wenxue*, 103.

37. Lu Xun, *Lu Xun yiwen ji* 10:575.

38. Lu Xun, *Lu Xun yiwen ji* 10:576.

39. See Lu Xun, "'Renxing de tiancai: Jiaerxun' yizhe houji," 13. See also Zhang Zhuyun, "Wuxiang yu xiangzheng," 49, and Li Chunlin, "Liangwei 'renxing tiancai,'" 45.

40. "Changming deng," *LXQJ* 2:68.

nepodvizhnym goriachim bleskom);[41] Lu Xun mentions several times that the madman's eyes emit a crazed, flashing glow (*shanshuozhe kuangre de yanguang* 閃爍著狂熱的眼光).[42] But here the similarities between the two works end, and it is in the changes that Lu Xun makes to Garshin's story, in both content and form, that a gulf of hopelessness and glimmers of potential hopefulness may be found. At a formal level, Lu Xun changes the figurative underpinning of the story's plot, the narratorial perspective, and the tone of the narration, while at the level of content he alters the madman's fate as well as the nature of his fundamental difference from the people whom he wishes to succor.

In 1929, Lu Xun commented that Garshin is a writer who invests his entire being to "bear the burden of the world's suffering" (*dan renjian ku* 擔人間苦) as someone oppressed under the reign of Alexander II.[43] Lu Xun thus read "The Red Flower" as growing out of this state of national darkness. It is therefore fitting that his own story, modeled after "The Red Flower," should allegorize the circumstances of the nation. This is the major difference between the stories. Unlike Garshin's madman, Lu Xun's is not trying to sacrifice himself for the good of all humanity. Lu Xun's madman wishes to save a more specific subset of humanity, the villagers, who are representative of China. His struggle to extinguish the light of the Chinese temple, the locus of longstanding religious practices, is symbolic of the attempt to pull down the tottering edifices of Chinese tradition and erect a modern, educated nation grounded upon rational scientific thinking—the project of luminaries such as Lu Xun in the New Culture Movement. That Lu Xun's madman decides to fight fire with fire (in his desire to burn down the temple) is symbolic of the fact that it is the scion of a landowning family at the top of the traditional social hierarchy who contends against this very social order—and this is true not only of the madman but also of Lu Xun himself in his project of writing this story. The fact that the madman ultimately fails in his endeavor and finds himself locked in a room closely resembling the iron house is another expression of the ambivalence that Lu Xun felt toward his endeavor to save China by writing fiction.

The gap between the madman and those around him is something Lu Xun develops in his story. Garshin's madman is misunderstood by the guards and medical professionals in the asylum because they cannot gain access into his

---

41. Vsevolod Garshin, "Krasnyi tzvetok," 172, translation mine.
42. "Changming deng," *LXQJ* 2:64.
43. Lu Xun, *Lu Xun yiwen ji* 10:576. Lu Xun saw Garshin as someone who supported humanism and universal love in the midst of a benighted Russian society (Li Chunlin, "Liangwei 'renxing tiancai,'" 47).

thought processes.[44] This is true as well in "Lamp of Eternity," but Lu Xun makes it clear that the chasm between the madman and his fellow villagers is augmented by the former's status as a member of a literatus family. In other words, Lu Xun brings in the problem of social class and its metonymic marker, literacy. Lu Xun gestures at this when the proprietress of the local teahouse mentions that the fifth brother of the Liang family (Liang wu di 梁五弟) lit the hallowed lamp, having misunderstood the legend referring to the homophonous Emperor Wu of the Liang dynasty (Liang Wu di 梁武帝) who did the sacred deed. Here, Lu Xun is noting the gulf between spoken and written language, between those who have access to education or literacy and those who do not.[45] Indeed, the narrator notes that the proprietress keeps accounts by drawing pictures on the wall rather than by using words and numbers.[46] The madman and his fellow villagers are separated not only by the inscrutability of presumed mental illness but also by differences in social status. Lu Xun is thus interrogating whether the many Chinese people who cannot read or understand his writing will be able to appreciate his wish to reform their allegedly backward mentalities.

Garshin's madman is misunderstood by those around him, but at least the narrator of the story has access into the character's interiority, describing his suffering sympathetically. This is another major formal change that Lu Xun makes in writing his story. In "Lamp of Eternity," the exposition of the madman's history and thoughts is done by gossiping villagers, none of whom is sympathetic toward the madman's state. The narrator describes the madman comedically, noting the straw sticking out of his hair. Neither does Lu Xun's narrator seem sympathetic toward the uneducated villagers, who are described sardonically and comically as well. Like the Chinese onlookers to the execution in the lantern slide that Lu Xun describes in his preface to *Outcry*, these villagers, and the madman's uncle, are keen to spectate violence, for as they contemplate how to stop the madman, they discuss with approval the murder and assault of an unfilial son in another village the year before.[47] Garshin's story maintains a tone of solemnity and even of reverence as it describes the unswerving determination of his madman, but Lu Xun changes the mode of narration to one of comedic mockery, of both the madman and those whom he wishes to aid.

---

44. In his 1920 preface to *Yuwai xiaoshuo ji*, Lu Xun remarks that Garshin's characters are singular and difficult to comprehend, especially for Chinese readers so divorced from the original Russian context; see Lu Xun, *Lu Xun lun waiguo wenxue*, 104. He harnesses this notion of the protagonist's incomprehensibility in his own story.

45. In her chapter in this volume, Xiaoyu Xia problematizes the materiality of this discrepancy between haves and have-nots in a different context.

46. *LXQJ* 2:61.

47. *LXQJ* 2:65.

Whereas Garshin's madman succeeds in his Christlike martyrdom to destroy the red flower, Lu Xun's madman is incarcerated in a version of the iron house before he can take action. Yet Lu Xun makes one final change to Garshin's plot that may inject a modicum of hope into the work. Garshin's story ends with the madman's burial, but Lu Xun keeps his madman alive, perhaps in a profound state of futility in the iron house. Importantly, though, he is not voiceless in the end. The madman's cries from his prison in the temple do not fall on deaf ears. The children playing outside hear his exhortations to set the place on fire, and they incorporate this language into their songs and riddles:

白帆船，對岸歇一歇。
此刻熄，自己熄。
戲文唱一出。
我放火！哈哈哈！
火火火，點心吃一些。

The white-sailed boat rests on the opposite shore.
Blow it out this moment, I'll blow it out myself.
Sing a little opera.
I'll start a fire! Ha ha ha!
Fire fire fire, eat some snacks.[48]

Their riddle becomes nonsensical, but they have taken up the madman's refrain. Perhaps this is the reformer's way of "saving the children," as the earlier protagonist of Lu Xun's "Diary of a Madman" enjoined. Lu Xun, like his madmen, aims to tear down the false idols of superstition and tradition, and here expresses a forlorn hope that in some way future generations will hear his injunctions and internalize them. This story goes a step farther than the ending of "Diary of a Madman": there, the madman's exhortation lingers at the end, trailing off in ellipses, but here it is taken up by other exuberant young voices.

Conclusion

At the level of content, Lu Xun's stories are ambivalent about the ability of the educated outsider to return to his native home and reform society and culture there. At a formal level, however, Lu Xun confidently employs literary techniques gleaned from outside China to reform the state of Chinese culture. In general terms, these three stories share a plot structure: someone wishes to shake up the foundations of society, but those around him find this incomprehensible and alarming. They conspire to muffle his voice. In each of these stories, Russian intertexts provide Lu

---

48. *LXQJ* 2:68, translation mine.

Xun the plot devices to highlight the protagonist's ineluctable psychological distance from the people around him: from Gogol, the form of the madman's diary, which deprives the protagonist of credibility; from Andreev, the perspectival and temporal structure which emphasizes the inability of the self-absorbed individual, preoccupied with bodily pain, to heed world-historical events; and from Garshin, the opacity of the madman's interiority to those around him. At the same time, Lu Xun adapts from these writers the means to indicate that there may be some possibility of communication after all: the madman's final exhortation that is not cut off at the end of "Diary," in contrast to the final absurdity uttered by Gogol's madman; the wreath and the crow, added in from Andreev's texts, even if they were not there to begin with (in the case of the wreath) or not at all hopeful in their original context (in the case of the crow); the madman's voice that is not silenced, and that even finds an echo in the voices of children, as opposed to the irrevocable death of Garshin's madman.

Although Lu Xun's three stories share broad similarities, each makes a distinct contribution to the development of a new modern Chinese short story form. Lu Xun does not merely combine components from his Russian sources; he "grabs" from Russian literature while making careful changes in these materials. In "Diary of a Madman," for instance, Lu Xun introduces to Chinese literature the fictionalized diary form, while innovating upon Gogol's model by adding the preface. Similarly, in "Medicine," he experiments with perspective and figuration inspired by (mis)translations of Andreev's work; with "The Lamp of Eternity," he riffs on Garshin's use of narratorial voice and omniscience.

Lu Xun's intertextual relationship with Russian literature often means that a single source provided textual DNA for several of his stories. For instance, the wreath at the end of "Medicine" is made of red and white flowers, forming a visual rhyme with Garshin's red flower, which also is echoed by the red flower that the homecoming intellectual tries to bring Ah Shun in "Upstairs in the Tavern."[49] Garshin's story has left an imprint on several of Lu Xun's texts. "The Red Flower" is also a plausible intertext for "Diary," whose madman is likewise fixated upon one locus of figuration (cannibalism) in his attempt to save those around him. Lu Xun's intertextual engagement sometimes has the opposite effect, too, whereby several different Russian sources informs the writing of a single story, as in the case of "Medicine." The work of grabbism is multilayered and richly generative in Lu Xun's oeuvre.

---

49. Ah Shun dies of illness before he can give it to her, so it becomes a symbol of the fundamental disconnect between the social underclass and the educated intellectual whose ideals of reforming Chinese society are doomed. At the same time, the red flower that blooms in the courtyard of the wine tavern, bringing life to the barren snowscape, is perhaps a breath of hope in the otherwise gloomy story.

Lu Xun famously called Russian literature "our guide and friend" (*women de daoshi he pengyou* 我們的導師和朋友) and, in the same essay, acknowledged Russia's invasions onto Chinese soil.[50] This duality of intimacy and alienation makes it fitting that Russian texts mediate Lu Xun's exploration of connection and disconnection in his fiction. To gain purchase on the problem of social otherness within China, Lu Xun experiments with literary techniques from the foreign other. Thus, the stories exhibit the dialectics of pessimism and optimism toward the project of an outsider reforming the native, by using techniques that Lu Xun gleaned from outside of native Chinese soil.

---

50. See "Zhu Zhong E wenyi zhi jiao," *LXQJ* 4:473.

4
What Happens after a Text Leaves Home?

Lu Xun, Ibsen, and Ichiyō

Satoru Hashimoto

Even as Lu Xun prolifically translated foreign literary and critical works into Chinese, some of his own texts were rendered into several languages during his lifetime.[1] "The True Story of Ah Q" (1921–1922), for instance, was quickly translated into French (1926), English (1926), Japanese (1928), Russian (1929), Korean (1930), Esperanto (1930), and Czech (1937). A German translation is said to have been completed in the early 1920s but did not get published at that time.[2] Lu Xun penned prefaces to some of the early translations of his works and reflected on their reception in broader worlds. Among these texts, the preface dated 1925 to the Russian translation of "The True Story of Ah Q" develops his thoughts on the work and its readership in a remote culture. This essay is instructive for illustrating the theoretical implications of Lu Xun's works for the understanding of world literature that I explore in this chapter.

In the preface, Lu Xun, as if to anticipate the later characterization of his work as a national allegory,[3] reveals his intention to express "the soul of the nation."[4] His self-conscious presentation of his work to a Russian audience as an example of national literature, however, is counterbalanced by the acknowledgment of an intense difficulty of producing just such a work in contemporary China. Lu Xun attributes the difficulty to the fact that China is "an old country"—the contention he will reiterate in his well-known writings such as "Voiceless China" (1927) and "Amateur Talk on Literature" (1934). China's alleged premodern status is ascribed in the first place

---

1. For Lu Xun's works of translation, see Wang Yougui, *Fanyijia Lu Xun*.
2. For the early translations of "The True Story of Ah Q," see Xie Miao, "'Shijie wenxue' zhong de 'A Q zhengzhuan' zaoqi yijie"; Lin Minjie et al., *Lu Xun yu ershi shiji Zhong-wai wenhua jiaoliu*.
3. Cf. Fredric Jameson, "Third-World Literature in the Era of Multinational Capitalism."
4. Lu Xun, "Ewen yiben *A Q zhengzhuan* xu ji zhuzhe zixu zhuanlüe," *LXQJ* 7:84.

66   What Happens after a Text Leaves Home?

to the absence of a nation per se due to the age-old social hierarchy erecting high walls among its people and numbing their sense of empathy for each other. The disintegration of the people is aggravated by the lack of a common medium for their self-expression due, as he claims, to the use of Chinese characters, which are "awfully difficult" to learn and thus prone to appropriation by the elites at the cost of popular literacy. He concludes, "Though I try my best to explore people's soul, I often regret after all that I feel certain estrangement [*gemo* 隔膜]."[5] This confession of feeling a sense of "estrangement" from the people whose soul he is supposed to depict for a foreign audience strikes a paradoxical note.

Yet the recognition of such estrangement—or to put it in general terms, the inadequacy of the medium to the subject of representation—indeed underlies formal experiments in Lu Xun's works including, most notably, "The True Story of Ah Q." This work features a narrator who, professing the "absolute difficulty" of writing a story of Ah Q, ruminates on the very nature of his writing that does not seem to belong to any generic configuration of valuable writing as he knows it, leading to a makeshift solution to write it as a parody of the traditional genre of the *zhuan* 傳 (biography).[6] Above all, the salient unsuitability of the representation to the represented is embodied in the narrative perspective itself, which is focalized through the point of view of the villagers of Weizhuang, whose collective gaze creates the ideological closure where Ah Q is unable to express his voice and bound to be sacrificed for their spectatorship.[7] Even as the story represents that which needs to be "revolutionized" in China or its "national character,"[8] "The True Story of Ah Q" adopts a form that self-consciously calls into question the adequacy of just such representation. It is from such a self-critical *difference* it inscribes in the existing realm of literary writing that this text derives a force to carve out a novel expressive capacity, one through which it tells a story of such an "unworthy" subject as Ah Q whose life has never received serious treatment in Chinese writing before.

This leads to the second point that Lu Xun broaches in the preface to the Russian translation: his "great interest" in the prospect that "The True Story of Ah Q" "could perhaps evoke a different kind of sight in the eyes of Russian readers who do not share 'our traditional thought.'"[9] The expectation he harbors for foreign reception is indeed an antidote to the criticisms leveled against this work by contemporary domestic critics. He derided them, for instance, in a 1926 essay where he targeted the kinds of readings that judged its value based on certain aesthetic standards, took it allegorically as a satire of a particular person, or focused merely on the identity of

---

5.   Lu Xun, "Ewen yiben *A Q zhengzhuan* xu ji zhuzhe zixu zhuanlüe," 84.

6.   Lu Xun, "*A Q zhengzhuan*," 512–13.

7.   See Satoru Hashimoto, *Afterlives of Letters*, 118–25.

8.   See Lu Xun, "*A Q zhengzhuan* de chengyin," 397; Lydia H. Liu, *Translingual Practice*, 69–76.

9.   Lu Xun, "Ewen yiben *A Q zhengzhuan* xu ji zhuzhe zixu zhuanlüe," 84.

the author.[10] Lu Xun also downplayed authorial design with regard to Ah Q's final execution and emphasized a certain amount of contingency that had led the story to end that way. These claims converge on a single argument: "The True Story of Ah Q," while set in the era of the Republican Revolution (1911), a decade and a half before he wrote this essay, was about the Chinese society in the present. "I'm afraid that what I saw was not at all what precedes the present, but indeed what follows it, or even what happens in twenty or thirty years from now."[11] He thus suggests that as much as it portrays a regrettable situation of the society several years earlier, this story indeed represents China's current reality; and for that realism to function for the Chinese audience in 1926, the kinds of modes of literary appreciation that the critics tend to employ must be bracketed out. Be it a preconceived aesthetic standard, a mimetic relationship to reality, or the author's autobiographic identity, an existing mode of reading that helps paraphrase the significance of this work in an established critical language should be set aside for the sake of a self-critical mode of reception—one that destabilizes the existing ideological frames of reference and makes the reader perceive the present reality in novel light. As Lu Xun insists, "I have nothing to say or write; I just have a kind of a self-deprecating temperament and sometimes cannot help emitting a few outcries, hoping to have people make some noise [*renao* 熱鬧]."[12] His tongue-in-cheek proclamation encapsulates the critical stakes of his works, which presents them as "outcries," or a disquieting voice that resists its harmless reduction to a content ("[something] to say or write") and prompts the reader to challenge ("make some noise") the culturally ingrained discourse that keeps them from perceiving "grotesque"[13] aspects of reality.

Lu Xun's characterization of "The True Story of Ah Q," therefore, indicates the ambivalence of this work's status as literature—the ambivalence that he encapsulated by calling this work a "rapidly perishable writing" (*suxiu de wenzhang* 速朽 的文章).[14] This work achieves its status as literature by means of a fundamental breakaway it creates from the established modes of literary reading and writing in its home culture—the breakaway that became a real possibility when the text left home for Russia, which he observed did not share "our traditional thought." The high expectations Lu Xun expressed for the Russian translation amid disappointing cultural situations at home in the mid-1920s thus indicate a key notion that must be kept in mind in understanding the significance of cross-cultural circulation for his works. To the extent that their status as literature depends on the differences they create in the notion of literature in their home culture, their circulation abroad and

10. Lu Xun, "*A Q zhengzhuan* de chengyin."
11. Lu Xun, "*A Q zhengzhuan* de chengyin," 397.
12. Lu Xun, "*A Q zhengzhuan* de chengyin," 394.
13. Lu Xun, "*A Q zhengzhuan* de chengyin," 399.
14. Lu Xun, "*A Q zhengzhuan*," 512.

68   What Happens after a Text Leaves Home?

engagement with foreign texts must also be understood without premising those processes on a certain accepted idea of literature. Lu Xun's works need to be understood in a broader cross-cultural context in a way that does not tame the forces of the "outcries" texts emit to dislocate and expand the notion of literature at home.

These preliminary reflections prompt us to revisit the concept of world literature as it relates to Lu Xun's works. Against the backdrop of globalization, scholarship on world literature in the past two decades has shifted away from the classical great books model and reconceptualized it as a mode of circulation. This paradigm shift has been articulated by David Damrosch in his well-known argument that a work's status as world literature derives from its circulation out into a broader world following its recognition "*as* literature" in its home culture.[15] Lu Xun's works take issue with this understanding, for their distinction as literature *already* implies a critique of that notion in its home culture. Just as they are read as literature in its cultural point of origin, so should they be already open to a world beyond it, or to the possibility for the literary realm to be demarcated *otherwise*. The difference that a work creates in the idea of what is to be read as literature constitutes the condition of possibility for its status as literature in the first place—the paradoxical structure that informs literature in its modern sense at large, as an institution that, in Eagleton's words, has "no 'essence' . . . whatsoever."[16]

Lu Xun's discourse on "The True Story of Ah Q," therefore, indicates an opportunity to examine his works in a comparative context to put forward an alternative conception of world literature that is capable of doing full justice to the fundamental ambiguity of the significance of what literature is in modern times. In this chapter, I pursue this opportunity by exploring a case of literary encounters between works by Lu Xun, Henrik Ibsen (1828–1906), and Higuchi Ichiyō (1872–1896). My examination is inspired by the sensational reception of Ibsen's *A Doll's House* (1879) in modernizing China and Japan; yet it is more specifically concerned with the tangential relationships that Lu Xun's and Ichiyō's works create with the play through the theme of gendered suffering in marriage—the relationships that, as I will argue, resonate with Ibsen's reflections on the boundaries of literature bespoken in *A Doll's House*. With a particular focus on Lu Xun's short story "Regrets for the Past" (1925) and Ichiyō's "Jyūsan ya 十三夜" (The thirteenth night, 1895), I will examine comparative textual moments suggesting that literature in a broader world be conceptualized on what I call a resemblance model. I specifically adapt Wittgenstein's notion of "family resemblances" to consider the relationship between literary works without relying on a presumed concept of literature, and try to propose a new way of understanding world literature.

---

15. David Damrosch, *What Is World Literature?*, 5–6.
16. Terry Eagleton, *Literary Theory*, 8.

Lu Xun and Ichiyō vis-à-vis Ibsen

My examination of the cross-cultural relationship of literary texts in this chapter is thus underpinned by the question, What happens after a text—such as *A Doll's House*—leaves home? Here, I am alluding to the seminal speech Lu Xun gave to the Literature and Arts Society at Beijing Women's Normal College in December 1923: "What Happens after Nora Leaves Home?" The speech was delivered in response to the inaugural performance of *A Doll's House* in China put on by an all-female cast at this college in May of the same year.[17] In it, Lu Xun argued for the economic rights of women, contending that Nora would need money if her departure from home were to result in anything other than the predictable outcomes: her returning home or becoming a prostitute. He famously concluded, "Dreams are fine, but otherwise money is essential."[18] His position is as much informed by the actual tragedies of women who had to confront toxic patriarchy in post–May Fourth China as it is indicative of his critical perspective on the class structure detrimental to women's rights.[19] Yet at the same time, his argument also indicates a particular mode of engagement with Ibsen's text as literature. As he writes,

> However, Nora ends up leaving home. What happens to her afterward? Ibsen gave no answer, and now he's dead. Even if he weren't dead, it wouldn't be his responsibility to answer the question. For Ibsen was writing poetry, not raising a problem for society and providing an answer to it. It's like the golden oriole, which sings for itself and not for the amusement or benefit of human beings.[20]

As Lu Xun interprets the text, Nora represents someone awoken to a crippled reality of society for which "we cannot find a way out," society whose problems are so deeply ingrained that even "hope" would prove too "costly." Such hope would make "people . . . more sensitive to the depths of their own suffering, while their souls would be summoned to witness their own rotting corpse." "What we need," then, is precisely "falsehoods and dreaming" that spare you such a taxing realization.[21]

In his characteristically ironic tone, Lu Xun sees Ibsen grappling with the same kind of "iron house" as he figured in explaining what made him venture to write fiction in the first place. As is well known, Lu Xun in the preface to *Outcry* rejected positive hopes that would vainly enlighten people stuck in old society at the cost of their peaceful death from suffocation in it and had recourse to a kind of double

---

17. Zhang Chuntian, *Sixiangshi shiye zhong de "Nuola,"* 24–25.
18. Lu Xun, "Nuola zouhou zenyang," *LXQJ* 1:167.
19. See Kwok-kan Tam, *Chinese Ibsenism*, 109–13; Zhang Chuntian, "Cong Nuola chuzou dao Zhongguo gaizao."
20. Lu Xun, "Nuola zouhou zenyang," *LXQJ* 1:166.
21. Lu Xun, "Nuola zouhou zenyang," *LXQJ* 1:166–67.

negation to affirm the stakes of his literary endeavor: "I cannot obliterate hope, for it belongs to the future."[22] "Hope" resides outside of the bounds of that which can be spoken of and listened to in the present order of discourse—i.e., the "iron house"— where his writing is also situated and thus can only be defended through double negation. Lu Xun saw in Nora's departure an exercise of this kind of hope—hope that does exist, though not for the present. He contends that Nora's departure does not so much concern "raising a problem for society and providing an answer to it," as it constitutes a "poetry," conveying, like a "golden oriole," a voice that can only be heard by dislocating the boundaries of what the normative "human beings" are able to hear in present society. The hope that it envisions, or Nora's future, can thus become achievable only through practice without a conceivable path where money becomes the necessary means to continue the fighting.

Lu Xun's interpretation of *A Doll's House* betrays its idiosyncrasy when considered in the context of the play's avid reception in contemporary China. While as early as 1907, Lu Xun penned some of the earliest Chinese-language essays to mention Ibsen, it was a 1918 special issue of the May Fourth flagship journal *Xin qingnian* 新青年 (New youth) that ignited widespread interest in the writer among progressive intellectuals.[23] The issue included a translation of *A Doll's House* by Luo Jialun 羅家倫 (1897–1969) and Hu Shi 胡適 (1891–1962), as well as the latter's "Yibusheng zhuyi" 易卜生主義 (Ibsenism). In that essay, Hu Shi first and foremost attributed Ibsenism to "realism": "I have said in the beginning of this essay that Ibsen's view of life [*renshengguan* 人生觀] is but realism. Ibsen writes down all the actual situations of family and society so that he moves the reader's minds, making them realize how dark and rotten their family and society are and that they truly must be reformed and revolutionized. This is Ibsenism."[24] Hu Shi illustrates his point by deploying a medical metaphor and comparing Ibsen to a physician making a diagnosis, suggesting that the playwright's work reflects the function of society's intrinsic immunity. He claims that just like the human body,

> the health of society and state also depends entirely on those white blood cells that never feel satisfied or content and always declare wars with evil and dirty elements. Therein resides hope for reform and progress. . . . If we make sure that society always has this kind of white blood cell spirit, then there is no way society does not reform or progress.[25]

Hu Shi not only reads Ibsen's work as an embodiment of realism in the society fraught with the corrupt powers of law, religion, and morality, but he also draws from it a

---

22. Lu Xun, "Nahan zixu," *LXQJ* 1:441.
23. Chengzhou He, "Chinese Ibsens."
24. Hu Shi, "Yibusheng zhuyi," *Hu Shi quanji*, 1:612.
25. Hu Shi, "Yibusheng zhuyi," *Hu Shi quanji*, 1:616.

metanarrative of an inherent predilection of society in general toward progress that exists in China and elsewhere just as it does in Norway. If Ibsen's work represents the kind of literature (i.e., realism) to be introduced into China, then the function of literature is delineated by the understanding of a universal working of society (i.e., social evolution) comparable to that of a biological immune system. Ibsen's text not only provides an object of interpretation but also a framework thereof. It at a time gives a "diagnosis" *and* "hope"; its "realism" constitutes a "view of life."

Following the *New Youth* special issue, Ibsen's plays began to serve as a model for the modern genre of spoken play (*huaju* 話劇) in China, while *A Doll's House*, and especially the character Nora's decision to leave her husband Torvald, became a crucial source of inspiration for the discourse of the new woman.[26] Although Hu Shi's "Ibsenism" by no means summarizes this rich reception history, it helps put into relief the significance of Lu Xun's engagement with the Norwegian playwright in the contemporary context. Hu Shi's medical metaphor reminds one of the preface to *Outcry* in which Lu Xun recounted his youthful idea of using literature as a means to "reform the spirit" of the nation by analogy to medicine "improving [its] physical health." Yet this positive function was to be negated so that he affirmed through double negation the paradoxical significance of modern fiction—the significance that he attributed to his own work and, as we have seen, also recognized in Ibsen's play.[27] Lu Xun's reading of Ibsen's work in this sense squarely undercuts a general framework—be it "progress" in general or "social evolution" in particular—establishing a notion of literature by means of its function in society and instead leads to affirming the futility of maintaining, positively or negatively, such a framework.

A similar idiosyncrasy, I contend, resides in the relationship of Higuchi Ichiyō's work with Ibsen's. The arche-figure of women's writing in Meiji Japan, Ichiyō did not write about Ibsen herself; yet the possible interplays between their works are suggested in Mori Ōgai's 森鷗外 (1862–1922) well-known accolade of Ichiyō. Having penned some of the first essays to introduce Ibsen to Japan in 1889 and having translated four of his plays, including *A Doll's House* in 1913, into Japanese, Ōgai was instrumental in the early Japanese engagement with the playwright.[28] In his criticism coauthored in the style of a trilogy with two other contemporary writers, Ōgai expressed profuse praise of Ichiyō's "Takekurabe" たけくらべ (Growing up, 1895), her seminal short story of school-age children growing up in Yoshiwara, Tokyo's largest red-light district, by referring to Ibsen as well as Zola.

---

26. Chengzhou He, "Chinese Ibsens"; Kristine Harris, "*The New Woman* Incident," 287–88.

27. Lu Xun, "Nahan zixu," *LXQJ* 1:439–42.

28. Yōichi Nagashima, "From 'Literary Translation' to 'Cultural Translation'"; Reiko Abe Auestad, "Japanese Ibsens," 239–44. The first Japanese translation of *A Doll's House*, by Shimamura Hōgetsu 島村抱月 (1871–1918), was published in 1911.

72   What Happens after a Text Leaves Home?

It is not especially remarkable that this author, a member of a literary field in which the naturalist school is said to be enjoying a vogue, should have chosen to set her story in this place [i.e., the Yoshiwara red-light district]. What *is* remarkable is that the characters who haunt this area are not the brute beasts in human form—the copies of Zola, Ibsen, and the rest—presented by the assiduous imitators of the so-called naturalist school, but human beings with whom we can laugh and cry together. . . . At the risk of being mocked as an Ichiyō-idolator, I do not hesitate to accord to her the name of "poet" [*shijin* 詩人]. It is more difficult to depict a person with individual characteristics than a stereotype, and far more difficult to depict an individual in a milieu than a special person all by himself. This author, who has painted the "local coloring" of Daionji-mae [in Yoshiwara] so effectively that one might say it has ceased to exist apart from "Growing Up," without leaving any trace of the efforts such portraiture must have cost her, must truly be called a woman of rare ability.[29]

Ōgai positions Ichiyō tangentially to the "literary field" centered on "the naturalist school" that took shape in Meiji Japan through the introduction of Western writers such as Ibsen and Zola.[30] While Ichiyō benefits from the new mode of literary representation breaking away from the classical "stereotype[s]" and capable of exposing a bare tableau of the red-light district without outdated moralistic constrains, she also distances herself from the emergent literary field, which Ōgai denounces as full of the bland characters of "brute beasts in human form" produced by "assiduous imitators." Whereas Ōgai himself spearheaded literary reform in Meiji Japan through his avid translations of European creative and critical works, it is rather in Ichiyō's distance from its established mode in his times that he saw the kernel of her work, her ability as a "poet" to delve into "human beings with whom we can laugh and cry together" and to derive "poetic taste" from "the most vulgar of the vulgar world" of Daionji-mae.[31] Ichiyō's poetry consists in her dwelling in the "milieu" of the red-light district defying the purview of the established literary field and drawing from it "local colors" that are so unique to that location that it would "cease to exist" apart from her fiction. While Ōgai was credited with conceptualizing and practicing modern literature in Japan, he saw in Ichiyō a defiance of its normalization, an embodiment of its original poetic spirit to pursue an ever-newer mode of representation in the face of present reality.

---

29. Mori Ōgai, "Sannin jōgo," in *Ōgai zenshū* 23:488. Ōgai's interlocutors are Kōda Rohan 幸田露伴 (1867–1947) and Saitō Ryokuu 斎藤緑雨 (1868–1904). I use, with modifications, translation by Donald Keene in *Dawn to the West*, 1:180.

30. For the Japanese engagement with naturalism, see Christopher L. Hill, *Figures of the World*.

31. Mori Ōgai, "Sannin jōgo," 23:488. For Ōgai's role in the formation of modern Japanese literature, see Richard John Bowring, *Mori Ōgai and the Modernization of Japanese Culture*.

In Japan, Ibsen's initial introduction was followed by theater productions beginning in 1909, which played an integral role in the development of modern theater (*shingeki* 新劇) in that country. Early twentieth-century Japanese literature saw an Ibsen boom, and *A Doll's House* was discussed particularly avidly by emergent feminist writers gathered around the journal *Seitō* 青鞜 (Bluestockings), which published a special issue on the play in 1912.[32] Despite her reputation as one of the earliest successful female writers in modern Japan, Ichiyō is but marginally mentioned in the incipient formation of Japanese feminist literature to which Ibsen's work provided major inspiration. Yet Ōgai's criticism encourages a comparative reading that discerns a fundamental relationship between Ichiyō and early feminist literature in Japan, one that is underpinned by their common defiance of the accepted modes of literary writing.

Ichiyō's critical relationship that Ōgai reconstructs to the normalized "Ibsen" transposed to Japan resonates with Lu Xun's ironic response to *A Doll's House*. In both cases, the relationship with Ibsen calls into question literary practice itself, even one that is informed by the introduction of Ibsen himself. Just as Ōgai perceives in Ichiyō a "poet" defying mainstream literature, so does Lu Xun draw an idea of "poetry" that challenges what normative "human beings" are capable of discoursing in the present literary culture. Lu Xun's and Ichiyō's engagements both prompt a fundamental rethinking about what is accepted as literature in the discursive situations where they wrote. As it evokes such radical reflections as pertain even to its own status as literature, Ibsen's text undergoes as precarious a fate abroad as Nora must do after her departure.

Translating Silence: "Regrets for the Past"

Lu Xun's engagement with *A Doll's House* is most notably developed in his 1925 short story "Regrets for the Past." The story is presented as a note left by the modern-style young intellectual named Juansheng recounting the tragic outcome of the short-lived romance with his deceased lover Zijun. The private form of the account indicates the immense moral conflict that their audacious pursuit of free love caused with the social norms of the time. The narrative begins with a recollection of their rendezvous at Juansheng's humble abode, which would be filled in Zijun's lovely presence with his discourse on cutting-edge intellectual subjects: "the dictatorship of the family, the destruction of old habits, gender equality, Ibsen, Tagore, Shelley." Imbued with the May Fourth zeitgeist, Zijun comes to defy the interventions from her father and uncle to stay true to her love of Juansheng. Declaring, "I belong to

---

32. See Toshiko Nakamura, *Nihon no Ipusen genshō*. See also Kiyoko Horiba, "*Seitō*" *jyosei kaihō ronshū*, 34–83.

myself! They do not have any rights to meddle with me!"[33] she clearly resonates with Nora's pivotal realization: "I believe I am first and foremost a human being."[34] Zijun's transformation deeply moves Juansheng, convincing him that "she has completely understood" all his "opinions, experiences, and shortcomings" and that "Chinese women are not hopeless as the pessimists would like to believe, and they will see a glorious future before long."[35]

Juansheng's idealism and Zijun's audacity lead to a new life. Yet the couple's cohabitation out of wedlock immediately clashes with the orthodoxy of society, and Juansheng is soon fired from his clerkship job due to his damaged reputation. Initially modest yet happy, their life begins to face crippling economic hardship. Juansheng, however, takes the challenges as a chance for starting a truly new life, determined as he is to overcome them by cashing out his knowledge through publication, tutorship, and translation. But he soon realizes the futility of his plans because of the meager compensation he receives for his first publication. Meanwhile, he sees Zijun stuck in the endless routines of housework, which becomes a Sisyphean burden in a deteriorating household, turning her increasingly pale and downcast. He finally begins to see her presence as a hurdle for his envisioned new life. The account cruelly illustrates the precarity of Zijun's existence by depicting her as a remainder after they have consumed their chickens and expelled their dog. As Juansheng finally tells her that he does not love her anymore, Zijun is taken home by her father, and he soon learns that she is dead.

Lu Xun's characterization of Juansheng—familiar with modern notions and newly introduced foreign authors yet so insensitive to the suffering of his lover as to drive her to death—has drawn considerable critical attention. Lydia Liu reads his mistreatment of Zijun as a sign of "the modern notion of love, whose male centered discourse ironically reproduces the patriarchy it aims to overthrow,"[36] while Eileen Cheng attributes this irony to the man's "propensity for appropriating New Culture rhetoric haphazardly."[37] Embodied in this character, accordingly, is an allegory of China's incomplete modernity that would misuse modern ideas in old habitus, appropriating free love and women's liberation for male interest.[38] His self-reflecting "notes" then invite the contemporary reader, expected to share the May Fourth ideals with this man, to undergo moral "self-scrutiny."[39] "Regrets" becomes Lu Xun's biting satire of a post–May Fourth culture in which Ibsen's text is "egregious[ly]

---

33. Lu Xun, "Shangshi," *LXQJ* 2:114–15.
34. Henrik Ibsen, *A Doll's House*, 184.
35. Lu Xun, "Shangshi," *LXQJ* 2:115.
36. Lydia H. Liu, *Translingual Practice*, 194.
37. Eileen J. Cheng, *Literary Remains*, 121.
38. Lydia H. Liu, *Translingual Practice*, 167.
39. Theodore Huters, "Blossoms in the Snow," 72.

misuse[d]"[40] to produce a Chinese youth who is no better than another Torvald aggravating society's deep-seated patriarchy.

Juansheng's "notes," however, expose his interiority that makes his perpetuation of toxic patriarchy even more ironic. Quite unlike Torvald, Juansheng is a figure of thorough defiance. If Torvald embodies society's dominant morality—male "honor"—that is adjudicated in the existing legal system, Juansheng self-consciously tackles such normalized morality throughout the account. Just as he was defiant of norms when he dared to begin cohabitating with Zijun, so does he remain unrelenting in his abandonment of her and continued struggle for a new life. As he convinces himself, "It is not that the world does not open a way forward for those who struggle for it. I have not yet forgotten how to flap my wings, although they are much weaker than before."[41] His wings should take him to a battleground, whose players he visualizes: "a fisherman fighting the waves, a soldier in the trench, a VIP in his motorcar, a speculator in the foreign concession, a bandit hero in the wilderness, a professor at the lectern, a political activist at dusk, a thief at night."[42] If Torvald has an honor to uphold, a family to support, and a society to defend, then Juansheng is to venture out into existential struggles on an open-ended field straddling social and legal boundaries in search of a desired new life. If Torvald admonishes Nora, "You talk like a child. You don't understand the society you live in,"[43] then Juansheng, despite the obvious moral self-contradiction that eventually causes the tragedy, keeps pressing Zijun to live up to Nora's unbending spirit and leave him: "To start the conversation, I intentionally broached our past, mentioning literature and touching on foreign writers and works, like *A Doll's House, The Lady from the Sea*. I praised Nora's courageous resolve."[44] Therefore, while society blinds Torvald to Nora, it is "Nora" that blinds Juansheng to Zijun.

The tragedy of "Regrets" derives not so much from Juansheng's failure to live up to the revolutionary spirit of *A Doll's House*, as from the exclusory forces that even such an emancipatory discourse can exert. As such, "Regrets" is a meta-tragedy of literary reception itself. If Ibsen's work provided an idea of literature to be practiced, then "Regrets" lays bare the exclusions it produces once it has been normalized— exclusions exposed when Juansheng makes the same reference in blatantly contradictory ways, first to convince Zijun to move in with him and second to expel her. The tragedy arises precisely from the fact that literature—as valuable, exemplary, or "progressive" as it may be—can be used in a way that blinds the reader to the reality it is supposed to uncover and change. At the heart of Lu Xun's engagement

---

40. Eileen J. Cheng, *Literary Remains*, 124.
41. Lu Xun, "Shangshi," *LXQJ* 2:124.
42. Lu Xun, "Shangshi," *LXQJ* 2:124.
43. Henrik Ibsen, *A Doll's House*, 185.
44. Lu Xun, "Shangshi," *LXQJ* 2:126.

with Ibsen's work is this self-reflection about possible exclusions inherent in that very act—self-reflection that precisely indicates a refusal of normalizing the idea of literature that he transposes. The tragedy of "Regrets" does not arise from deficiency vis-à-vis a norm but from such a normalizing reading itself.

The haunting absence of Zijun, therefore, serves as a powerful prohibition against the normalization of what Nora's departure would signify, for Zijun's death was a direct result of just such a normalization. Yet at the same time, Zijun's absence also constitutes a *repetition* of Nora's departure, the termination of conversation at the end of the play, which is "the product of a different mode of interaction with the world, one drastically different from the one underlying the norms and criteria previously at work."[45] Nora's final departure reveals the limits of what can be represented in the play's fictional framework, while Zijun's absence likewise points to that which Juansheng's notes are unable to account for. Zijun's absent voice calls into question the existing norms and criteria of literary representation itself, even those drawn from "foreign writers and works." By leaving Zijun's voice silent, Juansheng's "notes" embody the inherent limits of their representational capacity so as to utter a moral call for a completely new mode of representation—a call sounding all the more blaringly as Zijun's voice remains silent. If one were to point out an ethical significance of "Regrets," therefore, it would not consist in an attempt at giving voice to Zijun—not even through images of "dead souls" or "hell"[46]—within the available regime of representation, but rather in a paradoxical attempt to *embody* the structural exclusion or forgetting that inheres in that regime itself, in the hope of changing it. Hence, the inscription of the imperative on "the first step toward a new life": "I must forget."[47]

It is thus through silence—the absence of Zijun's voice and the unspoken whereabouts of Nora—that "Regrets" most fundamentally resonates with *A Doll's House*. Lu Xun, in other words, engages with Ibsen's work precisely at a moment that it calls its value as "literature" into question. Such a moment occurs when Juansheng alludes to *A Doll's House* for the second time to persuade Zijun to leave him:

> *A Doll's House, The Lady from the Sea.* I praised Nora's courageous resolve . . . All this we had spoken of last year in that shabby room in my hostel, but my words now rang hollow [*kongxu* 空虚]. As they left my mouth and entered my ears, I often suspected that there was an invisible urchin, behind my back, maliciously and spitefully parroting all I said.[48]

---

45. Leonardo F. Lisi, *Marginal Modernity*, 153.
46. Lu Xun, "Shangshi," *LXQJ* 2:133.
47. Lu Xun, "Shangshi," *LXQJ* 2:133.
48. Lu Xun, "Shangshi," *LXQJ* 2:126.

As it is mentioned by Juansheng for the second time, Ibsen's work begins to lose the power it possessed, ceasing to be the literature that had such currency the preceding year that it inspired the young couple to envision their new life. The same text that was read as powerful literature in one form of life ceases to be read as such in another, merely ringing "hollow." The uncanny "parroting" of "an invisible urchin" behind his back exposes what Juansheng's subjective engagement with the foreign text—his blind following of the spirit of progress embodied in "Nora"—has suppressed: the fundamental openness of literature as a concept, thanks to which a text that gained literary distinction once can lose it now. And it is precisely such openness that Zijun's absent voice demands, as it calls for a renewed realm of literary representation, a demand echoing Nora's departure, which likewise reveals the limits of that which can be written about in the literature that Ibsen's play is. When Lu Xun engages with Ibsen's work, therefore, he does so by embracing the work's inherent critique of the medium and thus rejecting its appreciation *as* literature in its normalized sense.

Ichiyō: Critique of "Literature"

Having left home, Ibsen's work is received by Lu Xun in such a way that the significance of its being read as literature is fundamentally interrogated. Ōgai pointed out similar dynamics in Ichiyō's work as he admired it as a much-needed excess in the contemporary literature produced, in the name of the "naturalist school," on the model of European literature. Once brought in dialogue with Ibsen, Ichiyō's work indeed reveals itself as often self-reflexively marked by the exteriority of the literary representation that she practices, which is rhetorically indicated by the frequent use of ellipses and narratologically suggested by the enchanted moments of holidays and festivals that suspend social norms.

Ichiyō's two-part short story "The Thirteenth Night" thematically speaks directly to *A Doll's House*. The story takes place on "the thirteenth night" (the thirteenth day of the ninth month of the classical lunar calendar), the auspicious night of the second moon viewing of the year, which follows the first occasion on the "fifteenth night" (the fifteenth day of the eighth month). For the first time since she got married seven years ago, the heroine Oseki returns to her parents' house during the night. Her unexpected return delights her parents, who enthusiastically welcome back their well-dressed daughter, who has "risen in the world" as the wife of the high official Harada Isamu, to their humble rented house. To her parents admiring her success in life and thanking her husband for his help in the promotion of their unmarried and introverted son Inosuke, Oseki hesitantly reveals the real purpose of her sudden homecoming: to get their permission for divorce. She calls her husband "a devil" and reveals to them how much psychological maltreatment she has had to

78 What Happens after a Text Leaves Home?

endure since giving birth to their son Tarō. As she tells, Harada's attitude toward her is hostile, indifferent, and dehumanizing:

> He starts in at me at the breakfast table, and it never stops. In front of the maids even he complains how I can't do anything right, how ill-bred I am. . . . He slights me for my lack of learning. . . . You know, for the first six months or so after we were married, he was always at my side, doing everything he could for me. But as soon as Tarō was born—it's frightening how much a man can change! . . . At first I thought he must be teasing. But then I began to understand: he had tired of me, and that was that. He bullies and bullies me in the hope that eventually I'll run away or ask for a divorce.[49]

Oseki that night was fed up with the unhappy marriage and made up her mind to take advantage of the husband's absence and leave their household.

Oseki is a Nora figure, and yet her departure turns out to be bafflingly short-lived. Her mother is sympathetic, showing indignation at Harada, who at first begged Oseki for marriage but lost interest in her so quickly, and even suggests arguing with him, though they have so far refrained from visiting him out of consideration for class difference between the two families. Yet the father overrides the mother's opinion, emphasizing that people in disparate social statuses have different ways of thinking and that Harada may not find satisfactory what Oseki does in her best effort to please him. At the end of the day, it is for her parents, her brother Inosuke, and her son Tarō that she has to fulfill "a wife's duty" and bear the hardships of her marriage to a man of such high social standing.[50] The narrative sets the stage for successful persuasion, depicting Oseki's mind wavering between the wish to be freed from a torturous marriage and her motherly affection toward Tarō, whom she would not be able to see again if divorced.[51] And Oseki finally admits that she was selfish and declares, "From tonight I will consider myself dead—a spirit who watches over Tarō." She convinces herself that she is Harada's wife and her body belongs to him and that she should do whatever he says.[52] She decides to return to her husband at the end of the first part of the story, terminating her momentary defiance.

Oseki's disappointing conclusion stands in stark contrast to Nora's realization that she is "first and foremost a human being" before being a wife or mother, and to Zijun's declaration, "I belong to myself!" Having left her husband, Oseki is sent back to him by her father, imprisoned in the iron house of patriarchy. This saliently frustrating ending corroborates Lu Xun's remark about the difficulty of living an entirely

---

49. Higuchi Ichiyō, "Jyūsan ya," in *Zenshū Higuchi Ichiyō*, 2:159–60. I use, with modifications, Robert Lyons Danly's translation.
50. Higuchi Ichiyō, "Jyūsan ya," 164–65.
51. Higuchi Ichiyō, "Jyūsan ya," 164.
52. Higuchi Ichiyō, "Jyūsan ya," 166.

new life and suggests that the narrative framework of "The Thirteenth Night" accords with the stubborn confines of society's patriarchal ideology which perpetuates on countless women's sufferings. Yet thanks to the existence of its second part, Ichiyō's work indeed performatively exposes or makes tangible, rather than constatively affirms, its obviously regrettable accordance with the repressive social norms. By implying through ellipses a possible, happier life that the heroine would have lived, the story throws into relief the coterminous limits of the forms of life that the heroine can afford to live, on the one hand, and of that which is representable in the literary medium at the author's disposition, on the other hand.

The second part of "The Thirteenth Night" verges on melodrama. Oseki takes a rickshaw to return home, but its puller for no obvious reason abandons the work and insists that she get off and find another car to continue her way. The bewildered Oseki examines the puller to find out from his moonlit silhouette that he was indeed her childhood boyfriend Takasaka Rokunosuke, or Roku. Like Oseki, Roku had agreed to an arranged marriage and had a daughter, but he grew increasingly nihilistic and began to indulge in dissipation, abandoning his family's tobacco retail business and secluding himself from society. Now living alone from hand to mouth by pulling the rickshaw, he would sometimes be overwhelmed by cynical thinking and stops working out of the blue. This chance meeting reminds Oseki of her past:

> She used to imagine what it would be like to sit behind the counter of the tobacco shop, reading the paper and waiting on customers. But then a stranger came along and asked her to marry him. Her parents pressed her, how could she defy them? She had always hoped to marry Roku, though he had never made any overtures, it was true. In the end, her parents persuaded her, and she told herself that her dreams of helping Roku run the shop were only that—the dreams of a schoolgirl, puppy love. She put him out of her mind and resigned herself to marrying Harada.[53]

The unrequited love is a prevalent theme in Ichiyō's oeuvre. Just to name a few examples, be they between Midori and Shin'nyo in "Growing Up," Oriki and Genshichi in "Nigorie" にごりえ (Troubled waters, 1895), Yukiko and Uemura Rokurō in "Utsusemi" うつせみ (The cicada shell, 1895), or Okyō and Kichizō in "Wakare michi" わかれ道 (Separate ways, 1896), the romances in Ichiyō's work do not have a resolution in the stories. Structurally, these couples' affairs have no place in society due to their conflicts with various social norms. As it is the case in most of Ichiyō's stories, the woman first enters the realm of society, entangled in social relations including the duty to parents, arranged marriage or engagement, and bondage to prostitution. The woman's socialization has to put an end to their affection that can only exist temporarily in liminal spaces and has no way to materialize in a viable

---

53. Higuchi Ichiyō, "Jyūsan ya," 172.

80   What Happens after a Text Leaves Home?

form of life without paying too high a price. Ichiyō's storytelling is not concerned with following their amorous fates, either through tragic or melodramatic imaginations; yet it consists in a rejection of doing so, implying through ellipses a possible social reality that her literature chooses *not* to depict.

This rejection is best illustrated, for instance, in the final scene of "Separate Ways," where the hero Kichizō begs the heroine Okyō, who has agreed to an arranged marriage and ends their ambivalent yet happy relationship that has not gone much beyond an affinity between elder sister and younger brother, saying, "Take your hands off me, Okyō."[54] Okyō hopes Kichizō understands and approves her decision, whereas Kichizō, given his low social status as an outcast, knows that he is unable to stop her. Okyō is introduced into society, while Kichizō remains on its periphery. "Separate Ways" refrains from justifying either of their situations and instead embodies the sheer impossibility of realizing a new life that could reconcile their incompatible ways. Likewise, in "The Thirteenth Night," Ichiyō concludes the story with the symbolism of "one headed east, and the other south,"[55] positioning her writing in the midst of an unjust society where difference in status—class, gender, age, roles in the family, and so forth—is insurmountable. Ichiyō's characters are as trapped in this banal society as they are in the purview of accepted literary expressions in its culture that her works conform to, and their unrequited romances indicate that which is excluded from the fictional spaces of her works.

I contend, therefore, that "The Thirteenth Night" does not simply represent a short-lived, failed version of *A Doll's House* in a stubbornly patriarchal society. Instead, the two works speak to each other through their elliptical endings, where they reveal the boundaries of literary representation in their respective cultures—the former through Oseki's separation from Roku and the latter through Nora's departure. If Nora's unrecounted whereabouts indicate a world where she would live a totally new life to enact a notion of "humanity" that is "not what we have seen so far,"[56] then Oseki's unrealized romance bespeaks a world where she would find herself in an entirely different set of social relations where she is finally free.

Ichiyō envisions this radical future through the image of the thirteenth night. Oseki's return to her parents on that night has such an enchanting power that it suspends her social status and manners; it allows her to take part in the moon-viewing ritual of offering beans and chestnuts with her parents. Her fortuitous comeback even supersedes the long-held belief that considers observing only one of the two moon-viewing dates of the year to be a taboo. Knowing that Oseki must have missed the year's first occasion on the fifteenth night in Harada's modernized household,

---

54. Higuchi Ichiyō, "Wakare michi," in *Zenshū Higuchi Ichiyō*, 2:202.
55. Higuchi Ichiyō, "Jyūsan ya," 173.
56. Leonardo F. Lisi, *Marginal Modernity*, 155.

her mother nevertheless invites her to eat her beans and chestnuts, which are simultaneously ritual offerings and "mother's cooking":

> It's like a dream, that you've come tonight. It's as if you read my mind! You must have all kinds of sweets to eat at home, Oseki, but it's not often you can have your mother's cooking, is it? Let's see you eat some beans and chestnuts—you used to like them so when you were little. Tonight you can forget you're a married woman. Be your old self, don't worry about your manners.[57]

The enchanted occasion of the thirteenth night provides Oseki, who gladly eats the food, a magical relief from being a wife and mother and allows her to be her "old self" (*mukashino Oseki* 昔しのお関), which even cuts across being a "daughter" defined in the patriarchal institution. Embracing the ritualistic moment that suspends the social relations, Oseki recovers her ambivalent "old self"—as undefined as the significance of the "human" that Nora realizes she is. The serendipitous reenactment of a happy relationship, here materialized between the mother and the daughter, indicates an opening toward a new form of life that only exists in the present as a question for the accepted order of literary representation.

Conclusion

I began this chapter by pointing out an opportunity to reconsider the concept of world literature through an examination of Lu Xun's work in a comparative context. Lu Xun's engagement with *A Doll's House* fundamentally dislocates a normalizing understanding of literature, and this mode of textual interplay is also observed in Ichiyō's "The Thirteenth Night" as it relates to Ibsen's same play through exclusion inherent in their representations of marriage. These textual relationships are structurally contingent on the sheer impossibility of postulating a common realm of literature under which to subsume the literatures that these works are read as.

The way in which the texts that I have explored relate to each other thus depends on the irreducible possibility that a work of literature can cease to be read as such when it leaves a culture for another. This leads to the question, How should we conceptualize the relationship between multiple literatures when that relationship depends on the impossibility, in this broad context, of defining what constitutes "literature" writ large? I would like to propose to understand such a relationship in terms of Wittgenstein's notion of "family resemblances." Wittgenstein used this notion to conceive of the relationship between different games where a general definition of what constitutes a "game" is unavailable. A broad exploration of different games—such as "board-games, card-games, ball-games, athletic games,

---

57. Higuchi Ichiyō, "Jyūsan ya," 156.

82   What Happens after a Text Leaves Home?

and so on"—results in a mere "complicated network of similarities overlapping and criss-crossing: similarities in the large and in the small," he argued.[58] The "family resemblances" indicate the impossibility for the players to conceptually define the game they are playing so that it inevitably opens itself, through "resemblances," to another game unbeknownst to them. The fundamental openness of the concept of literature on which the works and their relationships we have examined in this chapter depend on, therefore, invites us to consider literature in terms of a form of Wittgensteinian "game." Just like a broad examination of different games dislocates a definition of what a game is, our comparative reading of literatures across cultures yields an observation that they resist subsumption under a general concept of literature and display mere resemblances among them. Lu Xun's works in a broader cross-cultural context point to a reconceptualization of world literature through a resemblance model, a conceptual ambiguity that is tantamount to doing full justice to the critical diversity of what is taken as "literature" across cultures.

---

58. Ludwig Wittgenstein, *Philosophical Investigations*, 36.

5

Guarded Pages, Borderless Books

Lu Xun and the Revolution of the Book in Modern China

Xiaoyu Xia

In 1927, a Chinese librarian penned a fiery public letter complaining about an onerous chore. Fang Chuanzong 方傳宗 had spent two laborious hours cutting open pages in the books shipped from Shanghai publishers to the library in Fujian where he worked.[1] But one man's pain could be another man's pleasure—these unopened pages constituted a novel source of entertainment for modern Chinese readers. The word *maobian* 毛邊 (literally "feathered fringes") refers to this kind of book in which pages are intentionally uncut and fused together. The common use of *maobian* in fact conflates two distinct book forms in Western traditions: the "uncut" book in which pages are rough-edged (customarily referred to as "deckle-edged") and the "intonso" book wherein pages are unopened.

The librarian's frustration about these *maobian* books points us to the contention on the physical form of the book in early twentieth-century China. This contention culminated in the late 1920s in tandem with the heated debate on "revolutionary literature." Spreading across various venues (including the leading literary journal *Yusi Kaiming* 語絲開明), discussions of the *maobian* book turned attention from the politics of writing to the politics of reading. It was precisely Lu Xun's rebuttal to the 1927 letter from Fang Chuanzong that escalated the debate.[2] Readers were immediately polarized into pro- and anti-*maobian* camps.[3] These debates lasted into

---

1. Fang Chuanzong, "Maobian zhuangding de liyou," 180.
2. Lu Xun, "Kou si zagan," 268.
3. For the opinions from supporters of *maobian*, see comments from Yuan Shimin, "Maobian zhuang-ding yulun"; Lin Yi, "Guanyu zhuangding"; Wang Fen, "Duzhe de yijian"; Lin Yu, "Yijian de yijian"; Yin Huai, "Wo de yijian zhi pianpian"; Shen Baojun, "Duiyu zhuangding yu paiyin zhi guanjian"; and Xu Jiu'an, "Wo de yijian zhi pianpian de buchong." For criticisms of *maobian*, see Huang Ruyi, "You guanyu maobian zhuangding"; Tan Zhenxiang, "Guanyu zhuangding"; Xu Bochun, "Guanyu zhuangding"; Leng Yan, "Yige yong shujia zhe de pianjian"; Gu Jun, "Yeshi guanyu maobian shu"; Du Yong, "Wo yelai tantan zhuangding"; and Qi Guang, "Maobian shu yu zazhi."

84 Guarded Pages, Borderless Books

the early 1930s, yet neither side was able to win over the other. Lu Xun's brother Zhou Zuoren, also a champion of the bibliographic revolution, may have been correct when he made the democratically minded comment, "Some want *maobian*, and some do not. It is a matter of personal preference, not something that can be solved in theory."[4]

To situate these polemics surrounding *maobian* in a larger context of the revolution of Chinese book culture, this chapter will trace a trajectory from the *maobian* craze in modern Chinese books to the international Arts and Crafts Movement, thereby revealing the revolutionary longings initially invested in these rough edges.[5] I will show how Lu Xun wielded these marginal features of book design and manufacture as a tool to retrain Chinese readers and to reform Chinese minds. This transnational lineage of *maobian* sheds light on a key yet oft-neglected route through which Lu Xun engaged with foreign literary inspirations—a route mediated by the book as a material object. It was precisely in the materiality of *maobian* books that Lu Xun embedded his utopian longing for a boundless world of letters. As such, *maobian* signified a bibliotopia—an attempt of worlding through books.

By placing Lu Xun's utopian *maobian* project in a global context, this chapter seeks to offer a new vantage for our understanding of Lu Xun's lifelong endeavor as a translator. Echoing other contributors to this volume, I see translation as crucial to Lu Xun's literary legacies. I further propose that Lu Xun's experimentations with foreign book forms should be seen an integral part of his translatorial undertaking. Through this material translation, Lu Xun not only inherited the project of critiquing modernity from Western and Japanese promoters of deckle-edged books but also attuned *maobian* to aspirations and anxieties specific to early twentieth-century China. The *maobian* debate in the 1920s manifests the conflicted visions of revolution underlying this imported book form, while also pointing us to the bounds of Lu Xun's seemingly boundless bibliotopia.

Maobian as Modernity Critique: From William Morris to Natsume Sōseki

To make sense of the librarian's frustration with *maobian* volumes, we need to understand that this form of binding was a relatively new introduction to the Chinese publishing industry. Indeed, the deckle-edged form had a long and contested history in Europe before it turned into *maobian* books and reached the hand of Chinese readers. These signature rough edges were originally caused by a technical defect in

---

4. Zhou Zuoren, "Qi Ming an," 20.
5. Scholar He Min has explored a similar territory in her recent articles. See He Min, "Jixie fuzhi shidai de meijie nigu" and "Xiandai shijie wenxue huanliu zhong de 'jingmei' yu 'yuyu' zhiwu."

handmade papers, as the pulp often seeps under the wooden rims that are deployed to hold the paper mold. In the times of handpress printing, deckle edges were manually cut away by the binder, and untrimmed codices were an object of contempt. Yet what was initially a defect would become a fetish. Collectors of antique books began to use the deckle edge as evidence of the pristineness of a book—for the very presence of the edges would assure the reader that the book had never been rebound or irreversibly trimmed. As a result, deckle-edged books became a symbol of status and taste. Despite or perhaps due to the boom of industrial papermaking in France and Great Britain during the first quarter of the eighteenth century, deckle-edged books continued to be popular among bibliophiles, fulfilling their longing for the bygone era of handmade paper.[6]

This kind of nostalgic sentiment culminated in the British Arts and Crafts Movement of the nineteenth century, an international movement that would lay the ground for the global art nouveau style. A central figure in this movement was the writer, painter, and printer William Morris, whose Kelmscott Press was famous for its consistent and stylistic use of deckle edges.[7] The deckle-edged form encapsulated Morris's socialist agenda to resist the alienation of labor in the capitalist printing industry. If industrial printing was threatening to obliterate craftsmanship and subjugate the hand of the writer, binder, press worker, and papermaker to the streamlining and standardizing forces of printing machines, Morris enshrined deckle edges as an emblem of the handicraft tradition, even "a utopian space of ideal workmanship."[8]

The critical connotations that Morris consciously associated with the deckle-edged form were inherited by Japanese book designers. Released in 1905, the first volume of the novel *I Am a Cat* (*Wagahai wa neko de aru*) was one of the earliest and most celebrated deckle-edged books in Japan.[9] The author, Natsume Sōseki, who was to become the most seminal writer in modern Japanese literature, was quite deeply involved in the process of supervising the visual arts and physical form of the

---

6. See Dard Hunter, *Papermaking*, 456. See also Alexander Starre, "The Pleasures of Paper," 131–32.
7. William S. Peterson, *The Kelmscott Press*, 109. See also Starre, "The Pleasures of Paper," 132.
8. Starre, "The Pleasures of Paper," 132. For William Morris's understanding of art and labor, see Ruth Kinna, "William Morris," 493–512.
9. The novel was initially serialized in the journal *Hototogisu* in 1905. The second volume was released in 1906 and the third volume in 1907. All three volumes were printed by the Shueisha and released by Ōkura Shōten in Tokyo. For more on this printing press, see Suzuki Keiko, "Kindai nihon shuppan gyō kakuritsu ki ni okeru Ōkura Shōten," 101–13. Other deckle-edged books printed in the early 1900s include Ueda Bin's *Mi wo tsukushi* (Tokyo: Buntomokan [printed by Tōkyō tsuiji gappan seizōsho], 1901).

book.[10] Not only did he send multiple letters to illustrators,[11] but Sōseki also took pains to inform the typographer, Hashiguchi Goyō, of his preferences for certain types of paper.[12] No wonder, then, that *I Am a Cat* presents a perfect merger of visual and typographic arts (Figure 5.1). The cover features the title in the form of a seal imprint, printed in gold in relief, beneath which there is an illustration featuring a pair of cats, their tails connected to form the shape of a book. In contradistinction to the title, the cats are printed in vermillion ink in the style of an intaglio impression. As if to better imitate these diverse seal forms, both the title and illustration are rendered with wavering strokes and undulating borders, which not only evoke the aura of an artist's carving hand but parallel the deckle-edged border of the book.

When Natsume Sōseki and his friends experimented with the deckle-edged form in 1905, this style of binding was still rather unfamiliar to Japanese readers. Anecdotally, one contemporary reader of *I Am a Cat* had a particularly difficult time

Figure 5.1: Cover of Natsume Sōseki's *I Am a Cat*

10. According to scholar Pedro Bassoe, Sōseki became interested in book design during his stay in England from 1900 to 1903. See Pedro Thiago Ramos Bassoe, "Judging a Book by Its Cover," 160. For more on Japan's reception of William Morris, see Shuichi Nakayama, "The Impact of William Morris in Japan, 1904 to the Present," 273–83.
11. See Natsume Sōseki's letters to Hashiguchi Goyō on January 18 and February 12, 1905, and his letter to Nakamura Fusetsu on August 7, 1905. Natsume Kinnosuke, *Sōseki zenshū*, 22:374, 384, 421.
12. See Natsume Sōseki's letter to Hashiguchi Goyō on August 9, 1905. Natsume Kinnosuke, *Sōseki zenshū*, 22:422.

reading the book while he was hospitalized. Because the pages in the book were unopened, he had to ask his nurse to help him cut open these leaves. Due to her inexperience in handling deckle-edged papers, the nurse ended up ruining the book. The infuriated patient thus concluded that Natsume Sōseki was a habitual "trouble-maker" (*tesū wo kakeru*)—not only did he quit his doctoral program in London and thus brought trouble to the Japanese Ministry of Education, but he was now ready to begin a new business to torture readers. Shibata Shōkyoku observed that the "paper knife"—a necessary companion to the deckle-edged book—was still a foreign object to Meiji readers.[13]

This anecdote illustrates the foreignness of the deckle-edged book to Japanese readers even after decades of Westernizing Japanese books since 1870s.[14] To the extent that deckle edges allowed William Morris to distinguish his books from mechanically mass-reproduced ones, these same edges served as a sign of distinc-tion for Sōseki and his book design team. Indeed, the feathered fringes of *I Am a Cat*, I suggest, signaled a departure from the conventionalized look of Westernized Japanese books. Although the glossy texture of industrial paper might have been a shocking sensation to early Meiji readers, for the generation of Japanese readers in the 1900s, Western-style books should have already become an everyday expe-rience. With recourse to uneven edges and unopened pages, the design team of *I Am a Cat* snapped readers out of their growing overfamiliarity with the Westernized look of the Japanese book, in turn reattuning Japanese readers to the foreignness that had been internalized in their experience of reading. Such an attempt to alert readers to the imprints of Western modernity on Japanese culture—imprints that were originally shocking and alienating yet familiarized and naturalized toward the end of Meiji—was not only a central motif in *I Am a Cat* but an enduring endeavor throughout Sōseki's literary career. The deckle edges on the book *I Am a Cat* thus shed light on a transnational lineage from Morris's defiance of industrial capitalism to Sōseki's critique of Japanese modernity.

The Deckle-Edged *Anthology of Fiction from beyond the Border* and the Open Future of the Open Book

Published four years after the release of the first volume of *I Am a Cat*, the collec-tion of foreign stories translated by Lu Xun and Zhou Zuoren, *Anthology of Fiction from beyond the Border* (hereafter, *Anthology of Fiction*), inherited this lineage of

---

13. Shibata Shōkyoku, "Peepaanaifu," 278.
14. According to Shōji Sensui, Western-style bookbinding technology was brought to Japan in 1873 by an Englishman named W. F. Patterson. Shōji Sensui, *Insatsu bunka shi*, 231.

modernity critique.[15] Lu Xun was not exaggerating in his retort against librarian Fang Chuanzong when he identified himself as the culprit of China's *maobian* fever.[16] As arguably one of the earliest extant *maobian* books in China, *Anthology of Fiction* was printed in 1909 in Tokyo by a Kanda Press (located in today's Jinbōchō neighborhood, which has been a hub of publishers and bookstores since the Meiji era). This Japanese origin of the Chinese *maobian* book implies Lu Xun's participation—as the designer of the book—in the transnational lineage from Morris to Sōseki.

The critique of modernity is first and foremost manifested in the choice of language in *Anthology of Fiction*. Translations in this collection are rendered neither in vernacular Chinese nor in the style of *guwen* (ancient-style prose) popular in the market of translated literature in China at that time. Lin Shu, the epitome of the prevalent guwen-style translation, often combed classical syntax with newly imported neologism, thus masterfully resolving the tension between traditional Chinese writing and modern Western vocabularies.[17] By contrast, Lu Xun and Zhou Zuoren viewed translation as a chance to remold the Chinese language itself.[18] Instead of papering over the conflict between the foreign and the Chinese, *Anthology of Fiction* attunes readers to these gaps and incongruities. Whereas Lin Shu's *guwen* would have read smoothly for his anticipated readers (considering their previous training in the institution of the imperial examination), Lu Xun and Zhou Zuoren's translations, interlaced with extremely esoteric characters, could pose a challenge even for an erudite reader of Confucian classics.[19] Such a difficulty of reading signals Lu Xun and Zhou Zuoren's endeavor to retain the "foreignness" of foreign literature without prematurely assimilating these foreign narratives into the hegemony of classical Chinese. Therefore, *Anthology of Fiction* unsettles the ossified conventions of Chinese writing and, perhaps more important, pries open a critical distance between the linguistic and epistemic systems of China and the West.

---

15. Scholar He Min also suggests that Lu Xun and Zhou Zuoren's experience in Japan might have inspired them to experiment with the *maobian* form. See He Min, "Jixie fuzhi shidai de meijie nigu," 29.

16. Lu Xun, "Kou si zagan," 268.

17. On Lin Shu's translation strategies, Michael Gibbs Hill, *Lin Shu, Inc.*, 49.

18. Lu Xun, "Xu," *Yuwai xiaoshuo ji* (1921), 1. The preface was initially published under Zhou Zuoren's name, yet according to Zhou Zhuoren's own accounts, it was penned by Lu Xun. See the first footnote to the preface in *LXQJ* 10:163–64. On Lu Xun's lifelong practice of "literal translation," see Wenjin Cui, "'Literal Translation' and the Materiality of Language," 393–409.

19. As Lu Xun admits in the 1920 preface to the reprint of *Anthology of Fiction*, the 1909 edition includes some quite "archaic" characters. These characters were removed from the 1921 edition to save "the printers from the trouble casting these characters." Lu Xun, "Xu," *Yuwai xiaoshuo ji* (1921), 2.

The difficulty of reading, moreover, is materialized in these unopened pages of *Anthology of Fiction*—yielding an experience that would have been entirely new for Chinese readers in the late 1900s. For the first time in their lives, reading became a laborious manual process; cutting open leaves was the first step toward prying open a textual gateway to a foreign land. Just as the page border can serve as a metaphor for national and linguistic borders, reading can in turn be seen as a transgressive act. This border-negating connotation is also underscored by the cover of *Anthology of Fiction* (Figure 5.2). Like Natsume Sōseki, Lu Xun was hands-on in designing the book. Recalling the seal impression on the cover of *I Am a Cat*, the title *Yuwai xiaoshuo ji* is rendered in the same style of seal script.[20] Paired with the script is an art nouveau illustration in which a Greek woman is playing the harp in face of the rising sun.[21] Here, the harp might remind readers of the violin in the first piece of the collection—a translation of Henryk Sienkiewicz's short story "Janko Muzykant." In the story, the protagonist Janko's yearning for a violin drives him to break into

Figure 5.2: Cover of Lu Xun's *Anthology of Fiction from beyond the Border*

---

20. See Cui Wendong, "Qingnian Lu Xun yu deyu 'shijie wenxue,'" 194. See also Dong Bingyue, "Wenzhang wei meishu zhiyi," 21–30.
21. Thanks to scholar Cui Wendong's masterful detective work, we now know that the illustration came from the fifth volume of the German literary journal *Aus fremden Zungen* published in 1905. See Cui Wendong, "Qingnian Lu Xun yu deyu 'shijie wenxue,'" 194.

someone else's house.[22] His transgression of borders, in a sense, parallels Lu Xun and Zhou Zuoren's valorization of translation as a means to steal art from other countries. For Lu Xun and Zhou Zuoren, translation represents a hope to enrich the allegedly impoverished world of Chinese literature. The harp player on the front cover may be seen as a stand-in for the translator. But is she playing the harp to perform a hymn to the rising sun, or more radically, is her music what awakens and brings up the sun? The translator is thus imagined as an Apollonian figure whose words would enlighten the dark horizons of national literature.

The light of the sun, moreover, dissolves the inner border of the illustration. Whereas the left half of the illustration is framed by border lines, the right half of the image is left borderless—as if light and the sea would extend infinitely beyond. This illustration foregrounds a dialectic between a bounded form and boundless flows, between the finite frame of the harp and infinite reverberations of music.

The dissolved borders in the illustration, I suggest, correspond to the negation of paginal borders. The unruly edges of the deckle-edged book embody a utopian promise to emancipate readers from the confined space of the page. This liberatory tone is attested by the introduction (*Lüeli* 略例) of *Anthology of Fiction*. Stressing that the book is "bound in the new style" (*zhuangding juncong xinshi* 裝訂均從新式), Lu Xun describes how "all three sides of the book are left as they naturally [*benran* 本然] are and untrimmed [*bushi qiexue* 不施切削]."[23] As the uncut and unopened pages of *Anthology of Fiction* represent an ideal natural state, the conventional technical process of book trimming acquires a repressive connotation.

The physical form of *Anthology of Fiction* can thus be seen as Lu Xun's resistance against a repressive regime of text. Following the description of the uncut pages in the introduction is a note on the intentionally blank spaces in *Anthology of Fiction*—"margins of paper are all very wide and expansive."[24] Precisely because the page is untrimmed, the margin is wider than usual, hence capable of entertaining readers' jottings. Thus, these blank spaces anticipate readers' participation in the making and remaking of the book. As discussed earlier, the deckle-edged form was initially deployed to allow readers to rebind and redecorate books by themselves. Likewise, the deckle-edged *Anthology of Fiction* is made with the expectation that the book would be eventually disassembled. Lu Xun even takes pains to explain why "the first and last page of each story are separate from those pages in other stories."[25]

---

22. Zhou Zuoren, "Yueren yaoke," *Yuwai xiaoshuo ji*, 1–10. As scholar Dong Bingyue has pointed out, this image of a Greek woman playing the harp harks back to the image Lu Xun chose for the inaugural (and only) issue of *Vita nova* (*Xinsheng*), an aborted journal of translations Lu Xun previously established in Tokyo. Dong Bingyue, "Wenzhang wei meishu zhiyi," 23.

23. Lu Xun, "Lüeli," *Yuwai xiaoshuo ji*, n.p.

24. Lu Xun, "Lüeli," *Yuwai xiaoshuo ji*, n.p.

25. Lu Xun, "Lüeli," *Yuwai xiaoshuo ji*, n.p.

According to Lu Xun, this design would allow readers to rebind these stories "in the future" with other works from the same country or period.[26] In other words, Lu Xun longed for a future dismembering of his book, for such dissolution would be a testament to the profusion of translation in China. He counted on readers to bring that future into being through their rebinding and remaking of the book. The openness of the future is promised by the openness of the book.

Rescuing Chinese Readers from the Textual Iron House

The openness of *Anthology of Fiction*, moreover, prefigured Lu Xun's consistent contemplation of the relationship between the physical form of the book and the mental life of Chinese people. Unlike his precursor Sōseki whose infatuation with the deckle-edged form seems rather short lived,[27] Lu Xun remained a lifelong adherent of *maobian*. In a letter to publisher Cao Juren written in 1935, a year before Lu Xun's death, Lu Xun asked if it would be possible to leave ten copies of his *Uncollected Work* uncut. "I was a member of the *maobian* faction ten years ago," Lu Xun confessed, "and my preference has never changed."[28]

What do we make of the divergence between Sōseki and Lu Xun? Scholar Pedro Bassoe notes that unlike its European counterparts, Sōseki's book design was "never overtly political."[29] Indeed, out of his entire oeuvre, the deckle-edged volumes are tinged with what Sōseki himself identified as a comic *haikai* taste.[30] The deckle-edged form of *I Am a Cat*, in this sense, affords a ludic experience of reading, resonating with early Sōseki's playful style of writing. This take on the book as a space for play can be detected in the intentionally blank pages attached to the end of volumes 2 and 3 of *I Am a Cat*—presumably intended as a space for jottings.[31] These flyleaves were introduced to Meiji Japanese readers as an unfamiliar feature of Western books. The way in which the flyleaf is referred to in Japanese—*asobigami* (literally "pages for play")—underscores the ludic nature of these empty pages.

If Sōseki's interest in the physical form of the book was mostly ludic and apolitical, Lu Xun was invested in the politics of reading. Although not mentioned in the introduction, *Anthology of Fiction* was also printed with a couple of blank pages at the

---

26. Lu Xun, "Lüeli," *Yuwai xiaoshuo ji*, n.p. He Min discerns in the practice of rebinding an homage to traditional ways of reading and editing. See He Min, "Jixie fuzhi shidai de meijie nigu," 34–35.

27. In addition to the three volumes of *I Am a Cat* published in 1905–1907, the collection of short stories *Drifting in Emptiness* (*Yōkyoshū*) (Tokyo: Ōgura shoten, 1906) was likewise printed with deckle edges.

28. Lu Xun's letter to Cao Juren, April 10, 1935, *LXQJ* 13:436.

29. Pedro Thiago Ramos Bassoe, "Judging a Book by Its Cover," 161.

30. See Joel R. Cohn, *Studies in the Comic Spirit in Modern Japanese Fiction*, 22.

31. The 1906 *Yōkyoshū* (Drifting in emptiness) and the 1907 *Uzurakago* (Quail basket) also included this kind of blank pages.

92   Guarded Pages, Borderless Books

end of the book. Lu Xun was in fact quite insistent on making these flyleaves a convention of Chinese books. In a 1925 article, Lu Xun frowned upon Chinese books of his day for the lack of flyleaves; he faulted contemporary Chinese books for their unbearably narrow top and bottom margins. "Even if readers want to write down their thoughts or some other stuff, there will be no space," Lu Xun complained. For Lu Xun, the overcrowded layout of the Chinese book was culpable for the absence of breathing spaces or leisure (*yuyu* 餘裕) in Chinese life.[32]

As scholar Dong Bingyue is quick to notice, Lu Xun's use of the word *yuyu* echoes the notion of *yoyū* in Japanese—a notion often attributed by Lu Xun to Sōseki.[33] This invocation of *yoyū* might appear as evidence of Lu Xun's attachment to the literati culture of leisure—and that might well be part of the story. Nevertheless, Lu Xun's critique of the Chinese book can also be read in relation to his famous criticism of Chinese society. It is in this sense that the insertion of flyleaves in Lu Xun's books departed from the ludic connotation of these *asobigami* in Sōseki's early books. Indeed, when Lu Xun complained about the sense of suffocation he felt when facing the crowding together of movable metal type, it is hard not to think of the all-too-famous allegory of the windowless iron house that stands in for a slumbering and moribund Chinese society.[34]

The insertion of blank pages and empty margins in *Anthology of Fiction* can hence be interpreted as an attempt to enable more mental space for Chinese readers through the enlargement of paratextual and even nontextual spaces. These empty spaces, as Lu Xun saw it, would not only allow readers to jot down their thoughts and opinions but give them a chance to let their minds wander freely into unprogrammed spaces. Whereas the overpowering dominance of the written word signals the author's monopoly over the book, the increased nontextual space, as Lu Xun hoped, would empower Chinese readers and emancipate Chinese minds. This explains the divergence between Sōseki's dabbling with deckle edges and Lu Xun's lasting insistence on *maobian*. For Sōseki and his book design team, deckle edges were deployed momentarily as a shocking effect to defamiliarize the Westernized appearance of the Japanese book. For Lu Xun, the persistent adoption of *maobian* was intended as a long-term training course for Chinese readers—a training toward readerly freedom.

---

32. Lu Xun, "Huran xiangdao (er)," 8.
33. In *Collection of Modern Japanese Books (Xindai Riben xiaoshuo ji)* edited by Lu Xun and Zhou Zuoren and published in 1923, Lu Xun praised Sōseki's style as a "literature with *yuyu*" (*you yuyu de wenxue*). Lu Xun, "Guanyu zuozhe de shuoming," *LXQJ* 10:216. See Dong Bingyue, "Wenzhang wei meishu zhiyi," 29. See also He Min, "Jixie fuzhi shidai de meijie nigu," 35–36; He Min, "Xiandai shijie wenxue huanliu zhong de 'jingmei' yu 'yuyu' zhiwu," 44–45.
34. Lu Xun, "Na han zi xu," *LXQJ* 1:441. In the aforementioned 1935 letter to Cao Juren, only few paragraphs prior to his note on *maobian*, Lu Xun again mentions the iron house allegory. See *LXQJ* 13:436.

Page, Space, and the Temporality of Reading: *Maobian* and Print Capitalism in the 1920s

The liberatory affordances of *maobian* envisioned by Lu Xun, however, clashed with the book market in the 1920s. Perhaps because of its radical departure from the linguistic style and the physical form of the book that were familiar to its contemporary readers, *Anthology of Fiction* was a complete failure in the Chinese book market.[35] These rough edges accompanying the book almost disappeared from the public eye throughout the 1910s—until Lu Xun's rise to fame in the late 1910s and early 1920s brought the deckle-edged form back to life. In fact, the production of *maobian* books surged in the mid-1920s.[36]

The debate on *maobian*, in this sense, was a response to the popularity of this book form in the 1920s. What came to the fore in this debate was the tension between these uncut, unopened pages and the infrastructures undergirding the production and consumption of books. The librarian Fang Chuanzong's laments about the inconvenience of unopened pages, for example, revealed the multiple ways in which *maobian* could be deemed unfit for modern libraries. The problem, first and foremost, resided in the conflict between a private reading experience and the institutionalization of reading as a public activity. One major appeal of the *maobian* book to its readers was the sense of a pristine, private ownership.[37] The process of separating pages and revealing the inside of the book was a process of imprinting oneself on the surface of the book, and in so doing, personalizing the book. What *maobian* books entertained was thus an intimate readership. This sense of intimacy, however, conflicted with the newly public nature of books as part of the circulation system of public libraries. The guarded pages of the *maobian* book hence became an impediment to the book's entry into public use.

In addition to *maobian*'s clash with immediate library circulation, this book form created troubles for the shelving system of both public and private libraries. A number of readers complained that the *maobian* book was often too large to fit into bookshelves; the differing sizes of *maobian* books irritated those who preferred an orderly look to their book collections.[38] The popularization of the term *maobian* resulted in the coinage of an inverse term, *guangbian* 光邊 (literally "smoothened

---

35. According to Lu Xun's 1920 preface to the reprint of *Anthology of Fiction*, it only sold a meager twenty copies in Tokyo and another twenty-odd copies in Shanghai. Lu Xun, "Xu," *Yuwai xiaoshuo ji*, 2.
36. See Wang Yanting, "Guojia tushuguan baocun benshuku minguo maobian shu diaoyan," 51–52.
37. This discourse of pristineness was manifested in the introduction to the 1909 *Anthology of Fiction*; Lu Xun already praised the *maobian* form for its capacity to stay unsoiled despite multiple rounds of reading, as deckle edges would make timeworn or thumb-worn traces less visible.
38. See Leng Yan, "Yige yong shujia zhe de pianjian," 259–60.

border").[39] Evoking a sense of streamlined smoothness and polished shininess, the word *guang* underscored the superiority of the trimmed book and its easy, efficient entry into the standard space of modern bookshelves.

The standardization of modern bookshelves, moreover, was contingent on the rise of a standard system of page sizes. Concomitant with the debate on *maobian* was the codification of a set of new vocabularies for the size of the page—namely, the system of *kai* 開. In two articles printed in the journal *Kaiming* 開明 in 1930, an author publishing under the pen name Shuixian 水仙 (literally, Narcissus) divided contemporary publications into two categories: "regular" and "irregular" sizes. Here, *regular sizes* refers to volumes that follow the geometric division of standard printed papers: a printing sheet folded once is *duikai* 對開; twice is 4 kai; thrice is 8 kai, and so forth up to the extremely unusual 256 kai.[40] *Irregular sizes*, by contrast, refers to those that are not modeled on a geometric sequence with a first term and ratio of 2—including 6 kai, 9 kai, 12 kai, 15 kai, 18 kai, 20 kai, 23 kai, 25 kai, 40 kai, 46 kai, and 50 kai.[41] As Shuixian noted, the biggest problem with irregular sizes was that they were "hard to print," "hard to fold," and "hard to bind." All these difficulties compounded themselves to the detriment of printshop workers.[42] It was also widely believed that the geometric kai system was the most economical means of using stocks of paper, while irregular kai sizes unavoidably yield a certain percentage of paper waste. The kai system epitomizes how Western technologies of industrial printing imposed a standardizing effect on the physical form of modern Chinese books.[43] The geometric logic of the kai system was even internalized into the practice of literary criticism. Critics of mid- to late-1920s China were remarkably well versed in the vocabulary of book production.[44]

Meanwhile, as Shuixian acknowledged, despite the codification of page sizes, writers and publishers continued to play with irregular page sizes to defamiliarize the habituated look of Westernized Chinese books and to furnish readers with a feeling of novelty.[45] The unruly edges of the *maobian* book constituted a flight from an allegedly universal system of pagination. While the kai system presupposed a

39. See Du Yong, "Wo yelai tantan zhuangding," 765–66; Yu Gong, "Wo yelai gongxian yidian yijian," 243. A guangbian supporter even named himself "Qi Guang" (literally "even and smooth"). See Qi Guang, "Maobian shu yu zazhi," 4.
40. Shuixian, "Tan kaiben (shang)," 1–2.
41. Shuixian, "Tan kaiben (xia)," 1–2.
42. Shuixian, "Tan kaiben (xia)," 1.
43. Despite these attempts, the kai system remains unstandardized in China. See Xiao Chun, "Guanyu shukan kaiben," 39; see also Xu Rong, "Tan kaiben ji kaiben zhulu," 31–32.
44. See, for example, Sun Fuxi, "Chuban shiye de yishu," 25; Jing Si, "Chuban shiye de yishu," 8; Yin Huai, "Wo de yijian zhi pianpian," 655.
45. Shuixian, "Tan kaiben (xia)," 1–2. See also Shen Min, "Kaiben zuowei yizhong biaoshu yuyan," 56–58.

seamless commensurability with the global book market, *maobian* destabilized the smooth borders of the expanding empire of print capitalism.

The *maobian* form's potential to unsettle the capitalist apparatus was manifested not only in the spatial logic of pages but also in choreographing an alternative temporality of reading. In his 1927 letter to the magazine *Yusi*, the librarian Fang Chuanzong lamented the enormous amount of time to be wasted nationally on *maobian* books: "Suppose that there are fifty thousand readers in China reading *maobian* magazines and books, and every day one spends ten minutes on cutting open pages, it would cost ordinary readers nationwide more than eight thousand minutes per day, and over four million minutes per year."[46] Whereas Fang invoked the Taylorist rhetoric of efficiency and productivity, Zhou Zuoren, then the chief editor of *Yusi*, retorted that unlike America, readers in China did not need to give in to the Franklinian moral of "time is money." "Reading costs time," Zhou opined.[47]

The *maobian*, in this sense, can be seen as the time of reading materialized. Whereas some readers complained about how unopened leaves slowed down their reading speed and interrupt their experience of reading,[48] one adherent of *maobian* argued that unopened pages would allow one to pause and reflect on the previous page.[49] These two opposite attitudes on *maobian* foreground two distinct temporalities of reading—one is fast, linear, uninterrupted, and the other is slow, circular, and punctuated by both paginal division and contemplation. The former resembles the industrial clockwork wherein time is quantified and monetized. The rough edge of *maobian*, by contrast, disrupts the streamlined flow of time with dilated, unproductive pauses, which attune readers to the tangible here and now, rescuing time from devolving into homogeneity and emptiness.[50]

Leisure or Labor, Pleasure or Pain: *Maobian* and the Paradox of Revolution

Although the materiality of deckle-edged leaves seemed to afford readers with the revolutionary possibility of disrupting the capitalist abstraction of time, as *maobian* turned into a fetish item in the 1920s, the same materiality became bound up with issues of privilege and class. A critic concluded that the debate on *maobian* in the

---

46. Fang Chuanzong, "Maobian zhuangding de liyou," 180.
47. Zhou Zuoren, "Qi Ming an," 180.
48. See Huang Ruyi, "You guanyu maobian zhuangding," 20; Tan Zhenxiang, "Guanyu zhuangding," 46; Xu Bochun, "Guanyu zhuangding," 46; Gu Jun, "Yeshi guanyu maobian shu," 764; Qi Guang, "Maobian shu yu zazhi," 4.
49. Lin Yu, "Yijian de yijian," 238–39.
50. My interpretation of the punctuated temporality characteristic of *maobian* books is inspired by Walter Benjamin's notion of *jetztzeit*. See Walter Benjamin, "On the Concept of History," 395.

1920s boiled down to the rhetoric of utilitarianism. Readers who opposed *maobian* dismissed it as a waste of space (page space and the space of bookshelves) and time, thus useless and superfluous; members of the *maobian* party, by contrast, enshrined uselessness as beauty in its purest form.[51] This binary of utility and beauty, moreover, can be translated into a binary between labor (which is directed toward production) and leisure (which is by definition unproductive).

The tension between labor and leisure came to the fore in the contemporary debate on "revolutionary literature." In response to that debate, Lu Xun again invoked the notion of "leisure"—*yuyu*. In his 1927 talk "Literature in a Revolutionary Age," Lu Xun claimed that literature was essentially "a product of yuyu."[52] The word *yuyu* thus signals a fundamental gap between literature and revolution.[53] As a material expression of leisure, blank spaces in books—though previously valorized by Lu Xun as a means to enable more breathing spaces in Chinese minds—became indexical of the privilege of the leisure class. The poetry collection *Recollection* (*Yi* 憶) printed in 1925, for example, was faulted for its waste of page space, which made it unaffordable for lower-class readers.[54] As it turns out, blank spaces also cost money.

By the same token, deckle edges could be lucrative. The marginal profit of the deckle-edged form can be traced to one alleged tradition of this form of binding. To this day, deckle-edged books are referred to in Japanese interchangeably as "uncut books" (*ankatto hon* or *misai hon*) and "French binding" (*furansu sō*), indicating the French root of this form of binding. Although the contemporary typographer Ōneki Shinju frowned on the term "French binding" as a misnomer,[55] critics of 1920s China likewise traced *maobian* to France. The French-trained artist Sun Fuxi penned the article "The Art of Publishing" (*Chuban shiye de yishu*) in 1926; according to Sun, the deckle-edged form was initially meant to grant readers the freedom to rebind the book and redecorate the borders of leaves (often with deluxe golden or marbled patterns).[56] This luxurious taste is exemplified by Sōseki's *I Am a Cat*, which

---

51. Yu Gong, "Wo yelai gongxian yidian yijian," 243.
52. Lu Xun, "Geming shidai de wenxue," *LXQJ* 3:439, 442.
53. Similar criticisms can also be found in other contemporary essays by Lu Xun, such as the 1927 "Revolutionary Literature" (*Geming wenxue*) and the 1928 "Arts and the Revolution" (*Wenyi yu geming*). *LXQJ* 3:567–68, 583–84.
54. Criticisms of the poetry collection *Recollection* were mostly printed in the journal *Hongshui* (Flood). Note that the journal itself was printed with rough edges and uncut pages. See Gu Fengtian, "Wo duiyu yi," 375–76; Yi Ren and Quan Ping, "Guanyu 'Yi,'" 36–39; Jun Shi and Quan Ping, "Duiyu yi de gongdao hua," 128–29.
55. Ōnuki Shinju, *Seihon tansaku*, 85; see also Onchi Kōshirō, *Sōhon no shimei*, 225.
56. Sun Fuxi, "Chuban shiye de yishu," 25. See also Leng Yan, "Yige yong shujia zhe de pianjian," 260.

boasts gilded top edges; the book was so exorbitantly priced that these unopened pages virtually shut the door on common readers.[57]

For all its potentials to disturb the capitalist print industry and book market, the deckle-edged form was equally capable of colluding with the capitalist logic of scarcity and rarity; thence arises the paradox of revolution. What's enjoyed by some as part of a ludic, leisurely experience of reading was subjected to others as a tedious if also painful chore. Such dialectics of leisure and labor was already prefigured in Morris's bookwork. Despite his socialist ambitions, Kelmscott books were decried by his contemporaries as "the epitome of an artificial upper-class aesthetic of hand-made goods."[58] In his 1899 book *The Theory of the Leisure Class*, Thorstein Veblen looked down on Kelmscott books with a mixture of contempt and amusement. Note how he ridiculed the feigned crudeness of these books—"We have a somewhat cruder type, printed on hand-laid, deckle-edged paper, with excessive margins and uncut leaves, with bindings of a painstaking crudeness and elaborate ineptitude."[59] Veblen thus hinted at Morris's fetishization of labor as a selling point. In fact, it is said that the pressmen who worked for Morris detested these deckle edges because these edges often cut their fingers.[60] The violence inflicted on the laborer's hand debunks Morris's wish to make labor "pleasant," lending a disturbing twist to the leisurely pleasure one derives from the materiality of these deckle edges.[61] Likewise, the librarian who was assigned the laborious chore to cut open thousands of pages in one shift was not the one who got the leisure to enjoy these books himself.

What is evaded in Lu Xun's utopian interpretation of the *maobian* form is precisely the question of accessibility. One laborer's encounter with the *maobian* book might serve to expose the border of Lu Xun's bibliotopia. In a 1936 article, proletarian writer identified as Ah Lei reminisced about an unforgettable meeting in his life. It was 1932, a rainy noon. Between work shifts, he finally had the leisure to explore the neighborhood of the Hongkew Park in Shanghai. He decided to visit the famous Uchiyama Bookstore that Lu Xun was known to frequent. What immediately caught his attention was Lu Xun's translation of Alexander Fadeyev's *The Rout*, titled *Destruction*. He was eager to read Lu Xun's postface, only to find that the pages in the book were unopened. Left with no choice, he gathered up courage to ask Mr. Uchiyama how much the book cost. The price was much higher than he could

---

57. Each volume cost 90 sen, while other novels of similar length published in these years were consistently priced around 30 sen. Sōseki even states in a 1905 letter to Nakagawa Yoshitarō that all he wanted is to have a "magnificent" book regardless of whether the book would be too expensive and would not sell. Natsume Kinnosuke, *Sōseki zenshū*, 22:423.

58. Alexander Starre, "The Pleasures of Paper," 131–32.

59. Thorstein Veblen, *The Theory of Leisure Class*, 108.

60. William W. Peterson, *The Kelmscott Press*, 96.

61. See William Casement, "William Morris on Labor and Pleasure," 351–82.

afford. "Too expensive," he said. "Expensive? Look at the paper." Mr. Uchiyama ran his thumb over the cover of the book. *Chilachila*. The sound was enchanting. The cover was wrapped in a kind of grayish green cotton, and the inside was printed on thick foreign paper (*yangzhi* 洋紙). Holding the book in his palms, the laborer felt a sense of comfort, but he did not have enough money. As the laborer was about to leave the bookstore full of disappointment, Lu Xun showed up. "Do you want the book?" "Yes." He felt as though overwhelmed by the fatherly warmth exuding from Lu Xun's already sickened body. Finally, he was offered the book—together with another translation by Lu Xun—at an affordable price.

Published in the wake of Lu Xun's death, this article alternates between an elegiac tone and a more revolutionary voice. "Whenever I was tortured and beaten up by people . . . I would raise my head and say to myself: 'Mr. Lu Xun is always with us!'"[62] This impassioned call to class solidarity would make the article one of the most remembered of Lu Xun's many hagiographies, and for decades it has been a staple piece in the national elementary school textbook. Intriguingly, the part in which the laborer reverently addressed Mr. Uchiyama in the first person as *sensei*, together with the detailed descriptions of the look and sensation of the book are carefully redacted in the textbook. The reference to "foreign paper," for example, is replaced simply with "paper" (*zhizhang* 紙張).[63]

Editors of the national textbook were quick to detect the jarring contradiction between the deifying depictions of Lu Xun and the exotic, excessive materiality of the book he had translated. The removal of such material details in the textbook paralleled the systematic elimination of *maobian* books in socialist China.[64] Although the fetishistic pleasure the laborer derived from the texture of foreign paper might still be attributed to his longing for knowledge and literature despite material poverty, the irony is hard to miss when the laborer is denied access to the book by these *maobian* pages. In this vignette, not only does the *maobian* form epitomize a book fetish shared by the leisure class and a proletarian bibliophile alike, but it fatally undercuts the claim that Lu Xun had always stood with the poor and downtrodden. These guarded pages, in a tangible way, materialize the invisible wall between writer and reader, the haves and the have-nots.

---

62. A Lei, "Yimian," 297–99.
63. See Zhu Yongfang, "A Lei sanwen 'yimian' xiugai pingxi," 21. Although Zhu saw this revision as an attempt to improve the rhythm of the sentence, I suspect that the problem might have involved the "foreignness" (*yang* 洋) of the paper.
64. According to data collected by Wang Yanting, the spike of *maobian* books in the 1920s was followed by a drop in the 1930s and 1940s and a near extinction since the 1950s. Wang Yanting, "Guojia tushuguan baocun benshuku minguo maobian shu diaoyan," 51–52.

Part 2: Lu Xun into the World

6

(Geo)politics of Aesthetics

Transculturation of Lu Xun in Korea

Shijung Kim

In November 1916, the controversial founding figure of modern Korean literature, Yi Kwangsu (1892–1950?), serialized "What Is Literature?" (*Munhak iran hao*) in the newspaper *Daily News* (*Maeil sinbo*). The essay, though perhaps best known for having propagated an aestheticized and translingual definition of literature, is also symptomatic of what Andre Schmid has referred to as Korea's "decentering" or "demoting" of China at the turn of the nineteenth and twentieth centuries.[1] About halfway into the essay, Yi Kwangsu proposes a cultural divorce from China by equating the country with the past (as opposed to his vision of the future as consisting of "Westernization") and by likening its historical impact on Korea to that of "accumulated dirt" (*kugu* 舊垢).[2] The possible irony of his remarks is that they resort to a projection of fears of being backward compared to Japan or the West, when there could have easily been a case of identification. In other words, at this point Yi Kwangsu does not appear to realize that Chinese intellectuals were currently posing similar questions in their own struggle to integrate themselves into a changing world order and what they perceived to be the progressive temporality of modernity. What would Yi Kwangsu or any other member of the modern Korean literati have written had they been exposed to, say, Lu Xun's outcries in the preface to *Outcry*?

This chapter approaches this question by way of a critical overview of Korean literary transculturation of Lu Xun from the 1920s to the present day. In using the

---

1. "The shift in the definition of civilization ... away from one hegemonic system with its geographical locus in China toward another, centered on the West." Andre Schmid, *Korea between Empires*, 57. To this definition one can add that Japan, too, became a regional center.
2. "How sad that Koreans still admire the Chinese script and Chinese classics without trying to escape from Chinese influence. Recently, a new Western culture is flooding our land. It is beyond dispute that Koreans must shed their old clothes for new, and wash away the accumulated dirt." Yi Kwangsu, "What Is Literature?" 302.

term "transculturation," I follow Sylvia Spitta in looking at how cultures and their products as they cross most notably national frontiers and undergo "many different processes of assimilation, adaptation, rejection, parody, resistance, loss, and ultimately transformation."[3] Most common textual modes of transculturation include literary criticism, translation, and intertextualization, and as Karen Thornber observes in her work on East Asia that draws on Spitta's notion, one advantage of embracing the paradigm of transculturation rather than that of influence is that the former allows for a less hierarchical and reductively causal map of transmission, while another advantage involves its sensitivity to the geopolitical dimension of transnational artistic exchange.[4]

At present, not much English-language scholarship exists on the transculturation of Lu Xun in Korean letters. There are passages from Thornber's book and a few journal articles concentrating on the colonial and postliberation eras, in addition to a chapter on Lu Xun and Kim Saryang (1914–1950) in Satoru Hashimoto's forthcoming *Afterlives of Letters: The Transnational Origins of Modern Chinese, Japanese, and Korean Literatures*. In Korean, numerous papers cover a wider chronological range, as well as two monographs exclusively dedicated to the subject, Hong Sŏkp'yo's *Lu Xun and Early Modern Korea: Imagination for the Sake of East Asian Coexistence* (*Lu Swin kwa kŭndae Han'guk: Tong Asia kongjon ŭl wihan sangsang*, 2017) and Ch'oe Chinho's *Imagined Lu Xun and Modern China: The Question That Is Lu Xun in Korea* (*Sangsang toen Lu Swin kwa hyŏndae Chungguk: Han'guk esŏ Lu Swin iranŭn murŭm*, 2019). A variety of articles are also available in Chinese, together with three anthologies, *Collected Papers in Korean Lu Xun Studies* (*Hanguo Lu Xun yanjiu lunwenji*, 2005), *From Korean-Chinese Dialogues in Lu Xun Studies toward East Asian Luxunology* (*You Han-Zhong Lu Xun yanjiu duihua zouxiang Dongya Lu Xun xue*, 2008), and *A Selection of Korean Lu Xun Studies* (*Hanguo Lu Xun yanjiu jingxuanji*, 2016).

To expand the chronological scope of existing anglophone scholarship, I incorporate an array of recent publications in Korean and Chinese. Doing so makes available for the first time in the English language a relatively comprehensive survey of Korean literary transculturation of Lu Xun. The century of Korea's interaction with Lu Xun will be hereafter divided into five phases: the era of Japanese colonial rule, the "liberation space" (*haebang konggan*) between 1945 and 1948, the first half of the Cold War, South Korean social movements from the 1970s to the 1980s, and finally, the decades following the Sino-Korean normalization of diplomatic relations in 1992. Some flexibility with the periodical organization of texts has been maintained for thematic clarity. As will be seen, the introduction of Lu Xun in Korea

---

3. Sylvia Spitta, *Between Two Waters*, 750.
4. Karen Thornber, *Empire of Texts in Motion*, 4, 11.

Japanese Colonial Rule

Until the end of the Japanese colonial rule, China continued to occupy a demoted status in the Korean psyche. Many Koreans internalized Western and Japanese imperialist ideas about China and sometimes even sided with the dominant gaze, presumably in the hopes of escaping their own national inferiority complex. But as the news of China's Republican Revolution (1911), the May Fourth Movement (1919), and so on led to the development of the trope of a new China, a more positive image of the country as a companion and model of modernization and anti-imperialist endeavors also spread, and along with it formed the earliest generation of Korean readers, critics, scholars, and translators of Lu Xun.

The first-ever mention of Lu Xun in Korean letters dates to February 1921, when novelist and translator Yang Paekhwa (1889–1944) published in the periodical *Genesis* (*Kaebyŏk*) an installment of "China's Literary Revolution Centered on Hu Shi" (*Ho Chŏk ssi rŭl chungsim ŭro han Chungguk ŭi munhak hyŏngmyŏng*). The article was a translation of Japanese sinologist Aoki Masaru's 青木正児 (1887–1964) "Literary Revolution Revolving around Hu Shi" (*Ko Teki o chūshin ni uzumaite iru bungaku kakumei*, 1920) and contained a passing laudatory remark on Lu Xun. Seven years later, independence activist Yu Kisŏk (1905–1980)—whose pen name Suin (樹人) consists of the same characters as Lu Xun's official given name, [Zhou] Shuren [周]樹人—presented his translation of "A Madman's Diary" in an issue of *Eastern Light* (*Tonggwang*). Then followed a rendering of "The Story of Hair" in *Collected Chinese Short Stories* (*Chungguk tanp'yŏn sosŏlchip*, 1929)[5] as well as Yang Paekhwa's serialization of "The True Story of Ah Q" in *Korea Daily* (*Chosŏn Ilbo*) during the early months of 1930.

Although significant for its introduction of Ah Q to the Korean public, Yang Paekhwa's 1930 translation was wrought with linguistic errors, not least because it had based itself on a Japanese version by Inoue Kōbai 井上紅梅 (1881–1949). A student in China from the mid-1920s to the early 1930s, Chŏng Naedong (1903–1985) advocated instead for unmediated contact with the country's literature, thereby reflecting the epoch's transition away from the practices of relay translation

---

5. Erroneously attributed to Yang Paekhwa for a long time, the translation might be by a certain Kim Hongsŏn. See Ch'oe Ch'angnŭk and Zhao Yingqiu, "Kaebyŏksa 'Chungguk tanp'yŏn sosŏlchip' ponyŏkcha sogo."

(*chungyŏk* 重譯) and translation narration (*yŏksul* 譯述)[6] and contesting Japan-centric modes of circulation. He translated "Regrets for the Past," "The Passerby," and "Kong Yiji" in 1930, 1932, and 1934, respectively, and published what was arguably the most systematic analysis of the author at the time in Korea, "Lu Xun and His Works" (*No Sin kwa kŭ ŭi chakp'um*, 1931). For Hong Sŏkp'yo, the singularity of Chŏng Naedong as a reader of Lu Xun can be seen in his 1931 valorization of *Wild Grass* as "the finest crystallization of Lu Xun's entire art."[7]

By the same token, Chŏng Naedong was not exactly representative of Korean Lu Xun criticism in the 1930s. His dislike of Marxism separated him from many of his peers, whose attention to China revolved around leftist politics and revolutionary literature, as was the trend of Chinese and Korean letters at the time. More typical in this regard was literary historian Kim T'aejun (1905–1950), who once rhapsodized over "a newly rising China! . . . in the midst of a battle to reform everything" after a 1930 visit to Beijing.[8] Heavily influenced by Qian Xingcun 錢杏邨 (1900–1977), Kim T'aejun largely set Lu Xun aside, thinking the writer belonged to an inadequately engaged, thus "bygone age." Conversely, anti-colonial activist and journalist Sin Ŏnjun (1904–1938) promoted Lu Xun as a proletarian and revolutionary, going so far as to overstate a few details in the process. In an article recording his May 1933 interview with the author in Shanghai, "Visiting Lu Xun, the Literary Giant of China" (*Chungguk ŭi taemunho No Sin pangmun'gi*, 1934), Sin Ŏnjun wrote, "Every aspect of [Lu Xun's] life replicates that of the proletariat. Not only does he cry out for the proletariat by his mouth and brush but also embraces the proletarian way by his body and life."[9]

Lu Xun also inspired the resistance poet Yi Yuksa (1904–1944), who, days after Lu Xun's death, serialized in *Korea Daily* "Eulogy to Lu Xun" (*No Sin ch'udomun*). Part memoir and part literary criticism, the eulogy paints Lu Xun as a model to the colonial Korean literati, particularly in his navigation of aesthetics and politics: "For Lu Xun, not only is art not a slave of politics, but also, at the least, art is the forerunner of politics; [their relation] is neither that of fusion nor division."[10] Later that year, for the journal *Morning Light* (*Chogwang*), Yi Yuksa translated "Hometown," probably relying on Satō Haruo's 佐藤春夫 (1892–1964) earlier Japanese version,[11] and in "Unexpected Misfortune" (*Hoengaek*, 1939), he intertextualized "Miscellaneous

---

6. Hong Sŏkp'yo, *Lu Swin kwa kŭndae Han'guk*, 110–14.
7. Cited in Hong Sŏkp'yo, *Lu Swin kwa kŭndae Han'guk*, 134. All translations from Korean and Chinese are mine unless otherwise noted.
8. Cited in Hong Sŏkp'yo, *Lu Swin kwa kŭndae Han'guk*, 153.
9. Sin Ŏnjun, "Chungguk ŭi taemunho No Sin pangmun'gi," 150.
10. Yi Yuksa, *Yi Yuksa chŏnjip*, 209, 216.
11. For a side-by-side comparison of the two, see Hong Sŏkp'yo, *Han-Chung munhak ŭi taehwa*, 67–82.

Talk after Illness."[12] As Hong Sŏkp'yo points out, Yi Yuksa's "Hometown" stood out for its creative mastery of the target language,[13] and his involvement with Lu Xun in general likely functioned as a decisive turning point in the further politicization of his poetry in the latter half of the 1930s.[14]

Although not quite known for his resistance, Yi Kwangsu also transculturated Lu Xun. His short piece narrating the construction of his Hongji-dong residence, "Building" (Sŏngjogi, 1936), features the clownish personage of Pak Sŏndal, whose life, Yi Kwangsu notes, "shares some similarities with that of Lu Xun's Ah Q."[15] Sixty years old, a bit of a drunkard, foul-mouthed, vain, and always eager to pick on younger individuals, Pak Sŏndal suffers from "a physiological defect" that made more than ten wives run away within a few days of marriage.[16] Another reference to Lu Xun's character can be found in "The Stance of Wartime Writers" (Chŏnjaenggi ŭi chakkajŏk t'aedo, 1936), which describes how "China today has no Achilles, but only Ah Q. Guan Yu and Zhang Fei have degenerated into Ah Q and Kong Yiji."[17] Twenty years after "What Is Literature," Yi Kwangsu appears to have maintained his opinion of China, reading Lu Xun's story less as an act of self-critique than as a confirmation of the country's backward and degenerate condition.

Liberation Space

During the final decade of colonial rule, due in part to the Second Sino-Japanese War (1937–1945), the introduction of Chinese literature in the peninsula decreased dramatically, with Lu Xun's works appearing on the list of banned books by 1938. Other than the 1938 stage production of Ah Q that may have been permitted for war propaganda, or Kim Saryang's bilingual intertextualization of the character as "Count Wang" (Wang paekchak) and "Count Q" (Q hakushaku) in the early 1940s, there are few examples of Korean transculturation of Lu Xun from this period. The circumstances, however, took a different turn in the "liberation space" between the 1945 Japanese surrender and the 1948 formation of two Korean regimes. During that short period, the country witnessed a relative renaissance of Lu Xun transculturation.

The most consequential event of the era involving Lu Xun may have been the publication of Collected Short Stories of Lu Xun (No Sin tanp'yŏn sosŏlchip) in August and November 1946. Co-translated by Kim Kwangju (1910–1973) and Yi Yonggyu,

---

12. Hong Sŏkp'yo, Lu Swin kwa kŭndae Han'guk, 208–10.
13. Hong Sŏkp'yo, Han-Chung munhak ŭi taehwa, 82.
14. Hong Sŏkp'yo, Lu Swin kwa kŭndae Han'guk, 238–39.
15. Yi Kwangsu, Yi Kwangsu chŏnjip, 256.
16. Yi Kwangsu, Yi Kwangsu chŏnjip, 256.
17. Yi Kwangsu, "Chŏnjaenggi ŭi chakkajŏk t'aedo."

106   (Geo)politics of Aesthetics

the book gathered "A Happy Family," "Hometown," "Kong Yiji," "A Passing Storm," "Master Gao," "Dragon Boat Festival," "The Misanthrope," "A Madman's Diary," "Soap," and "The True Story of Ah Q." Whereas little is written about Yi Yonggyu, future *wuxia* novelist Kim Kwangju's presence in the history of Lu Xun transculturation in Korea is conspicuous. In effect, Kim Kwangju had also translated "Upstairs in the Tavern" back in 1932, and in 1948 he published "Lu Xun and His Works" (*No Sin kwa kǔ ǔi chakp'um*). In an essay that same year, "What Is New" (*Saeroun kŏt*), Kim Kwangju invoked Lu Xun's reflections on progress and evolution from "Impromptu Reflections No. 49" as a better alternative to what he judged were left-leaning ideals, prolonging perhaps the legacy of anti-Marxist readings by Chŏng Naedong.

Offsetting Kim Kwangju's political penchant, literary historian Yi Myŏngsŏn (1914–1950) continued Kim T'aejun's leftist line of Lu Xun criticism. Educated, like Kim T'aejun, at Keijō (Kyŏngsŏng) Imperial University's Chinese Language and Literature Department, Yi Myŏngsŏn likened Lu Xun to an unyielding revolutionary "warrior who spent his life in combat" in "The Unfinished Works of Lu Xun" (*No Sin ǔi misŏng chakp'um*, 1940).[18] In the liberation space, Yi Myŏngsŏn edited and translated *Selected Modern Chinese Short Stories* (*Chungguk hyŏndae tanp'yŏn sosŏl sŏnjip*, 1946) as well as the unpublished *Selected Miscellaneous Prose of Lu Xun* (*No Sin chapkammun sŏnjip*). The former book entailed "Hometown," and its preface hypothesized that had Lu Xun been alive during the Sino-Japanese War, he would have been in the vanguard of resistance. As for the foreword of the second collection, it interpreted the later Lu Xun's preference for miscellaneous prose over fiction as a choice that weaponized literature.

Beyond the Kim Kwangju–Yi Myŏngsŏn dyad, whose ideological bifurcation foreshadowed the impending war, Korea University's Association of Dramatic Art Research (Kŭk yesul yŏn'guhoe) staged a performance of *Ah Q* in 1946, commemorating the tenth anniversary of Lu Xun's death. In 1947, a series of public lectures on Lu Xun took place at Seoul National University, with the participation of Chŏng Naedong and newspaper editor Song Chiyŏng (1916–1989). Noted modernist Kim Kwanggyun (1914–1993) published the poem "Lu Xun" (*No Sin*, 1947) in which a wistful apostrophe to the Chinese author gives way to an image of a solitary yet steadfast lamplight. Last, on August 10 of the same year, critic and novelist Hong Hyomin (1904–1976) tried to redress the "demoted" standing of China by calling attention to Lu Xun's literary achievements in his article "Chinese Literature and Korean Literature" (*Chungguk munhak kwa Chosŏn munhak*): "Just as Chosŏn [Korean] people have the habit of looking down on Chinese people for no reason, the Chosŏn literary scene has the habit of placing not much importance on Chinese

---

18. Yi Kwangsu, *Yi Myŏngsŏn chŏnjip*, 56.

literature. This is a grave mistake. Did we really ever produce a man of letters like Lu Xun or Guo Ruomo [*sic*]?"[19]

Cold War Rivalries

With the outbreak of the Korean War (1950–1953), the surge in Lu Xun transculturation came to a premature end. Relevant activities did eventually start again, but throughout the subsequent couple of decades, they never quite managed to dissociate Lu Xun from Cold War ideologies. For many South Koreans of the period, Lu Xun had to be either condemned or severed radically from "the menacing monster" that was, in the eyes of historian Kim Chunyŏp (1920–2011) writing in 1961, the People's Republic of China (PRC).[20]

Despite the limited amount of accessible material, it may be safe to surmise that the systematic introduction of Lu Xun resumed faster in North Korea than in its southern counterpart. This to all appearances reflected the Democratic People's Republic of Korea's geopolitical ties with the PRC, where Lu Xun was hailed and canonized. From 1956 to 1957, the National Press (Kungnip ch'ulp'ansa), located in Pyongyang, published at least three volumes of *Selected Works of Lu Xun* (*No Sin sŏnjip*). The volumes translated not only the usual trio of *Outcry, Hesitation*, and *Wild Grass* but also writings from *Hot Wind, Inauspicious Star, Sequel to Inauspicious Star, Graves, And That's All, Dawn Blossoms Plucked at Dusk*, and *Old Tales Retold*.

Also in 1956 in North Korea, on the twentieth anniversary of Lu Xun's death, the review *Korean Literature* (*Chosŏn munhak*) allotted roughly twenty pages of its October issue to the writer, presenting translations of "Thoughts on the League of Left-Wing Writers" and "On Our Literary Movement at Present." The issue also included two pieces of literary criticism, "Lu Xun and Korean Literature" (*No Sin kwa Chosŏn munhak*) and "Modern Chinese Literature and Lu Xun" (*Chungguk hyŏndae munhak kwa No Sin*). One memorable moment from the former piece is when novelist-politician Han Sŏrya (1900–1976) claims to have intertextualized "A Madman's Diary" and "Kong Yiji" in his own short stories. However, scholar Chŏn Hyŏngjun cautions against accepting this claim at face value since Han Sŏrya would have had much to gain from being associated with Lu Xun.[21] In other parts of the essay, Han Sŏrya valorizes the later Lu Xun's miscellaneous prose for its "deepening of Marxist-Leninist aesthetic"[22] and quotes a passage in praise of the author from Mao Zedong's "On New Democracy" (*Xin minzhu zhuyi lun* 新民主主義論, 1940).

---

19. Hong Hyomin, "Chungguk munhak kwa Chosŏn munhak."
20. Cited in Ch'oe Chinho, *Sangsang toen Lu Swin kwa hyŏndae Chungguk*, 161.
21. Chŏn Hyŏngjun, *Tong Asiajŏk sigak ŭro ponŭn Chungguk munhak*, 84.
22. Han Sŏrya, "No Sin kwa Chosŏn munhak," 191.

108   (Geo)politics of Aesthetics

By contrast, no major translation of Lu Xun emerged in the Republic of Korea in the 1950s, possibly because his works were forbidden due to their ties to the PRC. Nevertheless, South Korean readers did occasionally discuss him, though they did so while exhibiting the curious habit of connecting the author to Taiwan, despite the censorship of his oeuvre under Chiang Kai-shek. In a 1963 essay, Chang Kigŭn (1922–2011), who was then professor of Chinese literature at Seoul National University, imagined that were Ah Q to come alive, he would have "passed through Hong Kong to go to Free Taiwan or some other place under the sun" in order to avoid reexperiencing his "doglike death" in China.[23] He also wrote, "as a bourgeois intellectual rooted in evolutionary thought, Lu Xun consciously refused to become a Communist until the very end."[24] Somewhat more subtly, in a 1966 anthology of world literature that he coedited with Cho Yŏnhyŏn (1920–1981), Kim Kwangju constructed a genealogy of modern Chinese literature that began with Lu Xun and ended with three Taiwanese authors, including Wang Lan 王藍 (1922–2003), and a Hong Kong author, Xu Su 徐速 (1924–1981).[25]

It was only in 1963, ten years after the armistice, that a new book of Lu Xun translation saw the light of day: scholar of premodern Sino-Korean literature Yi Kawŏn's (1917–2000) The True Story of Ah Q: Selected Stories of Lu Xun (A Q chŏngjŏn: No Sin sosŏl sŏnjip). This volume included translations of "Medicine," "Tomorrow," "The Rabbits and the Cat," and "New Year's Sacrifice." His early reviving of Lu Xun notwithstanding, Yi Kawŏn was not free of Cold War ideologies either. Not only did he present Lu Xun solely as an enlightenment reformer, but he also handpicked Kim Kwangju and Yi Yonggyu as his predecessors in Lu Xun translation, omitting all mention of Yi Myŏngsŏn. As Chŏng Chonghyŏn observes, the possibility of Yi Kawŏn's unfamiliarity with Yi Myŏngsŏn was improbable, given the latter's renown in the field until the war. More likely was the erasure of Yi Myŏngsŏn's legacy due to his choosing the north.[26] In any case, in 1964, Chŏng Naedong followed Yi Kawŏn's lead by co-translating A Brief History of Chinese Fiction, whose publication, as Pak Chaeu reminds us, was possible only after being deemed compliant with the government's anti-communist measures.[27]

Around this time, the novelist Pak Kyŏngni (1926–2008) appropriated "Ah Q" in her essay "To Mr. Q" (Q ssi ege, 1966), giving rise to one of the most lyrical Lu Xun intertexts in the Korean language. After reminiscing about the time she spent "drunk with works such as 'Kong Yiji,' 'Hometown' and 'The Misanthrope,'" she moves on

---

23. Chang Kigŭn, "Chunggong ŭi A Q," 183.
24. Chang Kigŭn, "Chunggong ŭi A Q," 182.
25. Chŏng Chonghyŏn, "Lu Swin ŭi ch'osang," 76.
26. Chŏng Chonghyŏn, "Lu Swin ŭi ch'osang," 71.
27. Pak Chaeu, "Xuyan," 6.

to the more private reason behind her "stealing" the letter Q from Lu Xun.[28] She says that the unknown sinograph behind Q stands for the indeterminate addressee of the epistolary essay, or maybe even, one might infer, of all acts of writing: "To tell the truth Mr. Q might not be human. He could be the sky outside that window or these walls that surround me on four sides or perhaps everything that I face"; "Mr. Q, how could I expect you to echo this call. I do not even possess a language lucid enough to convey my thoughts truthfully."[29] Several years later, novelist Yi Pyŏngju (1921–1992) integrated the more orthodox image of Lu Xun as "a man of determination" into *Mount Chiri* (*Chirisan*, 1972–1978).[30] He also penned a long piece of criticism, "Lu Xun" (*Luu Sin*, 1979), which discussed China's overdeification of the author, as well as the necessity of reading him regardless.

Social Movements

In the 1970s, a couple of new developments altered the reading of Lu Xun in South Korea. One was the thawing to a slight degree of Cold War tensions at the international level after the "ping-pong diplomacy" initiatives between the United States and the PRC. The other was the growing dissatisfaction within the nation toward the Park Chung Hee regime, whose chief traits included anti-communism, authoritarian rule, and rapid economic growth. Under these conditions, there appeared efforts to reject uncritically anti-communist approaches to Lu Xun, and some social activists found inspiration from the author in their struggle against the government.

Journalist and activist Yi Yŏnghŭi (1929–2010) embodied both of these trends in Lu Xun transculturation. Writing retrospectively in "Lu Xun and I" (*No Sin kwa na*, 1988), Yi Yŏnghŭi explains that the story of the iron house from the preface to *Outcry* determined "the substance and direction and purpose" of his life: like Lu Xun, he was to "wake" Koreans up from the "irrational anti-communism" of the Park Chung Hee regime which, for him, "in every aspect resembled China under Chiang Kai-shek."[31] What is interesting about this recollection is that during the actual Park Chung Hee era, Yi Yŏnghŭi, at least as reflected in his texts, concentrated more on Mao Zedong than on Lu Xun, supporting the Cultural Revolution and being sentenced to prison in the process. Only from the 1980s onward did he publish the bulk of his writings on Lu Xun. As Li Dake and Chŏn Hyŏngjun show, Yi Yŏnghŭi may have assimilated Lu Xun's oeuvre to Mao Zedong Thought and vice versa, at times

---

28. Pak Chaeu, *Q ssi ege*, 11.
29. Pak Chaeu, *Q ssi ege*, 12.
30. Cited in Chŏng Chonghyŏn, "Lu Swin ŭi ch'osang," 84.
31. Yi Yŏnghŭi, *Chayuin, chayuin*, 321.

110   (Geo)politics of Aesthetics

comprehending the latter through the former's enlightenment ideas, at other times internalizing the latter's expounding of the former.[32]

Literary critic Im Hŏnyŏng (1941–) was another activist of the era harboring admiration for Lu Xun. Like Yi Yŏnghŭi, he spent time in jail, notably due to his participation in the late 1970s underground organization South Korean Liberation Front (Namjosŏn minjok haebang chŏnsŏn), which aimed to establish a more democratic and socialist country. He read Lu Xun in prison and later shared his fondness for the "gratifying" treatment of the "dictator" in "Forging Swords" in his correspondence with Pak Chaeu.[33] Although less engaged than Im Hŏnyŏng during the 1970s, intellectual, activist, and farmer Chŏn Uik (1925–2004) can be mentioned here as well, given the inflection of his thought. His essays "Democracy Made of Diverse Individuals Bringing Their Forces Together" (*Tayang han kaein i him ŭl hapch'yŏ irun minju chuŭi*, 1990) and "Respected Monk and Lu Xun" (*Sŭnim kwa No Sin*, 1990) described Lu Xun as a promoter of veritably human and nonslavish existence and as a thinker who wanted the common people (*minjung*) to become self-reflective subjects of politics.

Park Chung Hee was assassinated in 1979, but authoritarianism and anti-communism persisted under military strongman Chun Doo Hwan throughout most of the 1980s. At the same time, pro-democracy movements and the desire for critical reexamination of Cold War ideologies also intensified, resulting in, as Ch'oe Chinho puts it, "a contradictory era" that both demanded and silenced China-related discourses.[34]

In addition to a series of Yi Yŏnghŭi's writings on Lu Xun, such as "It's Arrived!" (*Lairŏ*, 1982), "The Opportunism of Intellectuals" (*Chisigin ŭi kihoe chuŭi*, 1987), and "No Fair Play for Fascists" (*P'asisŭt'ŭ nŭn p'eŏ p'ŭllei ŭi sangdae ka anida*, 1988), the decade yielded some events in translation. In 1983, Pak Pyŏngt'ae's (1957–1981) rendering of *Letters between Two Places* was posthumously published as *Respected Teacher Lu Xun* (*No Sin sŏnsaengnim*). It comprised the correspondence, a chronology of Lu Xun's life, a preface and a postface by other scholars, as well as a remark indicating that Pak Pyŏngt'ae had also translated *Two Hearts* and *Three Leisures* but that "adverse circumstances"—probably censorship—had prevented their printing.[35] Then from 1985 to 1987 appeared Korean relay translations of Takeuchi Yoshimi's 竹内好 (1910–1977) *Collected Writings of Lu Xun* (*Ro Jin bunshū*, 1976–1978), introducing *Dawn Blossoms Plucked at Dusk* and approximately 150 pieces

---

32. See Li Dake and Chŏn Hyŏngjun, "Lu Xun zai Hanguo shehui biange yundong zhong de jieshou fangshi."
33. Pak Chaeu, "Qi, bashi niandai Hanguo de biange yundong yu Lu Xun," 42.
34. Ch'oe Chinho, *Sangsang toen Lu Swin kwa hyŏndae Chungguk*, 231.
35. Cited in Ch'oe Chinho, *Sangsang toen Lu Swin kwa hyŏndae Chungguk*, 228.

of miscellaneous prose to the country for the first time.[36] To be sure, even before *Collected Writings*, Takeuchi had been a part of Korean transculturation of Lu Xun. Both Yi Yŏnghŭi's and Im Hŏnyŏng's initial exposures to Lu Xun were indebted to the Japanese critic.[37]

Perhaps because of its democratic spirit, the 1980s also saw an increased practice of the woodblock print, an art form with the potential of mass diffusion, and Korean critics devoted a handful of articles to Lu Xun's relation to art and the Chinese woodcut movement. Novelist Hwang Sŏgyŏng (1943–) would later write about this phenomenon in *Old Garden* (*Oraedoen chŏng'wŏn*, 2000), which fictionalizes pro-democracy movements in the 1980s. In a scene set in the decade, one of the characters says, "Roughly in that period I belatedly took an interest in the craft of the woodblock print that had developed around China's Lu Xun and was engrossed in my work on a plain-looking engraving."[38]

In the academic sphere, the 1980s entered what Pak Chaeu terms "the period of rapid growth" in Korean Lu Xun studies, generating more than sixty research papers on the author and fostering scholars whose input is still heard to this day, such as Pak Chaeu (1954–) himself and Chŏn Hyŏngjun (1956–).[39] Apart from the circulation of previously banned books starting from 1987, no doubt relevant to this boom was the founding of the Korean Society of Modern Chinese Literature (Han'guk Chungguk hyŏndae munhak hakhoe) in 1985. Concurrently with the inception of the society, specialized publications on the subject started to flourish, and much of the research favorably viewed Chinese leftist literature.

Although it is not feasible to provide a similarly detailed overview of Lu Xun's reception in North Korea, scholar Sin Chŏngho notes that Lu Xun may have been the sole modern Chinese author to be translated and published in North Korea from 1967 to 1983.[40] One of the new editions was Pak Hŭngbyŏng and Yi Kyuhae's *Selected Works of Lu Xun* (*No Sin chakp'umsŏn*, 1964), which gathered forty-eight pieces of writing and a translators' preface.[41] Another was a collection of twelve works titled *Blessing* (*Ch'ukpok*, 1979) of which fifty thousand copies were printed.[42] Beyond the domain of translation, in 1970, Kim Il Sung delivered a speech affirming the fitness of Lu Xun's oeuvre for the revolutionary cause, and in 1972, a reference book on literature and arts reproduced the same ruler's 1959 extolment of Maxim

---

36. Pak Chaeu, "Xuyan," 9.

37. Pak Chaeu, "Qi, bashi niandai Hanguo de biange yundong yu Lu Xun," 41–42.

38. Cited in Kim Yangsu, "Tong Asia ŭi munhakchŏk t'ongno rosŏŭi Lu Swin," 167.

39. Pak Chaeu, *Hanguo de Zhongguo xiandai wenxue yanjiu tonglun*, 62–64.

40. Sin Chŏngho, "Pukhan ŭi Chungguk munhak yŏn'gu (1949–2000)," 349.

41. Cui Xiongquan, "Jieshou yu piping," 59.

42. Sin Chŏngho, "Pukhan ŭi Chungguk munhak yŏn'gu (1949–2000)," 349. It is unclear if the title alludes to Lu Xun's "New Year's Sacrifice."

112   (Geo)politics of Aesthetics

Gorky and Lu Xun as required readings for everyone.[43] In 1981, the Academy of Social Sciences (Sahoe kwahagwŏn) hosted a symposium to commemorate the centennial of Lu Xun's birth.[44] Given these indications, it might be safe to presume that Lu Xun's prestige in North Korea stayed undiminished until the end of the century.

From the 1990s Onward

The beginning of the final decade of the twentieth century marked yet another period of transition: the Soviet Union collapsed in 1991, China and South Korea officially normalized diplomatic relations in 1992, and Kim Young Sam assumed presidency in 1993 as the nation further consolidated its nascent democracy. At the same time, the two most ubiquitous and mutually contrastive Korean tropes of China—China as an ideological adversary of the Cold War and as a model for left-wing social activism—began to fade.

At the early stage of these shifts, the legacy of Korea's social activist Lu Xun remained perceptible and culminated in the popular success of *Morning Flowers Collected in the Evening: Collected Prose of Lu Xun* (*Ach'im kkoch'ŭl chŏnyŏge chupta: No Sin sanmunjip*, 1991). Translated and edited by Yi Ugyŏn (1963–), the book brought together about sixty of Lu Xun's essays that were not necessarily included in the homonymous Chinese collection, with the aim of underscoring what its foreword articulated as Lu Xun's "boundless love for the common people [*minjung*] of China."[45] In 1991, a newspaper article summarized the book's message as a critique of the ruling class,[46] and in 1992, another announced that it had sold more than thirty thousand copies in two months.[47] The contemporary consensus is that Yi Ugyŏn's edition played a sizable part in the spread of Lu Xun among the general public.

But soon after, intellectuals put forth readings of Lu Xun with fewer direct ties to the social movements of the previous decades. For literary critic To Chŏngil (1941–), as he argued in "The Globalization of the Cultural Sphere or the Ah Q Phenomenon" (*Munhwa yŏng'yŏk ŭi segyehwa ttonŭn Ak'yu hyŏnsang*, 1997), residents of Seoul in the 1990s were practitioners of Ah Q's "spiritual victories" inasmuch as they are in a denial about the loss of their cultural identity (*chŏngch'esŏng*) in the midst of globalization. Although resistance to homogenization is relatable, To Chŏngil's adherence to the logic of identity as opposed to, as sinologist Anne Cheng has suggested, that of affiliation (*appartenance*) leaves one hesitant to

---

43. Sun Qilin, "Lu Xun he ta de Chaoxian duzhe," 433–39.
44. Cui Xiongquan, "Jieshou yu piping," 59.
45. Yi Yŏnghŭi, "Lu Swin egesŏ palgyŏn hanŭn onŭl ŭi uri," 7.
46. Yi Yŏnghŭi, "Chungguk munhak chakp'um chal p'allinda."
47. Ch'oe Chinho, *Sangsang toen Lu Swin kwa hyŏndae Chungguk*, 259.

wholly espouse his adaptation of Ah Q.[48] From this perspective, legal scholar Pak Honggyu's (1952–) cosmopolitan Lu Xun in *Free Man Lu Xun: Portrait of a Great Intellectual* (*Chayuin Lu Swin: Widaehan chisigin ŭi ch'osang*, 2002) offers a useful counterbalance.

Lu Xun thus became somewhat implicated in discussions addressing the issues of globalization and nationalism. The author also became a presence in academic debates around the notion of East Asia, and research on him included more than a hundred papers between 1997 and 2004.[49] Among scholars active at that time, Hong Sŏkp'yo (1966–) was also a prolific translator, and during the first decade of the twenty-first century he rendered into Korean "The Power of Mara Poetry," *Inauspicious Star, Sequel to Inauspicious Star, Graves*, and "Outline of the Literary History of the Han." In 2007, a dozen researchers came together to form the Korean Committee on Translation of Lu Xun's Complete Works (Han'guk Lu Swin chŏnjip pŏnyŏk wiwŏnhoe), and in 2018, they accomplished the eponymous goal of making the writer's entire oeuvre available in the language. Currently in progress is another large-scale translation project by a separate yet overlapping set of contributors—namely, a series titled *Selected Eminent Works of Chinese Lu Xun Studies* (*Chungguk Lu Swin yŏn'gu myŏngga chŏngsŏnjip*, 2021–) of which the tenth and final volume currently awaits publication.

To paraphrase the preface to *The Complete Works of Lu Xun* (*Lu Swin chŏnjip*, 2010–2018), the milestone achievements listed above illustrate that Lu Xun's writings have acquired the status of a "classic" (*kojŏn*) in twenty-first-century South Korea. "The True Story of Ah Q" alone boasted more than twenty versions by 2009 in such varied forms as children's graphic novel, young adult study guide, and Chinese-language manual.[50] But whereas Lu Xun is now regularly on required reading lists for college students, he seems to generate less spontaneous enthusiasm from the younger generation than in the 1990s,[51] and what is more, based on data from major online booksellers from 2005 to 2015, Yu Hua 余華 (1960–) surpassed Lu Xun as the best-selling Chinese fiction writer in Korea.[52]

A couple of factors may have contributed to this decrease of Lu Xun's appeal. One is a feeling of the diminished potency of Lu Xun's oeuvre in an age of transnational capitalism and consumerist culture.[53] The other is interlaced more generally

---

48. Anne Cheng, "La Chine pense-t-elle?"
49. Pak Chaeu, *Hanguo de Zhongguo xiandai wenxue yanjiu tonglun*, 73.
50. Sŏ Ŭnsuk, "Han'guk tokcha ŭi Chungguk munhak pŏnyŏngmul e taehan insik kwa p'yŏngga yŏn'gu," 533.
51. Sŏ Ŭnsuk, "Han'guk tokcha ŭi Chungguk munhak pŏnyŏngmul e taehan insik kwa p'yŏngga yŏn'gu," 528.
52. Ch'oe Ŭnjŏng, "Chungguk hyŏndae sosŏl ŭi pŏnyŏk hyŏnhwang mit tokcha suyong yangsang," 113.
53. Pak Chaeu, "21 shiji Dongya yujing li de Lu Xun jiazhi," 233.

114 (Geo)politics of Aesthetics

with the fate of modern Chinese literature in Korea. Despite the 175 percent surge in the publication of China-related books in 2007, signaling the country's rise on the global stage and the imminence of the 2008 Beijing Olympics, Korean readers by far prefer literatures from Japan and the United States, according to statistics from 2008 to 2014.[54] Only 201 translated literary works from China were published in 2014, which is lower than 883 from Japan, 467 from the United States, 268 from Britain, and 231 from France.[55] Apparently, the Korean public frequently finds modern Chinese literature alienatingly foreign in terms of its historical background.[56] The consequences of the Cold War cleavage still seem to linger, and the more recent image of China as a purveyor of hegemonic Sinocentrism, which surfaced along with that of the nation as an economic opportunity and neighboring partner, might exacerbate the situation.

For at least two readers, however, not all is lost for Lu Xun in twenty-first-century Korea. Yi Ugyŏn, for one, considers Lu Xun to be a living classic who transcends time to assist people in honing their skills of critical discernment vis-à-vis their own reality, and he puts that belief into practice in *Nights Reading Lu Xun, Hours Reading Myself* (*Lu Swin ingnŭn pam, na rŭl ingnŭn sigan*, 2020).[57] The book interweaves commentary on Lu Xun's texts with Yi Ugyŏn's personal thoughts on diverse societal topics related to contemporary Korea, such as generational conflict, gender inequality, perverse usage of social media, imperfections of democracy and interpersonal competition as a means of survival. In "The Value of Lu Xun in the Context of Twenty-First-Century East Asia" (*21 shiji Dongya yujing li de Lu Xun jiazhi*, 2008), Pak Chaeu, for another, contends that Lu Xun can facilitate struggles against the negative effects of market-oriented economy, the retrograde escalation of nationalism, the inhumanity of neoliberalism, the estrangement and polarization of people, and so forth. He also wishes for an increase in intra-East Asian and global intellectual dialogue through the figure of Lu Xun, in the collective and allusively phrased aim of "resisting despair" (*fankang juewang* 反抗絕望).[58]

* * *

From the preceding discussion, we may observe several recurrent patterns in the transculturation of Lu Xun in Korean letters since the 1920s. One of those patterns is the inseparability of Korea's imagined Lu Xun and the shifting landscapes

---

54. Data from 2013 are missing. Son Chibong, "21-segi Chung-Han munhak pŏnyŏk ŭi hyŏnhwang kwa chŏnmang," 74, 67.
55. Son Chibong, "21-segi Chung-Han munhak pŏnyŏk ŭi hyŏnhwang kwa chŏnmang," 67.
56. Sŏ Ŭnsuk, "Han'guk tokcha ŭi Chungguk munhak pŏnyŏngmul e taehan insik kwa p'yŏngga yŏn'gu," 528.
57. Yi Ugyŏn, *Lu Swin ingnŭn pam, na rŭl ingnŭn sigan*, 5.
58. Pak Chaeu, "21 shiji Dongya yujing li de Lu Xun jiazhi," 233.

of geopolitics, from Japanese imperialism, the Cold War rivalries to China's latest ascent on the global stage. A large part of this interconnectedness was probably enhanced by Lu Xun's reputation as "the sage of modern China," which led to the confusion of the writer and the nation, a confusion that was all the more avowed when there were hectic efforts to dissociate the two. In addition to in-depth readings of individual translations, criticisms, and intertexts, a future direction of anglophone Korean-Chinese scholarship might be to juxtapose the transculturation of Lu Xun with that of other Chinese writers who are less likely to be conflated with the PRC.

Another pattern to be gleaned from the above overview is the afterlives of Lu Xun's texts as creative catalysts. In "Intra-Asian Reading; or, How Lu Xun Enters into a World Literature" (2022), Satoru Hashimoto articulates Takeuchi's engagement with Lu Xun as a processual event of "self-transformation" that generated a new plane of universals and literariness, or in a word, a new world literature.[59] That is to say, Hashimoto makes a subtle adjustment to David Damrosch's well-known definition of world literature—"all literary works that circulate beyond their culture of origin, either in translation or in the original language"[60]—so as to more explicitly account for not only quantitative or extensive circulation, but also qualitative or intensive transformation.[61] Hashimoto's observation regarding world literature proves pertinent to the transculturation of Lu Xun in Korean letters as well. As with Yi Yuksa's self-dedication to resistance poetry, Yi Yŏnghŭi's turn to social activism, or Yi Ugyŏn's method of self-reading, Korean literati's encounters with Lu Xun actualized and set in motion novel modes of existence that were themselves pathfinders of transculturation trajectories to come. Korean readers may have hybridized Lu Xun in accordance with the overarching geopolitical landscapes, but when they did so, they were also already entangled in the process of what can be dubbed in Deleuzo-Guattarian as becoming-Lu Xun.

Hence, the transculturation of Lu Xun in Korean letters from the 1920s onward, which illustrates world literature's multiple and ongoing self-actualizations, is at once a matter of what Deleuze and Guattari call molarity and molecularity—where molarity consists of "locking singularities into systems of resonance and redundancy"—in other words, of stable orders and meanings, including stereotypes and clichés about China that reproduce geopolitical dynamics—and molecularity stands for "intensive multiplicities composed of particles that do not divide without changing in nature"—in other words, for processual creations of the new, including

---

59. Satoru Hashimoto, "Intra-Asian Reading," 98.

60. David Damrosch, *What Is World Literature?* 4.

61. By "extensive" and "intensive," I follow Deleuze's reading of Leibniz. The extensive means quantities "divisible into equal parts," as in the Cartesian *res extensa*, while the intensive means "relatively indivisible" quantities, or quantities "which do not change without changing their nature" or quality. Gilles Deleuze, *Difference and Repetition*, 331.

116 (Geo)politics of Aesthetics

singular events with less obviously perceptible political and aesthetic ramifications that result from exposures to Lu Xun.[62] "Every society, and every individual, are thus plied by both segmentarities simultaneously: one molar, the other *molecular*," Deleuze and Guattari write, "every politics is simultaneously a *macropolitics* and a *micropolitics*."[63] Indeed, even Yi Kwangsu's interaction with Lu Xun, which may have been one of the most heavily determined by molarity, did not preclude the invention of Pak Sŏndal, a character whose comic relief brings about a dose of subversive and molecular vitality to quotidian stuffiness.

---

62. Gilles Deleuze and Félix Guattari, *A Thousand Plateaus*, 40, 33.
63. Deleuze and Guattari, *A Thousand Plateaus*, 213; emphasis original.

7
Belated Reception and Residual Influence
Lu Xun and Spain

Carles Prado-Fonts

In *What Is Global History?* Sebastian Conrad insightfully proposes an attention to transnational interactions that is based on integration. He suggests that our understanding of the world as a globality should neither try to embrace the "history of everything" nor fetishize exchanges and connections that sometimes are explanatory but sometimes are not. Instead, he argues, global history should be approached by focusing on the causalities that explain how some transnational processes and structures integrate one into each other.[1] Despite the remarkable conceptual and methodological advances that have taken place in the past few decades in translation studies and comparative literature, the study of translations and cross-cultural representations has often been based on the kind of superficial circulation questioned by Conrad. In recent decades, scholars have traced all sorts of flows, transfers, and entanglements as the features that characterize the interactions between literatures around the world. David Damrosch's influential definition of world literature as including all works that circulate beyond their culture of origin illustrates—and is taken as the foundation of—this notion of circulation.[2] However, Conrad's approach reminds us of the need to look for the significance within the quantitative, referential circulation. Rather than paying attention to the connections that emerge out of global flows, we would do better by asking whether these transnational movements have caused any changes in the different cultures implied. After all, as Stefanie Gänger has shown, the use of circulation

---

1. Sebastian Conrad, *What Is Global History?*
2. David Damrosch, *What Is World Literature?* 4.

as a metaphor to understand how literatures or cultures interact has always been quite inconsistent.[3]

In this chapter, I examine the translation of Lu Xun's works in Spain in this light. I contextualize, describe, and interpret some of the Lu Xun's works that have been translated into Castilian, Catalan, and Galician while paying close attention to the relevance of these translations to Spain's literary context. As we will see, with more than twenty translations published in different editions over the past fifty years, Lu Xun is probably the *most* translated modern Chinese author into Spain's various languages. These translations include all the genres cultivated by Lu Xun: essays, poetry, and fiction. In other words, Lu Xun's works have reached Spain in a complete and remarkable way—compared to other important (modern) Chinese authors. From the perspective of mere circulation, then, Lu Xun in Spain could be taken as a case of success.

But what have been the results of this remarkable circulation? How have Lu Xun's works been read and interpreted in Spain? Have they impacted on Spain's literary developments? Have these translations opened new views on China or modern Chinese literature in Spain? Have Lu Xun's works engaged with local intellectual debates? Has Lu Xun become a recognizable literary and intellectual figure for Spanish readers? Have these pieces opened new avenues in Spain's publishing industry? In other words, do these translations of Lu Xun show any causality or traction that goes beyond their individual and quantitative significance?

In the following sections, I address these questions. First, I contrast the reception of Lu Xun's works, which began in the 1970s, with the attention to China in Spain during earlier decades. Second, I survey some of the translations of Lu Xun in Spain, and although I do not comment on all of them, the reader can consult the final bibliography section for a more complete list. Third, I outline some features that characterize the reception of Lu Xun's works in Spain and that not only may help address the questions posed above but also help reveal some of the predicaments for the translation and reception of modern Chinese literature in Spain. While the following sections do not present a particularly hagiographic treatment of Lu Xun, I hope that as Xiaolu Ma rightly pointed out in this volume's introduction, the "ripples, refractions, and differences" that will be presented will "shed new light on our understanding of world literature more broadly."

I should note that I focus here on Spain, and Latin America is largely outside the scope of this chapter. Of course, given that Spanish is a shared language between Spain and Latin America and that the publishing industry has partially unified these two regions, some connections are inevitable. We will see, for instance, how some translations move from one place to another. However, the Latin American context

---

3. Stefanie Gänger, "Circulation."

(and its different cultural and national contexts) deserves a more specific study of its own.[4]

China in Spain before Lu Xun

There are almost no references to Lu Xun in Spain's press and intellectual circles until the 1970s. This absence is even more striking when compared to the abundant representations of China in Spain during that same pre-1970s period. Between the mid-nineteenth century and the 1930s, for instance, China was in Spain "the burning question, the topic of the day."[5] During this period, China was frequently covered in newspapers, magazines, and books.[6] During the last decades of the nineteenth century, diplomats such as Sinibaldo de Mas, Eduard Toda, Enrique Gaspar, and Luis Valera turned their experiences in China into important literary writings.[7] In later decades, authors such as Vicente Blasco Ibáñez, Federico García Sanchiz, and Luis de Oteyza published successful works of fiction and nonfiction based on their experiences in China, too.[8] The popularity of China in Spain was such that not only authors who had visited China wrote about the country, but important writers like Ramón Gómez de la Serna, Pío Baroja, and Federico García Lorca who had never set foot in China also included Chinese topics or images in their works.[9] In Catalonia, canonical poets such as Josep Carner, Josep Maria de Sagarra, Carles Riba, and Marià Manent acted as translators, imitators, and critics of East Asian lyrics. China's presence in Spain's culture was not restricted to literary and intellectual circles. Chinese references were also frequent in popular culture, including theatrical plays and memorabilia.

---

4. It is worth mentioning, for instance, that Lu Xun was already examined in an article published in 1968 in *Estudios Orientales*, the journal from El Colegio de México, a solid sinological venue that began in 1966 and that in 1975 became *Estudios de Asia y África*, still in publication. Sen Ma, "Lu Xun, iniciador de la literatura china moderna."

5. Francisco Peniche de Lugo, "China y Europa," xx.

6. Between 1911 and 1926, there were at least forty-seven monograph publications about China in Spain. Between 1927 and 1940, the number increased to fifty-eight. See Xavier Ortells-Nicolau and David Martínez-Robles, "Publicaciones históricas."

7. Sinibaldo de Mas, *L'Angleterre et le céleste empire*; Sinibaldo de Mas, *L'Angleterre, la Chine et l'Inde*; Sinibaldo de Mas, *La Chine et les puissances chrétiennes*; Eduard Toda, *La vida en el celeste imperio*; Enrique Gaspar, *El anacronópete*; Luis Valera, *Sombras chinescas*.

8. Vincente Blasco Ibáñez, *La vuelta al mundo*; Federico García Sanchiz, *La ciudad milagrosa*; Luis de Oteyza, *El diablo blanco*.

9. Ramón Gómez de la Serna, *Los dos marineros*; Ramón Gómez de la Serna, *Caprichos*; Pío Baroja, *Yan-Si-Pao*; Pío Baroja, *Los pilotos de altura*; Pío Baroja, *La estrella del capitán Chimista*. For Lorca's use of Chinese images throughout his career, see Yue Zhang, "Evolución de las imágenes chinas en la poesía de Lorca."

120   Belated Reception and Residual Influence

Given such a sustained and exuberant interest in China during the first decades of the twentieth century in Spain, why did Lu Xun remain almost unknown there until the 1970s? One could argue that it is only natural that references to Lu Xun did not appear in Spain until his works had been translated into Spain's languages. However, the idea that cross-cultural interaction depends on translations is not quite accurate.[10] The effervescence of representations of China in Spain during the last decades of the nineteenth century and the first decades of the twentieth century took place even though the volume of translations of Chinese literature into the languages of Spain at that point was still very low. And, in fact, the same argument could hold true the other way around: translations of Lu Xun may had appeared if references to him had already been made in Spain's cultural circles. In any case, the question remains, why was Lu Xun absent in Spain until so late?

In my view, there are at least two reasons for Lu Xun's absence in Spain until the 1970s. First, the Cold War and the Franco dictatorship created a new context for interacting with China in the West in general and in Spain in particular. The richness and intensity of representations of China in the first decades of the twentieth century decreased in the 1940s and 1950s. Lu Xun's official enthronement as a model revolutionary writer in China did not easily fit in the new political context of reception in Spain. Second, the tendency in Spain of interacting with China in an indirect way (primarily via the mediation of British and French agents) did not favor the translation of Lu Xun's works in Spain when he was not widely popular in other Western contexts. Spanish writers were often more interested in exhibiting their command of English and French sources that talked about China than in engaging with China itself.[11] Moreover, such preference for an approach to China that was mediated by Western agents reached a stage in the 1930s and onward in which Western figures such as Pearl Buck or André Malraux were valued as the true facilitators of new views on Chinese society and culture. As Ramon Vinyes observed, Western writers like Buck "make the real China known as it has not been made known by Chinese writers themselves."[12] As a consequence, it was thought that Chinese writers deserved less attention as less reliable information providers.

In fact, one of the very few references to Lu Xun in Spain before the 1970s points precisely to this kind of unreliability. Having read a few short stories by Lu Xun (probably in Edgar Snow's 1937 edited volume, *Living China: Modern Chinese Short Stories*), Catalan literary critic Ramon Vinyes compares Lu Xun's style with that of Sherwood Anderson—identifying his fiction with a kind of psychological, modernist literature that does not portray China in a realist way. Instead, Vinyes

---

10. Carles Prado-Fonts, *Secondhand China*, 179–88.

11. Prado-Fonts, *Secondhand China*, 10.

12. Ramon Vinyes, "Xina," 5.

claims that "only Pearl Buck, alone, without Chinese roots, has presented to me the realist, vivid China, that I think can be found in the Chinese fighters, in its patriots, in its heroes, in its martyrs."[13]

As we will see below, the interpretative inclination to look at modern Chinese literary works for a realist reflection of China would persist in later decades after Lu Xun's works finally began to be translated in Spain.

Lu Xun in Spain

The trajectory of Lu Xun in Spain can be roughly divided into three stages: the first consisting of references and translations that, around the 1970s, replicate the Maoist view of Lu Xun as a revolutionary writer; a second period between the 1990s and the 2010s when a more nuanced view of Lu Xun is enhanced—mostly through the efforts of his translators in their paratexts; and the contemporary period in which the translations of Lu Xun's works have blended into the development of a new publishing industry in Spain.

Lu Xun, the revolutionary icon

The first translations of Lu Xun's works into Spanish appeared in 1960, but it was in the 1970s when they began to gain a certain visibility in Spain. These were the first translations not only of Lu Xun's works but also of modern Chinese literature into Spanish. In 1960, Ediciones en Lenguas Extranjeras (Foreign Language Press) published *Novelas escogidas* (Selected short stories) in China. It was translated indirectly from English and French by the diplomat Luis Enrique Délano. The collection included the preface to *Outcry*, as well as "Diary of a Madman," "Kong Yiji," "Medicine," "Tomorrow," "An Incident," "A Passing Storm," "My Old Hometown," "The True Story of Ah Q," "Shexi," "New Year's Sacrifice," "Upstairs in the Tavern," "A Happy Family," "Soap," "The Misanthrope," "Regrets for the Past," "The Divorce," "The Flight to the Moon," and "Forging Swords."

The impact of this first translation of Lu Xun in Spain was relatively unremarkable, as the volumes from the Foreign Language Press were not available in bookstores at the time and hardly circulated beyond small circles of Spaniards in China. However, this translation subsequently gained importance for two reasons. First, *Novelas escogidas* was republished (under different titles) in 1961, 1962, 1972, and 1984 by the Foreign Language Press in Beijing and Havana. Moreover, some short stories collected in the original volume became part of other anthologies—of Lu Xun's work or of modern Chinese literature—in Spain or Latin America. For

---

13. Vinyes, "Xina," 5.

122   Belated Reception and Residual Influence

instance, in 1971 Salvat Editores published *La verdadera historia de A Q y otros cuentos* (The true story of Ah Q and other stories). Although it was the first work by Lu Xun published by a Spanish press, the collection was based on the short stories included in the 1960 Foreign Language Press edition. Second, this institutional translation of Lu Xun's work under the auspices of a revolutionary agenda in Beijing became the reference against which future translations of Lu Xun's works in Spain attempted to provide an alternative vision of Lu Xun—as an author with literary merit. Future translators who promoted Lu Xun's work with a less political and a more literary agenda (Sergio Pitol, Iñaki Preciado, and Laureano Ramírez) worked or were associated with Beijing's Foreign Language Institute, home of the Foreign Language Press.

These first translations of Lu Xun in Spain coincided with a growing interest in Maoist China in Spain at the time of the Cultural Revolution. A crucial reference in this trend is Baltasar Porcel's series of articles "Una revolución en pie: La China de Mao" (A revolution on foot: Mao's China). The series was written for *Destino*, a prestigious and popular weekly magazine at the time. Founded in the 1930s as a platform for Francoism in Catalonia, *Destino* gradually shifted to a more liberal ideology in the 1960s. In 1973, the magazine was already in continuous tension with the Franco regime and sent Porcel, then a young writer and journalist, to report on Mao's China. Porcel wrote a series of fifteen pieces that were published between June 30, 1973 and October 20, 1973. The series included articles from places such as Canton, Tibet, Shanghai, and Beijing and covered topics such as the Great Wall, the industry, Sun Yat-sen and Chiang Kai-shek, the Forbidden City, and Chinese women.

In his articles, Porcel frequently refers to Lu Xun's work—mostly to provide evidence for some social commentary. Lu Xun's authority is backed up with his popularity in China, which Porcel even quantifies: he quotes an intellectual noting that after the Cultural Revolution, each edition of Lu Xun's works increased from around three thousand to around three hundred thousand copies.[14] Porcel also projects the official view of Lu Xun as a revolutionary quoting Lu Xun himself on the topic of revolution.[15] At the same time, however, Porcel notes the tension between Lu Xun as a revolutionary, politicized author and Lu Xun as a "literary" writer, as well as his proverbial iconoclasm. He mentions, for instance, Lu Xun's speech "Geming shidai de wenxue" (Revolutionary period literature) given on April 8, 1927 at the Whampoa Military Academy in which Lu Xun "analyzes with clarity the contradictions and concerns of the time," and adds long quotes in which Lu Xun expresses his

---

14. Baltasar Porcel, "El frente cultural," 37.
15. Baltasar Porcel, "Shanghai (y 2)," 6.

concern for those writers who rely only on revolution and become worthless from a literary point of view.[16]

Porcel's series was later republished as a book.[17] Given the prestige and wide readership of *Destino* at the time, Porcel's reportage projected Lu Xun's figure and works from an excellent platform. It was probably the most outstanding position that Lu Xun held in Spain in terms of public exposure, which, as we will see, did not have the same kind of continuity in later decades. The tension between politics and literature expressed in Porcel's series did remain a constant frame for interpreting Lu Xun's work in Spain—as it was certainly the case in other Western contexts.[18]

Lu Xun, the universal writer

The official view of Lu Xun as a revolutionary symbol was joined in the following decades by the publication of other translations of Lu Xun that presented a different view—sometimes using the same texts. In 1971, for instance, Tusquets published *Diario de un loco* (Diary of a madman) translated indirectly by the diplomat and writer Sergio Pitol. In addition to "Diary of a Madman," the collection only included "The True Story of Ah Q" and "The Lamp of Eternity." This collection was republished in 1980 in Spain and later in Mexico (by Universidad Veracruzana in 2007) and Colombia (by Taller de Edición Rocca in 2009). Pitol, who had worked as an English translator at the Foreign Language Press in 1962, prepared the publication of Lu Xun's translations while he lived in Barcelona and directed the series Los Heterodoxos at Tusquets at the beginning of his literary career.

The preface (which is uncredited but was probably written by Pitol himself) explicitly contrasts the reading of Lu Xun emphasized by the Foreign Language Press edition with a more complex and critical interpretation. The preface notes that Lu Xun's texts

> cannot be classified with docility. The comparison of Lu Xun with other European figures shows how far the discrepancies can go. During his lifetime Lu Xun was already called the Chinese Chekhov, the Chinese Gorky, and the Chinese Nietzsche: three personalities who are difficult to combine. The Cultural Revolution made his name news again. Lu Xun suddenly appeared clad in all the attributes of a red guard.[19]

It is not clear why Salvat and Tusquets decided to publish their volumes almost simultaneously. Maialen Marín-Lacarta has speculated that the notice of Pitol's

---

16. Porcel, "El frente cultural," 36.
17. Baltasar Porcel, *China, una revolución en pie.*
18. See, for instance, Fang Gao, "Idéologie et traduction," for the case in France.
19. Lu Hsun [Lu Xun], *Diario de un loco,* 9.

124 Belated Reception and Residual Influence

edition at Tusquets may have incited Salvat to publish Délano's version from the Foreign Languages Press.[20] The coincidence may also indicate a lack of systematicity.

In 1973, Edicions Tres i Quatre in Valencia published *Sobre la classe intel·lectual* (On the intellectual class). It was a relay translation from the Italian by Joan Francesc Mira into Catalan and included pieces such as "Why 'Fair Play' Should Be Deferred," "Revolutionary Era Literature," "About the Intellectual Class," and "From Satire to Humor." The volume's introduction by Jenaro Talens, the scholar who had commissioned the translation, deserves special attention. Talens, a cultural theorist without any sinological background, shows what, at the time, was an unusually deep and mature understanding of Lu Xun. While he mentions the two 1971 anthologies of Lu Xun's fiction published in Spain, Talens admits having gathered information about Lu Xun from English, French, and Italian sources. (He also seems to have consulted Wang Chengru's dissertation *Lu Hsün: Sein Leben un sein Werk* [Lu Xun: His life and work] in German.) Talens mentions the increasing interest that Lu Xun has raised in the West—writing, as Porcel, from the assumption that Lu Xun is the most important writer in modern Chinese literature. He also refers to the biased understanding of Lu Xun and the appropriation of his works and figure by socialist historiography and literary criticism. Yet Talens goes beyond a mere survey of the reception of Lu Xun and takes the author as a case study for exploring the role of the artist in a revolutionary period and its problematic relation with tradition. The complexities and ambiguities of Lu Xun's thought and his particular position as an iconoclast and critical thinker are compared, for instance, to Chekhov, with Lu Xun's "cold lucidity" being contrasted with Chekhov's' "desperate nostalgia."[21] While the piece acts as a preface for the translation of Lu Xun's essays, Talens productively includes a reading of some of Lu Xun's short stories, too.

In 1978, Alfaguara published *Grito de llamada* (Outcry), translated by Iñaki Preciado and Miguel Shiao. It was the first direct translation into Spanish that took Lu Xun's original Chinese writings as a source text. It was also the first complete translation of *Outcry* into Spanish. The paratext indicates that Lu Xun's short stories combine universal topics with the depiction of an exotic, radically different world. The collection was reviewed in *El País*, a major newspaper in Spain that belonged to the same media group as Alfaguara. The reviewer, Pablo Lizcano, first goes over Lu Xun's biography and the political views that consider him a revolutionary hero. But he later adds, significantly, that "those who read Lu Xun will be surprised," as his writings go beyond mere political propaganda.[22] While Lu Xun's complexity is used

---

20. Maialen Marín-Lacarta, "Mediación, recepción y marginalidad," 174.
21. Jenaro Talens, "Revolució de la literatura i literatura de la revolució," 28.
22. Pablo Lizcano, "Lu Sin."

as a strategy to attract readers, it is a contrapuntal reading that still depends on Lu Xun's canonical role in the Maoist consideration.

In 1982, Edicións Xerais de Galicia published *Flores e leña* (Flowers and firewood), an anthology of modern Chinese literature. It was a direct translation by Fernando Perez-Barreiro Nolla. It included the first translation of Lu Xun's works into Galician. The collection includes "Diary of a Madman" and "A Passing Storm." The paratext stresses the literary value of the selection and presents the anthology as a supplement to revolutionary literature—a work "to be enjoyed," as it brings to the European cultural sphere a "truly significant tendency of modern literary creation."

In 1994, Edicions 62 published *Mala herba* (Wild grass) in its prestigious series *Els Llibres de l'Escorpí*, devoted to twentieth-century universal poetry. It was a direct translation by Seán Golden and Marisa Presas and was the first translation of Lu Xun's works into Catalan, appearing in a bilingual edition with the original and the translation side by side. The translation was commissioned by the series director, the poet and scholar Joaquim Sala-Sanahuja, who had read Lu Xun's poems in both French and English. In the preface, Golden and Presas offer a complete survey of Lu Xun's life and historical context. They also stress the aesthetic, universal value of Lu Xun's prose poems. They argue that these poems, given their "radical ambiguity and the existential hesitations they exhibit, could not fit in the biased interpretation of Lu Xun's work by the Party." They add that the artistic value of this work has started to be reinterpreted in China regardless of any ideological consideration.[23]

In 2001, Azul published *Breve historia de la novela china* (A brief history of Chinese fiction), which was a direct translation by Rosario Blanco Facal. The text had previously been published in Venezuela by Monte Ávila Editores in 1997 and was the first translation of Lu Xun's nonfiction into Spanish. Blanco Facal's preface surveys Lu Xun's trajectory, contextualizes the origin of Lu Xun's original text, and summarizes the contents of the book. The book flap refers to Gao Xingjian's recent Nobel Prize and to "China's millennial literary tradition." It presents Lu Xun's book as having "the fundamental coordinates to situate such a wide legacy."

Also in 2001, Hiperión published *Contar nuevo de historias viejas* (Old tales retold), which was translated by Laureano Ramírez, who had proposed the project to the press. The translation, which was republished in 2009, amplified Golden and Presas's sinological portrait of Lu Xun. In a paratextual apparatus that includes a preface and abundant annotations, Ramírez surveys not only Lu Xun's life and works but also the different editions of Lu Xun's original *Old Tales Retold*. Lu Xun and his texts are projected as objects with a literary and philological interest, besides having a universal resonance. Ramírez contextualizes this work against the assumption that Lu Xun's *Outcry* or *Hesitation* are his most representative works. He argues that

---

23. Séan Golden and Marisa Presas, "Lu Xun en el seu temps," in Lu Xun, *Mala herba*, 22.

126   Belated Reception and Residual Influence

Old Tales Retold "portrays with greater fidelity and consistency than other works the consciousness of an author who is split between classicism and modernity, the guidelines of a universalist thought that is headed toward the future without the easy recourse of disdaining the past, his own ethics of life in the changing times he had to live."[24] Ramírez's preface strikes a perfect balance between the universal value of Lu Xun's work and its cultural specificity, which he does point out but, at the same time, makes sure not to turn into a major obstacle for the nonspecialized reader.

In 2007, Edicions de 1984 published *Diari d'un boig i altres relats* (Diary of a madman and other stories), which was a direct translation into the Catalan language by me (Prado-Fonts) and includes the preface to *Outcry*, "Diary of a Madman," "Kong Yiji," "Medicine," "A Passing Storm," "The True Story of Ah Q," "New Year's Sacrifice," "Soap," "The Misanthrope," and "Regret for the Past." The project for this translated volume—which emphasized Lu Xun's canonical position in China and the need to have his short fiction available for Catalan readers—was awarded the second prize in the Premi de Traducció Vidal Alcover in 2001. In a review for *El País*, Manel Ollé, a Catalan sinologist and literary critic, attempted to universalize Lu Xun's work by citing Sōseki, Dostoevsky, Nietzsche, Freud, Darwin, Gogol, Heine, and Bergson as authors with whom Lu Xun could be compared. He also mentioned Fredric Jameson's views on Lu Xun as a point of legitimation. In a previous review of *Mala herba* for *La Vanguardia*, Ollé had also added Byron and Petőfi to the list.[25] In contrast to Ramírez's attempt to "sinologize" Lu Xun, here we see an attempt to, also from a sinologist's position, universalize Lu Xun's works for the general reader.

Lu Xun in a new publishing context

In the 2010s, the publishing industry in Spain and, particularly in Catalonia, gradually shifted toward a new configuration. The emergence of a wide array of small publishers (or micropresses) created a more dynamic context that, in principle, seems more favorable to alternative or non-Western literatures: these new publishers targeted at more specific niches and readerships and seem to be more eager to incorporate Chinese authors to their catalog. Most of the recent translations of Lu Xun's works have appeared in this new kind of venues. For example, in 2013, Bartleby Editores published *La mala hierba* (Wild grass) in a direct translation by Blas Piñero Martínez; in 2014, Kailas published *Diario de un demente y la auténtica historia de Ah Q* (Diary of a madman and The true story of Ah Q) in an indirect translation by Néstor Cabrera López y Puerto Barruetabeña; in 2017, Miraguano published *Gritos: Diario de un loco y otros relatos* (Cries: Diary of a madman and

---

24. Laureano Ramírez, "Prefacio," in Lu Xun, *Contar nuevo de historias viejas*, 9.
25. Manel Ollé, "Supervivències"; Manel Ollé, "Mala herba."

other stories) in a direct translation by Iñaki Preciado; and in 2021, Lamola Press published *Colección de un errante* (A wanderer's collection) in a direct translation of *Panghuang* by Wang Liyun and Dídac Masip.

The new configuration of the publishing industry and the emergence of new translators opened the way for translations in new formats. This is the case of Manuel Pavón Belizón's accurate translation of the short piece "Congmingren he shazi he nucai" into "El inteligente, el tonto y el siervo" (The wise man, the fool, and the slave) in the online platform *China traducida y por traducir* (China translated and to be translated), published in 2020. These recent translations of Lu Xun's works have been joined by translations of a heterogeneous group of modern Chinese authors including Eileen Chang, Shen Congwen, Xiao Hong, Lao She, Ding Ling, and Xu Dishan.

Lu Xun: Residual or Emergent?

The translation of Lu Xun's works in Spain over the past fifty years illustrates at least three aspects that may also characterize more generally the translation of Chinese literature in a larger context.

First, many of the publications were driven by translators themselves: it was often the case that the translator had the project in mind, looked for a press, and saw the project to completion. This is what I would call translations by spontaneous generation,[26] without a consolidated stimulus beyond the translators' intervention. It can be explained by a combination of factors such as the lack of a solid sinological tradition in Spain and the lack of engaged publishers. This tendency may have slightly changed in recent decades, due less to an increasing interest in Chinese literature after the Nobel Prize was awarded to Gao Xingjian in 2000 and to Mo Yan in 2012 or to the increased social perception of China as a major geopolitical agent and more to the new configuration of the publishing industry in which small new presses have been more active in searching for new avenues of development.

Second, the reception of Lu Xun's works in Spain has historically depended on previous translations of Lu Xun into other languages, mostly into English or French. This dependence is expressed in two interrelated ways. On the one hand, at a purely linguistic level, many of the translations of Lu Xun's works are relay translations of previous translations into other languages, mostly English and French. Whereas during the 1970s and 1980s, it could be argued that the practice of relay translation was due to a lack of Chinese-Spanish translators, the situation from the 1990s onward does not justify that practice anymore. Yet this is a practice that still characterizes the translation of modern and contemporary Chinese literature in Spain and has been

---

26. Carles Prado-Fonts, "Del xinès al català, traduccions per generació espontània."

128   Belated Reception and Residual Influence

rigorously analyzed.[27] On the other hand, at a more epistemological level, since the mid-nineteenth century onward Spain has been understanding China through the mediation of cultures such as British, French, and German. It is not a coincidence that Spanish publishers and intellectuals became interested in Lu Xun after having come across his work in other languages and cultural settings. For instance, Joaquim Sala-Sanahuja commissioned the translation of *Mala herba* following his encounter with Lu Xun's work in Paris. Jenaro Talens commissioned the translation of *Sobre la classe intel·lectual* after having been introduced to Lu Xun's figure through English, French, and Italian references. The influential publisher Jaume Vallcorba (Quaderns Crema, Acantilado) confessed that his curiosity for Lu Xun was raised by Simon Leys's mentions and translations.[28]

Third, perhaps the most salient feature that can be observed in the translations of Lu Xun's works in Spain is their nonliterary interpretation. Lu Xun's fiction writings have often been credited with providing documentation to illustrate China's society and culture. Baltasar Porcel's influential pieces in 1973, for instance, refer to "A Happy Family," "New Year's Sacrifice," and even "The True Story of Ah Q" as transparent depictions of the social situation in China. The case is particularly striking with Ah Q—a sarcastic and hyperbolic fictional account that is taken as a realist reflection.[29] Paratexts and critical apparatuses in later publications of Lu Xun's works sustain similar interpretations. Alfaguara's 1978 edition highlights how Lu Xun's writings offer an image of life in Chinese society. This kind of realist, mimetic interpretation is enhanced with the information provided in the paratexts, which usually focus on Lu Xun's life and historical context—something that easily leads to assume an autobiographical correspondence.[30] This tendency has not changed over time. We can find a recent example in the translation published by LamolaPress, which still emphasizes the use of Lu Xun's stories as social data: "This collection offers a panoramic perspective of the mentality and behavior of Chinese citizens of all social classes during the first decades of the last century." To be sure, this phenomenon can be generalized to the translations of modern Chinese literature in Spain, and even to a larger field such as world literature.[31] Many translators of Lu Xun into Spain's languages have been well aware of this limited interpretation of Lu Xun as a

---

27. Marín-Lacarta, "Mediación, recepción y marginalidad."
28. Vallcorba refused to publish a Castilian translation of Lu Xun's short stories given their "reduced readership" and concern about it "not being a very commercial book." Personal communications May 2008 and January 2009.
29. Baltasar Porcel, "Canton (2)," 8; Baltasar Porcel, "China," 25–26; Baltasar Porcel, "Del doctor Sun al general Chiang," 18.
30. The publication of Cheng Jing's biography of Lu Xun confirms this tendency: Cheng Jing, *Lu Xun*.
31. Carles Prado-Fonts, "Orientalismo a su pesar"; Maialen Marín-Lacarta, "La recepción de traducciones literarias por su valor documental." For the same issue in world literature, see Gloria Fisk, *Orhan Pamuk*.

mere data provider. Their stress on the literary value of Lu Xun's works should be understood as a deliberate attempt to counterbalance this dominant interpretation that undermines the complexity of Lu Xun's works.

We may conclude by returning to Sebastian Conrad's idea of causality in transnational interactions: Has the presence of Lu Xun in Spain over the past fifty years had any traction? Has it turned the individual and quantitative significance of Lu Xun's translations into Castilian, Catalan, and Galician into something else? Needless to say, all these translations have helped make the works of one of the founding fathers of modern Chinese literature available to new readers in Spain, particularly in a time when translations of Chinese works were scarce. And some (such as Ramírez's or Golden and Presas's) are distinguished by their literary sensibility and sinological rigor. But a more collective assessment is perhaps less optimistic. Unfortunately, the sum of these individual significances has not produced any major change in Spain— neither in a wide recognition of Lu Xun as a major world intellectual figure nor in the understanding of China and Chinese literature. Not only the main patterns in the translation of Chinese literature in Spain (a spontaneous generation of translations, a dependence on English and French sources, a denial of literariness in the name of a documentary interest) have remained the same, but no major changes have followed in terms of readership and industry involvement. No wide readership has been attained, as the sales of these translations have always been moderate. No major engagement from Spain's literary cliques has been achieved, as most of these translations (published by prestigious presses such as Tusquets, Alfaguara, Edicions 62, and Edicions de 1984) have passed relatively unnoticed by media or by critics and authors in Spain. No consequences in the publishing industry have followed, as these publications have neither had a continuity in their respective presses nor have they encouraged the publications of other Chinese authors. Here is an illustrative example: Preciado and Hsiao's 1978 translation at Alfaguara was announced to be the first of three volumes of Lu Xun's works, and the volume's complete title was *Obras I: Grito de llamada* (Works I: *Outcry*), as it was to be followed by *Obras II: Vagabundeos* (Works II: *Wandering*) and *Obras III: Viejos cuentos contados de nuevo* (Works III: *Old tales retold*). However, works II and III were never published, and their announcement, still visible on the pages of Preciado and Hsiao's volume, stands as evidence of the marginalized position of—and the lack of commitment for—modern Chinese literature in Spain.

To Chinese literature scholars in Spain, the general indifference toward Lu Xun's works ironically echoes Lu Xun's lament over the deep sense of desolation that comes after a *nahan* (outcry) that has received no response. But as Lu Xun's somehow affected but still confident words in the same text emphasize, there may still be hope in the future and children can still be saved. Things may already be changing. In recent years, more Chinese literary works have been translated into

130   Belated Reception and Residual Influence

Castilian and Catalan as a result of the new configuration of the literary industry, even if the pace is very slow compared to, for instance, the translation of Russian literary works due to a much stronger support by grants from the Institute of Literary Translation and other Russian institutions. The consolidation of sinology and the opening of degrees in East Asian Studies at Spanish universities in the 2000s may be creating a new sustained and engaged readership, too. New presses specialized in Chinese literature have appeared such as LamolaPress; Edicions Bellaterra has a series dedicated to modern Chinese literary works; and prestigious independent presses such as Libros del Asteroide, Males Herbes, or Club Editor seem to show a growing interest for Chinese and Sinophone authors. If these developments fructify and Chinese literature becomes a more solid presence in Spain's literary system, Lu Xun stands—as an already translated author—in a right position to exhibit his historical significance and reclaim the literary sophistication of his texts.

In any case, time will tell whether, echoing Raymond Williams, the current residual position of Lu Xun and, more generally, of modern Chinese literature in Spain will turn into an emergent form, even if, as Williams reminds us, "definitions of the emergent, as of the residual, can be made only in relation to a full sense of the dominant."[32] In fact, the current impasse of Lu Xun's position in Spain confirms Williams's suspicion about the difficulty to assess these historical transitions and what, going back to Conrad, could be considered the potential traction of these emergences. Indeed, "it is exceptionally difficult to distinguish between those which are [in fact] elements of some new phase of the dominant culture . . . and those which are substantially alternative or oppositional to it: emergent in the strict sense, rather than merely novel."[33]

In the meantime, given the current state of affairs, one is tempted to look at the residual position of Lu Xun's works in Spain from a less dialectical and rather more environmental perspective: their trivial addition to Spain's literary system seems an actual residue left out by a wide but hollow circulation of global, transnational world literature.

---

32. Raymond Williams, *Marxism and Literature*, 123. For Williams, the residual "is usually at some distance from the effective dominant culture, but some part of it, some version of it—and especially if the residue is from some major area of the past—will in most cases have had to be incorporated if the effective dominant culture is to make sense in these areas"; and the emergent are "new meanings and values, new practices, new relationships and kind of relationships" that are continually being created.

33. Williams, *Marxism and Literature*, 123.

8
Penitence, Mercy, and Conversion
Lu Xun as a Topos of World Literature

Xiaolu Ma

David Damrosch describes world literature as being not "a set canon of texts but a mode of reading,"[1] signaling an approach that prioritizes the significance of texts over that of their authors. Seen as a mode of reading, accordingly, world literature is already at the mercy of others, thereby giving readers comparatively greater control over how the work is evaluated or interpreted. In principle, such a vision of world literature should render authorship relatively invisible. Yet, in today's global publication industry, the names of the authors are often the best label for marketing. People may not remember the title of a novel, but they can generally recall the names of some of the world's famous writers, and they will often search for an author's name when looking for a book to read. The charm of the author's name brings us to Lu Xun. Rather than treating Lu Xun simply as a creator of literature, this chapter explores how he enters world literature as a literary figure. How has Lu Xun been canonized as a Chinese writer within world literature? How has he contributed to his own presentation or configuration?

In his biography of Tolstoy, Romain Rolland comments, "In him life and art are one. Never was work more intimately mingled with the artist's life; it has, almost constantly, the value of autobiography."[2] Rolland's verdict applies equally well to Lu Xun. Lu Xun's canonization rests on his ability to render the plight of Chinese intellectuals, which reflects his own predicament. Biographers have pieced together Lu Xun's life not only through his diaries, letters, and the recollection of acquaintances but also through his literary works, including his essays, poetry, and fiction. The personal details Lu Xun included in his publications have shaped scholarly re-creations of his life and status as the leading Chinese modernist, and thus, he contributed

---

1. David Damrosch, "Introduction," 4.
2. Romain Rolland, *Vie de Tolstoy*; Romain Rolland, *Tolstoy*.

132   Penitence, Mercy, and Conversion

to the crystallization of his image as a great modern Chinese writer. The resulting abundance of materials has allowed Lu Xun's admirers within and beyond China to envision stories and anecdotes leading to his canonization. In this way, Lu Xun has consequently become a topos within world literature, an entity open to constant reworking and renewed representation throughout the twentieth century. Not only his works but also his image—whether as an unyielding nationalist fighter or an agonized wandering soul—have prompted his readers both in China and abroad to inquire into his significance as not only a modernist but also as a human being. This interest has helped construct his unique place in world literature.

The contemporary global focus on eminent writers also aligns with Lu Xun's own approach to world literature. In his "On the Power of Mara Poetry," an essay that draws on poets in both Western and Eastern Europe, Lu Xun extolls these so-called Mara poets for maintaining their distinctive national features and resisting social hegemony. Such poets, he argues, are capable of striking deep chords in the generations to come.[3] The essay includes references to authors such as the British Romantic poets Lord Byron (1788–1824) and Percy Bysshe Shelley (1792–1822), while recollecting their life experiences and highlighting their individuality as unflinching defenders of truth, in opposition to conformists who flatter the masses.[4] It is not only these poets' masterpieces that attracted Lu Xun. He was perhaps even more inspired by their ideas and deeds. Lu Xun treats them as the essential foundation of the nation of human beings (*renguo* 人國)—in other words, a humanist nation. As this essay suggests, the key elements of world literature for Lu Xun are not works or texts but poets or authors with noble characters and the charisma to change the world—individuals he assimilates to Friedrich Nietzsche's figure of the *Übermensch* (superman). As Eileen J. Cheng observes, "The radical individualism Lu Xun espouses here is not an antidote to an oppressive tradition premised on a teleological view of history, as later promoted by his New Culture peers; rather, it is an embodiment of a universal human spirit that crosses boundaries of space and time, one that opposes all systems of hegemony, modern or traditional."[5] In fact, Lu Xun himself apparently aspired to become precisely this sort of Mara poet.

In "Mara Poetry," Lu Xun also comments on the contemporary Chinese mental state, remarking that "everyone is talking about 'reform,' which becomes the voice by which people confess their sins from all time, as if they are saying, 'We repent.'"[6] The motifs of guilt, confession, and rehabilitation appear consistently as some of the central themes in Lu Xun's autobiographical writing, making him the prototypical

---

3. Lu Xun, "Moluo shili shuo," 68.
4. Lu Xun, "Moluo shili shuo," 101.
5. Eileen J. Cheng, "'In Search of New Voices from Alien Lands,'" 592.
6. Lu Xun, "Moluo shili shuo," 102.

modern Chinese intellectual. These features have in turn been further elaborated in others' visions and reimaginings of Lu Xun both within and beyond China; new motifs such as mercy and pardon have been added, thus transforming the story and departing from Lu Xun's own vision. Not only did the fate of Lu Xun's literary works finally escape his control, but so too did his image as a world literary figure.

As a crucial mode of self-examination, confession in the modern era has become what Peter Brooks called "a dominant form of self-expression, one that bears special witness to personal truth."[7] By presenting his private self to his readers, Lu Xun provides them with intimate material possible for envisioning—and molding—a modern Chinese intellectual. The Chinese national character, or "Chineseness," is often taken to be the origin of sin in Lu Xun's writing. However, when his work enters world literature—and particularly as it travels to Japan—these social dimensions are reinterpreted. In particular, Japanese writers depart from Lu Xun's struggle with Chineseness, instead offering opportunities of reconciliation.

This chapter begins with Lu Xun's autobiographical writing, focusing on two incidents involving an accusatory letter from his Japanese classmates and a lantern slide image, to tease out the author's complicated responses triggered by Russo-Japanese-Sino social and political entanglement. Next, I explore how these moments are reimagined in narratives of Lu Xun's life by Japanese writers Dazai Osamu 太宰治 (1909–1948) and Inoue Hisashi's 井上ひさし (1934–2010), thus refashioning Lu Xun in an idealized manner. Spotlighting Lu Xun allows these two Japanese writers to anchor their texts in a specific moment of Sino-Japanese transculturation. Their works not only strengthened Lu Xun's national identity as a dedicated Chinese modernist but also wove the character Lu Xun into the Japanese literary realm, making him an organic component of modern Japanese literature. Surprisingly, in their respective texts, Dazai and Inoue suggest similarities between Lu Xun and other renowned writers such as Tolstoy. Through such varied and constantly renewed renderings of Lu Xun across languages and cultures, the image of the author has gained complexity and versatility and continues to facilitate transcultural negotiation, thereby making him a valuable case study in the development of world literature.

An Unexpected Encounter

In his 1926 essay "Mr. Fujino," Lu Xun recalls his experience at the Sendai Medical Academy in Japan during the 1904–1905 Russo-Japanese War. Tensions were running high, and Lu Xun describes an incident in which a group of classmates accused him of cheating on the final exam after Lu Xun—a Chinese student in an

---

7. Peter Brooks, *Troubling Confessions*, 9.

134   Penitence, Mercy, and Conversion

anatomy class taught in Japanese—scored higher than half of his Japanese class-mates. The accusatory letter, sent anonymously by Lu Xun's Japanese cohorts, included a phrase borrowed from the title of Leo Tolstoy's (1828–1910) 1904 letter about the ongoing war: "bethink yourselves."[8]

A more literal translation of both Tolstoy's Russian title, "*Odumaites'!*" and the biblical Greek term Tolstoy was explicitly citing, μετανοεῖτε,[9] would be "Repent!" Whereas the original Greek term was conjugated in the second-person plural imperative, the Russian title was grammatically ambiguous—potentially function-ing either as second-person plural or as second-person honorific singular. Similarly, in isolation, the Japanese translation of the title, "Kui aratameyo" 悔い改めよ, could theoretically be in either the singular or the plural (the Japanese grammar here does not distinguish between the two). In Lu Xun's essay, meanwhile, his Chinese trans-lation of the students' Japanese translation of Tolstoy's Russian translation of the original Greek—*ni gaihui ba* 你改悔罷—complements the verb with a pronominal subject, *ni* 你, thereby unambiguously specifying that the verb is functioning here in the second-person singular. In this way, Lu Xun's Chinese translation clarifies that the verb—originally used in the New Testament by Jesus to refer to "men" and later in Tolstoy's text to address both sides in the Russo-Japanese War—is being used by the Japanese students in a phrase attacking a single person: Lu Xun.

Moreover, it is ironic to find Lu Xun, a Chinese man, as the target of an accu-sation that invokes the language of Tolstoy's essay on the ongoing war, given that China was the most vulnerable of the three key players in the Russo-Japanese War that Tolstoy was condemning. The war was the result of long-running geopolitical frictions in Northeast Asia, and even though Japan had won the Liaodong Peninsula in Manchuria during the Sino-Japanese War of 1894–1895, it was subsequently forced to cede it back to China under pressure from Russia, Germany, and France. Ultimately, Russia gained control over the whole peninsula in 1898, when it received permission from China to use Port Arthur as an ice-free port for its Pacific fleet. This consolidation of Russian power in Manchuria threatened Japan's position in Korea, where Japan wanted to maintain its predominance after having eliminated rival Chinese claims. In 1900, Russian troops invaded and occupied Manchuria on the pretext of helping quell the Boxer Uprising but did not withdraw after the conclusion of the Boxer Rebellion, as had other foreign troops. Negotiations between Japan and Russia over the division of power in Korea and Manchuria continued for the next few years until negotiations broke down in January 1904, and the Russo-Japanese

---

8.   Lu Xun, "Tengye xiansheng," 316.

9.   "Two thousand years ago John the Baptist and then Jesus said to men: The time is fulfilled and the Kingdom of God is at hand; (μετανοεῖτε) bethink yourselves and believe in the Gospel (Mark i. 15); and if you do not bethink yourselves you will all perish (Luke xiii. 5)." (L. N. Tolstoy, *"Bethink Yourselves." Tolstoy's Letter on the Russo-Japanese War*, 16.)

War erupted. The resulting territorial dispute centered on both nations' attempts to lay claim to portions of the Qing empire's territory, yet the Chinese were forced to remain neutral by their relative weakness.

On June 27, 1904, Tolstoy published his "Bethink Yourselves" appeal in the *London Times*, attacking war in general and the Russo-Japanese War in particular. His anti-war statement was soon translated in Japan by news agencies, and "Bethink Yourselves" became a catchword during the Russo-Japanese War.[10] It is therefore not surprising that Tolstoy's words were borrowed by Lu Xun's Japanese classmates. At the same time, understanding the implications of this idiosyncratic calque demands scrutinizing the positions of Russia, Japan, and China during the Russo-Japanese War. If we take into consideration the vulnerability of China's political situation, as battles between Russia and Japan were fought on Chinese soil, then Tolstoy's wish for peace becomes particularly striking. After Japan's decisive victory in the Sino-Japanese War of 1894–1895, many Japanese came to view China as a weak country with inferior people. When war broke out between Russia and Japan a decade later, the moral high ground was reserved for the two formal antagonists, while China found itself a passive victim of the conflict, unable to defend itself and facing moral judgment by the two rivals.

The accusatory letter directed at Lu Xun by the students thus carries complex geopolitical implications, even as it marked the first indirect encounter between two great literary figures in Russia and China—Tolstoy and Lu Xun—in a foreign land, Japan. It was not a pleasant encounter, as Tolstoy's accusation of imperialism and militarism was transformed into an attack on a representative of the neutral side in the Russo-Japanese War, namely China.

At the same time, Lu Xun's reference to the letter in "Mr. Fujino" has generally been overshadowed by the essay's reference to the renowned lantern slide incident.[11] During a break in a microbiology lecture, Lu Xun saw a slide of a Chinese spy accused of working for the Russians, who was being executed by Japanese soldiers. Lu Xun claims that he was shocked by the apathetic expressions of the spy's Chinese countrymen in the image, and that this experience was the catalyst for his subsequent decision to abandon his medical study for literary pursuits. Eileen J. Cheng contends that Lu Xun's description captures the "originary moment of modern Chinese literature," which "has been invested with an almost mythic significance in the annals of literary history."[12] As Takeuchi Yoshimi 竹内好 (1910–1977) characterizes it, the incident captured all of the human debasement and cultural isolation that Lu Xun

---

10. Ozaki Hotsuki, *Ro Jin to no taiwa*, 113–14.

11. Lu Xun, "Tengye xiansheng," 317.

12. Eileen J. Cheng, "Recycling the Scholar-Beauty Narrative," 7.

136   Penitence, Mercy, and Conversion

experienced in Japan and that led to his "conversion" (*kaishin* 回心).[13] Leo Ou-fan Lee argues that the incident should be regarded as a metaphor or a moment of truth rather than as a discrete impetus.[14]

Regardless of how the lantern slide is viewed, an understanding of the life trajectory that led Lu Xun to become a crucial figure in modern Chinese literature must also take into account his experience prior to this pivotal incident, including the accusatory letter. It is also important to highlight these incidents' transcultural significance. During the Russo-Japanese War, Sendai was not merely a remote and secluded Japanese city, but rather, it was also the site of an internment camp for Russian prisoners, which was located not far from Lu Xun's boarding house.[15] Moreover, although it is not clear whether Lu Xun was himself mobilized, given that he was the only Chinese student in the medical school, we do know that many Japanese staff members from his school were drafted.[16]

Under these circumstances, nationalism and patriotism became a pressing issue with which Lu Xun had to grapple. It was not easy to take sides as a Chinese citizen living in wartime Japan. This is also one of the reasons that the citation of Tolstoy in the accusatory letter was so memorable and haunted Lu Xun for at least twenty years until his composition of "Mr. Fujino." It seems clear that Lu Xun documented this unexpected encounter in his autobiographical writing because he meant it to carry specific historical significance. The implications of the dramatic tension among different cultures allow the moment to be amplified for further examination and allegorical interpretation.

Many scholars have acknowledged the near impossibility of conclusively verifying the existence of the slide Lu Xun describes. Its unverifiability is further complicated by Lu Xun's multiple renditions of the same incident, which appears not only in Lu Xun's essay "Mr. Fujino" but also in his preface to *Outcry* as well as his lengthy introduction to the Soviet sinologist Boris Vasil'ev's translation of "The True Story of Ah Q."[17] Significantly, while in the preface the spy is about to be beheaded, in "Mr. Fujino," the spy is instead about to be shot, and this inconsistency brings into question the overall reliability of Lu Xun's accounts. David Der-wei Wang suggests that the slide may be entirely fabricated. He argues that the image of supposed decapitation suggests how fiction and history are interwoven at the beginning of modern Chinese literary history, when Lu Xun refashioned and even manufactured his personal experience for literary purposes.[18] Wang's conclusion might be applied

---

13. Takeuchi Yoshimi, *Ro Jin*, 69–71.
14. Leo Ou-fan Lee, *Voices from the Iron House*, 18.
15. Ozaki, *Ro Jin to no taiwa*, 95–96.
16. Ozaki, *Ro Jin to no taiwa*, 91–92.
17. Lu Xun, "Nahan zixu," 438; Lu Xun, "Ewen yiben *A Q zhengzhuan* xu ji zhuzhe zixu zhuanlüe," 85.
18. David Der-wei Wang, *The Monster that Is History*, 21.

not only to the lantern slide incident but also to that of the accusatory letter. In the latter case, a well-documented historical moment—the circulation of Tolstoy's anti-war appeal—lends authenticity to a private recollection from China's leading modern writer. Lu Xun's repeated retelling of his experiences during the Russo-Japanese War exposes a complex of emotions, with an emphasis on the feeling of guilt among Chinese in the Russo-Japanese War and a profound criticism of the Chinese national character. To a certain extent, Lu Xun's multiple attempts at confessional rewriting became an emblematic redemptive performance of a Chinese intellectual in the modern era. The details mattered much less than the confessional gesture itself that allowed Lu Xun to probe into his interior darkness and to selectively expose a portion of his past to the targeted readers.

Dazai Osamu's Recapitulation

Both the accusatory letter incident and the lantern slide are reimagined in the Japanese writer Dazai Osamu's 太宰治 (1909–1948) 1945 novel *Regrettable Parting* (*Sekibetsu* 惜別), a work of fiction about Lu Xun's early years in Japan.[19] Although Dazai claims that he wrote this novel independent of governmental influence,[20] it was a project commissioned by the wartime Japanese Cabinet Information Bureau and the Japanese Literature Patriotic Association to express the ideals of the *Great East Asia Joint Manifesto*,[21] and the novel's theme is amity among the East Asian countries. In Dazai's story, Lu Xun is transformed into a Tolstoyan Christian who espouses values of neighborly love and expresses his gratitude toward Japan by declaring that "Japan fought the [Russo-Japanese] War to defend China's independence."[22] Dazai also revises Lu Xun's reaction after seeing the lantern slide; in the novel, Lu Xun remarks, "I do not understand the feelings of people who become military spies for our enemy [Russia], while the whole country of Japan as our ally is bravely fighting against it."[23] The Japanese figures, too, are adjusted in obedience to the Christian duty of self-reflection: in the novel, Yajima 矢島, the ringleader behind the accusatory letter, apologizes to Lu Xun for his rashness. Lu Xun not only forgives Yajima's act of racial humiliation but even calls him "a person of integrity."[24] Overall, the contested historical narratives among Russia, Japan, and China, which serve as the background to both incidents, are strategically reframed in Dazai's work. Japan becomes a rapidly modernizing role model that Lu Xun deeply admires; at the same time,

---

19. Dazai Osamu, *Sekibetsu*, 7.
20. Dazai Osamu, *Atogaki*, 7, 130.
21. Angela Yiu, "Delivering Lu Xun to the Empire," 324.
22. Dazai, *Sekibetsu*, 7, 44.
23. Dazai, *Sekibetsu*, 7, 123.
24. Dazai, *Sekibetsu*, 7, 100.

138   Penitence, Mercy, and Conversion

unsurprisingly, neighborly love is limited to East Asian nations: China and Japan's mutual neighbor Russia—which acts as a representative of the West—is regarded as the source of evil.

Although Dazai reimagines Lu Xun as a Tolstoyan figure, it is worth noting that Lu Xun viewed Tolstoy less positively than he did many other Russian writers. As the Lu Xun scholar Sun Yu points out, Lu Xun cared mostly about Tolstoy's weaknesses, especially his limits as an intellectual,[25] and he never fully embraced Tolstoyism. He first mentions Tolstoy's name in his 1908 article "Toward a Refutation of Malevolent Voices"[26] in which he compares Tolstoy with Augustine and Rousseau as writers of confessions who were willing to reveal their inner world. He praises Tolstoy for his humanism and pacifism but also points out his impracticality: "What he says is good as an ideal, but when it is realized, the outcome strays from the original ideal."[27] In a speech at Shanghai Jinan University in 1927, Lu Xun similarly observes that although he admires Tolstoy's courage to challenge authority, he considers Tolstoy's nonresistance theory feeble against real war. He describes humanists like Tolstoy as people who live in an ideal world, yet sympathizes with those suffering real plight and who wish to offer ideas that might help the poor change their situation. As a result, such humanists may come into conflict with politicians. However, instead of eulogizing Tolstoy for waking up the Russian people, Lu Xun instead concludes that these literati will get themselves killed for the social unrest they generate.[28] When Lu Xun turned to leftist literary criticism in his later years, he further highlighted Tolstoy's elite background as his "original sin." In an article published in 1930, for example, Lu Xun criticized Tolstoy as an aristocrat who did not support class struggle.[29]

Despite Lu Xun's cautious attitude to Tolstoyism, Dazai chose to convert Lu Xun into Tolstoy's disciple to correspond with the political agenda of Dazai's novel. Dazai began developing the narrative in 1943, when public discourse in Japan was already shifting toward pan-Asianism, which espoused the emancipation and independence of all Asian countries.[30] The novel *Regrettable Parting* is among the works in which Dazai espouses themes from the *Great East Asia Joint Manifesto*, including mutual prosperity, independence, and pan-Asian affinity with Japan, cultural elevation, economic prosperity, and contribution to the world progress.[31] Dazai uses the figure of Lu Xun to embody this idealistic vision and draws on Tolstoy's pacifism and nonresistance as the perfect philosophical fit to capture the manifesto's spirit.

---

25. Sun Yu, *Lu Xun yu Eguo*, 226.

26. Lu Xun, "Po e sheng lun," 29, 33, 35.

27. Lu Xun, "Po e sheng lun," 34.

28. Lu Xun, "Wenyi yu zhengzhi de qitu," 117–18.

29. Lu Xun, "Yingyi yu wenxue de jiejixing," 208–9.

30. Fujii Shōzō, "Dazai Osamu no 'Sekibetsu' to Takeuchi Yoshimi no 'Rojin,'" 56–57.

31. Angela Yiu, "Delivering Lu Xun to the Empire," 334.

Indeed, Dazai himself stated that he wrote the novel to support "complete Sino-Japanese peace" (*Nisshi zenmen heiwa* 日支全面平和).[32]

In the narrative, Dazai relentlessly promotes Japanese-style modernity in contrast to Western modernity. As Christopher Robins summarizes, "In this imagined world order, Japan serves as a bulwark against Western imperialism in Asia and presents itself to China as a role model for modernization, integrating Western knowledge without jettisoning some vaguely conceived notion of pan-Asian cultural values guided by Japanese spiritual principles."[33] Dazai explicitly emphasizes a sense of cleanliness (*seiketsu-kan* 清潔感) as one of the key virtues that differentiates Japanese culture from Western culture.[34] The simplicity and purity highlighted by Dazai not only signify modern Japan's superiority but also suggest the magnificence of Japan's cultural legacy. Dazai's overt nationalism and unabashedly patriotic tone infuriated Chinese readers, and Chinese scholars denounced Dazai's political stance, calling him a state-hired writer.[35] These readers felt that Dazai had turned Lu Xun into a mouthpiece for Japanese imperial and military propaganda, an unacceptable move in which Dazai distorted Lu Xun's political views.[36]

Although the message of pan-Asian affinity with Japan and independence from the evil West (represented by Russia) is clear, Dazai also attempts to maintain distance between the patriotic narrator and Dazai as a writer capable of independent thinking, thereby opening room for his own creative autonomy. By modeling his novel's narrative structure on Lu Xun's "Diary of a Madman"—in which the madman's journal is preceded by a short preface penned by a former friend—Dazai frames the narrative through the viewpoint of a fictitious old country doctor, Tanaka, who was a compassionate classmate of Lu Xun's in Sendai. Dazai draws clear lines at the beginning and end of the story to differentiate his own voice from that of Tanaka.

Moreover, Dazai uses the conversation between a journalist and Tanaka to expose the political publication agenda of his time: to promote articles about the friendship between Japan and China.[37] Unwilling to serve as a simple mouthpiece, Tanaka pens the story about his interactions with Lu Xun because he is frustrated by the distortion of his narrative by the journalist. Thus, the novel implies that beyond Tanaka's version represented in its own pages, there actually exists another even more politically driven version published in a Japanese newspaper. In this way, the narrator tries to convince his readers that the version he provides, transcribed directly from Tanaka's handwritten account, is more intimate and faithful than the

---

32. Dazai Osamu, *"Sekibetsu" no ito*, 10, 282.
33. Christopher Robins, "Japanese Visions of Lu Xun."
34. Dazai, *"Sekibetsu" no ito*, 10, 281.
35. Wang Xiangyuan, "'Yaxiya zhuyi' 'Dadongya zhuyi' jiqi yuyong wenxue."
36. Robins, "Japanese Visions of Lu Xun," 4.
37. Dazai, *Sekibetsu*, 7, 6.

140   Penitence, Mercy, and Conversion

journalist's report based on his interview with Tanaka. Before Tanaka's memoir begins, he even apologizes for his hazy memory about things that took place forty years ago, explaining that the purpose of the memoir is "to correct the remembrances of my teacher and my friend."[38]

Whereas the old doctor's recollections sound subjective and sentimental, Dazai keeps the tone of the narrator detached. To create further distance from Tanaka's narrative, he even includes Lu Xun's own words, as translated by Matsueda Shigeo 松枝茂夫 (1905–1995).[39] Dazai thereby presents at least four layers of narration— Tanaka's, the journalist's, the narrator's, and the translator's. This polyglossia renders the core narrative less definitive and reminds readers of the complex layering of any form of historical narrative, including Lu Xun's own autobiographical account.

In addition to these narratological devices, Dazai avoids presenting Tolstoy's doctrine in a mechanical or heavily politicized way. "Neighborly love" is a central virtue of Tolstoyism, and it is emphasized in Dazai's work as something equivalent to mutual respect, righteousness, or the original way of East Asia (*Tōyō honrai no michi* 東洋本来の道).[40] It is evident that an affinity forms among Lu Xun, Tanaka, and their teacher Mr. Fujino out of one mutual weakness shared by all three: the inability to speak formal Japanese properly. While Lu Xun could not speak Japanese well given that he was a foreigner, Tanaka and Mr. Fujino both speak Japanese with heavy rural accents, which makes them a target of mockery by other Japanese students. In Lu Xun's original account, he describes Mr. Fujino as speaking "in a slow tone with strong cadence" that provokes other students' laughter.[41] Dazai elaborates on this aspect further, creating a common bond of "otherness" through Mr. Fujino's Kansai accent, Tanaka's rural accent, and Lu Xun's foreign accent. Social segregation thus becomes the foundation of their friendship: the awkwardness in communication forges a connection among these three outsiders. In this way, Tolstoy's universal love is replaced by a more selective and specifically targeted affection. Indeed, Dazai's special attention to the weak and downtrodden in his version echoes Lu Xun's own literary practice.

Dazai described his novel as a picture of adolescence "portraying young Zhou Shuren [i.e., Lu Xun] in a fair and tender manner, carrying a pure, independent, and amiable attitude."[42] For readers like Angela Yiu, Dazai provides a "portrait of an

38. Dazai, *Sekibetsu*, 7, 9.
39. Matsueda Shigeru was a friend to Lu Xun's brother Zhou Zuoren and also collaborated with Masuda Wataru and Takeuchi Yoshimi in translating Lu Xun's work. He primarily approached Chinese literature based on his aesthetic taste, and his translation of Lu Xun's writing avoided politically motivated changes. Therefore, although Dazai draws on Matsueda's translation of Lu Xun's account, the narrative alterations are Dazai's.
40. Dazai, *Sekibetsu*, 7, 53.
41. Lu Xun, "Tengye xiansheng," 314.
42. Dazai, *"Sekibetsu" no ito*, 10, 282.

awkward young man struggling with commonplace problems at an extraordinary moment in a euphoric and pompous Japan on the cusp of victory in the Russo-Japanese War."[43] Dazai has achieved this portrait by weaving in his own college experience as a student coming to Tokyo from Tsugaru Domain in northeastern Japan. It may be argued that Dazai has made the story too personal by incorporating his own experience, jeopardizing the narrative's geopolitical and social implications.[44] However, the tale of an adolescent's anxiety and befuddlement, told as a bildungsroman, readily provokes readers' empathy and makes Lu Xun appear more accessible.

Inoue Hisashi's Parody

Once Lu Xun's autobiographical details are in print, other readers, like Dazai, have the same ability as Lu Xun to interpret them. Forty-six years later, another Japanese writer picked up the same autobiographical details and elaborated on them in a different manner. Published in 1991, Inoue Hisashi's play *Shanghai Moon* (*Shanhai mūn* シャンハイムーン) tells of the friendship between Lu Xun and a couple named Uchiyama at whose bookstore he took refuge to avoid the Kuomintang's persecution of pro-Communist Chinese in 1934. At the start of the play, Inoue quotes one of the lines he has written for Lu Xun, which grants Inoue permission to construct his own version of Lu Xun's life: "I have no right or obligation to stop your recklessness. Do as you please."[45] Inoue uses this invented quotation to imagine Lu Xun giving him permission to compose a play about his life completely in Japanese, performed by Japanese actors, and watched by Japanese audiences.[46] Read by actors of Inoue's play, this line was blended with real quotations from Lu Xun's works, creating a layered space of encounter: a character representing the playwright Inoue exchanges letters with a character representing Lu Xun in which they discuss a play that describes Lu Xun's life in 1934, the year Inoue was born. One can even imagine Inoue preparing a seat for Lu Xun in the auditorium to show him the writer Lu Xun as played by a Japanese actor. Unlike from Dazai's distanced and cautious authorial voice, veiled behind many layers of narration, Inoue is more daring, making "Do as you please" the motto of his play.

Shanghai Moon focuses on the period when Lu Xun was involved with the League of Left-Wing Writers. However, in the play the conflicts within the leftist movement and Lu Xun's political predicament are barely mentioned. It is a dark comedy that instead foregrounds various illnesses including what Angela Yiu

---

43. Yiu, "Delivering Lu Xun to the Empire," 336.
44. Kawamura Minato, "'Sekibetsu' ron—'Daitōa no shinwa' no maboroshi."
45. Inoue Hisashi, *Shanhai mūn*, 11.
46. Inoue, *Shanhai mūn*, 12.

142   Penitence, Mercy, and Conversion

summarizes as "pathological paranoia, decay, nervous conditions, dementia, slurred speech, and hemorrhage that plagued the ailing Lu Xun."[47] As Christopher Robins points out, "many of [Inoue's] semi-fictionalized portraits of recent historical figures suggest a mischievous iconoclasm designed to subvert the foundations of Japanese conservative political ideology," but *Shanghai Moon* puts much greater emphasis on the Sino-Japanese friendship at the civilian level, "a forgotten facet of Japan's involvement in China during the war."[48] The kindhearted Japanese people's joint effort to cure Lu Xun's physical and spiritual afflictions becomes the main mission in the play. As a writer who appreciates the power of humor, Inoue portrays Lu Xun in a comical way, lightening the heavy topics that arise around the last years of Lu Xun's life, including his ailments and frailties, with a dose of laughter.

The play's black humor makes it difficult to pin down any concrete historical details. By making Lu Xun's body and soul a site of pernicious maladies, Inoue reminds readers of Lu Xun's allegorical treatment of ailments in stories such as "Diary of a Madman" and "Medicine." However, whereas Lu Xun takes a candid attitude toward his physical condition in his own writing, Inoue's play instead presents him as someone who refuses to see doctors for proper medical treatment. The play's ultimate diagnosis is chronic suicidal longing arising from Lu Xun's lingering guilt over his perceived betrayal of the people who trusted and supported him. In the play, those figures include his teacher Mr. Fujino, who trusts him with the future of Chinese medicine, his legal wife, Zhu An 朱安 (1878–1947), whose emotional needs Lu Xun ignores, and the female martyr Qiu Jin 秋瑾 (1875–1907) and imprisoned young radicals, to whose revolutionary passion Lu Xun fails to respond. The solution offered by Inoue's play is for Lu Xun to seek forgiveness from these people.

This type of absolution is more in line with Tolstoy's nonresistance than Lu Xun's intransigence. In the play, Inoue provides Lu Xun with the chance to achieve reconciliation with these figures through a temporary drug-induced haze, when Lu Xun misrecognizes people. A series of characters, the majority of whom are Japanese, impersonate these figures; in his haze, Lu Xun cannot tell the difference and so takes the opportunity for confession. Each impersonator announces that his or her character forgives Lu Xun, who unburdens his conscience and finds relief from his sense of guilt. Like Dazai, Inoue depicts Lu Xun and his Japanese friends to be magnanimous. Perhaps both Japanese writers see such magnanimity as the only solution to the spiritual wounds brought on by the Sino-Japanese War; and while Tolstoyism is not explicitly referenced in Inoue's play, Tolstoy—with his pacifism and call to end the war—serves as the best possible peace ambassador. At the same time, it seems

---

47. Yiu, "Delivering Lu Xun to the Empire," 340.
48. Robins, "Japanese Visions of Lu Xun," 12.

this rapprochement cannot be achieved without a complete misrepresentation of Lu Xun, whose own works and remarks make him seem like the last person to support compassion and reconciliation.

In his article "On the 'Why "Fair Play" Should Be Deferred,' that Should Be Slowed Down," Lu Xun makes it clear that he has little patience for people with ideas contrary to his own. He considers it necessary to vigorously pursue and subdue his enemies, never giving them the chance to fight back. His reasoning mostly concerns the ongoing Chinese revolution: He has witnessed too many Chinese revolutionaries sacrificing their lives to the future of China, while the conservative forces have taken advantage of tenderhearted "revolutionary supporters" to annihilate revolutionaries' efforts. As he puts it, "Perhaps for one moment the good people are ascendant, and the bad are supposed to fall into the water, but the sincere upholders of justice again call out: 'Do not take revenge!' 'Have mercy!' 'Do not resist evil with evil.'"[49] In Lu Xun's eyes, such a cry for justice, which carries the true spirit of Tolstoyism, is not very different from conniving with evil. His rejection of forgiveness persisted to the end of his life, and even in 1936, when he was seriously ill, he still refused to be reconciled with his enemies. He recalls the European practice of seeking mutual forgiveness on one's deathbed, yet decides that he would rather let his enemies maintain their resentment, nor does he wish to forgive anyone, especially those who hypocritically advocate mercy. He instead warns his relatives, "Never befriend those who destroy other people's teeth and eyes, yet [claim to] object to vengeance and support leniency."[50]

The attitude Lu Xun expresses in such texts was likely not acceptable to Inoue, who converted to Christianity at the age of sixteen and sought to live in accordance with Christian love. Inoue's religious faith also guided his rewriting of the famous lantern slide moment. Inoue makes it a life-changing moment for Sudō Iozō 須藤五百三 (1876–1959), Lu Xun's physician, but in a reversed manner: whereas in Lu Xun's account, he had abandoned his medical career after this incident, in Inoue's version Sudō gives up literature for medicine. Sudō notices a Japanese soldier in the corner of the slide praying for the executed Chinese spy like a true Christian. In the play, this soldier turns out to be one of Sudō's cousins, who later dies from illness on the battlefield.[51] Sudō calls him the future of the Japanese army and takes up medicine to strengthen the bodies of such people so they are not destroyed by the cruelty of war. Benevolence and sympathy are recognized by Sudō as the highest virtue of Japanese *bushido* (the proper way of Japanese warriors).

---

49. Lu Xun, "Lun 'fei'e polai' yinggai huanxing," 291.
50. Lu Xun, "Si," 635.
51. Inoue, *Shanhai mūn*, 160.

144 Penitence, Mercy, and Conversion

Inoue's treatment of the lantern slide incident is also paired with the death of Sudō's wife and daughter from typhoid, which leads Sudō to conclude that only good health can guarantee even the tiniest happiness in daily life. Thus, the lantern slide incident, with its weight implications in Lu Xun's autobiographical writing, is replaced by Sudō's determination to aid Lu Xun's physical recovery. Another Japanese character in the play, Okuda Aizō 奥田愛三, even suggests that Lu Xun's essays arguing with his detractors not only vitiate his literary talent but actually destroy his health and should therefore be stopped.[52] This speculation prioritizes physical health over mental struggle, subverting the essence of the lantern slide incident as Lu Xun originally presented it.

Inoue's reversal arises from the universal compassion embedded in the medical directive to do no harm. It is against the tenets of medical care to allow personal differences to interfere with treatment; it is even unclear whether the morality of one's patients should not be taken into consideration when a doctor is deciding on priorities for treatment. Sudō is proud of his impartial treatment of both Japanese and Chinese citizens, prioritizing those with real needs regardless of nationality. Yet, following the same logic, he cannot refuse to treat those Japanese soldiers who advocate war and the invasion of China—even those that have committed atrocities in the battlefield. If he heals the bodies of these soldiers, does he thereby support a war that is sending so many young men to the battlefield? Does that make doctors collaborators in waging war? Perhaps only Tolstoy's universal pacifism and nonresistance can explain Sudō's logic. Yet this type of discourse is exactly what Lu Xun resists.

Both Japanese authors altered decisive moments of Lu Xun's life, and although they may not have intended the connection, both have made Tolstoy's teachings the solution to Lu Xun's perplexity and the agony typical to Chinese intellectuals of his generation. In doing so, they turn Lu Xun's confessional moments into absolution. The logic of this approach might appear convoluted and even forced, but it seems to be the solution that arises for these Japanese writers facing the colossal moral burdens of the twentieth century.

By all accounts Lu Xun's autobiographical writings provide his readers with a window through which to glimpse his most private self. They offer him a chance for self-reflection and an opportunity to make himself known. Such writing is often seen as aspiring to moments of truth, yet it also has its performative aspects. This is particularly relevant to Lu Xun, who makes a considerable effort to take control of the discourse surrounding his stories, repeatedly rewriting the crucial moments of his life and canonizing them as crucial moments in modern Chinese literary history. His confessional gestures have in turn inspired Japanese readers to re-create key

---

52. Inoue, *Shanhai mūn*, 162.

moments in his autobiographical writings, evoking motifs of rehabilitation and reconciliation but ultimately diverging from Lu Xun's original narrative. Nonetheless, the Japanese authors' joint efforts help usher Lu Xun onto the world literary stage as a thought-provoking Chinese intellectual and a figure of becoming, open to further reimaginings.

9
Ghostwriting the Subalterns

Rereading Ah Q through Wong Bik-wan's *Lielaozhuan*

Wayne C. F. Yeung

"Autobiography"? But I am obviously not Ah Q.

—Lu Xun, "The True Story of Ah Q"

In 2004 I came up with the idea of writing about Hong Kong's prison history, thinking that historicity was just a matter of incorporating historical events into my novel. I began my research, reading newsclips and documents, and visiting former inmates. About two years later, however, I decided I didn't want to do that anymore, because *I* don't have the same immediacy. I am not them.

—Wong Bik-wan, on her writing of *Lielaozhuan* 烈佬傳[1]

If it seems out of place to juxtapose a contemporary Hong Kong female novelist with an author who has played an almost paternal role in the formation of modern Chinese literature, these two quotes placed together should bear out their allied concern for the literary problem of representing the Other. The first quote, drawn from the famous opening of "The True Story of Ah Q," depicts Ah Q's "quick-to-perish" life as a genre trouble. In a comical gripe, Lu Xun's classically educated yet modernized narrator complains that no available genres from the elitist Confucian textual tradition he inherited would be appropriate for the lowly, biographically unworthy Ah Q. He settles for the compromise "true story" (正傳), a stock phrase from vernacular fiction, but not before stating the obvious by adding that the story is not an "autobiography," given that the narrator is not Ah Q.

The second passage, coming from Hong Kong author Wong Bik-wan 黃碧雲 (1961–), describes the process by which she arrives at her ultimate choice to

---

1. Wong Bik-wan, "The Necessity of Forgetfulness," 37.

adopt the first-person perspective in her novel *Lielaozhuan* ("Biography of a Lad," 2012). Wong Bik-wan's novel has been compared to "The True Story of Ah Q," and commentators have noted that certain turns of phrases in *Lielaozhuan* are reminiscent of some of Lu Xun's well-known lines.[2] One critic went so far as to claim that *Lielaozhuan*'s "cultural bloodline" derives from Lu Xun's story, claiming that Ah Q is the archetype for Wong's protagonist.[3] Digging deeper into this comparison yields even more surprising results. Unlike Lu Xun's story, Wong's novel is presented as an autobiography of its protagonist. Written from a first-person perspective, the novel tells the story of Chow Mei-nan as he reminisces, well into his sixties, about his past life spent almost entirely in the criminal underworld in Hong Kong's Wan Chai district, various Hong Kong prisons, and a halfway house. Without an external narrator acting as the intermediary, *Lielaozhuan* also fits poorly into the category of allegory—another feature that distinguishes it from "The True Story of Ah Q." Wong's narrative is richly informed by history, but it writes against many historiographical conventions of Hong Kong literature as it gives short shrift to almost all major local historical events, such as the 1989 Beijing Spring and the 1997 handover. Foregrounding the protagonist's unique perspective as his worldview is highly constrained by his long-term incarceration and subaltern status, *Lielaozhuan* disorients the cosmopolitan Hong Kong identity with which local readers have come to be familiar.

This chapter's second epigraph explains Wong's creative decision. While prison history initially provided Wong with the novel's through line, she ultimately became dissatisfied with the way this conceptual framework presupposes a perspective from above, which is unlikely to come organically from her subjects who would not have the privilege to see this history as a whole. To write about Hong Kong's subalterns, she concluded, she had to think outside a generic template.

The two passages in this chapter's epigraph reveal our writers' shared scruples over representing subaltern alterity. Lu Xun's readers generally had little difficulty enjoying a text about a nameless character who satirizes Chinese culture's collective shortcomings and Chinese society's backwardness, and they therefore forget having been forewarned that it could not have come from Ah Q's perspective—that their pleasure of recognizing Ah Q as a cultural archetype is at least partially the result of narrative objectification, if not blatant ventriloquizing. Through her writing of *Lielaozhuan*, in contrast, Wong problematizes this lack of demographic proximity—an epistemic and ethical dilemma that took her seven years of interviews to overcome.[4] We are therefore confronted with an intertextual relation that does not fit

---

2. Cheng Yat-sze, "*Lielaozhuan*," 209.
3. Ling Yue, "Reconstituting Eastern and Western Cultures," 120.
4. Wong Bik-wan, "Speech Is Futile, Silence Hurtful," 15.

148   Ghostwriting the Subalterns

well with any simple notion of reception or linear concept of genealogical influence. Intertextuality is also intersubjectivity. Throughout her career, Wong has spoken frequently about her admiration for Lu Xun.[5] However, Wong's readings of Lu Xun rarely conform to the authorial image we have inherited from critical discourses on Lu Xun as a committed social critic and literary modernizer, no more than how her own literary practice lends itself to the temptation of collective allegory as the primary reason for Lu Xun's canonization. Consider the following remark made by Wong, speaking again of the creative process of *Lielaozhuan* to a local audience in 2014:

> We need not look beyond Lu Xun's works for this kind of compassion, of commiserating with the miserable. His novels were something I revisit often, and there I frequently came across something very small yet immensely touching to me. . . . Kong Yiji [in the final scene when he crawls to the winehouse] did not cry out in laments, but his suffering comes to full light through nothing more than the specks of mud in his palm when he hands out his meager four coins. Without compassion, Lu Xun could not have seen the mud he so gently described.[6]

Wong's suggestion that Lu Xun's empathy ultimately lies with the small-time, failed Confucian scholar wasted away among the callous crowd points us to an "other" Lu Xun, one far removed from the modern satirist of traditional Chinese society for which we have come to know him. As a reading practice rooted in Hong Kong, Wong's practice of reading Lu Xun "otherwise" amounts to an epistemological alternative to cultural nationalism.

This chapter examines Wong Bik-wan's reverse influence on Lu Xun (or at least on his canonically accepted reception) as an argument against viewing influence and reception as a one-way street. Theories of world literature and cultural circulation tend to take for granted the idea that the receiving end of cultural transfer—usually the periphery—is haunted with a sense of belatedness and subordination, acting only as a reactionary agent if not plainly passive recipient on behalf of the center. Wong's literary relationship with Lu Xun is a counterexample. If Wong appears to be free of any "anxiety of influence," hers is not so much an uncritical acceptance of literary nationalism as a localist self-confidence that the interpretative paradigms behind nation-centric canonization can be hacked and come undone when engaged

---

5. As early as 1998, Wong already expressed in an interview that she felt her own works to be (surprisingly, to the interviewer) so close to Lu Xun's to the point of plagiarism. Even Wong's own artworks featured in the book of *Lielaozhuan* were said to be inspired by Lu Xun. "The choice of woodcuts was because of Lu Xun. Woodcuts were the art of peasants, raw and primitive. *Lielaozhuan* is raw." Cited in Yuen Siu-cheung, "Wong Bik-wan," 173). The idea that *Lielaozhuan* is composed in conversation with Lu Xun, if not "The True Story of Ah Q" in particular, is inspired by these more or less proximal textual affinities.

6. Wong Bik-wan, "Moxiang shenghuo, wenxue yu shijie."

through the unique position of Hong Kong within or without the normative nation-state. Consequently, this literary dialogism is also a hermeneutic insurrection—a process of *reading back into*. Different from the postcolonial writing back, this process is governed by a cultural logic more complex than traditional dichotomies of source and reception, center and periphery. This chapter accordingly takes its lead from Wong Bik-wan to reverse-engineer a different Lu Xun—to reconstruct him as an author who, rather than constantly voicing the desperate call for national renewal and societal modernization, whispers inconsistently but ever so frequently in the minor tone of subaltern peoples and concrete locality at the periphery of the imagined community. The result, I argue, is that Wong Bik-wan and Lu Xun can be placed within a continuum of an unfinished project of *ghostwriting* empire's subalterns, to lend worldliness to their idiosyncratic voice and agency while wrestling with the discursive inequality between writer and subject.[7] Hong Kong culture thus compels a radical rethinking of the nation as our privileged unit of analysis, reflecting back on Lu Xun's novella as a text unconsciously preoccupied with the empire.

Ghostwriting Otherwise: Recuperating Subaltern Occlusions in National Allegory

The term *ghostwriting* has multiple meanings, the most obvious of which being the dictionary definition of "writing in proxy," which in turn precipitates a problem of puppeteering the Other and denial of intersubjectivity. But Wong and Lu Xun are also literally "writers of ghosts." Lu Xun's narrator begins by saying that he has been meaning to write Ah Q's story "for several years," and the thought of Ah Q "seems to have been haunting" him (彷彿思想裡有鬼) (102)—implying that the idea of Ah Q had been a years-long compulsion. Similarly, Wong suggests in her blurb that her biographical subject interpellates her into writing. "I marvel at the intensity that burns within him [懾於其無火之烈], and so I can only write *Lielaozhuan*."

---

7. My use of the term *subaltern* is informed by the decolonial critics Catherine Walsh and Walter Mignolo, who ask us to critically "confront the idea of historically excluded, subalternized, and racialized peoples as 'objects' of study" and instead "open consideration about the ways in which subjects, peoples, and movements who live the colonial difference not only act but also produce knowledge and construct theory" (Walter D. Mignolo and Catherine E. Walsh, *On Decoloniality*, 28.) Although I do not see their usage of the term as necessarily in conflict with postcolonial studies (which took the term from Antonio Gramsci), the larger, ongoing conversations about the convergences and divergences of decolonial and postcolonial studies is beyond my scope. Here, suffice it to say that by naming Ah Q as "subaltern" of a certain kind, we try to call attention to the historical silencing and sacrificial violence at work in the modernist and nationalist framing of his biography not wholly different from Gayatri Chakravorty Spivak's own analysis of widow burning (*sati*) between British imperialism and Hindu nativism.

150   Ghostwriting the Subalterns

Lielao does not read and can't write, he'll say, what are you talking about, making things so complicated, being human ain't that big of a deal, it comes and goes—taking hardship lightly, brushing off grandness in a slight, negating intensity by taking it to the extreme, [he did them] all on the land we grew up, for him it's Wan Chai, for us it's Hong Kong, the flailing island. The one for whom I sketch drawings and write biography, is little but a mere shadow.[8]

Lielao's shadowy existence comes from the unbearable lightness of his being when compared to the trial and tribulations history has thrown at him. Like Ah Q, lielao makes no claims on his position within the grand narrative of history. Both literary projects, accordingly, begin with a sense of interpellated obligation toward a specter of history.

Ah Q's spectrality has often been read in terms of his archetypal abstraction—his lack of specific identity makes him the perfect candidate to represent Chineseness in general. But within the text of "The True Story of Ah Q," this quality is also connected to the archival erasure of his true identity. Lu Xun's narrator is unable to ascertain any information crucial to Ah Q's identity, including his full name and place of origin which biographies should open with traditionally. This lack of informational certainty is caused by the unreliability of archival records.

As a last resort, I asked someone from my district to go and look up the legal documents recording Ah Q's case, but after eight months he sent me a letter saying that *there was no name anything like Ah Quei in those records*. Although uncertain whether this was the truth or whether my friend had simply done nothing, after failing to trace the name this way I could think of no other means of finding it. (105–6)

Lu Xun thus anticipates the Haitian anthropologist Michel-Rolph Trouillot's observation that the mediation of the archival order introduces preemptive silences into the production of historical narratives.[9] The narrator must begin by suspending his disbelief toward history as authenticated by the archive. Even the title "The True Story of Ah Q" is derived from the uncertainty surrounding Ah Q's identity—all biographical genres available from Confucian historiography are reserved for individuals with notable respectability, social significance, or family connections, leaving no appropriate genre for writing about small, nameless people like Ah Q. The narrator finds himself struggling within the Confucian discursive framework and ends up with a Frankenstein invention resulting from hybridizing Confucianism with a vernacular tradition: "So from the stock phrase of the storytellers, who are not reckoned among the Three Cults and Nine Schools [of classical Chinese thoughts]. 'Enough of this digression, and back to the true story!' I will take the last two words

---

8.   Wong, *Lielaozhuan*, back cover.
9.   Michel-Rolph Trouillot, *Silencing the Past*, 26.

as my title." Ah Q is ghostly because he is missing in relation to both state power as represented by archival records as well as social propriety as defined by Confucian values.

Lu Xun's project of writing Ah Q is constrained by the limits of written records and traditional parameters with which the author constantly negotiates. Wong, by contrast, has oral sources available to her, as we know from her experiences of visiting former inmates. Ultimately, the ethnographic method makes up for the blindness of written authority. She explains, "I continued my visits, I don't know why. Now I understand why I didn't want to write, or didn't feel right about what I came up with—because what I wanted to do is to write history, not the tool to explain it."[10] As opposed to Lu Xun having to meld Confucian genres with vernacular forms, Wong abandons the metahistorical framing altogether; actual encounters with the Other provide Wong with a conceptual toolkit unavailable to Lu Xun to solve the genre trouble of rendering subaltern life. The ethnographic encounter with otherness informing Wong's creative process is thus a critical reparation of a previous lack that condemned subaltern characters like Ah Q to be nothing more than a cultural stereotype. Informed by prolonged immersion in the lielaos' lifeworld, *Lielaozhuan* makes good on its promise of thick description and well-rounded personhood. When writing the novel, Wong categorically rejected the "exotic spectacle in a third-person perspective" of sensationalist Hong Kong gangster films through whose lens criminals and drug addicts are often portrayed.[11] For Wong, narrating lielao's biography in his own terms is predicated on a process of becoming the Other: "What is written in the novel is mostly from what I've heard or seen: I record, organize, fictionalize, and transform I into 'I.' This I-becoming-'I' is my most difficult task."[12] The first-person perspective of *Lielaozhuan* speaking through the ethnographically identified persona allows the protagonist to fully narrate his internal monologue. It puts in relief the descriptive thinness of the third-person perspective in "The True Story of Ah Q." Exemplifying—so perfectly that it borders on parody—the all-seeing objectivity of classical realism, Lu Xun's writing always leaves us at a superficial level of the character's mind, as Marston Anderson has observed concerning the novel's "paucity of interior monologue."[13] Ah Q is framed as an object of critique because we are allowed to observe him from a realist distance and spared from going through the same ordeal of becoming the Other as Wong invites her readers to do for the lielao.

---

10. Wong Bik-wan, "The Necessity of Forgetfulness," 37.
11. Wong Bik-wan, "Speech Is Futile, Silence Hurtful," 15–16.
12. Wong Bik-wan, "Epilogue," *Lielaozhuan*, 198.
13. Marston Anderson, *The Limits of Realism*, 83.

The idea of Ah Q being a negative, satirical caricature of the nation thus has an obverse side, a reading made possible only by denying Ah Q his personhood as a social outcast. The slang-inflected neologism lielao ("intense dude," a calque on *lienü* 烈女, from Wong's previous novel *Lienütu* 烈女圖 [Triptych of martyred women, 1999]) that Wong coined for these old ex-gangsters restores agency and personal perspective, even heroism, back to these small people: "In Wan Chai they all called me Shanghai Boy. My real name no one knew."[14] *Lielaozhuan* gives center stage to the micropolitics of subaltern survival. In the world of the protagonist Chow Mei-nan, blatant resistance is futile: "In the juvie I learned not to talk back. People say their stuff, I think my own stuff. . . . Say, yea, yea, gotcha. No sweat. Just words."[15] To retreat into his interiority, as the novel does into the protagonist's mind, the protagonist regains his dignity in a world that utterly demeans him. "Whether or not I'm worthless scum is not up to y'all to tell, you folks in blue shirt or not, takin' yourself as some friggin' big shots with a gun in the pocko, fallin' in line for your monthly dough. I picked this road. I paid my price too."[16] By contrast, "The True Story of Ah Q" has conventionally been read through how Ah Q follows the Confucian tradition of China against his as well as the country's macropolitical interest. However, taking inspiration from Wong's novel, we could also reread Lu Xun's story by focusing on how Ah Q survives in a class-based tradition that marginalizes him at a local level. We should be reminded that Ah Q is anything but a typical Confucian patriarch, having no kinsmen to do his biddings. In other words, he is the most awkward candidate to represent Confucianism. We can instead appreciate how he appropriates the Confucian ideology to express outrage that otherwise Ah Q, someone whose upbringing is so molded in the epistemic violence of Confucianism, does not have any other language to come to terms with. Whenever Ah Q cites a classical proverb, he gets it wrong—he tries to rationalize his being harassed by the local bullies by reassuring himself that they are but "his very sons," in comical distortion of plain facts. His use of the patriarchal discourse may well be illegitimate, but nevertheless he registers a real moral travesty for which no redress would be available to him anyway. When he claims to bear the same surname as the prestigious local gentry clan Zhao—the first surname on the list of the traditional compilation of Chinese surnames *Hundred Family Surnames* (*Baijiaxing* 百家姓), which is the origin of the Chinese term for "common people" (*lao baixing*)—Ah Q assigns himself a genealogy when the world gives him none, inserting himself as *one of the people*. But even this imagined vengeance is met with very real punishment from those possessing hereditary legitimacy. "Even if his surname *were* Zhao," reflects the narrator, "he

---

14. Wong Bik-wan, *Lielaozhuan*, 11.
15. Wong Bik-wan, *Lielaozhuan*, 21–22.
16. Wong Bik-wan, *Lielaozhuan*, 60.

should have known better than to boast like that in the presence of Old Master Zhao himself." (104) As a matter of fact, the remote possibility that Ah Q may indeed be a Zhao *does not* matter when the honor system of genealogical affiliation is policed by power (and negatively, shame); not getting this part right further confirms Ah Q's deviation from normative Confucianism. Like Shakespeare's Caliban ("You taught me language, and all I can do with it is curse"), Ah Q's distortive appropriation of patrilineal Confucianism is the only way he can speak back to a hostile tradition that deprives him of a proper place in society. Ah Q's "spiritual victory" is the subaltern's only way to see himself as more than the "worthless scum" despite those who call the shot around him.

It is through the lens of *Lielaozhuan*'s refusal of the allegorical impulse that Ah Q's supposed crystallization of the "Chinese characteristics" may be radically rethought.[17] As assessed above, *Lielaozhuan* is composed against the convention of the "Hong Kong novel" whose cosmopolitan purview often privileges the perspective and assumptions of the local middle-class citizenry. Born in Shanghai on the eve of the Cultural Revolution and speaking in an inflected Cantonese, Chow Mei-nan is a rather unlikely Hong Konger and defamiliarizes Hong Kongness as we know it; and yet his life, so structured by colonizing state powers, cannot but be read through the history of Hong Kong as existing at the periphery of imperial powers. By the same token, "The True Story of Ah Q" participates in the making of modern China, albeit in a sarcastic manner, through critically forging a backward "national character" in line with the May Fourth discursive onslaught of Confucian tradition and feudal institutions. But Lu Xun was always aware that Confucianism was an elitist philosophy having little truck with common people. In an essay on Confucianism in contemporary China originally published in Japanese (where the author could enjoy a bit of freedom from the presumptions of the Chinese-reading public), Lu Xun noted that "China's ordinary populace, especially the so-called ignorant mobs [愚民], call Confucius a saint without feeling so. They well may revere him, but they never feel intimate with him."[18] Moreover, before Confucianism became "Chinese" classics (as Confucius's early English translator James Legge called it in the nineteenth century), it had always operated as a *universalist* ideology circulating in the classical Sinosphere. In the same essay, Lu Xun expressed cognitive dissonance over finding out about a Confucius shrine in Tokyo. "I came to Japan [to study] out of despair over Confucius and his disciples. And here they worshipped him too? I was struck by such oddity, and *I believe I wasn't alone in thinking that*."[19] Had Lu Xun finished his thought here, he presumably would have said that since there was nothing

---

17. See Lydia H. Liu, *Translingual Practice*, 47–50.
18. Lu Xun, "Confucius in Contemporary China," 329.
19. Lu Xun, "Confucius in Contemporary China," 326; italics added.

particularly Chinese about Confucianism, the idea of an unchanging Chinese national character befuddled by rigid Confucian dogmas was but a presentism— a deceitful pretense his contemporaries should have known better than parroting. In "The True Story of Ah Q," Confucianism's civilizational status in history was underwritten in a narrational sleight of hand: the narrator ironically calls Ah Q "no doubt the proof of the superiority of *China's* spiritual civilization over the rest of the world," circumscribing Confucianism's imperial universality as national particularity. On the contrary, chauvinistic as he is about his cultural superiority, Ah Q himself never once uses the word *Zhongguo* 中國 (China) in the national sense, nor does he ever explicitly identify as Chinese. In the story, he "dismisses heterodoxy" (排斥異端; 119) but not foreignness as such (which is why there is an episode about Ah Q bullying a Buddhist nun). The narrator surreptitiously and ironically reveals that by writing "The True Story of Ah Q," he knowingly participates in the discursive remaking of empire into nation. To be legible to his new national readers, the Confucian-style yet modernized narrator must force his Whiggish anachronisms onto a subject for whom the idea of the modern nation-state has yet to take shape.

Wong's interest in Hong Kong's locality shows through the language used in *Lielaozhuan*, characterized by a mixture of standard Chinese, vernacular Cantonese, and underworld jargon with a smattering of Shanghainese and pidgin English thrown in. Hybridity of spoken Cantonese and written Chinese is evident already in the novel's first sentence: "In the [prison] sewing room I was lookin' at the sewing machine, for how long I dunno" (在車衣位我望著衣車有多久，我都不知).[20] On one occasion, the barely literate protagonist miswrites a Chinese character (writing 練 as "么柬") for his biracial Macanese inmate's prison correspondence, further highlighting the imperial entanglements between Sinitic characters and race, class, and colonial multilingualism.[21] In "The True Story of Ah Q," the town of Weizhuang 未莊 as a linguistically specific location is transubstantiated into a "neverville"—it could have been anywhere in China—but traces of local heterogeneities remain as the narrator evokes them in a backhanded way. Not only does Ah Q pronounce "to sleep" as *khunkao* 困覺 in Lu Xun's own Shaoxing Wu dialect instead of as *shuijiao* 睡覺 in Mandarin Chinese, but even Ah Q's name is a local sound inscribed as a textual lacuna. "I have given the question careful thought: Ah Quei—would that be the 'Quei' meaning cassia (*gui* 桂) or the 'Quei' meaning nobility (*gui* 貴)?" (106) May Fourth literature championed vernacular writing but largely preserved the Chinese script (though Lu Xun once advocated complete Latinization of written Chinese as a solution to mass illiteracy). "Quei," a romanization of a topolectal syllable, transcribes poorly into the Sinitic writing system that has long privileged traditional

---

20. Wong Bik-wan, *Lielaozhuan*, 7,
21. Wong Bik-wan, *Lielaozhuan*, 109.

elites with the cultural capital to follow elaborate naming conventions. However, Lu Xun's position is not the same as Western phonocentrism as some critics believed it was. If the objective is simply to transcribe a local pronunciation, then spelling out *Quei* would presumably be enough—but only for modern readers already familiar with phonographic writing. The further reduction of *Quei* to Q enables logographic readings (such as Ah Q's final signature on his confession paper, or the comparison to a man with a Manchu queue) whereby the illiterate Ah Q may have a little more hope to recognize himself. Further, the narrator jokingly notes that "the only thing that consoles me is the fact that the character 'Ah' [阿] is absolutely correct" (106), and this nonsemantic *Ah* is indeed the sound of an outcry—which is referenced in the title of Lu Xun's *Outcry*. Between sense and nonsense, "The True Story of Ah Q" gives the lie to the righteous May Fourth intellectual as full of sound and fury, signifying nothing. Lu Xun registers his self-aware complicity by highlighting that the name Ah Q is a catachresis, a creolized neologism created under the epistemological double-bind of modernity and nation building to circumscribe the unnamable subaltern—but not without his sonic revenge.[22] Building on this, Wong's slang-inflected coinage of lielao and his creolized language gives full expression to subaltern locality for those who eke an impossible living from the harshest corners of society so poorly understood by the many.

Empire, Nation, and Democracy

"The True Story of Ah Q" references a void at the cultural heart of national discourse in search of its postimperial identity. As a lowly character surviving under imperial ideology, he is in theory a subject of justice that the May Fourth call for democracy should have answered for. But once he rises out of anonymity and enters the "field of the sensible" (Rancière), the progressive gaze of nationalism finds him unvirtuous as one of the "people(-nation)." The fact that Ah Q falls between all stools as China transforms from empire to nation-state is registered even in the episodic form of "The True Story of Ah Q," originally published in newspapers as the crucible of national consciousness. "The True Story of Ah Q," originally serialized in the Jokes (開心話) section of a Shanghai-based journal, was meant to be consumed by urban

---

22. In an essay on misglossed characters (*biezi*), Lu Xun suggested that they are symptomatic of Sinitic writing itself—"borrowing" (*tongzhe*) was historically so widespread in classical writings that neither restorationism (relying on historical sources) nor presentism (defaulting to currently accepted written forms) would provide a coherent approach to grammatological legitimacy (see Lu Xun, "Talking around 'Misglossed Characters,'" 289–94). Although "The True Story of Ah Q" was written before this essay, one could see that Lu Xun, by giving his character the name Ah Q, was already preoccupied with tetragraphical anomalies—in this case, fear of catachrestic errors, ad extremum, leads paradoxically to the sinographic system ceasing to function.

intellectuals.[23] Ah Q himself was intended to be a laughingstock, a running gag for the educated people of the May Fourth generation who took themselves as the progressive reformist of an insufficiently modern, underdeveloped China. As Ah Q's story entered the format of modern journalism, it was divided into episodes, flattened into a caricatural comic strip meant as a linear series of jokes wherein the protagonist has no character development or plot progression to speak of (until the revolution arrives at Weizhuang). A deliberately failed bildungsroman, "The True Story of Ah Q" is originally meant to be "quick to perish" (速朽)—Ah Q's whole life is extracted for the sole purpose of entertaining readers for no longer than a day. As if making a mockery of Benedict Anderson's observation that the journalistic medium catalyzes national consciousness,[24] the episodic nature and linear temporality of Ah Q's "true" story (which in fact starts in medias res, misses significant details, and ends with his premature death) documents the epistemic violence perpetrated by the modern nation when "translating" subaltern life into consumer commodity and national narrative. In contrast, the nonlinear narration of Wong's *Lielaozhuan* restores to view how the subaltern would recollect his life story in his old years and unhinges his subjectivity from the tutelage of any ideological metanarratives. If the lielao's life too is ephemeral, mortality points instead to his subaltern resilience constituting the subject of Wong's biographical study. "My lielao, with his only perishable body [一己必壞之身], never says 'difficult,' and never uses words like 'the will,' but greets fate graciously."[25]

Wong's careful rendition of the lielao's interiority—an emotionally restrained monologue showing what prolonged confinement and repression do to one's expressivity—concerns the reparation for irreversible epistemic deprivation by foregrounding the lielao's specific ways of knowing. "After Stanley, it seemed the days in prison just got more and more, gettin' back in right after comin' out, I was spending more time inside than outside. Exactly for how long I dunno, I didn't count."[26] Wong refuses to see above her subject and fill in what he could not have known. For example, one of the most reported events in Hong Kong prison history, the Stanley Prison riot, is not particularly important to the narrator since he was then serving in

---

23. Lu Xun, "The Origins of *The True Story of Ah Q*," *LXQJ* 3:396.

24. Benedict Anderson, *Imagined Communities*, 32–35. Anderson, noting the "obsolescence on the morrow of [the] printing" of this so-called one-day bestseller that is the newspaper, implies that the juxtaposition of ephemeral individual stories imaginatively creates the "representative body" that is the imagined community. Lu Xun's phrase "quick to perish," one may argue, suggests that Lu Xun reflected on the ephemerality of his narration—and by extension Ah Q's "dead vagrant individuality" (B. Anderson, *Imagined Communities*, 32)—as a necessary condition for the daily continuation of the newspaper and its reading community.

25. Wong Bik-wan, *Lielaozhuan*, back cover.

26. Wong Bik-wan, *Lielaozhuan*, 54.

another prison and had only a few lines to say about it.[27] In contrast, he reports at an uncharacteristic length (about two pages) on an undated and undocumented unrest that he witnessed in another prison: "Tong Fuk became a rehab. People gone, place changed, not a trace left. Nobody remembered this happened"—except lielao himself.[28] Instead of emphasizing lielao's "ignorance," Wong lets him demonstrate the resourcefulness of having to live with deprivation. "At jail you see all sorts of folks. They're damn smart. If they got the materials my mates can make a plane, no joke."[29]

By contrast, Lu Xun writes as if the impossibility of knowing his subject intimately is the source of narrative ailment. The narrator never fails to rationalize Ah Q's actions with proverbial clichés (cited from vernacular plays), which he appears to follow without question: "I'll thrash you with a steel mace," "When two foes meet, their eyes flash fire." In citing these banalities, however, Ah Q's psychological motives are explained away rather than truly explicated. After Ah Q loses his odd jobs and is reduced to begging for food, he passes by some "familiar steamed bread" without pausing, because "it was not these he was looking for, although what exactly he was looking for he did not know himself" (127). What should surprise us is that there *is* psychological depth to Ah Q unavailable to him or to us—that physical hunger is against all odds not Ah Q's only preoccupations, when throughout the story he has not been shown to be beyond his most immediate needs. Like Wong, Lu Xun refuses to be an omniscient narrator, which reveals his urgent need to have Ah Q speak on his own terms. Unlike Wong, however, Lu Xun's narrator knocks on Ah Q's head repeatedly to find an inner world that will not open and only reflects Ah Q's ineffable blankness. All he could do is to underwrite, through the repetition of vernacular idioms and proverbial clichés, the violence of everyday language and epistemic deprivation in which Ah Q was raised, which wrecked Ah Q's personality development. Lacking Wong's ethnographic resources, Lu Xun writes as if to complain sorely about the descriptive thinness of national-allegorical realism.

Although Ah Q is incontrovertibly a flat character, Lu Xun hints time and again at how this flatness is overdetermined by the May Fourth discursive field—like Old Master Zhao, it slaps Ah Q's mouth shut for daring to proclaim that he too is part of the *demos*. Lu Xun's ironic self-awareness would culminate in the story's final scene. As bad as things are for him, old society still leaves enough crumbs between its fingers for Ah Q to live on. When the new revolutionary troops arrive, Ah Q tries but fails to surrender to them, for while he is attracted to the revolutionary promise of finally becoming a "somebody," the revolution clearly has no use of a vagabond "nobody" like him. Further enraged by the sight of the revolutionaries looting the

---

27. Wong Bik-wan, *Lielaozhuan*, 107.

28. Wong Bik-wan, *Lielaozhuan*, 91.

29. Wong Bik-wan, *Lielaozhuan*, 82.

158   Ghostwriting the Subalterns

prestigious Zhao family, Ah Q plans to tip them off for sedition. "So no rebellion for me, only for you, eh? . . . I'll turn informer, then see you dragged off to town to have your head cut off—your whole family executed" (147). But before this could happen, Ah Q is framed for the looting he has witnessed because the revolutionary government needs to establish credibility quickly by demonstrating efficiency. The death knell Ah Q imagines tolling for his enemies now tolls instead for him. Just before his death, the story takes a curious turn.

> Those eyes seemed to have melted together and had already begun to gnaw at his soul.
> "Help" (救命)
> *However, Ah Q had not spoken.* His eyes had already gone black, there was a buzz in his ears, and he felt his entire body disperse like fine dust. (153; translation modified; emphasis added)

This last plea for help of an unknown origin has generated multiple readings. Marston Anderson conjectures that the narrator here suspends his realist disinterestedness and presents his personal plea for Ah Q's salvation,[30] while Sebastian Veg suggests that it is Lu Xun the author interrupting the in-text narrator, who never breaks from the Confucian orthodoxy in judging Ah Q's actions.[31] Both readings attempt to close the gap between the subject and the narrator in the latter's favor, a tension that the narrative in fact leaves open. In a last-ditch effort to *make* the subaltern speak, Lu Xun resorted to putting words into Ah Q's mouth, paraphrased from the ending of his own "A Madman's Diary" ("save the children"). In reality, the subaltern remains incorrigibly silent, intractable to May Fourth's call for national self-strengthening. Lu Xun discloses the central paradox of May Fourth cultural vanguardism: the nationalist intellectuals must enlighten the locals because the Ah Qs will not enlighten themselves, but in doing so, they simultaneously deny the locals the capacity for spontaneous action.

We may juxtapose this ending to how Wong closes *Lielaozhuan*. After a life of incarceration, Chow Mei-nan is invited by the halfway house staff to take up a part-time job serving as a health counselor for addicts:

> Even the staff won't tell us to tell people to quit. They're on the job for long enough to know addiction isn't somethin' you talk people out of. Unless they decide to. . . . I dunno how exactly I stopped. The stuff's a rip-off now, there's no kick to it. And so once the kick's gone, it won't come back. One time, two times, again, and again, many, many times later, my heart grows dead.
> My heart's dead to the stuff. It can't tie me down no more. So I'm free.[32]

---

30. Marston Anderson, *The Limits of Realism*, 83–84.
31. Sebastian Veg, "Democratic Modernism," 41.
32. Wong Bik-wan, *Lielaozhuan*, 194.

There is no dramatic resolution to the broken life of lielao, no miraculous cure to his dependence or criminality, no pretension that external help can ever save one from oneself. All that is left is the rejection of futurity, of the endless search for "the kick." Ah Q's public execution—a spectacle hyped up by a bloodthirsty mass eager to see a sensational beheading only to fizzle out into the tedium of modern gunfire—mocks the readerly expectation for a "grand finale," as suggested by the chapter title. Wong, in contrast, dispensed with the need for narrative buildup altogether and concludes her novel with the lielao's deadening of his addictive, restless heart as he makes an unexceptional decision to which there is no witness but himself. Instead of the infinitely deferred promise of revolutionary salvation and national renewal that haunts Lu Xun's text, Lielaozhuan is instead interested in the ordinariness of choice and its irreversibility as the price each of us pays for our freedom. "To walk again—would I pick this road? But in life there ain't no walkin' again."[33]

In Lu Xun's story, Ah Q faces a show trial against which defense is futile, as the text itself served as a convenient scapegoat for urban nationalist intellectuals trying to explain away China's underdevelopment while bracketing their vested interest in competing over global modernity wrapped in a discourse of enlightenment. The unfree, mentally servile Ah Q is a source of national shame because he reminds them too well of China's compromised sovereignty. In any case, Ah Q's desperate assertion of his being one of the people is met with denial and rejection from all fronts. For a century of critical refrains harping on Ah Q's "slave mentality," Lu Xun reserved a special place in the narrative—a group of long-coated revolutionaries in the modernized court who warn Ah Q not to kneel and, flustered that he finally does out of fear, sneer out the insult "Slavish!" (奴隸性)—a May Fourth buzzword—but they "did not insist on his getting up" (149; translation modified). These revolutionaries are concerned more about their own moral supremacy than the subaltern's dignity, and it turns out they are quite content that the Ah Qs remain in their humiliating position. May Fourth progressives voice their "outcries" in words that alienate common people, then put the blame of the revolution's failure on those who have literally no say. This duplicity, rather than any speculations about China's cultural genetics or mass psychology, is Lu Xun's hidden analysis of the failure of China's democratic modernity. Not being able to see Ah Q as a rightful part of the democratic collective is precisely the representational injustice perpetuated by national organization. Rather than condemning Ah Q for his inability to become a democratic citizen for a modern polity, Ah Q's execution for a crime he did not commit and his dying a death no one would grieve should instead prompt us to ask which democracy is needed for Ah Q to be accepted as the rightful part of the *people* he so desperately tries to convince everyone that he is.

---

33. Wong Bik-wan, *Lielaozhuan*, 166.

160   Ghostwriting the Subalterns

Alternatively, Wong's lielao has no plea to make and wants nothing out of the court, thus denying it the power to judge his worth. Apparent acceptance to what may be thrown at him is his silent defense for his own respectability: "The judge asked, so you make no plea for lenience. I said I spent my whole life in jail, ain't beggin' for lenience ever."[34] To those progressive revolutionaries preening themselves on their vanguardist credentials, lielao would probably retort, "Between one person and another, how different can we be. We just like to think of ourselves like that, as different than others."[35] Ultimately, lielao retains the power to free himself and to be free, remarking, "Never will I know, if the road of my life's gonna be different, if he [lielao's father] found me that night [when he ran away from home for the first time]. I wake up, the bus has stopped. It's all gone. Ain't matter no more."[36] Turning Ah Q's public unlikability into subaltern pitilessness, the larger-than-life lielao represents a challenge of—but also an invitation to expand—democratic inclusivity. Wong emphasizes repeatedly that, marginal as the character himself is and idiosyncratic as his experiences are, lielao is in fact "very ordinary. This is what I need to write. He does not need cheap sympathy. He has dignity in his own terms. The difficulty lies in, how to write an ordinary person?"[37]

The fact that "The True Story of Ah Q" lends itself to national-allegorical readings still effortlessly testifies to the epistemological hold the nation has on us as it did for the May Fourth generation. It cannot be stressed enough that such classical readings are made possible only by forgetting that Ah Q comes to us the readers as someone stripped of any personal history. However, through small, seemingly harmless details, "The True Story of Ah Q" also signals the epistemic violence entailed in the representational conceit of performing cultural autopsy on Chineseness. These textual traces probably documented Lu Xun's reluctance to fully "obey the [May Fourth] commander's orders" as he describes himself in his preface to *Outcry*. Wong Bik-wan's *Lielaozhuan* puts into contrapuntal relief the epistemological limitations of nation-centric composition and interpretation. Clearly, Wong's novel is not a rewrite of Lu Xun's story, but indeed she grapples with the same representational challenges as he painstakingly did. *Lielaozhuan* does not represent Hong Kongness so much as it invites us to learn from the lielao about the Hong Kong he sees and lives. Although *Lielaozhuan* does not presuppose familiarity with "The True Story of Ah Q" to be intelligible, Wong's thick description of the subaltern eventually rubs into Lu Xun's narrative as well, revealing by way of contrast its poverty of local knowledge with respect to rural Shaoxing. This in turn shows how Lu Xun was hesitating between

---

34. Wong Bik-wan, *Lielaozhuan*, 182.
35. Wong Bik-wan, *Lielaozhuan*, 195.
36. Wong Bik-wan, *Lielaozhuan*, 196–97.
37. Wong Bik-wan, "Speech Is Futile, Silence Hurtful," 16.

the competing imperatives of literary democratization and national criticism. Ah Q is the butt of a nationwide joke created out of a bundle of political and cultural expediencies alien to the person as an end in himself. His personal biography does not matter in a "true story" about him. Ah Q's orality and locality, as well as the imperial history of Confucianism he imaginatively reconfigured from a subaltern perspective, must be erased to bring home a modernizing narrative and a national critique. May Fourth nationalism is in this sense deeply instrumentalizing, of which Lu Xun, by ever keeping his voyeuristic readers at the doorsteps of Ah Q's personal world without letting them in, was not wholly uncritical.

As empire's survivor, Ah Q has a history.

Conclusion: The (Unfinished) Project of Worlding Ah Qs

Lu Xun's initial plan to write Ah Q's biography amounts to nothing short of a project of worlding Ah Q. As it is used by Pheng Cheah[38] and Gayatri Chakravorty Spivak,[39] respectively, *worlding* can point to either the normative force of making marginal voices heard or to the imperialist violence of offering up the subaltern to the hegemonic discourse. The vernacular-inspired "true story" begrudgingly attributes to Ah Q a biographical worth that his is denied by Confucianism, but it does so by shoehorning him into the national gaze while ignoring his individual perspective and distorting his life experience. Within a different geographic and historical setting, Wong's *Lielaozhuan* asks the same question as Lu Xun did regarding how biography can be generically tweaked to unsilence the subaltern. Wong's rescripting of subaltern biography, prioritizing lived experience over collective injunction while refusing to impute discursive goals into ethnographic fictionalization, has the effect of teasing out a hidden transcript that marks Lu Xun's public role in literary nation making and cultural modernization as in fact riddled with unease, compromise, and feigned acquiescence. Hong Kong literature, borne out of a culture without nationality, performs the critical service of defamiliarizing national canon formation by questioning the teleology of China's transformation from empire to modern nation-state—it turns out that imperial concerns have never truly left Chinese letters, even (or especially) for its father figure who supposedly ushered in its modern revolution. As Wong reads "Kong Yiji" at the beginning of this chapter and as we read "The True Story of Ah Q" here, Lu Xun's ambivalent characterization of his rural-bound characters destined for history's dustbin intermittently betrays an ethical concern for those relegated to the margins of the Chinese empire. These nameless, homeless people populating Lu Xun's fictions—Ah Q, Kong Yiji, Xianglin's widow—are

---

38. Pheng Cheah, *What Is a World?*
39. Gayatri Chakravorty Spivak, "Three Women's Texts and a Critique of Imperialism."

162   Ghostwriting the Subalterns

routinely framed as lifeless examples of Confucian traditionalism, but this is possible only because modern readers can only know them through a misnomer that misrepresents their true character.

This repressed version of Lu Xun as a proto-Sinophone critic of empire has remained hidden to both the (socialist) nation and the (liberal) world but is visible to Hong Kong as a space of Sinophone extraterritoriality—a potential Lu Xun was implicitly well aware of, despite his overt criticisms of the colonial city, a factor arguably decisive for his widespread appreciation in other Sinophone literatures even despite their shared opposition to China-centrism (Carlos Rojas's chapter in this volume discusses precisely one such case from Malaysia). From the vantage point of extraterritoriality, we see the epistemological limits of national sovereignty as the hegemonic form of modern democracy, on one hand, and the critical site from which our work of intellectual democratization as well as cognitive decolonization should begin, on the other hand. Indeed, the project of world literature has by inception a troubled relationship with democracy, often conflated with nation thinking. Pascale Casanova, for one, devoted an entire chapter to discuss how small literatures "rebel" against the global literary hegemony through the "literary uses of the people" informed by a Herderian turn to national folklores and ethnographic root seeking.[40] Lu Xun would be (and in many accounts still is) the epitome of the cultural nationalist bent on reclaiming China's literary sovereignty; the untold half of the story is however that the nonmodern Ah Q functioned as the sacrificial chip in the bargaining of this gambit over the world literary Greenwich meridian. Reading Wong Bik-wan with and against Lu Xun gives us pause over the no-man's zone of such center-periphery conflicts and forces us to confront the hyphenation at the heart of the very amalgam of the "people-nation" as the center of modern political legitimacy. As people evicted from the nation, Ah Q and Chow Mei-nan will never be the modern citizen of liberal social contract, let alone the revolutionary subject of socialist progress. But as Wong Bik-wan teaches us, if we learn to see things from the subaltern's perspective, to learn from their intense struggle for life and self-realization against empire's odds, we may arrive at a conception of world literature alternative to the unending duel of periphery vying for the center, an understanding of democratic self-determination different from the desire for sovereignty. To paraphrase Albert Camus, *one must imagine Ah Q free*: to truly think the free people is to unthink the sovereign nation.

---

40. Pascale Casanova, *The World Republic of Letters*, 220–53, esp. 224–25.

10

"Each of Them Is a Lu Xun"

Lu Xun's Virtual Children in Southeast Asia

Carlos Rojas

On January 18, 1939, three years after Lu Xun's death in Shanghai, the prominent May Fourth author Yu Dafu 郁達夫 published an essay titled "Jige wenti" 幾個問題 (A few questions) in the Singapore newspaper *Sin Chew Jit Pao* 星洲日報, in which he cites Lu Xun's work as an example of the sorts of literary and artistic concerns that are often transported unaltered from China to Southeast Asia. Yu Dafu notes that many people in Shanghai have recently been consumed by what he calls Lu Xun fever, and he offers a pair of inverse hypothetical scenarios to consider how related issues might be addressed in Singapore: "If several dozen gentlemen were to participate in the discussion and each of them was a Lu Xun [個個都是魯迅], it would not be possible for them to avoid broaching these topics. On the other hand, if there were an event in which not a single Lu Xun appeared [連一個魯迅也不會再生], then what would be the point of discussing these issues at all?"[1]

Yu Dafu's 1939 essay captures an important tension that animated the author's own work in the final years of his life. After beginning his literary career while studying in Japan in the 1920s, Yu Dafu returned to China in 1922 and quickly established himself as a leading figure in the May Fourth/New Culture movement. He was working in Hangzhou when the Japanese invaded in late 1937, at which point he fled to Singapore, where he quickly became a vocal advocate for promoting Chinese-language literature in the Nanyang (South Seas) region. In this role, he attempted to support local literature while embodying the cultural authority of modern literature from mainland China. He was interested, in other words, in the ways in which Chinese literature might serve as a model for literature in the local southeast region but also in the ways in which the Chinese literary model might be transformed as it was introduced into the new cultural environment of the Nanyang region.

---

1. Yu Dafu, "Jige wenti."

164   "Each of Them Is a Lu Xun"

The Lu Xun fever that Yu Dafu mentions in his 1939 essay refers to the out-pouring of commemorative activities that followed Lu Xun's death in October 1936. Indeed, as historian Yang Bin 楊斌 has observed, Yu Dafu had been one of Lu Xun's most devoted mourners:

> After Lu Xun's death, Yu Dafu was unmatched among Lu Xun's friends and fellow warriors when it came to the frequency with which he commemorated Lu Xun. Scarcely a year would pass in which Yu Dafu did not write a piece commemorating Lu Xun, and he would attend virtually every commemorative event—up until the eruption of the Pacific War rendered such activities impossible.[2]

After Yu Dafu relocated to Singapore, however, he began to shift his attention from commemorating Lu Xun himself to helping promote the diasporic circulation of the literary traditions that Lu Xun represented. In particular, he became interested in promoting the development of a local Chinese-language literary field that might rival the literature coming from China and expressed the hope that Southeast Asia might one day produce an author capable of bringing global attention to Chinese-language literature from Southeast Asia. He, in other words, hoped that Southeast Asia might one day produce its own local Lu Xun.

In this chapter, I consider the Southeast Asian legacies of Lu Xun and the May Fourth tradition through an examination of the work of the contemporary Chinese Malaysian author and critic Ng Kim Chew 黃錦樹. Born and raised in Malaysia, Ng went to Taiwan for college, and after receiving undergraduate and graduate degrees in Chinese literature, he remained in Taiwan as a professor of Chinese literature while also establishing himself as an influential creative author in his own right. One theme that runs through many of Ng's works involves the ways Nanyang literature engages with the legacies of early twentieth-century Chinese authors, and particularly those of Yu Dafu and Lu Xun. In Ng's stories, these two figures represent the degree to which Chinese literature and culture continue to influence ethnically Chinese communities in Malaysia and throughout Southeast Asia, while also being continually transformed as they circulate through the Southeast Asian region and beyond. Below, I begin with a consideration of Ng's fictional engagement with Yu Dafu and his legacy, then turn to his parallel engagement with the transnational circulation of Lu Xun's own works and the values with which they are associated.

The Afterlives of Yu Dafu

In one of Ng's earliest literary works, the 1990 short story "M de shizong" M的失蹤 ("The disappearance of M), the protagonist is a Malaysian Chinese reporter

---

2.   Yang Bin, "Lu Xun yu Yu Dafu."

investigating a mysterious recent novel titled *Kristmas* that has received extraordinary praise from around the world.[3] Although the author of the novel is only identified by the letter *M*, there is circumstantial evidence that the author may be from Malaysia, and may even be ethnically Chinese. Literary figures throughout Malaysia respond enthusiastically to the possibility that one of their own may have produced a world-renowned work, and express their interest in solving the mystery of M's identity. After interviewing several leading Malaysian Chinese authors living in Malaysia and Taiwan, all of whom deny having written *Kristmas*, the protagonist has a reverie in which he encounters an old man claiming to be Yu Dafu, who suggests that he may be the true author of the anonymous novel in question. The story concludes on an ambiguous, metatextual note, without ever confirming the identity of the mysterious author.

After fleeing from Hangzhou to Singapore in 1937, the historical Yu Dafu fled Singapore in 1942 on the eve of the Japanese invasion and ultimately ended up in a Western Sumatran village called Payakumbuh, where he assumed the identity of a Chinese businessman named Zhao Lian while secretly working as a language interpreter for the Japanese military police. One evening in 1945, shortly after the end of the war, he was abducted and was never seen again, and although it was widely assumed that he had been assassinated by the Japanese military, his body was never recovered and his death was never materially confirmed. In "The Disappearance of M," Ng alludes to the possibility that Yu Dafu may have survived his abduction and continued living incognito for decades, eventually writing and publishing the novel *Kristmas*. Although the story does not definitively state that Yu Dafu was the anonymous author in question, it does explicitly raise this as a possibility.

Ng explores a similar premise in several other early works. In Ng's 1992 story "Si zai nanfang" 死在南方 [Death in the south], for instance, the narrator recalls how, when he was growing up in Sumatra, he had once met a man known as Zhao Lian (which is the pseudonym Yu Dafu adopted after fleeing to Sumatra). Later, as an adult in the 1980s, the narrator finds some unpublished texts that appear to have been composed by Yu Dafu long after his presumed death in 1945, and then attempts to confirm whether the May Fourth author might have survived his abduction and continued his literary work long after disappearing from public view. The story concludes with a description of the narrator uncovering additional troves of text that appears to have been written by Yu Dafu either before or after his nominal death in 1945, and as the narrator struggles to copy the textual fragments into his notebook, he observes that he "unconsciously transformed [himself] into the final reincarnation of [Yu Dafu's] deceased spirit," and adds that "as I penetrated deeper

---

3. Ng Kim Chew, "M de shizong"; Ng Kim Chew, "The Disappearance of M."

166 "Each of Them Is a Lu Xun"

into the life revealed in and outside his writings, his style became so familiar to me that I could easily imitate it."[4]

Ng's 2001 story "Buyi" 補遺 [Supplement] follows a Taiwanese documentary film crew who have recently completed a documentary on Yu Dafu as part of a series on contemporary Chinese authors, whereupon they happen to learn of the work of a Japanese scholar who contends that Yu Dafu may have survived his 1945 abduction. The film crew attempt to corroborate the Japanese scholar's claim, to determine whether they will need to add a supplementary segment to their documentary. The film crew ultimately find an elderly man, who has converted to Islam, and his Indigenous wife living on a small Indonesian island, and they come to suspect that the man is, in fact, Yu Dafu—though the man claims that his surname is actually not Yu 郁 but rather the graphically and phonetically similar character Du 都, short of Abdullah. Like "Death in the South," "Supplement" never confirms definitively that the old man is Yu Dafu, but it clearly presents the possibility that for years, the famous author has been living on the island incognito, his primary link to his May Fourth past being a private library "filled with old books in many different languages."[5]

All three stories feature texts (or textual fragments) that appear to have been composed by Yu Dafu long after his 1945 disappearance, and although none of the stories states definitively that the texts in question were written by Yu Dafu, neither do they rule out this intriguing possibility. Like Lu Xun, Yu Dafu began his literary career while studying in Japan, where he was based from 1913 to 1922. And like Lu Xun, Yu Dafu became a leading figure in the May Fourth movement after returning to China. Unlike Lu Xun, who died in 1936 while still in China, however, Yu Dafu fled the country in 1937 and spent the next eight years living in Southeast Asia, where he extended his dedication to commemorating Lu Xun's death into a commitment to promoting the development of a vibrant local literary tradition. In emphasizing the transregional and transtemporal circulation of textual fragments that resemble Yu Dafu's own writing, accordingly, Ng offers a suggestive commentary on the significance not only of Yu Dafu's relocation to Southeast Asia but also of the broader circulation of May Fourth literary traditions to Southeast Asia and beyond.

It is significant, moreover, that each of these contemporary stories revolves around the unexpected discovery of previously unknown texts or textual fragments. In each case, the textual fragment appears to bear a relationship with Yu Dafu's known writings—on account of its style, themes, linguistic virtuosity, and so forth—yet at the same time differs enough from those known writings that the provenance of the new texts cannot be verified with certainty. In this respect, the conundrum that

---

4. Ng Kim Chew, "Si zai nanfang," 182–210; Ng Kim Chew, "Death in the South," 47–68, 65–66.
5. Ng Kim Chew, "Buyi," 267–90; Ng Kim Chew, "Supplement," 209–36.

the stories pose regarding the potential afterlives of Yu Dafu's work, and of Yu Dafu himself, serve as a useful model for more general processes of textual transmission and literary dissemination.

The Afterlives of Lu Xun

More recently, Ng Kim Chew has explored similar issues of textual transmission through a focus on the literary legacy of Lu Xun himself. For instance, Ng's 2014 short story "Zhufu" 祝福 [Benediction] opens with a young woman called Xiao Nan—literally "Little South"—having just arrived in Malaysia's Kuala Lumpur airport.[6] Xiao Nan's father, who goes by the name Ah Fa, was an ethnic Chinese who was born and grew up in British Malaya, but after being arrested in the 1950s on account of his ties to the Malayan Communist Party, he was deported to China. In leaving British Malaya, the only home he had ever known, Ah Fa also had to leave behind the lover whom he had planned to marry and who, it turns out, was already pregnant with his child at the time. After being sent to China, Ah Fa repeatedly petitioned to be allowed to return to the nation that, after independence, becomes known as Malaysia, but was never given permission. Instead, he married a local woman and proceeded to raise a family in China's Henan Province. It was not until after Ah Fa's death decades later that Xiao Nan was finally able to realize his dream by bringing him (in the form of his ashes) back to the country that he regarded as his homeland.

When Xiao Nan lands in Kuala Lumpur with her father's ashes, she meets her paternal relatives for the first time—including her father's former lover, Lan, whom the narrator addresses as Auntie Lan, and a local man known as Ah Fu, whom Auntie Lan married after Ah Fa's involuntary departure. When Xiao Nan arrives at her relatives' home, Ah Fu immediately takes her upstairs to see his study, which is filled with Lu Xun's works and other memorabilia associated with the author:

> On the wall was hanging Lu Xun's postmortem portrait (the one with whiskers, and in the museum itself there was a photograph of Lu Xun's Japanese instructor, Fujino Genkuro), while the bookshelves next to the wall were filled with different editions of Lu Xun's works, including a Japanese-language edition of his complete works. On one of the bookshelves there was a volume of *Lu Xun's Handwritten Manuscripts*, and on one of the walls there were several texts handwritten by Lu Xun himself.
>
> Those handwritten texts and familiar stele-rubbings were ones that all of us who grew up in the People's Republic had studied in school. But where had all

---

6. Ng Kim Chew, "Zhufu," 15–39.

these original artifacts come from? From the kind of paper and the color of the ink, they did not appear to be reproductions.[7]

Just as Xiao Nan is wondering how Ah Fu could have possibly acquired so many of Lu Xun's artifacts and original works, Ah Fu abruptly exclaims, "That's right, these were all written by me!"

As an ethnically Chinese Malaysian, Ah Fu had long been fascinated with Chinese culture, and after having both of his legs amputated at the knee as a result of a war injury, he proceeded to devote himself to learning Lu Xun's distinctive calligraphic style—as though this sort of calligraphic practice could function as a compensatory substitute not only for his own amputated legs but also for the distant Chinese homeland that he had apparently never visited. Moreover, Ah Fu not only learns how to imitate Lu Xun's calligraphic style, but he also produces convincing replicas of many of Lu Xun's manuscripts and other textual artifacts, which he then uses to create a library that is a close replica of a Lu Xun memorial museum.

A mirror image of Xiao Nan's stepfather, Ah Fu, can be found in Xiao Nan's birth father, who is called Ah Fa. After being exiled from Malaya to China's Henan Province, Ah Fa developed an interest in the ancient script used in the oracle bone inscriptions that were discovered in Henan at the turn of the twentieth century. During the Cultural Revolution, Ah Fa devoted himself to copying Chairman Mao Zedong's poems in oracle bone script, but after the Chairman forbade him from continuing to use the Chairman's poems for this purpose, Ah Fa instead switched to copying titles and excerpts from Lu Xun's works—developing a particular fondness for the characters 祝福 *zhufu*, from the Chinese title of Lu Xun's story "Benediction," also known in English as "New Year's Sacrifice."

One of Lu Xun's best-known stories, "New Year's Sacrifice" describes how the narrator, after a long absence, returns to his hometown, where he feels a distinct sense of alienation, as though he were an outsider in his own home. The narrator's alienation is catalyzed by an encounter with a former family servant known as Xiang Lin sao (which literally means "Xiang Lin's wife," and the narrator notes that no one in his clan knew her real name). The woman, who is now a beggar, approaches the narrator shortly after his arrival and asks him what happens to people after they die and, specifically, whether they will become ghosts. The narrator initially hesitates, unsure how to respond, but ultimately decides that she must be asking this question because she hopes there might be a possibility of life after death, so he tells her that he thinks that ghosts might exist. The woman then asks him whether there is a hell, and whether family members who have died will ever see one another again. The narrator is flummoxed by these queries and feels deeply ashamed that he is unable

---

7. Ng Kim Chew, "Zhufu," 25.

to answer the woman's simple questions. He mumbles, "In this case . . . as a matter of fact, I am not sure. . . . Actually, regarding the question of ghosts, I am not sure either," and then quickly scurries off.[8]

This exchange turns out to be the last conversation that the narrator has with Xiang Lin's wife. Later that same day, the narrator learns that the woman has just died, which further reinforces the distress he feels at having been unable to answer her earlier questions about death and the afterlife. The narrative then switches to a retrospective overview of Xiang Lin's wife's tragic life. It turns out that shortly after when she began working for the narrator's clan as a servant, her husband had recently died. Her mother-in-law subsequently came to claim her to marry her off to another man, and even though she tried to kill herself on her wedding day, the marriage was eventually consummated and she later gave birth to a son. In relatively short order, however, her new husband died from typhoid fever and her young son was killed by a wolf, after which Xiang Lin's wife eventually resumed working for the narrator's clan, although by this point she was perceived to be deeply polluted by the tragedy she had endured and was therefore not permitted to participate in any of the clan's ritual celebrations. The narrator appears to be drawn to—yet is simultaneously alienated by—this memory of the hardships that Xiang Lin's wife had experienced, and in this respect his reaction to her story resembles that of his relatives after she resumes working for them after the death of her young son —in that the relatives would repeatedly ask her to repeat her abject story about how her son was killed by a wolf, appearing to derive some sort of cathartic enjoyment from her rote retellings of a tragedy that she herself has clearly not been able to fully process. Lu Xun's story concludes with the narrator waking up the next day to the sound of firecrackers, whereupon he allows the doubts and anxieties that had been triggered by his recollection of the hardships endured by Xiang Lin's wife to be "swept clean away by the atmosphere of celebration."[9]

Although Ng Kim Chew's story "Benediction" does not directly address the plot of the Lu Xun story from which it borrows its title, nor does it specify why precisely Ah Fa is so fascinated by the binome *zhufu* 祝福 that comprises the title of both works, Ng's story does note that when Ah Fa was forced to leave Malaya—and long before he became interested in Lu Xun's work—his lover at the time, Lan, had given him a volume by Mao Zedong inside which is hidden a copy of the Bible, on the cover of which Lan had secretly stitched the binome *zhufu* 祝福 (which is the title of both Lu Xun's and Ng Kim Chew's stories, though in this context it could be understood more literally as meaning "wishing you good fortune"). Meanwhile, Ah Fa and Lan never saw each other again after his departure, though the man Lan

---

8. Lu Xun, "Zhufu."
9. Lu Xun, "Zhufu."

subsequently married—so that her unborn child might thereby grow up with a father figure—learned about her attachment to Ah Fa and the secret message she stitched for him on his departure, and as a result decided to change his name to Ah Fu in acknowledgment of the fact that he was effectively functioning as a replacement for Lan's true "*fu* 福": her former lover, Ah Fa.

Ng's story concludes with Xiao Nan giving her auntie Lan a tortoise shell on which her father, before he died, had inscribed a series of oracle bone-style versions of the character *zu* 足, or "foot." On seeing this trail of virtual footprints on the shell's inner surface, Auntie Lan begins to sob and exclaims, "The world originally did not have a path, but as people walk through it" (世間本來就沒有路，但人走多了就——).[10] Here, Auntie Lan is paraphrasing a famous line from Lu Xun's 1921 story "My Hometown," which describes a narrator who, on returning to his hometown after a long absence, encounters a local man who had been his childhood friend, and the story concludes with the narrator privately critiquing his friend's superstitious faith in religious idols, which leads him to reflect that the sentiment he himself called hope "was no more than an idol I had created for myself." The narrator quickly qualifies this critique, however, suggesting that such a hope is not necessarily impossible: "Hope cannot be said to exist, nor can it be said not to exist. It is just like roads across the earth. The world originally did not have a path, but after many people walked over, it became a path" (世上本沒有路，走的人多了也就成了路).[11]

The challenge of maintaining hope in the face of despair is a theme that runs through much of Lu Xun's oeuvre, but whereas at the end of "New Year's Sacrifice" the narrator notes that his relatives ultimately decided to dismiss Xiang Lin's wife "because there was no hope of her improving," meaning to recover from her traumatic experiences, "My Hometown" instead concludes on a more ambivalent note, with the suggestion that hope can never be completely ruled out and instead may be produced through the very process of seeking it. The irony, however, is that it is precisely during a deeply alienating trip back to his hometown that Lu Xun's narrator has his epiphany about the importance of creating new routes, just as it is during a similar trip to a "hometown" she had never previously visited, that Ng's later protagonist appears to come to a similar realization.

In particular, Ng's "Benediction" pivots around a strategic inversion of the concepts of homeland and diaspora in that the ethnically Chinese Ah Fa considers himself to be in exile while in China and yearns to return to what he regards as his Malaysian homeland. Xiao Nan, meanwhile, arrives in Malaysia for the first time as an adult and meets an extended family to which she is related only by proxy (the only member of the Malaysian side of the family to whom she is directly related

---

10. Ng Kim Chew, "Zhufu," 34.
11. Lu Xun, "Guxiang."

is her half sister with whom Lan was pregnant when Xiao Nan's father was exiled to China). It is during this alienating visit to her father's homeland that Xiao Nan manages to reestablish a link between her father and her stepmother, Lan—a link that, as in Ng's Yu Dafu stories, is mediated by a trail of postmortem textual fragments and virtual quotes.

New Paths

Although Ng Kim Chew's "Benediction" features Ah Fu's elaborate replica of a Lu Xun memorial museum and Ah Fa's own multiyear project of using oracle bone script to reproduce Lu Xun's works, Ng's most detailed fictional exploration of Lu Xun's legacy in the Nanyang region can be found in his 2019 short story, "Ta shuo ta jianguo Lu Xun" 他説他見過魯迅 [He said he saw Lu Xun], which revolves around a search for what the story calls a "Nanyang Lu Xun" (a South Seas Lu Xun). In particular, the story's first-person narrator collaborates with some colleagues to interview a certain Mr. Zhou, who claims to have met an individual he refers to as a Nanyang Lu Xun. When the narrator and her colleagues arrive at Zhou's apartment, they find it contains a rare set of Lu Xun's complete works published in Singapore in 1938 and many prewar Malaysian Chinese literary works, including some that share the same title as Ng's own stories (including one book titled *Monkey Butts, Fire, and Dangerous Things* [*Houpigu, huo, yu weixian shiwu* 猴屁股，火與危險事物], which shares the same title as Ng's 2001 story about a Malaysian Chinese man exiled to a remote island in the Pacific). On a table, there are two volumes titled *Lu Xun in Southeast Asia* (*Lu Xun zai Dongnanya* 魯迅在東南亞) and *Another Side of a Literati* (*Wenren de lingyimian* 文人的另一面).

After a lengthy search, the narrator eventually succeeds in locating not one but three different middle-aged men who all identify as "Lu Xun." One of the men lives at home while the other two are long-term residents of mental institutions, and although none of them bears a particularly strong resemblance to the historical Lu Xun, they all sport iconic mustaches and Shaoxing accents resembling those of the famous author. Ng's story notes that another thing the three men have in common is that each of them insists that the narrator and her colleagues sing a song titled "We Are All Lu Xun's Children," which features the lyrics:

> We are literary and artistic youth, we are Lu Xun's children.
> Lu Xun, ah, is teaching us; and with a furrowed brow he is coldly pointing.
> In lockstep we follow Lu Xun, eternally heading toward truth, eternally heading toward the light.
> We are literary and artistic youth, we are Lu Xun's children.
> Lu Xun, ah, is teaching us; he bows down and is willing to be an ox.

In lockstep we follow Lu Xun, eternally heading toward victory, eternally heading
toward the light.

我們是文藝青年，我們是魯迅的子弟，
魯迅啊教育著我們；橫眉冷對千夫指
我們齊步跟著魯迅走永遠向真理永遠向光明！
我們是文藝青年，我們是魯迅的子弟，
魯迅啊教育著我們；俯首甘為孺子牛
我們齊步跟著魯迅走永遠向勝利永遠向光明！[12]

Although Lu Xun had only one son of his own, he was famously devoted when it came to supporting younger writers to the point that many progressive Chinese authors from the 1920s and 1930s could be viewed as his virtual offspring. When the three "Nanyang Lu Xuns" in Ng's story present themselves as Lu Xun's (virtual) children, accordingly, they are positioning themselves as inheritors of Lu Xun's literary legacy while at the same time emphasizing the open-ended nature of this system of intellectual and artistic inheritance. Not only does the story feature multiple individuals who all claim to be diasporic versions of Lu Xun, those Nanyang Lu Xuns also insist that the narrator and her colleagues join them in a song that figuratively includes *everyone* under the umbrella of Lu Xun's legacy.

In his 2008 essay "Marx & Sons," composed for a symposium held on the fifteenth anniversary of the publication of his influential 1993 study *Specters of Marx*, Jacques Derrida employs a similar trope of paternity and filiality to clarify his earlier assessment of Marx's political and intellectual legacy. He notes that "as a book on inheritance," *Specters of Marx* "analyzes, questions and—let us say, to save time— 'deconstructs' the law of filiation, particularly patrimonial filiation, the law of the father-son lineage."[13] In other words, Derrida emphasizes the lines of filiation that directly connect Marx's original oeuvre to the disparate ways in which it has been deployed by subsequent generations, while simultaneously underscoring the fundamentally flexible and fungible nature of that inheritance. One implication of this approach, Derrida argues, is that he has undertaken to "analyze and question the fantasy of legitimate descent (fathers, sons and brothers, etc., rather than mother, daughter and sister), attempting to throw it into crisis."[14]

In his deconstructive analysis of the lines of filiation that connect Marx's original oeuvre with that of his virtual "sons," Derrida emphasizes that "the question of woman and sexual difference is at the heart of this analysis of spectral filiation."[15] Meanwhile, we find a similar emphasis on issues of sexual difference in relation to

---

12. Ng Kim Chew, "Ta shuo ta jianguo Lu Xun," 109.
13. Jacques Derrida, "Marx & Sons," 231.
14. Derrida, "Marx & Sons," 232–33.
15. Derrida, "Marx & Sons," 231.

notions of filiation in the very language Ng uses in his description of the song that is sung by all three of the Nanyang Lu Xuns. The Chinese term that is translated here as "children" refers more literally to "sons and younger brothers" (子弟 *zidi*)—which is to say, younger males within the same patrilineal line. Although it is true that all three of the Nanyang Lu Xuns found by the story's narrator are male, however, the "We Are All Lu Xun's Children" song casts a broader net to include both men and women, as implied by the fact that each of the Nanyang Lu Xuns urges the story's narrator to sing along with them—effectively including the female narrator in the nominally male category as one of "Lu Xun's sons and younger brothers."

On the one hand, this gesture of including the female narrator within the nominally male category of Lu Xun's inheritors appears to reinforce a vision of the fundamentally fungible nature of Lu Xun's literary legacy as it enters new geographic regions and historical periods. On the other hand, Ng's story simultaneously points to areas of resistance in this attempt to cross the gender gap as seen, for instance, in an incident when the narrator falls ill and is sent to the hospital, where she babbles deliriously in her sleep (she is later told that it sounded as though she were reciting fragments from Lu Xun's prose poem collection *Wild Grass*). The nurses tie the narrator down to prevent her from ripping out her intravenous needle, and she subsequently recalls how she dreamed of having been sexually violated:

> My dreams were overlapping and broken, but I clearly recall being violated by a frightening middle-aged man. The man's skin was black and icy cold, as though it were made of cast iron, but it moved in a very lively manner, and was also rather brusque. It seemed he was coldly and dispassionately using his awl-like reproductive organ to pierce my body with countless openings, to the point that I almost bled to death. My period came. It was very heavy, and lasted much longer than usual, continuing for almost an entire month. This left me completely exhausted, making me feel as though I had just had a miscarriage.

The narrator then specifies the identity of the middle-aged man who violated her in her dream: "I clearly remember the angry face of that terrifying man who frequently appeared in my dreams and abused me. This is very difficult to say out loud, but it was the face of Lu Xun."[16]

The narrator's association of Lu Xun's spectral figure with a scene of sexual violence appears to be grounded not on any specific misogynist details from Lu Xun's biography but rather on the masculinist connotations of the underlying discourse of literary inheritance itself. In her delirious state, the narrator imagines her contact with Lu Xun's legacy as a form of sexual violation, where the famous author's specter attempts to transform her into a vessel for his own self-reproduction. In her dream,

---

16. Ng Kim Chew, "Ta shuo ta jianguo Lu Xun," 105.

174   "Each of Them Is a Lu Xun"

however, these repeated sexual violations result not in the conception of a child but rather in profuse bleeding, while in real life the narrator experiences an unusually heavy period, like a miscarriage—as though her body responds to the attempt to impregnate it by performing an aborted pregnancy.

The narrator explains that the only person she told about the dream was her roommate, who immediately advised her to go to a nearby temple to obtain a charm that would help calm her soul. At the temple, the narrator recorded a spell and brought back a Daoist charm containing the phrase, "A path is made by people walking over it," which is of course the famous line from the end of Lu Xun's "My Hometown" that is also paraphrased at the end of Ng's story "Benediction." This reference to the Daoist charm inscribed with the Lu Xun quote suggests that for the narrator, Lu Xun's specter represents not only malady but also potential cure—which is to say, it functions as a Derridean *pharmakon*.[17] For the narrator, the Lu Xun figure who assaults her in her dreams induces a condition that resembles a miscarriage, even as the charm she later receives to treat her condition contains one of Lu Xun's most famous expressions of the possibility of transformative hope. More generally, with respect to the broader phenomenon of Lu Xun's literary legacies, the story suggests that these legacies are simultaneously restrictive, attempting to produce a series of near-clones of the original and generative, encouraging a wide range of creative transformations that may stray far from their putative origin.

Meanwhile, the repeated allusion—both here and in Ng's earlier story "Benediction"—to Lu Xun's description of a path that is not yet a path offers a useful model for the transnational legacy of the May Fourth author's own oeuvre. Just as Lu Xun repeatedly reinvented himself during his own lifetime, after his death his image and his works have been continually appropriated for a variety of different purposes and objectives—from being an iconic symbol of Chinese national identity to embodying modern Chinese literature's cosmopolitanism and diasporic potential.

These questions of inheritance and transformation are perhaps most evident in Mao Zedong's strategic reappropriation of Lu Xun's legacy in his "Talks at the Yan'an Forum on Literature and Art," which he delivered in 1942, only six years after Lu Xun's death, in which he celebrated Lu Xun for the author's "burning satire and freezing irony" while at the same time suggesting that Lu Xun's couplet about serving children "like a willing ox," from "Laughing at My Own Predicament," could be taken as a motto for all contemporary revolutionary literary and art workers. On the other hand, even as Mao was holding Lu Xun up as a model of ideal filiation—wherein not only are younger generations expected to follow Lu Xun's paternal example, but furthermore that same paternal authority is expected to serve those same younger generations "like a willing ox"—he was simultaneously gesturing to

---

17. See Jacques Derrida, "Plato's Pharmacy."

Lu Xun's own concern about the potential breakdown of that filiational lineage, in his allusion to Lu Xun's concern that his son might fail to follow in his footsteps and instead grow up to be a "phony author or artist" completely lacking in talent.[18]

In *Routes*, James Clifford, who identifies himself as "a historical critic of anthropology," notes that although the concept of a dwelling is conventionally understood to be "the local ground of collective life, [and] travel a supplement; roots always precede routes," in practice this relationship between dwelling and travel—between roots and routes—needs to be strategically inverted to recognize that "cultural centers, discrete regions and territories, do not exist prior to contacts, but are sustained through them, appropriating and disciplining the restless movements of people and things."[19] In other words, Clifford suggests that the process following a route (or prospective path) can have the practical result of helping create new roots (or established paths). Although Clifford was discussing travel particularly as it pertains to the movement of actual people, he was also concerned with the parallel circulation of objects, ideas, and perspectives, as suggested by the first piece in his *Routes* collection, "Traveling Cultures," a title Clifford borrows from Edward Said's 1982 article "Traveling Theory."[20] In this respect, Clifford's point about how routes have the potential to generate new roots—like Lu Xun's postulate that the process of traversing a route has the potential to create a new path—has useful implications for our understanding of the worldwide dissemination and transformation of Lu Xun's works and ideas.

---

18. Mao Zedong, "Talks at the Yan'an Forum on Literature and Art"; Lu Xun, "Zichao"; Lu Xun, "Si."
19. James Clifford, Routes, 3.
20. Edward Said, "Traveling Theory" (originally published in *Raritan: A Quarterly Review* (1982) 1: 3, 41–67).

Part 3: Lu Xun and Worlding

Part 3: Lu Xun and Wording

11
Structure of Suspicion

Body, Time, and the Worlding of Nontranscendence in Lu Xun's and Guo Moruo's Fiction on Laozi

Kun Qian

In recent years, the notion of Chinese exceptionalism has increasingly attracted attention in politics and academia.[1] The seemingly successful China model of economic development has granted Chinese intellectuals and policymakers more confidence in questioning Western universalism and articulating a Chinese self-identity. Stressing the uniqueness of Chinese history and practice, the concept of Chinese exceptionalism affirms the positive influence of tradition—a view rarely promoted by intellectuals decades earlier. Although a comprehensive discussion of an inherited Chinese worldview is beyond the scope of this chapter, I suggest that a suspicion about Western universalism, including Marxism, has endured the entire process of China's modernization. The suspicion, embedded in the Western Enlightenment movement and articulated most influentially by Nietzsche, Freud, and Marx, has accompanied Chinese intellectuals' search for self-transcendence and a better future for China.

This chapter considers Lu Xun in relation to fellow May Fourth author Guo Moruo, focusing specifically on the spirit of suspicion and self-transcendence in two stories they wrote about Laozi: Guo Moruo's *Zhuxiashi ru guan* 柱下史入關 (The archivist entering the pass, 1923) and Lu Xun's *Chu Guan* 出關 (Leaving the pass, 1935). I have selected these Laozi-inspired stories because scholars have claimed that Lu Xun and Guo Moruo were influenced by Daoist correlative thinking, leading them to seek transcendence to combat nihilism.[2] However, the May Fourth authors'

---

1. Benjamin Tze Ern Ho, *China's Political Worldview and Chinese Exceptionalism.*
2. See Wenjin Cui, *Lu Xun's Affirmative Biopolitics,* and Joanness D. Kaminski, "Grafting German Romanticism onto the Chinese Revolution."

180 Structure of Suspicion

treatment of Daoism and Laozi reveals not an antithetical complementarity, the affirmation of opposites , or a double negation of opposites without potential for synthesis or reconciliation, that is often associated with Daoist dialectics. Instead, what can be discerned in their works is deeply ingrained self-doubt, a structure of suspicion that is alien to Daoist thinking. I suggest that their consciousness of self-doubt and nontranscendence corresponds to what Paul Ricoeur called a hermeneutics of suspicion. Employing the trope of double negation as a writing strategy, Lu Xun and Guo Moruo translated the modern Western spirit of suspicion into their work and life, revealing the temporal anxiety over an inability to transcend the present embodied by a cultural symbol that had long-lasting transcendent values.

This chapter has three objectives. First, I discuss the significance of Laozi and Daoism for Chinese intellectuals to seek self-transcendence. Second, I establish the influence of the masters of suspicion on Lu Xun and Guo Moruo, demonstrating how both writers internalized the spirit of doubt and developed a structure of suspicion in their stories on Laozi. Third, by contextualizing the theories of the masters of suspicion and Chinese reception of them, I show what I call "suspended temporality" and impossibility of transcendence of the present for Lu Xun and Guo Moruo. With the spirit of suspicion, they challenged not only Laozi and Daoism but also Western universalism, especially Marxism. The pass, as a symbol demarcating China and the West, past and future, figures as a lasting trope of suspicion in Chinese pursuit of modernity.

Laozi and Self-Transcendence

Lu Xun and Guo Moruo wrote about pre-Qin thinkers Confucius, Mencius, Laozi, Zhuangzi, and Mozi in stories that were included in Lu Xun's *Old Tales Retold* and Guo Moruo's fiction collection *Shiti* 豕蹄 [Swine trotters]. Despite many similarities in their personal experience, Lu Xun and Guo Moruo nonetheless had quite different personalities, styles, and reputations. For instance, whereas Lu Xun is known for his iconoclasm, pessimism, and ambivalence, Guo Moruo is associated with revolutionary romanticism and idealistic optimism. Their respective fascination with these ancient philosophers therefore reflects the general tendencies in the intellectual field and speaks to the temporal configurations within China and the world.

The pre-Qin thinkers in question are important intellectual sources of Chinese culture, and Laozi, the quasi-mythical founder of Daoism, has been seen as influencing both modern authors in their pursuit of self-transcendence. In her comprehensive study of Lu Xun, Wenjin Cui argues that Daoist correlative thinking informed Lu Xun's critical undertaking of the affirmative power of life to cope with nihilism.[3]

---

3.   Wenjin Cui, *Lu Xun's Affirmative Biopolitics*.

Similarly, Joanness D. Kaminski relates that Guo Moruo's rendition of Goethe's *The Sorrows of Young Werther* was to "complement the Daoist concept of creativity and to frame ancient and contemporary discussions of self-transcendence in China."[4] However, both writers' attitudes toward Laozi and Daoism remained ambivalent, even contradictory. Lu Xun recognized the value Laozi placed on peace through nonaction but criticized its impossibility on the grounds that the force of evolution is unstoppable,[5] and Guo Moruo celebrated the creative energy embedded in Daoism in his early years, yet ridiculed Laozi and Zhuangzi in his fiction. Jianmei Liu perceives Guo Moruo's radically changing attitudes toward Zhuangzi and Daoism as chameleonic adaptations to constantly changing external forces including political power.[6] The transcendence manifested in their writing and thinking, therefore, can only be understood in a negative mode: it is doubt or refusal that characterizes their thought process.

Self-doubt, often intensified as radical self-negation or satire, is absent in Daoist correlative thinking, which tends to embrace opposite forces and changes with ease. The optimistic acceptance of reality in Daoism stands in stark contrast to modern Chinese intellectuals' intense negation of reality. The self-negation is nevertheless characteristic of Western perception of one condition of modernity—that is, obsessive suspicion.[7] Modernity, in its wholehearted endorsement of science, observed Theodor Adorno and Max Horkheimer, begets a kind of neurotic obsessiveness in modern subjectivity.[8] Science's aim to interpret, organize, and control everything and simultaneous acknowledgment of its limitations, produces an obsessional condition of modernity, which subsequently institutionalizes doubt.[9] This obsessional desire to define the present and intrinsic self-doubt echoes what C. T. Hsia calls Chinese intellectuals' obsession with China,[10] and I argue that Lu Xun and Guo Moruo internalized this obsessive suspicion and translated it into a grammar of double negativity that resists transcendence. This is best captured in their stories on Laozi.

Lu Xun and Guo Moruo both picked the legendary episode of Laozi leaving the Hangu Pass as recorded in Sima Qian's *Shiji* 史記 (The records of the grand historian). *Shiji* describes Laozi as the keeper of the imperial archive in the Zhou dynasty, who left his text *Daodejing* 道德經 while venturing to the West. In 1923, Guo Moruo

---

4. Kaminski, "Grafting German Romanticism onto the Chinese Revolution."
5. Lu Xun, "Moluo shili shuo," 69.
6. Jianmei Liu, "Guo Moruo."
7. Jennifer L. Fleissner, "Obsessional Modernity," 34.
8. Robert M. Pippin, *Modernism as a Philosophical Problem*, 192. This is Pippin's reading of Horkheimer and Adorno's *Dialectic of Enlightenment*.
9. Fleissner, "Obsessional Modernity," 112.
10. C. T. Hsia, *A History of Modern Chinese Fiction*.

182   Structure of Suspicion

published a short story titled "Hangu guan" 函谷關 in *Creation Weekly* (*Chuangzao zhoubao* 創造週報), the journal he coedited for the Creation Society, but he later changed the work's title to "The Archivist Entering the Pass." The story imagines Laozi returning to the pass after an aborted journey in the western desert. More than a decade later, in 1935, Lu Xun wrote "Leaving the Pass," retelling Laozi's original journey to the West, only presenting it as a response to the threat of Confucius.

In accordance with their iconoclastic spirit, Lu Xun's and Guo Moruo's representations of mythical, sagely figures exhibit an attempt to critique traditional culture as it is normally observed. Yet as Lu Xun mentioned many times, reading Chinese classics gave him a peaceful mind, detaching him from troublesome reality.[11] The motivation for writing about ancient legends also came from a desire to avoid thinking about the present.[12] This effort to transcend reality, however, often resulted in a caricature of historical figures because real-life events often interfered with his creative process.[13]

Similarly, Guo Moruo's radical rewritings of historical tales are also reflections of his paradoxical disengagement with personal and political crises at the time.[14] Before committing to Marxism in 1924, Guo Moruo was seen as a zealous romantic rebelling against the established social order and traditions. As a founding member of the Creation Society, Guo Moruo is thought to have shared with his fellow Creationists the temperament of a wandering intellectual, taking a marginal stance and extremist attitude against cultural center. On the one hand, they were extremely proud of themselves, posing as enlightener and savior as if they were flawless saints; on the other hand, they could be extremely self-debasing, belittling themselves as if they were good for nothing.[15] Their volatile sentiment is a testimony to the unstable social environment as well as intellectual quandary they faced every day, thus the difficulty to transcend the present.

I suggest that this radical self-negation corresponds seamlessly with the spirit of suspicion found in Western thinkers such as Freud, Nietzsche, and Marx, who

---

11. In an article published in 1925, "The Necessary Books for Youth" (*Qingnian bi du shu*), Lu Xun stated that Chinese classics tend to give him a peaceful mind. In his often-cited preface to *Outcry*, Lu Xun also mentioned that he immersed himself in classical books for a long time to escape loneliness and desolation.

12. Lu Xun, preface to *Old Tales Retold*, 296.

13. Lu Xun admitted in the preface to *Old Tales Retold* that the contemporary events influenced his writing so that he "couldn't help a little simulacrum—in classical robes" to satirize reality. Preface to *Old Tales Retold*, 295.

14. In Guo's *Chuangzao shinian* (Ten years about the Creation Society), he mentioned his own escapist tendency when writing historical plays. See Guo, *Chuangzao shinian*, 135. I discuss Guo's methodology and philosophy of "borrowing history for the present" (借古諷今) and "virtual focus" (虛的焦點) for his writing of historical dramas in my book *Imperial-Time-Order*, 165–66.

15. Xian Liqiang, *Xunzhao guisu de liulangzhe*, 155.

have afforded legitimate voices to modern Chinese writers to articulate their own doubts. Moreover, as the philosopher Paul Ricoeur relates, these masters of suspicion provide a hermeneutics, a mechanism of interpreting the world via hidden structures.[16] I contend that Lu Xun and Guo Moruo internalized this hermeneutics, not only in their treatment of Laozi and Daoism but also in their readings of the Western masters' works. Although Lu Xun and Guo Moruo did not employ hidden structures in their stories, they portrayed Daoism as being so deceptive through double negativity as to compromise any affirmative reading. Meanwhile, unlike the Western masters who still attempted to arrive at totalizing narratives in their respective works, Lu Xun and Guo Moruo avoided synthesis or transcendence altogether.

Masters of Suspicion: Freud, Nietzsche, and Marx

Modern Western philosophy had been dominated by Cartesian dualism predicated on our capacity for conscious thought, and further developed by Kant for whom transcendental reason can grant us knowledge and judgment. According to Ricoeur, Freud, Nietzsche, and Marx challenge Descartes as three "protagonists of suspicion who rip away masks and pose the novel problem of the lie of consciousness and consciousness as a lie."[17] In their radical negation of Kantian consciousness, all three figures developed a method of suspicion through interpreting hidden structures: Nietzsche discovered the false consciousness of slave mentality through his genealogy of morality, Freud unraveled the unconscious mind that compromises rational cognition, while Marx uncovered alienation of labor and surplus value that characterize capitalism. Although people tend to understand these thinkers in relation to their respective fields, Ricoeur contends that they all share a view that takes immediate consciousness primarily as *false* consciousness.[18]

Ricoeur's reading of the three masters reflects structuralism's challenge to absolute truth but also sheds light on Chinese intellectuals' earlier reception of these same thinkers during the Republican period. Since Chinese reception of Western thought was often selective and fragmentary, as characterized in Lu Xun's essay "Grabbism," Chinese intellectuals' acceptance of these Western thinkers was accompanied with doubt from the very beginning. I would suggest that the intellectuals' abandonment of certain ideas is symptomatic of this intrinsic doubt inherent in the Western thinkers themselves.

All three of Ricoeur's masters of suspicion were well known to Lu Xun and Guo Moruo. Leaving aside Marx, who will be discussed later in their fiction on Laozi, let

---

16. Paul Ricoeur, *Freud and Philosophy*.
17. Ricoeur, *Freud and Philosophy*, 127.
18. Alison Scott-Baumann, *Ricoeur and the Hermeneutics of Suspicion*, 44.

184   Structure of Suspicion

us focus first on Nietzsche and Freud. Not only did Lu Xun and Guo Moruo discuss these thinkers directly, but they even sometimes identified with them. For example, Guo Moruo once claimed that his poetry showed an "anti-normal" personality (*fan renge* 反人格), "like the personality of the German Nietzsche."[19] Lu Xun translated Nietzsche's prologue to *Thus Spoke Zarathustra* and was found to be influenced by Nietzsche's affirmative biopolitics.[20]

As for Freudian psychoanalysis, both figures took the unconscious as a source of vitality and creativity. Lu Xun acknowledged that his story "Mending Heaven," about the creation goddess Nüwa, was inspired by Freud's "theory of creation—the creation of both life and literature."[21] Similarly, in his article about literary criticism, Guo Moruo defended his short story "Can chun" 殘春 (Withering spring) by showing his portrayal of the unconscious. He noted psychanalysts such as Freud and Jung for their discovery of the unconscious and their interpretation of dreams as a "combination of repressed desires in the unconscious as well as intense emotions and opinions, revealed in dreams for lack of censorship by consciousness during the day."[22]

However, Lu Xun's and Guo Moruo's perception of Nietzsche and Freud was mostly critical. Although Lu Xun admired Nietzsche's iconoclastic spirit, calling it "profoundly thoughtful and deeply insightful in revealing the falsity and prejudice of early modernity,"[23] he nevertheless characterized Nietzsche as just another human unable to achieve what he desired: "Nietzsche used to claim that he was a sun, emitting boundless light and heat . . . yet, he was after all not a sun. He went mad."[24] He also saw Nietzsche's construction of the overman as hopelessly distant, not as accessible as his own creation of the madman.[25] By juxtaposing Nietzsche's philosophy with Nietzsche the philosopher, the all-powerful overman with the debilitated madman, Lu Xun questioned the efficacy of Nietzsche as a modern iconoclast.

Similarly, Lu Xun mocked Freud's reduction of everything to repressed sexual drive, satirizing Freud for living an affluent life, never worried about starvation, as people's demand for food must precede their sexual desire. He was also not convinced that children's attachment to their parents of the opposite sex is due to repressed sexuality because infants first need to eat for survival.[26] In another article, Lu Xun criticized Freud's interpretation of literary works in a seemingly scientific

---

19. Guo Moruo, "Lun Shi," 113.
20. Wenjin Cui, *Lu Xun's Affirmative Biopolitics*, 6.
21. Lu Xun, preface to *Old Tales Retold*, 295.
22. Guo Moruo, "Piping yu meng," 131.
23. Lu Xun, "Wenhua pian zhi lun," 50.
24. Lu Xun, "Nalaizhuyi," 39.
25. Lu Xun, "Zhongguo xinwenxue daxi xiaoshuo erji xu," 247.
26. Lu Xun, "Tingshuo meng," 483.

manner that reduces poetry to mechanical signs, thus putting him in the camp of "enemies of poetry."[27]

Likewise, Guo Moruo criticized Nietzsche for his individualism, suggesting that he jeopardized German culture.[28] He also critiqued Freudian theory, describing instead how dreaming results from interactions between the peripheral and central nervous systems from physiological perspectives. The bioscientific way of interpreting dreams juxtaposed with Freud's theory, instantly compromised the credibility of psychoanalysis.

Selective and critical as it was, Lu Xun's and Guo Moruo's response to these masters of suspicion captures the genuine doubt intrinsic in those theories. And the doubt carries not only the masters' challenges against the dominant discourse in nineteenth-century Europe but also the suspicion of their own interpretations because they are, after all, just one among many possible interpretations. Engaging with Paul Ricoeur's analysis of the three masters of suspicion, Andrew Dole suggests using the term "suspicious explanation" in place of Ricoeur's "hermeneutics of suspicion."[29] For Dole, suspicious explanation invokes both "hiddenness" and "badness." The former is easy to understand as all three masters reveal hidden structures of society or life by reinterpreting overlooked evidence. The latter involves ethical valuations, as they can appeal to purportedly universal moral valuations or to recognizably nonmoral values. Attempting to explain large-scale social phenomena, suspicious explanations can be cognitively appealing and cognitively ensnaring.[30]

It is in this sense of a double suspicion—hidden meanings and ethical valuation—that I propose a structure of suspicion. I demonstrate that in their intense desire to transcend the present, Lu Xun and Guo Moruo developed a grammar of suspicion, a structure of double negativity in their writings. In fact, their critical readings of the three masters already reveal this suspicion. Doubtful of using one theory in place of the others, they refused to accept any overarching narrative about the world. In terms of creative writing, this double negativity is best manifested in their stories on Laozi. Making Laozi interpret his own theory while negating the ethical valuation of Laozi's own statements, Lu Xun and Guo Moruo managed to externalize the spirit of suspicion.

---

27. Lu Xun, "Shige zhi di," 246.
28. Guo Moruo, "Lun Zhong De wenhua shu," 157. In this article published in 1923, also a letter to Zong Baihua, Guo compared Laozi with Nietzsche, suggesting that they had a lot in common, both individualistic and both causing damage to their own home cultures.
29. Andrew Dole, Reframing the Masters of Suspicion.
30. Dole, Reframing the Masters of Suspicion, 4.

Entering the Pass: Guo Moruo's Discovery of Body in Double Negativity

Guo Moruo's "Entering the Pass" is a radical denunciation of the possibility of Daoism, where Laozi lays bare the condition of his theory and confesses his hidden motive that is self-serving hypocrisy. In the story, the famished and exhausted Laozi recounts his experience in the desert where he cut his beloved ox's artery and drank its blood to survive. The ox died of blood loss, "sacrificing his life" to teach Laozi a lesson. "Ah, although my ox died for me," Laozi exclaims, "he drew out the conscience of me-the-hypocrite. The ox is in fact my teacher. He taught me that one should not leave the mundane human world. There is no life outside the human world. Talking about the 'Way' and 'Virtue' in the desert cannot compare with growing some greens in the human world."[31]

In contrast to the Daoist conception of oneness, Guo Moruo revealed the hidden centrality of the human body for basic survival. Through Laozi's own interpretation, he criticized the Daoist philosophy of body: "I perceive life as precious, but I said there is nothing to worry about without a body. Ah, I am such a hypocrite!"[32] Nature is presented in such an inhospitable way that antagonizes all living beings within it, directly opposed to the Daoist advocacy of harmony between body and mind, man and nature. The Daoist body, as noted by scholars, is the quintessential form of microcosm. The body is the visible expression of the universal flow of energy, consubstantial with the bodies of ancestors and descendants and all the people around. The boundless organism is like an extended network, connecting many different organic structures within each individual and outwardly with numerous others.[33]

In the story, however, Laozi's body is a discrete, concrete unit separate from the surrounding environment. As a former medical student, Guo Moruo would have been familiar with modern scientific conceptions of the body, and this conception of the human body as constantly at war with the environment is in accord with the law of the jungle in the social Darwinism familiar to modern educated Chinese. Guo's Laozi recalls his violent attack on his beloved ox in which he slashed the ox's artery, sucked its blood, and cut its tail. By assailing his own philosophy, Laozi discredits the spiritual principle that would have any positive effect on the body.

Laozi's defense of the body is triggered by the guard Yinxi's flattering comments on his *Daodejing*, which Laozi wrote before venturing into the desert. Yinxi tells Laozi that this book has become a kind of essential bible of life for him that

---

31. Guo Moruo, "Zhuxiashi ru guan," 156.
32. Guo Moruo, "Zhuxiashi ru guan," 156.
33. Livia Kohn, *Daoism*, 50.

inspires tranquility and serenity amid this chaotic world. "Whenever I spread open your book," Yinxi tells Laozi, "this hot world, this foul world, immediately disappears from my eyes, and a breeze arises from my mind to ease every vein of my body. My soul then flies out of this body to approach the mystical forces of nature." Yinxi's remark testifies to the transcendent effect of Daoist doctrine as it literally transforms the physical world people live in. The environment confines the body, yet the mind can liberate the body. The transformative power of Daoism in Yinxi's remarks highlights the cross-fertilization of body and mind.

However, Laozi is unmoved by this praise. He insists on separating body and mind. The truth is that human life is important, Laozi asserts, and material desire is an intrinsic part of life. The so-called harmony with nature, the alleged transcendence, is but a lie that dismisses the beauty of the mundane human world. After a distraught castigation on his own character and philosophy, Laozi conveys to Yinxi that he is going home to his wife to enjoy life in this human world: "Unfortunately I do not have any other ways than the knowledge of history to support myself. Perhaps I will need some self-reform to make a living. I am willing to sweep the floor or wash clothes for people. I will never again pride myself in talking about the self-serving 'Way' or 'Virtue'!"[34]

Laozi's radical self-negation offers a powerful rhetoric to criticize Daoism for its fondness for paradoxes and impossibility while reasserting the condition of life. Yet why would Guo Moruo, the enthusiastic promoter of Daoism in his early career, attack Daoism so severely here? In his early works, especially his poems "The Goddesses" (女神) and "The Nirvana of the Feng and Huang" (鳳凰涅槃), Guo mobilized all natural, cosmic elements, transforming them into the revolutionary forces able to blast open a new world. Shu-mei Shih argues that the pantheism embedded in Guo's poetry lays the ground for his later universal cosmopolitanism, enabling him to grasp modern temporality as a world citizen.[35] Daoism, with its nonanthropocentric worldview, is an integral part of pantheism for Guo Moruo, in which he saw the rejuvenating energy that had renewed Chinese culture. In fact, in 1923, a few months before he wrote "Entering the Pass," Guo published an article in a Japanese journal hailing Laozi as a "revolutionary" and Daoism the forerunner of a Chinese Renaissance.[36] For Guo, ancient Daoism was a regenerating movement that "subverted the religious, superstitious, and other-disciplined ruling thoughts in the Xia, Shang, and Zhou dynasties"—a period Guo regarded as the equivalent to the European Middle Ages, while Daoism awakened, recovered, and

---

34. Guo Moruo, *Zhuxiashi ru guan*, 159.
35. Shu-mei Shih, *The Lure of the Modern*, 98.
36. Guo Moruo, "Zhongguo wenhua zhi chuantong jingshen," 135–40.

188   Structure of Suspicion

developed hibernated national spirits, the free thoughts prevalent before the three dynasties.[37]

However, a few months later, Guo seemed to have completely abandoned his assertion about Daoism in the story "Entering the Pass." Critics have noted that Guo at the time was undergoing a transition from believing pantheism to embracing Marxism.[38] After returning to China from Japan in the same year, in 1923, Guo transformed himself into a wholehearted literary revolutionary, devoting his entire energy to building the status of the Creation Society and participating in literary debates. He joined forces with Cheng Fangwu 成仿吾 and Yu Dafu 郁達夫 editing *Creation Weekly* (創造週報) and *Creation Quarterly* (創造季刊). For Guo, however, this otherwise active and lively period was a lonely, wandering, and reclusive time. He largely confined himself in a dingy Shanghai apartment, composing explosive articles to "bomb" the conservative literary field, which nonetheless "never affected the opposing camp, but only left ourselves badly battered."[39] The feeling of futility was further compounded by economic distress. The idealistic literati men in the Creation Society were shy about negotiating finances with Taidong Tushu Ju—the publisher they collaborated with; consequently, it was hard for them to make ends meet. Guo Moruo was no exception. His Japanese wife, Guo Anna (Tomiko Sato), was not used to life in Shanghai, and young children often created chaos in the narrow apartment that hardly provided a quiet space for his writing.[40] The group of young people to which Guo belonged often exhibited in themselves an extreme, and it was also hard to maintain unity among them.[41] After a while, some cofounders expressed a desire to withdraw from the group, further shattering Guo's dream of enacting change with his writing.

In this context, it appears reasonable to relate Guo Moruo to Laozi. The disillusioned philosopher in "Entering the Pass" mirrors the disillusioned author. Criticizing Laozi is then self-mockery, and abandoning Daoism paves the way for accepting Marxism.[42] Even Guo himself confessed in his autobiographical narrative *Chuangzao shinian* 創造十年 (Ten years about the Creation Society) that the reclusive experience in his Shanghai apartment revealed to him the vain attempt to reform the world:

> Philosophically, I was in a quandary. I had always had leftist leanings, having articulated radical ideas in the *Creation Weekly*, calling for "going to the military," and "going to the masses," yet after all these talks I was still on the upper floor of

---

37. Guo Moruo, "Zhongguo wenhua zhi chuantong jingshen," 136.
38. Zhu Yuhong, *Gushi ruhe xinbian*, 43.
39. Guo Moruo, *Chuangzao shinian*, 153.
40. Xian Liqiang, *Xunzhao guisu de liulangzhe*, 149–52.
41. Xian Liqiang, *Xunzhao guisu de liulangzhe*, 155.
42. Zhu Yuhong, *Gushi ruhe xinbian*, 47.

the apartment in Min hou nan li. All talk but no action. Endless guilt increasingly overwhelmed me. My previous belief in pantheism, the so-called development of individuality, freedom, and expression, had gradually undergone invisible liquidation. The Marx and Lenin that had been on the margin of my mind then gradually replaced Spinoza and Goethe and became the center of my thought.[43]

Indeed, much evidence suggests that this was a period of self-negation for Guo. Laozi's radical self-negation then reflects Guo's criticism of his own "all talk but no action," and the importance of material things certainly looms large in his thought. Yet such a reading closes the gap between fiction and reality, creating a linear time retrospectively accounting for Guo's transformation. In contrast, a closer look at the story "Entering the Pass" would yield a more complex reading, which implies a different temporal frame and multiple referentiality. First, Laozi's narrative appears to be untrustworthy. The incoherent, radical self-debasement, triggered by the loss of his beloved ox, shows symptoms of traumatic distress. Can one take his words literally in his extreme guilt and grief? Moreover, Laozi's self-criticism is mostly centered on his character as selfish and hypocritical. Can an ethical evaluation of one person completely negate the validity of an otherwise transcendent theory? After all, Yinxi's initial response to it testifies to the value of his book, which is inspiring for people who are tired of the daily tedium, offering an escape from the quotidian entanglement in the mundane world. Furthermore, the ending of the story also destabilizes the meaning of Laozi's negation since Yinxi refuses to believe his story. Depicted as an irritable old man with the appearance of someone suffering from Basedow's/ Grave's disease,[44] Yinxi offers a response that creates a double for Laozi's narration, a stated counterpart that negates Laozi's negation.

This structure of doubling generates an effect of negativity, a term coined by Wolfgang Iser to describe the experience of literary text. Iser asserts that our aesthetic appreciation of literature pretty much depends on the deformation, negation, and defamiliarization of imagined objects, because such negation also challenges us to imagine that which is negated. The formulations of the text and the negated background together construct a "double," which is called negativity. "Unlike negations, [negativity] does not negate the formulations of the text, but—via blanks and negations—conditions them. It enables the written words to transcend their literal meaning, to assume a multiple referentiality, and so to undergo the expansion necessary to transplant them as a new experience into the mind of the reader."[45]

---

43. Guo Moruo, *Chuangzao shinian*, 166.

44. Guo Moruo deliberately chose the appearance of a Basedow/Grave patient to depict Yinxi. See the footnote in "Entering the Pass," 153.

45. Wolfgang Iser, quoted in Winfried Fluck, "The Search for Distance," 185.

190   Structure of Suspicion

In light of this theory, Laozi's radical yet untrustworthy negation already creates defamiliarization and negativity that conditions his statement, and Yinxi's reception further literalizes and doubles the negativity. This double negativity not only gives rise to the distance from Laozi's own narrative but also allows the reader to disassociate from Yinxi. The open ending of the story thus leads to an experience of a state of in-between, a nonidentity, which consequently poses a challenge to Guo Moruo's retrospective assertion of his abandoning pantheism and Daoism at the time.

Indeed, "Entering the Pass" suggests a temporal doubling and a spatial suspense, leaving no solution for the crisis experienced by two protagonists. Perhaps it is this sense of despair that best captures Guo Moruo's experience of time. The separation of body from mind does not legitimize the body's centrality, failing to capture the materialist essence advocated in Marxism. Rather than a linear progression from one worldview to another, or a rupture that points to a better future, the failed escape/return in his works suggests a suspense, a temporality stuck in its own negativity. While the rhetoric of negation implies an aesthetic transcendence that shows the modern intellectual's attempt to organize traditional thought, the innate negativity in the text only reinforces suspicion and cancels out that transcendence.

Leaving the Pass: Lu Xun's Double Resistance to Time

A similarly radical rewriting of Laozi, involving the structure of double negativity, appeared in Lu Xun's story twelve years later. This time, however, Laozi is not entering but leaving the pass. Lu Xun's story consists of three parts: Confucius's visits to Laozi's residence, Laozi's experience at the Hangu Pass, and the guards' mockery of him. Frustrated that various state rulers have rejected his theory of state governance, Confucius comes to seek advice from Laozi, who informs him that those rulers' reactions are only natural because the six classics Confucius has been promoting are just the dead remains of the past sages' teachings and not the teachings themselves—the same way that shoeprints are not shoes. Then Laozi describes different ways that insects mate and reproduce and concludes that "nature is unchangeable; fate is unalterable; time is unstoppable; the Way is unblockable. Once the Way is within your grasp, all will go your way. Without it, you are lost."[46] These mysterious remarks result in a long silence on Confucius's part, and only three months later does he return to visit Laozi. This time, he implies that he has decoded the Way as Laozi had suggested, and from now on he will be willing to embrace change. Confucius's departure prompts Laozi to leave immediately for the West, for he senses Confucius's impending conspiracy against him. At the Hangu Pass, it is requested that he share his wisdom with the scouts and customs officials, and he delivers a lecture on his

---

46. Lu Xun, *Chu guan*, 372.

philosophy, one that his audience finds tedious and incomprehensible. Although bored, the audience further demands a written version of his teachings, which then becomes the *Daodejing*.

Like Guo Moruo, Lu Xun emphasizes Laozi's frail physique, clumsy movement, and incomprehensible speech. However, Lu Xun paid more attention to the representation of time. It takes Confucius three months to decipher Laozi's teaching, but it takes eight minutes for Laozi to realize the time for his departure has come. For Laozi's audience, his lecture is seen as "the longest dream of their lives." Laozi's old age is emphasized a few times through his toothless mouth and motionless posture that resembles "a block of wood." The portrayal of time as an indicator of wisdom and physical deterioration creates a contradictory juxtaposition of values and the hopeless urgency to (re)act. Meanwhile, the riddle-like exchange between Confucius and Laozi and the disinterested responses from the guards form a double writing that sets the two philosophers apart from the ordinary people, who measure the value of Laozi's book by rolls of bread, no different from other confiscated goods piled up on the shelf.[47] The ethical valuation and explicit double negativity manifest what Andrew Dole would call a suspicious explanation of Daoism: just like theories by Nietzsche, Freud, and Marx, it delineates a process of decoding and can be misused by others (such as Confucius) against Laozi the founder.

Given the story's obvious parodic dimensions, many readers initially responded by attempting to match the fictional characters with real individuals. Some speculated that Lu Xun was satirizing Fu Donghua 傅東華, the editor in chief of *Literature Monthly* (*Wenxue yuekan* 文學月刊),[48] while others believed that the sympathetic image of Laozi mirrored Lu Xun himself, who must have painted a self-portrait with this old man's image drenched in loneliness and sadness.[49] Lu Xun's response to these critiques, however, was denial. In 1936, he published an article titled "The 'Pass' in 'Leaving the Pass,'" declaring both types of comments are misreadings of his work. Not only is the act of matching fictional characters with real individuals groundless, but he also intended to criticize Laozi as well as Confucius. Therefore, a distance must be perceived between Lu Xun the author and Laozi the character. The fact that Laozi's leaving for the desert was triggered by Confucius's threat, Lu Xun explained, was derived from Zhang Taiyan's 章太炎 comments on Confucius and Laozi.[50] Lu Xun was not completely convinced by Zhang's interpretation, yet he still accepted Confucius's triumph as inevitable—on the grounds that Confucius was a goal-driven activist who would try to make everything impossible possible, whereas

---

47. Lu Xun, *Chu guan*, 381.
48. Lu Xun, "*Chuguan* de 'guan,'" 541.
49. Qiu Yunduo, "'Haiyan' duhou ji."
50. Zhang Taiyan, *Zhuzi xue lüeshuo*, 292.

192 Structure of Suspicion

Laozi was a big talker who would do nothing in order to do everything.[51] Moreover, in response to the Marxist-oriented remark of the critic Qiu Yunduo 邱韻鐸, calling for Lu Xun–like lone writers to join the collective effort to form a "boundless force" for social reform, Lu Xun saw only wishful thinking, for "boundless force" is as impossible as "doing everything by doing nothing." Qiu's pro-Laozi reading of the story thus forecloses his negative depiction of Laozi with "an abstract gigantic seal," reducing it to a didactic piece irrelevant to the author's original intentions.[52]

Lu Xun's article ends with a negation, without offering a more affirmative reading of his story. Even though the title of his article is "The 'Pass' in 'Leaving the Pass,'" he never really addressed the meaning of the pass itself. Instead, Lu Xun's article compounds the story's suspicious explanation, responding to both textual and ethical questions while reinforcing the structure of suspicion. Like Guo Moruo, Lu Xun also reversed his early relatively positive opinion of Laozi. In his well-known text "On the Power of Mara Poetry," Lu Xun had acknowledged Laozi's philosophy as creative and transformative:

> The core of Laozi's five-thousand-word book is "Do not disturb anyone's mind," which requires one first to make deadwood of his mind and propagate inaction; acts of inaction transform society, and the world has peace. What an art![53]

Although he saw Laozi's philosophy as antithetical to the unethical killer instinct prevalent in social Darwinism, Lu Xun's reading of Laozi was nonetheless contradictory, wavering between evolution versus ethics and perception versus agency, as he later thought of Laozi's inaction as impractical. "Laozi extoled inaction yet aspired to govern all-under-Heaven; his inaction meant to act on everything."[54]

In fact, "Leaving the Pass" could be read as a commentary on elements of social Darwinism present in the works of two ancient thinkers who broach questions of evolution, ethics, and agency. Despite Lu Xun's criticism of Laozi in his essays, his story presents the philosopher in a largely sympathetic light, which also stands in contrast to the story's negative portrayal of Confucius and the ignorant audience at the pass. The hierarchy of wisdom as indicated in the portrayal of time, in opposition to power and vitality as suggested by physical and material strength, establishes a perspective of the defeated wiseman that undermines the legitimacy of evolution. Confucius, as an unlikely symbol of evolution, was attacked again—this time not for his enslaving people's minds for centuries but for his unethical killer instinct.

This negation of Confucius and Laozi reveals a double negativity that defamiliarizes and questions them. In a sense, Lu Xun's "Leaving the Pass" could be seen as

---

51. Lu Xun, "*Chuguan* de 'guan,'" 540.
52. Lu Xun, "*Chuguan* de 'guan,'" 540.
53. Lu Xun, "On the Power of Mara Poetry," 101.
54. Lu Xun, *Han wenxueshi gangyao*, 374.

counterpart to Guo Moruo's "Entering the Pass," but whereas Guo Moruo stressed the centrality of the body and of material necessity embedded in Marxism, Lu Xun instead challenged the boundless power of material force advocated by Marx. The intertextuality of their stories and the paratextuality of their essays reflecting on these works only compound the negations and suspicions of any overarching theory or ideology, which exemplifies the suspicious explanation that nullifies any hope for transcendence.

The Pass: Suspended Temporality and the Worlding of Nontranscendence

Guo Moruo's and Lu Xun's demystification of the sages does not simply serve the iconoclastic function of paving the way for the reception of Western ideologies, but it also expresses the intrinsic suspicion embedded in modern Western thinkers. The reworkings of historical stories, then, reveal a unique temporality that corresponds to a trending denunciation of transcendence in the West. Since the Enlightenment movement, along with the development of modern science wherein empiricism was granted a central status in Western thought, philosophers such as Nietzsche, Freud, and Marx began reflecting on the universality of any religious claims and transcendental values. However, each of these three thinkers proposed a universal theory, which makes them objects of suspicion in their own right, especially when they were received in a non-Western context.

This renunciation of transcendence was coupled with a recognition of particular historicity that shapes human actions and experiences. During the same period, we observe the rise of a historical consciousness such that humans are seen as historically definable subjects whose thoughts and behaviors are conditioned by their own cultural limitations; therefore, a universal truth seems to be hard to access. As Glenn Hughes points out, "the affirmation of transcendence has come to be seen as contradictory to a proper regard for the historicity of language and culture as well as to the nurturing of a proper appreciation of tolerance and pluralism."[55]

In early twentieth-century China, the so-called obsession with China foregrounded a particular Chinese historicity. Consequently, what is adopted by Chinese intellectuals is none other than the intrinsic suspicion and anti-transcendence. Although Nietzsche, Freud, and Marx all sought to propose a totalizing theory, the reception of their theories was already localized in a Chinese context and appears to be suspicious. Not only Nietzsche and Freud, whose reception in China remained selective and critical, but even Marx was received in China with deeply ingrained suspicion. While Guo Moruo embraced Marxism and promoted it in later years, his

---

55. Glenn Hughes, *Transcendence and History*, 8.

194　Structure of Suspicion

entanglement with Chinese history and tradition reveals what Pu Wang describes as a constant reinvention of tradition and transcoding of the foreign.[56] Guo's revolutionary practice is consequently full of unstable occasions and permanent crisis "within which subjectivity figures and simultaneously vanishes, is intensified and simultaneously instrumentalized."[57] The mixing of Chinese thinking and Marxism, such as Guo's Confucian-style moralistic reading of Marxism, betrays Guo's underlying doubts about Marxism.[58] Similarly, Lu Xun questioned the universality of all totalizing theories, including Marxism.[59] The double negativity expressed in their stories therefore constitutes a structure of suspicion. The pass—a signifier that separates this world from that which lies beyond—interrogates the material foundation of human existence and transcendent values as well as Chinese particularity and Western universalism, especially Marxism. As a geographic and philosophical concept, or an ontological and epistemological marker, the pass exhibits an in-between space and a suspended temporality. It can be viewed as a symbol of worlding in that it is a paradigmatic boundary zone but also marks a space of transregional, transcultural, and transtemporal connections. Lu Xun's and Guo Moruo's stories on Laozi, by way of constructing a structure of suspicion with double negativity, represent Chinese intellectuals' practice to localize the anti-transcendent spirit in the world and their doubts about any universal theory, whether Chinese or Western.

---

56. Pu Wang, *The Translatability of Revolution*, 285.
57. Pu Wang, *The Translatability of Revolution*, 295.
58. For Guo's moralistic interpretation of Marxism, see Kun Qian, *Imperial-Time-Order*, and Xiaoming Chen, *From the May Fourth Movement to Communist Revolution*.
59. Qian Liqun, "Lu Xun yu Zhongguo xiandai sixiang wenhua."

12

Beyond Oneself

Writing and Effacement in *Wild Grass* and *Morning Blossoms Gathered at Dusk*

Eileen J. Cheng*

Why did Lu Xun write? Or more appropriately, why did he start translating and introducing world literature in 1903? Looking back twenty years later in his preface to *Outcry* (1923), Lu Xun wrote that he initially did so with the intent to transform the spirits of his people.[1] This narrative, it turns out, rings hollow in light of the events that followed. In the second half of the preface, Lu Xun notes how his plan to launch a journal of translations failed and his translations mostly go unnoticed. The preface paints a portrait of a dejected and disillusioned middle-aged man: While new youths were promoting a new culture to rejuvenate the nation, Lu Xun remained ensconced in his room copying ancient inscriptions, seemingly oblivious to both the violence around him and the voices agitating for change. In Lu Xun's self-portrayal here, he appears more like the image of the apathetic Chinese that first prompted him to take up his pen than a literary warrior awakening the soul of his people.[2]

---

* The ideas in this essay were presented in two venues. The first is an online workshop on "Lu Xun and World Literature," organized by Xiaolu Ma and Carlos Rojas and sponsored by the Hong Kong University of Science and Technology, held in July 2021. The second is a virtual forum on "Lu Xun and World Literature: The Task of Translation," organized by David Der-wei Wang and sponsored by the Department of Comparative Literature and the Fairbanks Center for Chinese Studies, Harvard University, held in October 2022. I thank Hu Ying and David Der-wei Wang for their insightful comments and Carlos Rojas for the fine editing.

1. Lu Xun, "Nahan zixu," 437.

2. After he began writing under the pseudonym Lu Xun, Zhou Shuren had largely repudiated the image of the poet-rebel that he espoused in early essays he wrote in classical Chinese and published in the journal *Henan* in 1908. For an examination of Lu Xun's promotion and later repudiation of radical individuality and the image of the poet-warrior, see Eileen J. Cheng, "Performing the Revolutionary."

196   Beyond Oneself

Narratives that turn themselves inside out with the continual deferral of certainty where both the self and the narration turn out not to be what they proclaim is typical of Lu Xun's writings once he began writing creatively in 1918. The idea of a self-knowing "I" is deconstructed. Saviors often turn out to be victims, victims may turn out to be oppressors, and borders between self and other are broken down. What to do with a text with an unreliable narrator where the world is almost never what it appears to be? Drawn into the intriguing world of the text, readers are prompted to look beneath the surface and read between the lines. It also invites us, as readers, to think critically about our own limits and the narratives we tell about ourselves and the world, while keeping in mind the possibilities of a world that could be, and should be, otherwise.

Toward the end of the preface, Lu Xun portrays himself as a reluctant writer for the progressive journal *New Youth*. Unable to turn down an insistent friend's requests to contribute to the journal, he wrote "Diary of a Madman." His foray into creative writing, Lu Xun notes, was accidental. With no books on hand to write scholarly articles or foreign texts to translate, he ended up writing a short story, and others followed.[3] These stories reflect his dejected spirits from his failed aspirations and doubts over the prospects for social reform. The society portrayed in these works is like the iron house described in the preface to *Outcry*—a hermetically sealed room with no windows or doors, where sleeping inhabitants are slowly suffocating to death. In the insulated towns, superstitions are rife and old cultural practices remain firmly entrenched; those who speak out about the ills of society and call for reform are ostracized, persecuted, or, as in "Diary of a Madman," deemed insane.

Cognizant of the long history of the ruling class's wielding of language and texts as systemic tools of domination, Lu Xun was also wary of the act of representation itself. In his mind, the new arbiters of culture may wind up perpetuating yet another elitist system. Ever self-critical, his stories with intellectuals as narrators—which might be seen as traumatic retellings of his own failed aspirations at transforming people's spirits—almost invariably present these narrators as unreliable. As Marston Anderson has noted, Lu Xun's stories reveal his anxiety over the propensity of narratives to distort and be used for self-serving purposes, which might inadvertently replicate and reify the injustices of the world in second-order form.[4]

To conform to his "general's orders"—referring to the leading voices of the New Culture Movement, calling for the destruction of traditional culture and rejuvenation of the nation through radical linguistic, literary, and cultural reform—and to

---

3. Lu Xun, "How I Came to Write Fiction."
4. As Marston Anderson notes, Lu Xun held intellectuals morally accountable as agents of social order and as arbiters of culture through which societal norms are disseminated. Marston Anderson, *The Limits of Realism*, 86.

avoid infecting his readers with his own pessimism, Lu Xun added hopeful "distortions" (*qubi*) to the conclusions of his bleak stories. However, his sleights of pen—such as the line "Save the children" at the end of "Diary of a Madman"—do little to convince readers of the possibility of a better future. Almost all evidence points to the persistence and perpetuation of the same oppressive system. The analogy of the iron house with no escape might well reflect Lu Xun's sense of paralysis and his entrapped mind, the madman's sense of terror mirroring the author's own as he ponders his own complicity in the predatory system he condemns.[5]

The aesthetic and philosophic sensibilities *Wild Grass* (1927) and *Morning Blossoms Gathered at Dusk* (1928) depart markedly from those of Lu Xun's short stories and reveal a new trajectory in his creative writings. Informed by Buddhist ideas of the ephemeral nature of forms and the interdependence of all things, Lu Xun deliberately pushes beyond the limits of representation. He experiments with new forms, styles, and linguistic registers and explores the worlds *beyond*—the world of memories, dreams, the fantastic, and the imaginary. The exploration of these other realms is accomplished in part through a deliberate process of self-effacement, going beyond the limits of a conditioned mind and the egoistic nature of the writing self. I will consider four manifestations of effacement in *Wild Grass* and *Morning Blossoms*: self-effacement and defacement as means of self-discovery; effacement as form, a process of becoming and decaying; effacement as a recognition of the shared nature of existence; and effacement as a surrender to the other. Going beyond oneself, many of Lu Xun's writings in *Morning Blossoms* and *Wild Grass* give in to uncertainty and in the process look outward to an array of speculative possibilities, enabling different ways of seeing, hearing, and being in the world.

Effacement, Defacement, and Self-Awakening

Lu Xun had premonitions about his eventual canonization. In the last decade of his life, he vehemently rejected the labels given by friends and foe alike, including "spiritual warrior," "mentor for youth," and "celebrity scholar." He claimed he could not serve as a guide or mentor since he was certain only of one destination: the grave.[6] It is unlikely that he would have embraced his posthumous canonization as the father of modern Chinese literature, the soul of the people, and Mao Zedong's hailing of him as "the sage of modern China."[7] In contrast to such lionization, his

---

5. In a letter to Xu Shoushang dated August 20, 1918, Lu Xun points to the autobiographical impulses of the story, noting how it was after his reading of Sima Guang's 司馬光 *The Comprehensive Mirror to Aid in Government* (*Zizhi tongjian* 資治通鑑) that "I suddenly understood that the Chinese were a race of cannibals, and so I wrote 'Diary of a Madman'" (*LXQJ* 11:365).

6. Lu Xun, Afterword to *Graves*.

7. Mao Zedong, "On Lu Xun."

own self-representations are highly critical, exposing a flawed individual who was often conflicted, filled with self-doubt, and uncharitable to his literary adversaries.

Indeed, the ten loosely connected vignettes from his childhood and adolescence that appear in *Morning Blossoms* are remarkable for their ordinariness and deliberate distance from the biographical markers of the author (Figure 12.1).[8] The subject's name is mentioned in passing in the third piece and his hometown mentioned only in the last. No dates or descriptions of an illustrious clan are given; only a few family members appear and those who do are not identified by name. No particularly distinctive features, personality traits, or talents of the subject stand out. The account of childhood—fascination with folk tales and myths, love of drawing, adventures in the garden paradise, playing at the neighbors', navigating the complicated world of seemingly arbitrary adult rules—are experiences that would have been familiar to many, particularly those from elite families. Lacking specificity and marked by its ordinariness makes it all the more a universal story. The memoir is at once a celebration of the childlike nature that is open to myriad possibilities and the divine and a criticism of a society bent on destroying it.

Like entries in "Diary of a Madman," the memoir also consists of performative acts of critical self-introspection. The self that is depicted in the memoir is a

Figure 12.1: *Morning Blossoms Gathered at Dusk* (1928). Cover Design by Tao Yuanqing (1893–1929).

---

8. Ideas from this section are adapted from Eileen J. Cheng, "Vulnerable Subjects."

fractured one. We see not one self but rather multiple *selves*, as the I-now stands outside of itself to tell the story of an I-then. The narratives of these selves at times intrude and conflict with one another, as the past self is "subjected"—reconstructed through the eyes of others and the I-now. In a process akin to "defacement," prior understandings and images of the self and the world are readily torn down, shown to be partial and lacking.

Yet, like an odd variation of Oscar Wilde's *Picture of Dorian Grey*, there seems to be an inverse relationship between the private man—at least in Lu Xun's self-depictions—and his public image: however ordinary and flawed Lu Xun portrayed himself to be, his image became increasingly heroic after death. The more contradictory, convoluted, and elusive the self-portrait, the more readers and critics seemed compelled to delineate its outlines. Indeed, the experimental memoir has been mined extensively for biographical details, even as Lu Xun himself referred to it as a creative work, and gaps in the narrative are readily filled in by readers familiar with his background. Just as many of Lu Xun's stories have autobiographical elements yet are clearly fictionalized, the subject of the memoir, while clearly resembling the author, should not simply be equated with him. Aware of how the present mediates our remembrance of things past, Lu Xun was not singularly concerned with factual accuracy. He writes in the preface, "This is how I remember things now."[9]

The memoir is not a biography of a great man or the subject's triumphs over adversity but rather an account of a flawed individual still making sense of himself and the world through reconstructing the past. The memoir lays bare its anachronism: the understanding of the past and the self are not only partial but can only be reconstructed in the present. The narrative is not so much about the past as such as it is about how certain memories of that past—particularly traumatic ones the narrator prefers to forget—persist with lifelong effects and repercussions. The child narrator recounts how he was terrorized by didactic stories of filial piety, especially "Guo Ju Buries His Son" in which a filial son buries his infant alive to ensure that his elderly mother would have enough food to eat. This story instilled in the narrator a lifelong fear of his father and grandmother, adversely affecting his relationship with them both, "something that the Confucian scholar who gave me *The Illustrated Twenty-Four Exemplars* never would have anticipated."[10] Some thirty years after the event, the narrator recounts how he was forced by an authority on etiquette to wail at his father's deathbed against the patriarch's wishes. "Father's Illness" ends by reflecting how "even now I can still hear this voice of mine from then, and every time I hear it, I feel this was the greatest wrong I ever committed against my father."[11]

---

9. Cheng, "Vulnerable Subjects," 127.
10. Lu Xun, "The Illustrated Twenty-Four Filial Exemplars," 158.
11. Lu Xun, "Father's Illness," 189.

Beyond Oneself

Like many accounts of trauma, this voicing and reliving of memories is akin to a form of exorcism. It is a belated attempt at reordering, to put the past back in its place, if you will, to allow for the possibility of a regenerative present no longer haunted by it and a future in which such traumatic episodes would not be repeated. More than "a record of what 'really' happened," it functions more as what Janet Varner Gunn refers to as "an instrument of discovery," as the self is presented as one that is constantly unfolding to himself.[12] This process of revelation is one to which readers also bear witness. Through his performative introspection and retrospection, Lu Xun may have hoped to inspire in readers a similar quest for self-knowledge, which might in turn lead to a personal and social transformation. The defacement of the self and the world as he knows it and the epistemological breakdown the narrator confronts—however disorienting and confusing—awakens him to his preconceived notions of the self and society and the ways he has been conditioned to accept and perpetuate the normative ways of an inhuman world.

Effacement as Form: Becoming and Decaying at Once

While *Morning Blossoms* attempts to overcome the past's hold on the present, *Wild Grass* confronts the inevitable future that awaits all living beings—that is, death and how acknowledging and facing the prospect of death can transform the experience of the present (Figure 12.2).[13] The ephemeral nature of all forms—including the forms of texts—is addressed at the outset in the preface to the volume, which uses "wild grass" as a symbol for the pieces collected within:

> I hope the demise and rotting away of these wild grasses come swiftly.
> Otherwise, I will not have lived, something even
> more unfortunate than
> their demise and rotting away.
> Away with you, along with my inscriptions![14]

This same refrain is repeated in "Tombstone Inscriptions," where boundaries of the self and the world appear elastic and permeable as multiple I's converge—including I's from the past, present, and future, from the dream world and outside of it. The I-narrator recounts a dreamscape in which the I-in-the-dream comes across a dilapidated tombstone and a disemboweled corpse—presumably, the "I-in-the-future." The barely legible epitaph describes the failure of the I-corpse in his journey in search of himself:

---

12. Janet Varner Gunn, *Autobiography*, 104.

13. Ideas from this section are adapted from Eileen J. Cheng, "Bordering on the Divine," 7–27.

14. Lu Xun, "Inscriptions," Wild Grass *and* Morning Blossoms Gathered at Dusk, 32.

Figure 12.2: *Wild Grass* (1927). Cover design by Lu Xun.

... gouge out my heart and eat it, wanting to know its true taste.
The pain is so searing, how would I know its true taste?
... as the pain subsides, slowly consume it. But the heart now grown old and stale, how could I know its true taste? ...
... answer me, or else leave![15]

Just as the narrator is about to leave, the corpse conveys a message telepathically: "When I turn to dust, you'll see my smile!"

The search for self-knowledge, the tombstone inscriptions suggest, is inherently limited and painful. It is, however, imperative, even if self-defeating. Introspection, likened to a form of self-cannibalism, echoes Lu Xun's description of it as a process of "merciless self-dissection." As a metanarrative on the limits of writing, the cryptic tombstone inscriptions—referring to the story itself and the epitaph in the dream—fail to live up to their form or function, offering few facts about the subject they represent, focusing mostly on the subject's inscrutability. Yet the corpse and the inscriptions correspond uncannily with one another: indistinct, not entirely legible, and in the process of continued decay, they point to the ephemeral nature of all

---

15. Lu Xun, "Tombstone Inscriptions," Wild Grass *and* Morning Blossoms Gathered at Dusk, 74. Ellipses in the original.

forms. It reveals individual lives and texts to be forms that are ever changing, becoming and decaying at once.

The dreamer's confrontation with his own corpse highlights the inevitability of death and allegorizes what Lu Xun notes as the one and only certain destination in life: the grave. Laden with Buddhist overtones, death is portrayed as part of the inevitable cycle of life and a release from the suffering of existence. Lu Xun's playful take on the ephemeral nature of form and death as the ultimate destination of life is apparent in his illustration included in an essay collection he edited after completing *Wild Grass* and *Morning Blossoms*, titled *Graves* (1929) (Figure 12.3). The illustration depicts what appears to be a tombstone inscribed with two characters, "Lu Xun," under which is the larger character "grave." The years 1907–1925—the time span during which the essays in the collection were written—are visible in the frame below in black, to the right of which appears to be two trees. Lu Xun has written fondly about owls and used them as symbols of himself, as a "lover of the night" whose eyes and ears are particularly adept at seeing and hearing in the dark.[16] The comical-looking owl perched on what appears to be Lu Xun's tombstone, with head cocked and one eye open, may be a tongue-in-cheek self-representation—of the author as observer and writer, witnessing his own life and times as well as their demise, the essays serving as tombstone inscriptions chronicling this past.

Lu Xun in the afterword to *Graves* refers to himself as an intermediary, or more literally, a "thing-in-between" (*zhongjian wu* 中間物): "In the chain of evolution, everything is an in-between . . . things pass away and pass away, each and everything passes away quickly like time; they are passing away or will pass away—that is all

Figure 12.3: Illustration by Lu Xun, from the essay collection *Graves* (1929)

---

16. Lu Xun, "Ye song," 203.

there is to it, and I am perfectly content with it."[17] Referring to his essays, he notes, "I cannot firmly and decisively destroy them, wishing for the nonce to use them to observe the remaining traces from a life that has passed by. I only hope that readers partial to my work merely take this as a souvenir and know that within this small tumulus there is buried a body that was once alive. And after the passage of yet more time it, too, will transform into dust, and the memories will also vanish from the human realm, and I would have accomplished what I set out to do."[18]

Wild Grass and *Morning Blossoms* capture the dilemmas of existence—the difficulty of knowing oneself and others in a life filled with suffering that ultimately ends in death. In such despairing circumstances, where the writing that records this existence is filled with gaps and in a continual process effacement, why write at all? And just what was Lu Xun setting out to accomplish?

Singularity, Relationality, and Shared Existence

Morning Blossoms and *Wild Grass* give visibility and voice to a host of vulnerable subjects including children, servants, and social outcasts. In *Morning Blossoms*, some subjects are shown to be silent or reticent when conforming to unspoken rules of decorum. In the absence of patriarchs and superiors, however, readers also hear the laughter and chatter of children and the voices of the nanny and lower classes speaking in colorful vernacular. In the last two essays, the direct speech of the Japanese professor—in his quaint and halting drawl—and the unadorned and at times salty language of the narrator's friend Fan Ainong are refreshing contrasts to the highsounding and ornate language of the intellectual adversaries the narrator quotes with disdain in the first piece. The inclusion of different voices, speeches, languages, and linguistic registers add tone and variety, lending the memoir a polyphonous quality.

At the same time, *Morning Blossoms* shows how in this polyphonous world, lives are not just singular but relational, mutually constituted by the environment, objects, and the many others with whom we have come into contact in the past and the present—interactions that have ripple effects into the future. In particular, the memoir shows how we are irrevocably shaped by our memories, hopes, dreams, and imagination in ways we might not know. The first piece begins with Lu Xun's adversaries labeling him a cat hater. The long and rambling first part—recounting his petty squabbles with literary adversaries and their hypocrisy in using ornate language and rituals to cover up their selfish, self-aggrandizing motives for writing—is

---

17. Lu Xun, "Afterword to *Graves*," 31. The afterword was written half a year after the last piece in *Wild Grass*.

18. Lu Xun, "Afterword to *Graves*," 35.

a perplexing start to the memoir as a whole.[19] After a few digressions, the piece goes back in time to recount a tragic childhood episode that provides a possible reason for the narrator's cat hating: The nanny Ah Chang tells the boy that the house cat had killed his beloved pet mouse; the boy later discovers that the mouse had been stomped to death by Ah Chang herself.

Similar themes of loss, death, and betrayal appear in the essays that follow: the agonizing death of the father witnessed by a helpless, wailing child; a long-departed nanny, whose name and life story remain unknown; the death of a beloved friend, which the young adult narrator suspects is a suicide. In the world of the memoir, each of these lives—the child, the pet mouse, the nanny, the patriarch, the social outcast, the professor from a faraway land toiling away quietly—is at once singular and intimately interconnected with the lives of others. Each and every life, big and small, is meaningful and worthy of commemoration.

The creative pieces in *Wild Grass*—long noted for their themes of darkness and death—also teem with life and pulsate with sound. The "I" recedes and shares the stage with a host of vulnerable beings including the slave, the beggar, the outcast, and the prostitute. Beyond the human world, readers are invited into the intimate world beyond—of nature, dreams, the imaginary, populated by fauna, flora, the inanimate and the fantastic. In its delineation of a vibrant ecological web of existence and the suffering shared by all beings in the struggle for survival, the volume invites readers to reflect: What counts as a meaningful existence?

The tone of *Wild Grass* is established in the opening lines of the first piece of the collection, "Autumn Night": "Beyond the wall of my backyard, you can see two trees. One is a jujube tree, and the other is also a jujube tree."[20] The visual effect guides the readers' imagination, first presenting an expansive vista of the backyard with two trees and narrows to a close-up of each. The existence of each tree is relational and singular at once. However insignificant in readers' eyes, each jujube tree

---

19. Among the "estimable gentlemen" Lu Xun attacked in this essay are the literary critic Chen Yuan (1896–1970), the writer Lin Yutang (1895–1976), and the poet Xu Zhimo (1897–1931). The roots of his bitter disputes with Chen Yuan and his ilk stemmed from a series of protests between 1924 and 1925 at the Peking Women's Normal College. Lu Xun sided with the students who demand the right to political protest and opposed the restrictive policies of their American-educated principal, Yang Yinyu (1884–1938), who was supported by the minister of education, Zhang Shizhao (1881–1973), and backed by the Beiyang government warlord Duan Qirui (1865–1936). The public outcry over the dispute eventually led to the dismissal of Yang. Lin Yutang, in an attempt to mediate, called for a stop to the attacks against Yang and her supporters and claimed that "drowning dogs should not be beaten." "Dogs, Cats, Mice" harks back to Lu Xun's rebuttal to what he saw as Lin's use of empty slogans such as "fair play" and "public justice" in "Why 'Fair Play' Should Be Deferred" (1926), arguing that "drowning dogs" needed to be beaten, lest they rear their ugly heads from the water again. "Dogs," too, are used snidely as analogies for Chen, Lin, and their ilk, most of whom had studied in Europe or America, as "Western lapdogs."

20. Lu Xun, "Autumn Night," 33.

has a unique existence, one that is also mutually interdependent with that of others. Brimming with fruit in the late summer, the trees attract children who come to strike off the jujubes. With the arrival of autumn, the once vibrant trees wither and fall into neglect. Bereft of fruit and foliage, some branches curve into arcs, nursing scars left from the children's beatings; others stand tall and erect like iron rods that "pierce the odd yet high sky, causing the sky to blink his sinister eyes."[21] As each singular life transforms and struggles to survive, each in its own way leaves its mark on an inhospitable world.

Amid the suffering and the struggle to survive, signs of beauty, courage, and resilience abound in the world. In *Wild Grass*, the boundaries between different forms of existence are dissolved as plants, animals, objects—real and fantastic—are anthropomorphized and humans animalized and objectified. A similar affirmation of the capacity of often overlooked subjects to leave a mark on the world appears in "Tremors on the Border of Degradation," this time through the struggles of an abject woman. The narrator dreams of himself dreaming. In the first dreamscape, the I-in-the-dream encounters a scene in which a woman sells her body to buy food for her young daughter. Jolted awake, the I-in-the-dream enters a second dreamscape, a continuation of the earlier dream but after many years have elapsed. The now-adult daughter, ashamed of her mother's sordid past, heaps scorn and abuse on the old woman. Amid the jeers of her daughter and her family, the old woman walks out of the shed at night, deep into the boundless wilderness.

The simple storyline, ostensibly about an abject woman's oppression, is complicated by the descriptions of the woman's bodily sensations that permeate the multiple layers of the story. In the first dream episode, the woman's body is "trembling from hunger, misery, shock, humiliation, and pleasure." The "waves of pleasure, humiliation, misery, shock, and hunger" that "permeate and pulsate through the air" describe not only the woman's emotions and sensations but those of her child and male patron as well.[22] In the second dream episode, the old woman, rejected by family and society, walks out into the wilderness. The body of the woman—now removed from civilization, naked, alone, and stripped of all identity—again convulses as a medley of sensations and emotions overcomes her: "hunger, pain, shock, humiliation, pleasure . . . inflicting suffering, hardship, and dragging in others . . . devotion and estrangement, loving caresses and revenge, nurturance and annihilation, blessings and curses."[23] She enters a realm of consciousness that seemingly encompasses that of all humanity. The boundaries between self and other, oppressor and victim, past and present are dissolved as the abject woman becomes a transparent vessel of

---

21. Lu Xun, "Autumn Night," 34.
22. Lu Xun, "Tremors on the Border of Degradation," 75.
23. Lu Xun, "Tremors on the Border of Degradation," 77.

pure sensation and experience, her own intertwined with those of all others. The "border" referred to in the title, like the boundaries in the story, is itself blurred, as the line of degradation borders on the divine. The abject woman's primal scream—described as being "half-human, half-beast, and not of this world"—expresses a full range of emotions that is at once human, bestial, and divine.

Mutually interconnected with all things, the life force of this figure—simultaneously degraded and divine—traverses past and present and radiates out into an unfolding future:

> Her entire body—like a once great, noble statue, now wasted and withered—trembles all over. Each tremble resembles a tiny fish scale, each scale undulating like water boiling over a blazing fire. The air grew turbulent in an instant, like roiling waves in a vast sea during a thunderstorm.... Only the trembling disperses outward like the rays of the sun, instantly whirling around the waves in the sky, like a hurricane billowing in the boundless wilderness.

Her trembling body, the tiny "tremors on the border of degradation," emits a life force that pulses out into the universe, crossing and breaking down borders, bearing with it the potential for seismic change.[24]

Beyond Oneself: Surrender to the Other

Wild Grass and *Morning Blossoms* show how one's identity is not bound but inextricably intertwined with the existence of others. How, then, are we to coexist with, relate to, and represent these others whose lives are enmeshed with our own?

Many pieces in the memoir surrender to the story of others, appearing more biographical than autobiographical and minimizing the presence of the narrator while allowing the stories of others to shine. The nanny, the central character in "Ah Chang and the *Classic of Mountains and Seas*," appears in four of the eight essays. The presence of Ah Chang—comical, dominating, and at times domineering—often overshadows her young charge. The story of Ah Chang as seen through the child's eyes also provides an opportunity for the adult narrator to reflect on his own elite privilege and limited worldview and, hence, the partiality of his account. As the I-now writes, in spite of the dominant role that Ah Chang played in his childhood,

---

24. Alan Fox has noted the use of earthquakes in the "omniverse" of the *Flower Adornment Sutra* (*Huayan jing*) "as possible reminders to shake up and loosen or deconstruct fixed ontological commitments." A verse he quotes from the sutra resonates with Lu Xun's use of trembling in "Tremors on the Border of Degradation": "Then the ocean of worlds of arrays of flower banks, by the power of Buddha, all shook in six ways in eighteen manners, that is, they trembled, trembled all over, trembled all over in all directions." See Alan Fox, "The Practice of *Huayan* Buddhism," 264. Lu Xun was familiar and known to be fond of the *Flower Adornment Sutra*.

including inspiring his lifelong passion for collecting illustrated books, he knew neither her real name nor her life story, offering only the following speculation: "All I know is that she had an adopted son and was probably widowed from a young age."[25]

A similar surrender appears in the last two essays dedicated to two intellectual misfits, "Professor Fujino" and "Fan Ainong." The eponymous character in "Fan Ainong," initially looked down on by the narrator and others for his seeming arrogance and lack of social graces, appears to be a character far more worthy than the image-conscious young narrator. In hindsight, Fan Ainong is shown to be honest to a fault, uncompromising in manner, showing utter disdain for superficial displays, yet ever hopeful of the advent of a true revolution. In the end, dejected and ostracized by society, Fan Ainong, the narrator suspects, dies not by accident but by suicide. The penultimate essay provides a similar portrayal of Professor Fujino with a more hopeful ending. Critical of imperialist aggression and sympathetic to the plight of the oppressed, single-mindedly devoted to educating his students and overturning injustice, the Japanese professor presents a stark contrast to his lackadaisical student. Unimpeded by racial barriers and social hierarchies, Fujino—an embodiment of a universal human spirit that opposes all forms of oppression—inspires his student to keep attacking his literary enemies and carry on in his pursuit of realizing a more human and just society for all.[26] Both intellectuals, raised as exemplars, are obvious foils for the literary adversaries Lu Xun excoriated in the opening piece, shown to be more concerned with their own fame and status than exposing injustice and social reform.

Even as the essay highlights the partiality of the accounts—of the narrator's biases and large gaps in knowledge about the lives of those he memorializes—they attest that there has been a life—"a life worth noting, a life worth valuing and preserving, a life that qualifies for recognition."[27] Although the "real" life story of Ah Chang, the reasons for Fan Ainong's death, and the whereabouts of the professor remain mysteries in the end, the pieces point to the countless, nameless others

---

25. Lu Xun, "Ah Chang and the Classic of Mountains and Seas," 149.

26. Remarkably, "Professor Fujino" was published at a time of heightened anti-Japanese sentiment. The sentimental and uniformly laudatory portrait of his teacher, uncharacteristic of Lu Xun's writings, might have been a deliberate maneuver on Lu Xun's part to overcome the vociferous anti-Japanese sentiments at the time. His tribute at once humanizes and exalts Fujino's character, downplaying his race while playing up his significance as a humanitarian figure. For a more detailed examination of the "distortions" and Lu Xun's gesturing toward a paradigm of relationality that goes beyond national and colonial discourse in "Professor Fujino," see Eileen J. Cheng, "'In Search of New Voices from Alien Lands.'" The essay also notes how Professor Fujino—the epitome of benevolence and "a new voice from an alien land"—is portrayed as an exemplary Confucian gentleman.

27. Judith Butler, *Precarious Life*, 34. The quote here refers to the function of obituaries but is relevant to Lu Xun's essays memorializing the lives of others.

whose lives have been objectified, simplified, distorted, or rendered socially invisible in the world of the real and the world of narrative.

In the last decade of his life, Lu Xun became increasingly aware of his stature and influence in the literary field and used writing as a way to bear witness and to give voice to others. His writings about others function as what Thomas Couser has called "nobody memoirs" that may confer unexpected immortality on a hitherto anonymous but noteworthy person.[28] Other than the figures memorialized in his memoirs, a significant portion of Lu Xun's essays included tributes to the dead, including figures that would have otherwise faded into obscurity. Like fallen blossoms gathered at dusk, the memory and significance of the many lives Lu Xun commemorated are not left to languish, as traces of their lives continue to linger in those who are inspired by Lu Xun's written tributes to them.

* * *

In his essay "Inauspicious Star," Lu Xun writes, "I know great men have the penetrating vision to see the past, present, and future and apprehend all matters through contemplation because they have experienced great tribulations, tasted great happiness, and awaken great compassion for all living beings. But I also know that this kind of vision requires retreating deep into the mountains and forests, sitting under an ancient tree, quietly contemplating and reflecting, and opening one's divine eyes; the farther one's distance from the secular world, the deeper and wider the expanse of one's knowledge of it."[29] Even though this reference to "great men" is tongue in cheek, we sense in *Wild Grass* and *Morning Blossoms* contemplation that goes far beyond secular matters and merciless self-dissection. Transcending time and space, Lu Xun's exploration of the world of memories, imagination, and the speculative in forms beyond the short stories enabled different ways of seeing and being in the world.

Lu Xun's short stories, drawing attention to the elite nature of representation and its propensity to be manipulated, compulsively replay his own crisis of representation. Who has the power to represent? Is faithful representation possible or does representation potentially do injustice or violence to the other? In that case, why represent at all? *Wild Grass* and *Morning Blossoms*, however, open outward, going beyond the self, asking: If one has the power to represent, how can one represent through the perspective of others? How can representation enable the voices that

---

28. G. Thomas Couser, *Memoir*, 179.

29. The original term *tianyan tong* 天眼通, translated as "divine eye," is of Buddhist origin and refers to a line of sight that transcends time and space and penetrates the world of the visible and invisible.

have been silenced and submerged to be heard and to reverberate so that we can see and imagine a polyphonous world in which each life, however fleeting, is singular, relational, and part of an ecological web of shared existence? Resisting despair and embracing radical hope, *Wild Grass* and *Morning Blossoms* as a whole show Lu Xun's renewed faith in the power of creative art that continued into the last decade of his life—not just to expose injustice but also to awaken readers to the limits of the self and one's perception of the world.[30] The volumes give in to uncertainty and a sense of childlike wonder to see and imagine the possibilities of a world beyond the iron house.[31]

---

30. Evident as well in the stories collected in *Old Tales Retold* and his polemical essays, which formed the bulk of his writing.

31. Driven possibly by both a sense of mission and impending sense of death, Lu Xun threw himself with abandon into literary and artistic endeavors in the last decade of his life—translating, introducing, editing, and publicizing the written works of others, promoting woodcut art, while writing original works (mostly polemical essays and cultural criticism but also classical poetry and a handful of rewrites of old myths and legends in *Old Tales Retold*).

13

The Severe Style

Law, Irony, and the Absolute in Lu Xun

Roy Chan

Considering Lu Xun's relationship to both the "world" and "literature," one may speculate that the emergence of modern literature in twentieth-century China coincided with a deeply felt imperative that such literature should be congruent with a novel vision of universality. Literature ought to proffer an affective and cognitive disposition toward and address to the "world" but not the same "world" of the premodern normative, ritual order. Apart from the law of "Confucian" and "feudal" order, this literature should voice the new universal laws of modernity. If these premises hold weight, then it would follow that we cannot think the emergence of modern Chinese literature apart from questions of law and normativity.

However, appeals to universal laws, even novel ones, often find themselves beset by what Joseph Slaughter has termed their "paradoxes": the supposed universality of law finds itself plagued with inconsistences, hypocrisies, and outright fictions bearing little to no relation to practice.[1] The appeal to the transcendent authority of law, however modern, however enlightened, reveals itself to be deeply, internally

---

1. Joseph R. Slaughter, *Human Rights, Inc.*, 5–6. Kun Qian's contribution to this volume asserts that Lu Xun, alongside Guo Moruo, upheld a "structure of suspicion" that resists the possibility of transcendence: Qian, "Structure of Suspicion." I agree that the mature Lu Xun does not advocate an easy form of transcendence, but I also would not insist on a strict binary between skepticism and secular faith; I contend that Lu Xun's work appreciates the speculative unity of suspicion and belief. Pu Wang's contribution argues that Lu Xun's poetic practice constituted a normative form of world making that heralded an alternative to the contemporary logic of imperialism and domination; Lu Xun's engagement with world poetry and his production thereof was an attempt to envision a "radical normativity": Pu Wang, "Lu Xun, World Poetry, and the Poetic Worlding." I wonder if this slightly overlooks the issue of fully appreciating the difficult gap between aesthetics and actuality, of normative "oughts" (*Sollen*) and reality, and whether a notion like "radical normativity," however appealing, invites the same kind of internal discrepancies and diremptions that Lu Xun identified in the locution "revolutionary literature" (see my discussion toward the end of the chapter).

ironic, to the point that law risks foundering on its own instrumentalized cynicism: universal ends are unmasked as mere veils for particular interests. And yet we cannot wrest ourselves from pondering the modern law, even when it has always already been mired in ruins of its own making.

Lu Xun (1881–1936) engaged deeply with the ironies of law and norm in conjunction with China's troubled, traumatic integration into global capitalism and modern culture. During a period of fractured sovereignty under semicolonialism and imperialism, Lu Xun registered the felt effects of this ironic rupture in everyday life and culture. Apart from a wistful hope that a revitalized and modernized literature would promulgate a new law of the world, in Lu Xun's mature hands we observe instead a literature that bears witness to an already dirempted, estranged law. And yet in law's semicolonial disenchantment, I contend that Lu Xun still appealed to a horizon of normative possibility, even if it could not be fully stated or prejudged. Moreover, it was precisely by traversing through the actual ironies of law and norm in contemporary Chinese society that any hope of retrieving a more genuinely universal law would be possible.

This chapter leans on the philosophy of Gillian Rose (1947–1995) to illuminate Lu Xun's approach to literature, law, and norm during a period when ironies abounded, from the meaning of language, to debates about culture, and to questions of legitimate authority under semicolonial modernity. Rose's work may help to bring out what I contend to be Lu Xun's interest in the contentious, yet necessary, relationship between law, culture, and society. His stature as a philosopher and critic of modernity has long been recognized and notably by such writers as Takeuchi Yoshimi (1910–1977), who saw in Lu Xun a model for an agonistic modernity that seeks to overcome itself but avoid reinstalling the structure of hierarchical domination.[2] Bringing Rose to bear on Lu Xun may clarify how both found themselves in a similar position of agonistic equivocation vis-à-vis the aspirations of modernity and universality. In my reading, both were critical of modernity's constant discrepancies between ideal and actuality: they pointed out how claims to laws and universals come up short in light of lived experience and history. However, despite modernity's self-negations, neither was willing to give up the possibility of universality and the absolute—in fact, any hope for a true, concrete universality can only be obtained by grappling with modernity's gaps and contradictions. For Rose, this constantly anxious engagement with modernity's aporias was exemplified by dwelling in what she termed the "broken middle." For Lu Xun, who gave up the heroic, romantic idealism of his youth and contended with both personal and collective failures on the eve of the May Fourth movement, this anxious engagement was exemplified by a commitment to adhering to a constant struggle (*zhengzha* 掙扎) for truth without

---

2. Richard F. Calichman, "Preface," xi.

resting in any formulated dogma. For both writers, their fraught relationship to the question of authorship was always agonistic; the ultimate aim of writing was not to instruct from on high but to engage in a vigorous battle with one's own self, including one's own thought and commitments.

Rose's most significant contribution to modern thought was her retrieval of Hegelian speculative experience, one that proposed a nonfoundational Hegel against the stereotype of the arch-thinker of master narratives, linear history, universal systems, and stagist dialectic. Her insistence that Hegel's thought was at heart speculative and suppositionless led to a later productive engagement with Søren Kierkegaard that refused to posit these two thinkers as mutually exclusive. Departing from a clichéd approach that would hold up Hegel as the master philosopher of a closed, totalized system (with Marx as his materialist heir) against which insurgents like Nietzsche and Derrida would rail against in the name of contingency, indeterminacy, and/or *différance*, Rose sought to reveal a Hegel that in fact always militated against abstract, universal dogmas.[3]

For Rose, the dismissal of modernity and reason exemplified by postmodern thought was not a tenable position; for all of modernity's contradictions and pitfalls, simply giving up on modernity in favor of its transcendental "Other" (whether it be difference over sameness, *écriture* over *logos*, particular identity over universality, the "Other" over self) solved nothing except to maintain the artificial antinomy between dualistic terms. Rose refused to maintain such dualistic thinking—to authentically engage with modernity was to sit with the discrepancies between ideal and actuality and to use the experience of these gaps to instruct oneself further. This, for Rose, was the essence of Hegel's speculative method: to observe and experience the never-ending interplay of natural consciousness as it seeks to ascertain the world through its own understanding and categories, with philosophical consciousness, which reveals the insufficiency of such understanding and thereby moves closer to the truth.

Bearing Rose's approach in mind may help us better comprehend Lu Xun's own approach to modernity and writing. Previously marshaled by the Maoist establishment as their posthumous mouthpiece of heroic, nationalist poetics, scholarship of recent decades has sought to portray a more singular, ironic, personalized Lu Xun fearful of the law of the crowd. I contend that Lu Xun's life and thought reveal an intensely speculative thinker, one who used the weight of experience to reevaluate given laws, norms, and dogmas. However, despite his critique of modernity's abstractions, he did not then abandon a commitment to modernity in favor of an

---

3. Gillian Rose, *The Broken Middle*, 5–7. As she points out, in elevating the priority of "contingency," "difference," of the "Other," such philosophical rebels only further install the purported authority of Hegel as philosopher of "System."

esoteric flight into obfuscation. While demurring from a heroic arrogation of personalized authority, he nevertheless persisted with a commitment to authorship. While revealing the hypocrisies of abstract laws and norms as they were cynically instrumentalized in market society, he did not then suggest we do away with all law, or all norms. His commitment to eternal struggle revealed a philosophical appreciation of the imperfect tense, whereby norms and experience continually condition and modify each other. It may seem somewhat arbitrary to deploy the insights of a British philosopher active well after Lu Xun's death; nevertheless, I contend that their work displays mutual resonances in how both gave witness to the contradictions and promises of modernity without relying on any metaphysical or transcendent crutch, even that of skepticism.

Lu Xun's thought grappled intensely with an imperfect secularity: a disavowal of faded superstitions and beliefs and yet an awareness that modernity was full of its own empty transcendental postulates. And while Lu Xun positioned himself as a follower of a disenchanted, skeptical modernity, he nevertheless acknowledged the importance of the need and striving for immanence and meaning. Within, Lu Xun abided an intensely complicated spiritual secularity and for which writing became a vehicle in its pursuit. To borrow a term from Vincent Lloyd, a major commentator on Rose's work, Lu Xun could be said to be engaged in an "immodest jurisprudence." By this is meant a concern for law that goes beyond the specific parameters of legality; questions of law and norm cannot help but be speculatively related to the concerns of metaphysics, immanence, and meaning.[4]

The rest of this chapter will proceed as follows. First, I discuss Rose's conception of "the severe style," taken from her reading of both Hegel's *Elements of the Philosophy of Right* and his *Aesthetics* to show the possible relationship between aesthetic irony and social critique. I contend that this conception of the "severe style" may be constructively applied to how Lu Xun's texts both affirm and critique the realist impulse in May Fourth letters. I use Lu Xun's 1926 essay "Why 'Fair Play' Should Be Deferred" to provide a case study for how Lu Xun's severe style could dismantle an abstract notion of normativity as exemplified by the ideal of "fair play." Next, I focus on the central text of investigation, a longer 1931 essay, "A Glimpse at Shanghai Literature." I consider how Lu Xun offers an immanent critique of literature, law, and coloniality in Shanghai cultural production. Finally, my chapter concludes by wondering whether an absolute horizon of modern norm and law can be salvaged by traversing their ruins.

---

4. Vincent Lloyd, *Law and Transcendence*, 27–28.

Speculative Exploration and the "Severe Style"

In *Hegel contra Sociology*, Rose contended that Hegel's writings about politics and the state are often misread as ordinary propositions about what the state is and should be. In particular, the statement in the preface in *Elements of the Philosophy of Right* that "the actual is rational" has mistakenly been read as an affirmation of the status quo.[5] Rose argued that Hegel was not trying to give a full narrative exposition of society as it is; instead, Hegel's political writings are written in what Rose termed the "severe style," a category she drew from Hegel's *Aesthetics*. When written in the severe style, the narrative and historical attenuations between elements are not spelled out for the convenience of the reader; rather, the clash of contradictions and inconsistencies are highlighted in order to present a more authentic picture of reality:

> The severe style is concerned to give a true representation of its object and makes little concession to the spectator. It is designed solely to do justice to the integrity of the object. It is distinguished from a "lofty" or "ideal" style which maintains the integrity of the object, but is concerned, too, that the representation should harmonize with the meaning. An object in the lofty or ideal style receives a more "complete exposition" than an object presented in the severe style.[6]

Rose extended the use of the severe style to make a case for the value of aesthetic irony, although Hegel charged Romantic irony with indulging in "absolute subjectivity" at the cost of ascertaining reality.[7] For Rose, aesthetic irony has value in upending "pleasing" forms of art that pretend a "pseudo-integrity of meaning and configuration." Irony read as a form of severity reveals the diremption between appearance and essence.[8]

Rose's discussion of the severe style may help to better understand how to account for Lu Xun's particular irony—especially when it is read as Lu Xun's surreptitious rejection of realism. Clearly, Lu Xun's prose cannot sit easily within the category of realism—the sharp irony, the laconic narrative exposition, the questioning of observation all militate against an overarching realist pretention to represent actuality. On the other hand, neither have I been comfortable with readings of Lu Xun as a poet of modern, alienated individualism. Perhaps a more convincing account would be that Lu Xun sought a "true," or at least "truer," representation of its object (social reality) by highlighting and concentrating its contradictions, fragmentations, and fissures. Following Marston Anderson, Lu Xun's ironic style pointed to realism's

---

5. Gillian Rose, *Hegel contra Sociology*, 79–81.
6. Rose, *Hegel contra Sociology*, 51.
7. Rose, *Hegel contra Sociology*, 146.
8. Rose, *Hegel contra Sociology*, 147.

own internal impediments. But although Lu Xun may have abandoned the ambition of a narrative exposition pleasing to the reader, he intended to use his work to compel the reader to confront uncomfortable truths. Robert Moore's study of Lu Xun's late-Qing translations reveals how Lu Xun initially sought to deploy mass market publishing to teach readers about the world through accessible entertainment.[9] However, Lu Xun eventually grew skeptical to what extent commodified reading culture could actually educate readers about society. In the 1920s, Lu Xun no longer sought pleasing, marketable forms of literature; when it came to translating foreign works, he preferred a "hard" style that confronted readers with cultural difference to jolt them out of linguistic and epistemic complacency. As such, Lu Xun's mature writings may be described as both "severe" and "hard"; let us not forget that first and foremost, Lu Xun was most severe to himself. But we should avoid seeing Lu Xun's oft-cited figure of "self-dissection" as a morbid form of self-flagellation, an introversion into self and exaltation of a "beautiful soul" through egoistic martyrdom.[10] Instead, self-dissection may be more productively read as an initial step toward a speculative recognition of self and world.

Severe Overkill: Lu Xun on "Fair Play"

A look at an earlier essay, Lu Xun's 1926 "Why 'Fair Play' Should Be Deferred," sheds light on Lu Xun's critique of universal norms that reveal themselves to be internally estranged. Here, Lu Xun's use of caustic and absurd irony exemplifies how the severity of his style translates into a broader conceptual critique. Lu Xun wrote in response to an essay by Lin Yutang 林語堂 (1895–1976), whereby the latter bemoaned the lack of a spirit of "fair play" in Chinese public discourse. The immediate context was public denunciation of the leadership of Beijing Women's College that allowed students to be beaten and then forcibly expelled from campus following a protest over the college's proposed closure. Eventually, the students were allowed back to the college after significant public criticism of school administrators. Lin's essay argued that Lu Xun's vituperative criticisms went beyond a gentlemanly critique of ideas and veered into personal attacks. He continued that in a spirit of fair play, one should not "beat a drowning dog" or otherwise attack a person already lying down.[11]

Lu Xun's response to Lin's call for evenhandedness was ironically to go the other way: he declared that drowning dogs should and must be beaten to death. His refusal to abide by the rules of polite discourse and his insistence on doubling down on the

---

9. Robert Moore, "Paris by Way of the Moon," 61–68.
10. Borrowed from Goethe, Hegel deployed the "beautiful soul" to denote a subject's withdrawal from an immoral world to preserve their sense of moral purity; this only results in such a soul's withering and dissolution. G. W. F. Hegel, *Phenomenology of Spirit*, 380–81 (para. 658).
11. Gloria Davies also discusses this essay in *Lu Xun's Revolution*, 225.

216   The Severe Style

idea of beating a suffering dog to death were designed to shock. But his real target was the untenability of a universal "fair play" when the game was itself rigged. Lu Xun's critique of "fair play" was in essence a demystification of a universal, liberal norm that came too cheaply, blithely oblivious to material conditions on the ground. This demystification takes the form of severe irony brought to the point of cruel absurdity.

Lu Xun argued that it was simply "too early" for the Chinese to adopt such a normative standard. He acknowledged the charge that he might be advocating a "double standard" (*erchong daode* 二重道德) by stating that fair play should be deferred.[12] But he noted the prevalence of such double standards in a Chinese society that was internally divided "between masters and slaves, and between men and women."[13] One way of understanding this critique is the impossibility of imposing a single, universal norm on a reality that is internally estranged and divided; the result is a universal norm that is itself dirempted from within. The idea that such a universal norm ought to be "deferred" (*huanxing* 緩行) invites a sense of temporal estrangement—a transcendent norm that should lie beyond time is revealed to be temporally conditioned. There is also linguistic estrangement: it was Lin Yutang who deployed a transliteration to render "fair play" as *fei'e polai*, much in the same way an anthropologist extracts a term from a source culture and elevates it into a technical term in a disciplinary context (e.g., "potlatch," "*guanxi*," etc.).[14] However, in Lu Xun's hands, the linguistic irony was only bolstered by the temporal and semantic estrangements that he bundled into the term.

In his critique of the "gentlemen" (*shenshi* 紳士) who would presume to deliver moral and ethical judgments from on high, Lu Xun pointed out that they were irredeemably split between speech and intention, form and content: "We may put aside for the moment the maxims of those gentlemen whose hearts are full of naked self-interest [婆理] but speak loudly of 'justice in the public interest' [公理]."[15] Here, Lu Xun pointed out that the gentlemen's pronouncements of justice (公理) constituted precisely their opposite. Rather than state the presumed antonym ("naked self-interest"), he instead played with another meaning of *gong* (公) as "maternal grandfather." Its conjugal counterpart, then, would be *po* (婆), or "maternal grandmother." However, this very observation of the inversion of "justice" was itself "put aside for the moment" (暫且置之不論不義之列)—that is, bracketed for the time being in the set of things not to be discussed. If the gentlemen make timeless moral

---

12. Lu Xun, "Lun 'fei'e polai' yinggai huanxing," 1:291. For a translation, see Lu Xun, "Why 'Fair Play' Should Be Deferred," 161.
13. Lu Xun, "Lun 'fei'e polai' yinggai huanxing," 291; "Why 'Fair Play' Should Be Deferred," 162.
14. Michael Silverstein offers a discussion of this phenomenon in "Translation, Transduction, Transformation," 92.
15. Lu Xun, "Lun 'fei'e polai' yinggai huanxing," 291; "Why 'Fair Play' Should Be Deferred," 162.

pronouncements that are themselves ridden with hypocrisy, then Lu Xun openly disavows, downplays, or minimizes the force of his own untimely speech acts.

Lu Xun's contention that "fair play" ought to be "deferred" begs the question, when was law to begin? Lu Xun's use of a severe style gave witness to a zeitgeist deeply at war with itself, where ordinary language simply failed to render justice to the complex, contradictory actuality of the world. His discursive tone would seem to elicit another question, a more uncomfortable one in the immediate background of aspirations toward nationalist language reform: when was logos to begin? One wonders whether the discursive "deferral" Lu Xun speaks of was an eternal one, a bad infinity that extends with no resolution in sight.

Laws, Norms, and the Ethics of Revolution

Lu Xun's 1931 essay "A Glimpse at Shanghai Literature" might be an odd place to seek the writer's thoughts about laws and norms. And yet an attentive reading of this essay will demonstrate the centrality of questions of law in regard to the development of modern aesthetics. Law relates to modern Chinese literature in two ways: (1) by founding the juridical conditions through imperialism that allow novel market relations to flourish and that become the material basis for a new class of professional writers and (2) by compelling us to reconsider the norms of literary genre in relation to other social norms. What ostensibly begins as an attempt to lay out the history of a unique locale of literature develops into an ironic critique of laws and norms.

Rose contended that Hegel advanced a critique of bourgeois formulations of law predicated on the universal principle of property rights. Property, according to Hegel, could not be a universal principle, for it is already defined as "private"; hence, the concept of private property as the universal basis of law was contradictory.[16] Bourgeois law and property condition a form of ethical life that regards itself as absolute. However, the internal contradictions of this form of ethical life reveals that it is not absolute but relative. Rose explained that Hegel used the distinction between "relative" and "absolute" ethical life to reveal the contradictions of natural law.[17] What thought itself to be "absolute" was revealed to be "relative," thus setting the stage for the possibility of a more genuine absolute possibility of ethical life. As one contemporary commentator of Rose notes, "Hegel's idea of an absolute ethical life [*absolute Sittlichkeit*] . . . does not refer to a 'known' infinite; on the contrary, it refers to an infinite that is always present, but not yet grasped—an infinite that should not be dismissed from the outset as unknowable."[18]

---

16. Rose, *Hegel contra Sociology*, 57.
17. Rose, *Hegel contra Sociology*, 51–52.
18. Kate Schick, *Gillian Rose*, 31.

218   The Severe Style

Lu Xun's attempt to outline the history of Shanghai's literature quickly detours into a meditation on laws and norms. Although counterintuitive, this makes deeper sense when we think about modern Shanghai's genesis as a treaty port, the product of the violent conjuncture of war and law. This founding of Shanghai afforded possibilities for new kinds of cultural production, which Lu Xun was quick to appreciate and recognize. However, it was not an uncritical recognition; Lu Xun's relation to the modern form of art, and by extension, his own profession, was thoroughly speculative.

In the beginning of this essay (which began as a two-part lecture), Lu Xun noted the divide between the "gentlemen" (*junzi*) and the "talents" (*caizi*).[19] The former adhered scrupulously to the traditional norms of classical education and the eight-legged essay. The latter, however, quickly tired of the strictures of tradition and flocked to new market opportunities of literary production made possible by Shanghai's emergence as a treaty port. Their precocious creativity mingled with pecuniary opportunism, and Lu Xun labeled these "talents" as "scholar-cum-hooligans" (*caizi + liumang* 才子 + 流氓).[20] For Lu Xun, the ignored diremption between aesthetic creativity and the circumstances of market exchange constantly compromised the scholar-hooligan's claim to cultural and moral authority. They sought to supplant the outdated *junzi* who wasted their time on fussy, formulaic eight-legged essays. And yet, their complicity with the political economy of colonial modernity rendered their claim to such authority empty.

Lu Xun's use of the term "hooligan" (*liumang* 流氓) suggested a connotation of "outlaw," those who flout both legal and ethical norms. However, as Lu Xun showed later in the essay, hooligans do not merely flout laws; they operate in the shadows and cracks between them, either instrumentalizing or ignoring them whenever it is more convenient. Moreover, these hooligans are characterized by a disavowal of the ethical and formal norms of classical education. In rejecting the "eight-legged essay," they refused to be bound by outdated generic rules that pertain to both writing and living. Classical essays and poetry were discarded in favor of more lucrative scholar-beauty romances that indulged in the travails of desire and commerce. However, whereas early novels of this type documented the lovelorn scholar at the behest of a fickle courtesan, the apotheosis of this genre culminated into a "textbook" whereby a scholar-hooligan could learn to deceive and take advantage of prostitutes.[21] What culminated was not just a new genre of literature but also a new social type distinguished by its own normative traits as well, the most prominent among them being

---

19. Lu Xun, "Shanghai wenyi zhi yi pie," 4:298–315. See also Lu Xun, "A Glimpse at Shanghai Literature," 225–37. Gloria Davies gives a summary of this essay in *Lu Xun's Revolution*, 100–102.
20. Lu Xun, " Shanghai wenyi zhi yi pie," 299.
21. Lu Xun, "A Glimpse at Shanghai Literature," 226; "Shanghai wenyi zhi yi pie," 299.

the relentless pursuit of self-interest. According to Lu Xun, this scholar-hooligan was already given visual representation in the *Dianshi Studio Pictorial* (點石齋畫報) series. Characterized by shifty, slanting eyes, Lu Xun argued that this visual type underwent further development in the hands of artists like Ye Lingfeng 葉靈鳳 (1905–1975) and drew on other cultural traditions, including the decadence of English artist Aubrey Beardsley (1872–1898) and Japanese "floating world" *ukiyo-e* woodblock prints.[22] The modern visual representation of the "scholar-hooligan" was therefore overdetermined by both indigenous and transnational aesthetic influences in an increasingly interconnected and global commercial culture. Moreover, as a social type, the scholar-hooligan emerged as a species that operated according to its own laws in much the same way an aesthetic genre follows certain normative expectations. What the sprawling social ferment of Shanghai offered was an alternative form of cultural *Bildung*, replete with a new set of genres and social types. Alongside came a form of cultural authority that rivaled traditional learning but that seemed to operate in the unseemly shadows of market society.

Lu Xun traced the genealogy of the scholar-hooligan throughout Shanghai's history and finally identified the Creation Society (Chuangzao she 創造社) as their contemporary progeny. While his barbed critiques against the Creation Society could veer toward hyperbole, here what Lu Xun was trying to emphasize was the discrepancy between the appearance of cultural authority and the realities of market-based publishing. Although the Creation Society thought they had aesthetic preeminence in Shanghai, their publishers quickly turned on them, thus revealing the level of financial subordination of artists to their publishing bosses.[23] Further along in Lu Xun's account, the forlorn members of the Creation Society devoted themselves to the cause of "revolutionary literature" but only when real revolutionary forces had been heavily suppressed by the Guomindang after 1927. Lu Xun deflated the pretentions of a revolutionary literary movement utterly disconnected from its social base; for Lu Xun, the turn to revolutionary literature was not a genuine conversion to a revolutionary cause but another form of opportunism that followed the norms of the scholar-hooligan type.

Lu Xun excoriated the inflated pretentions of newly minted "revolutionary" writers who arrogated to themselves cultural and moral authority. To illustrate his critique, he offered an anecdotal example about how the "law" was opportunistically invoked not for the purpose of upholding a categorical ethical imperative but as a pretense for extraction:

---

22. Lu Xun, "A Glimpse at Shanghai Literature," 227; "Shanghai wenyi zhi yi pie," 300.
23. Lu Xun, "A Glimpse at Shanghai Literature," 230; "Shanghai wenyi zhi yi pie," 303.

> When a Shanghai hoodlum sees a man and woman from the countryside walking together, he'll employ Chinese law and say, "Hey! The way you're acting is an offense against decency. You're breaking the law!" When he sees a man from the countryside urinating by the street and says, "Hey, that's not allowed. You're breaking the law," he is using foreign law. But the result has nothing to do with the law; as long as he extorts some cash, the matter is over.[24]

The "law" is subjected to private use and self-interest. When "Chinese" law does not do the trick, "foreign" law can substitute for it. In this example, Lu Xun sent up the emptiness of semicolonial jurisprudence, one that can be manipulated to justify any kind of profit seeking.

Why does an essay ostensibly devoted to narrating the history of Shanghai literature become enmeshed with discussions of law, revolution, and hooliganism? Ultimately, for Lu Xun, a discussion of Shanghai's literature could not be divorced from a larger consideration of ethical life that encompassed concerns about laws, customs, and politics alongside aesthetics. Lu Xun was asking how a society, one thoroughly ruptured by a traumatizing encounter with colonial modernity, settles on new norms for living and creating. But the force of his inquiry went further—if semicolonialism subtended a deeply ironic sense of diremption between form and content, old and new, native and foreign, what, then, was the character of a norm or law that would see itself as universal? The outdated Confucian norms embodied by the genre of the eight-legged essay were now replaced by domestic and foreign "laws" that were themselves unreliable.[25] Would-be cultural revolutionaries were simply the latest avatars of opportunistic "hooligans."

Lu Xun's ironic mockery of the "revolutionary writer" resonates with Hegel's account of the "spiritual-animal kingdom" (*die geistige Tierreich*) in *Phenomenology of Spirit*. By this, Hegel denoted a scenario in which an individual commits their action to a "matter at hand" (*die Sache selbst*)—their work thereby participates in a universal endeavor through which the individual wins recognition from others. However, this turns out to be a deception; what seems to be a commitment to an objective "matter" in fact veils over not only the level of self-interest involved in assuming a certain kind of work but also how the individual seeks to exclude others from participating in this work. As Hegel noted, "A consciousness that brings into the open a fact instead learns from experience that others come hurrying over like flies to freshly poured milk, and they too want to know themselves to be busily engaged with it."[26] Because the work aspires to universality and mutual recognition it is "spiritual"; however,

---

24. Lu Xun, "A Glimpse at Shanghai Literature," 232; "Shanghai wenyi zhi yi pie," 304–5.

25. Takeuchi Yoshimi makes a similar point discussing Lu Xun's critique of "fair play" in *What Is Modernity?* 50.

26. Hegel, *Phenomenology of Spirit*, 241 (para. 417). For a fuller discussion of the "spiritual animal kingdom," see Hegel, *Phenomenology of Spirit*, 228–42 (paras. 397–417).

in actuality, it merely dissimulates a particular struggle for domination, and hence it is "animal." For Rose, the spiritual animal kingdom expresses the effect of formal property law and its establishment of legal personhood. Such a law "looks as if it recognizes the universal or ethical. But since it is really only acknowledging the world to the extent that it is determined by the formal law of private property relation, it is only really acknowledging its own particular interests.... The law is thus deceptive, and consciousness, too, deceives itself and others."[27]

Lu Xun's unending ironic deferrals are apt to lead to a nihilistic conclusion: laws and norms are meaningless because the ideal is always at variance with reality. Under such conditions, revolutionaries that emerge are always revealed to be self-promoting charlatans. Lu Xun's consistent use of irony cannot help but suggest a picture of eternal, unrelenting estrangement, if not utter hopelessness. He presents a world that is constantly fracturing into estranged antinomies, where no law, and no word, can escape ironic inversion. Is this not the most postmodern state of affairs avant la lettre, a realm where nothing can be uttered without being immediately emptied out of meaning?

Perhaps it is too easy to note the hypocrisy of "hooligan" writers who justify their self-seeking pursuits under cover of law. The law becomes a mere plaything, manipulated and recklessly deployed, and thereby emptied of whatever immanent aura it might have once had. And yet the diremption that Hegel pointed out through the "spiritual animal kingdom" in fact alludes to the inescapable necessity of invoking a form of spiritual universality. Indeed, for these hooligans, why mention the law at all? Their instrumentalization of law only serves to reinforce the extent to which we are still subject to the law's ostensible normative authority.

Lu Xun's work presents a "path of despair" that always risks utter, total dissolution. However, it also seems that only by venturing through this harrowing terrain of disillusioniment that any hope for meaning, redemption, or justice can be found. For Lu Xun, "revolution" was a term of great difficulty but one that was nonetheless necessary. Just because revolutionary writers were compromised does not mean that revolution loses its actuality. He upheld the possibility of genuine revolutionaries who do the hard work of living alongside the oppressed.[28] The fact that genuine revolutionary impulses were brutally repressed only served to confirm the existence of a more absolute horizon of ethical and political possibility. Lu Xun dismissed those superficial "revolutionary writers" who claimed the mantle of revolution only so they could become authoritative givers of universal law that benefit particular ends. However, his insistence that there was real revolutionary work to be done seems to

---

27. Rose, *Hegel contra Sociology*, 176–77.
28. Lu Xun, "A Glimpse at Shanghai Literature," 234; "Shanghai wenyi zhi yi pie," 307.

222 The Severe Style

suggest the possibility of a real transformation that would create laws and norms in greater consonance with a renewed ethical life.

On the other hand, this possibility of absolute ethical life, embodied by the genuine "revolutionary," is only inferred obliquely. Certainly, in 1931 and with genuine revolutionary forces at a low ebb, the ability to make visible the revolution seemed close to impossible. And at no point did Lu Xun imply that he himself was a model for an authentic revolutionary writer. If anything, his critique of the scholar-hooligan also partially enacted a self-critique, for in addition to his opponents in the Creation Society, he himself thrived on the professional career paths made possible by semicolonialism. And yet the horizon of the absolute remains, even if it can only be represented in mediated and deferred expression. The essay on Shanghai literature began with the invocation of the fussy, outdated Confucian "gentleman" (*junzi*). It ends by inquiring as to the possibility of the genuine "revolutionary." These allegorical figures of both the past and the future speculatively determine each other. The "gentleman" embodied commitment to ethical principles long since discredited. The "revolutionary" represents the possibility of a figure to come who will bring forth new laws for a transformed nation and community. The past "gentleman" and future "revolutionary" seem ungraspable within the flow of time, and yet their existence is necessary for making the broken middle of the present knowable.

Lu Xun was critical of the idea of revolutionary literature as a given unity: those who would proclaim themselves revolutionary writers failed to understand the speculative relationship of identity *and* its lack between politics and art:

> "Revolution" and "literature," whether separated or linked together, are like two boats floating side-by-side, one marked "revolution," the other marked "literature." A writer stands with each foot in separate boats. When the environment is relatively good, an author will step more firmly on the boat of revolution and make it clear that he is a revolutionary. But once the revolution is suppressed, then he'll step a bit more firmly on the boat of literature and transform to being just a writer.[29]

The link between revolution and literature was a speculative proposition: those who readily affirm the identity between the two conceal their opportunism of leaning on one term over the other based on conditions. A more genuine, honest attempt at being a revolutionary writer would be to admit the difficulty of balancing on these two boats and stay upright.

---

29. Lu Xun, "A Glimpse at Shanghai Literature," 232; "Shanghai wenyi zhi yi pie," 305.

Venturing the Absolute

Lu Xun's brilliance as a writer in large part stemmed from his deeply sensitive appreciation and recognition of the diremptions of spirit that attended Chinese culture's ordeals in the early twentieth century. He had a keen eye for the ironic splits between form and content, and appearance and essence, that proliferated within a nation under constant turmoil. On the one hand, he identified the source of these diremptions within the vicissitudes of colonial modernity itself. But he also refused to retreat into a close-minded nationalist mythology as a form of resistance. His promotion of "take-ism" in regard to foreign culture was only opportunistic in an ironic sense.[30] The real sensibility of take-ism was an exhortation to recognize actuality beyond dogmatic confines of "Chinese" or "other." China's actuality toggled between the frames of the national, the colonial, and the universal all at once.

For Lu Xun, any hope of emancipation could not derive either from a nativist rejection of colonial influence or from an uncritical embrace of abstract, universal norms. Instead, it was only in the constant equivocal working through of actuality, in all its complexities, complicities, and contradictions, that the future could become visible. His critique of empty, hollow norms did not cancel a commitment to the possibility of renewed ethical norms that would guide China and the rest of humanity. In Lu Xun's decolonial "resistance" lurked the enduring horizon of the absolute, the eternal struggle to reconcile the splits between self and other, China and the world.

To return to the work of Gillian Rose, her philosophy toward the latter part of her career responded against what she thought of as postmodernism's abandonment of law and reason as hopelessly empty and obsolete. Rose was well aware of the contradictions of universal law but held on to a renewed conception of law that did not deny its own misrecognitions. To reject all law and reason was to flail about in eternal, restless melancholia. Instead, Rose countered with the idea of "inaugurated mourning" as an act that would reaffirm the possibility of law.

> The law, therefore, is not the *superior term* which suppresses the local and contingent, nor is it *the symbolic* which catches every child in the closed circuit of its patriarchal embrace. The law is the falling toward or away from mutual recognition, the triune relationship, the middle, formed or deformed by reciprocal self-relations.
>
> The law, therefore, in its actuality means full mutual recognition, "spirit" or ethical life, but it can only be approached phenomenologically as it appears to us, modern legal persons, by expounding its dualistic reductions. . . . There is no word

---

30. Lu Xun, "Take-ism," 281–83; "Nalaizhuyi," 6:39–42.

in the *Phenomenology* which appears in section titles as much as *the law* in all its various historical adventures—*the comedy of misrecognition*.[31]

Law cannot be approached transcendentally as a given norm that lies outside time, space, culture, or history. Law must be approached precisely in all its misprisions through a phenomenology that recollects all its comedic errors and only then painstakingly comes to some kind of self-knowledge. Lu Xun's ironic approach, one that makes frequent use of temporal deferrals and semantic inversions, constitutes perhaps something close to a phenomenological approach to the world in which he lived, one that sees how given ideas and norms are always subject to inversion occasioned by historical conditions.

Rose's return to Hegel was in large part inspired by her critique of sociology, a discipline she charged with merely reproducing neo-Kantian antinomies rather than seek to think them through and perhaps overcome them. The discipline of sociology located its roots in German idealism; however, as it developed into its own autonomous field, it abandoned the philosophical questions that lay at its heart, in particular questions about how one can come to know and recognize the actuality of the social. In doing so, it entrenched the antinomian separation between validity and values, object and subject. For Rose, any knowledge of the social must embrace the possibility of thinking the absolute:

> Hegel's philosophy has no social import if the absolute cannot be thought.... The absolute is the comprehensive thinking which transcends the dichotomies between concept and intuition, theoretical and practical reason. It cannot be thought (realized) because these dichotomies and their determination are not transcended.[32]

Let us not lose sight of what Lu Xun himself was doing as someone struggling to come to grips with actuality through the means of writing. There is something instructive, something salubrious, about the anxiety with which Lu Xun sought to recognize and express the actuality in which he was embedded and the anxiety with which he approached his ability of whether he could do this work. All the while, he tried to maintain the hope that the actuality he sought to represent through writing could be transformed for the better. His work constituted an attempt to confront both the world and himself, to recognize their contradictions and diremptions but not losing sight of the possibility of an absolute.[33] If there was a social content to Lu Xun's own critique, it was never divorced from his own anxieties of how we come to know and commit it to writing. Lu Xun's polemical critique can never be divorced

---

31. Gillian Rose, *Mourning Becomes the Law*, 75.
32. Rose, *Hegel contra Sociology*, 204.
33. Eileen J. Cheng's contribution to this volume affirms the impulse in Lu Xun's writing to give voice to a world "beyond" the confines of self. See Eileen J. Cheng, "Beyond Oneself."

from his own equivocal relation to his authorship. His life and work evince a commitment to the possibility of an absolute but coupled with the relinquishing of individual, possessive mastery.

Both Lu Xun and Rose wrote up to their premature deaths, one from tuberculosis, the other from cancer. For them, writing was a practice of surviving under the brokenness of modernity that offered sustenance precisely due to writing's anxious but honest fragility. A month prior to his death, Lu Xun wrote a short essay on the topic. He eschewed needless commemoration and its expenses, and he did not seek forgiveness or closure from his enemies. But he was firm in exhorting his readers to stay true to themselves and avoid hypocrites, those who would "harm others yet profess to oppose retaliation and to advocate tolerance."[34] As she neared her own death, Rose produced a final testimony and titled her book and her lifelong endeavor as *Love's Work*. As its epigraph, she featured a quote from the Russian Orthodox monk Siluan (1866–1938): "Keep your mind in hell, and despair not."[35] Both Lu Xun and Rose lived and wrote out their lives in the throes of *agon* and, perhaps, preferred it that way.

---

34. Lu Xun, "Death," 67; "Si," 631–35.
35. Rose, *Love's Work*, epigraph.

14
Lu Xun, Nonhumans, and the Critique of Domination

Christopher K. Tong

Most students of modern Chinese literature are familiar with Lu Xun, and most readers of Lu Xun recall at least one reference to nonhuman animals in his work. Indeed, Lu Xun's writings contain hundreds of nonhuman references spanning the zoological realm from livestock to wild beasts, from terrestrial beings to marine creatures, and from fowl to critters.[1] Lu Xun himself was given a number of animal names by peers in the literary circles of Republican China. He was first called an "owl" for drawing one and putting it on the cover of his 1927 anthology *Graves*.[2] Lu Xun was also associated with wolves for his misanthropic tendencies: literary critics often call him a "wounded wolf," an allusion to the short story "The Misanthrope."[3] If not for misanthropy, Lu Xun was certainly recognized for incisive satires and criticisms. From the late 1920s to his death in 1936, he and Liang Shiqiu 梁實秋 exchanged a series of polemics on Chinese politics, making liberal use of animal epithets in the process. Lu Xun earned animal names from friends and foes alike. Lin

---

1. I have compiled a list to illustrate the diversity of nonhuman references in Lu Xun's writings. Terrestrial creatures include dogs, cats, cows, oxen, mice, wolves, hyenas, sheep, goats, monkeys, apes, pigs, wild boars, porcupines, bats, bears, rabbits, badgers, foxes, lions, tigers, donkeys, horses, and deer. Marine creatures include crabs, fish, shrimp, and eels. Fowl include owls, crows, eagles, ducks, chickens, sparrows, geese, magpies, and pigeons. Critters and insects include toads, snakes, scorpions, ants, flies, maggots, moths, spiders, fleas, bedbugs, beetles, silkworms, mosquitoes, bees, cicadas, crickets, mantises, butterflies, and fireflies. Jin Xinlai offers a rough estimate of approximately two hundred types of nonhumans in Lu Xun's work. Jin Xinlai, *"Ren" yu "shou" de jiuge*, 10.
2. Lu Xun was drawn to owls since his student days because he identified with them as harbingers of bad omen. Lu Xun, *Fen*, 225.
3. Lu Xun, "Guduzhe," *LXQJ* 2:110. Qu Qiubai even compared him to "Remus, who was raised on the milk of a [lupine] beast." According to legend, Remus was murdered for mocking his twin brother, Romulus, for building the city of Rome. As quoted in Qian Liqun, *Qian Liqun zhongxue jiang Lu Xun*, 85.

Yutang 林語堂 once likened Lu Xun to a "white elephant" for effecting little change with his powerful writing.[4] Meanwhile, Lu Xun's domestic partner Xu Guangping 許廣平 recalled him embracing the epithet: he even nicknamed their newborn son "Little White Elephant" (but later changed the color to red). Lu Xun's best-known epithet is arguably a "child's ox" (*ruzi niu* 孺子牛), which he calls himself in the poem "Laughing at My Own Predicament." Alluding to a classical Chinese story about a parent's love for a child, Lu Xun compares himself to an ox that serves the people of China, albeit somewhat reluctantly. Nonhuman animals play a prominent role in Lu Xun's literary writing and sociopolitical critique.

In this chapter, I show how Lu Xun's references to animals form a constellation of ideas that critiques domination across species, national, and ideological boundaries. More specifically, I argue that Lu Xun's discourse of animality—from "barbarians" and "savages" to "fowl and beasts [*qinshou*]"—condemns various forms of human domination, including imperialism, colonialism, nationalism, and racism. Moreover, I analyze Lu Xun's polemics with the Crescent School author Liang Shiqiu on the issues of class, ideology, and political affiliation. Their respective use of animal epithets in their exchange constitutes a lens through which one could scrutinize the limits of coexistence between classes, between the Kuomintang (KMT) and the Chinese Communist Party (CCP), and between Chinese people and the party state. It is through the discourse of nonhumans, I suggest, that Lu Xun forwards some of his most piercing criticisms of Western, Japanese, and Chinese domination. As such, Lu Xun's animal imagery can be interpreted as meditations on the menace of war and colonialism and the political disunion of Republican China in the early twentieth century.

Nonhumans and the Critique of Domination

While scholars often characterize Lu Xun as an avid reader of world literature, less known is his history of engaging with Western scientific literature about nonhumans. Lu Xun wrote about zoology and evolutionary theory as early as 1907: he summarized major developments by Western scientists in a classical Chinese essay titled "The History of Humankind."[5] As James Pusey claims, Lu Xun's essay, which cited the likes of Linnaeus, Lamarck, Cuvier, Darwin, Huxley, and Ernst Haeckel, was among the most sophisticated accounts of evolutionary theory in China at the time, "far surpassing anything written by [Yan] Fu or Liang [Qichao]."[6] Lu Xun also

---

4. Qian Liqun, *Qian Liqun zhongxue jiang Lu Xun*, 75.
5. Lu Xun, "Ren zhi lishi," *LXQJ* 1:12–13.
6. James Reeve Pusey, *China and Charles Darwin*, 205. Interestingly, Lu Xun suggested that Darwin's theory was more developed than Lamarck's. Other texts on evolutionary theory would appear in subsequent years. Yang Yinhang's *On the Struggle for Existence* (*Wujing lun*), a Chinese summary and

enjoyed reading entomological and zoological literature. Among his favorites were the *Book of Insects* (*Souvenirs entomologiques*) by the French entomologist Jean-Henri Fabre and *Brehm's Life of Animals* (*Brehms Tierleben*) by the German zoologist Alfred Brehm. In fact, Lu Xun enjoyed reading Fabre's work so much that from 1924 until his death in 1936, he bought multiple copies of Fabre's book, including English and Japanese translations.[7] Indeed, Lu Xun was a pioneer in reading and writing about the animal kingdom in the early twentieth century.

Lu Xun's interest in nonhumans extended from scientific literature to children's literature as well. His well-cited friendship with the Ukrainian-Russian writer Vasyl Yeroshenko (Vasili Eroshenko) marked a turning point in his creative process.[8] As Qin Gong observes, Lu Xun's descriptions of landscapes and nonhuman characters became more sophisticated and frequent after his translation of Yeroshenko's stories for young readers.[9] Lu Xun was responsible for the Chinese translation of many other European fairy tales featuring animals and nonhuman characters. The fairy tale that left the deepest impression on Lu Xun was arguably Frederik van Eeden's *Little Johannes* (*De kleine Johannes*), first serialized in 1887 in the literary journal *The New Guide* (*De nieuwe Gids*). Lu Xun became acquainted with van Eeden's work as early as 1906 in Tokyo and would ultimately complete the Chinese translation of *Little Johannes* in the summer of 1927 with the help of his friend Qi Shoushan 齊壽山.[10] Lu Xun also participated in other translation projects: for instance, when *Two Legs* (*Liang tiao tui* 兩條腿) by the Danish novelist Carl Ewald was first serialized in the *Morning Post* (*Chen bao* 晨報) in 1925, Lu Xun assisted by proofreading the Chinese translation and checking it against the German translation.[11] These understudied habits of Lu Xun as a reader, writer, and translator, with some spanning decades, illustrate how important nonhumans were to him and his creative process.

Although Lu Xun's nonhuman references have generated a host of interpretations among scholars of modern Chinese literature and culture, they remain understudied as a whole. Contemporary critics have tended to analyze Lu Xun's

---

translation of Katō Hiroyuki, was published in Yokohama, Japan in 1901, while Ma Junwu's Chinese translation of Darwin's *Origin of Species* was published in 1920. See R. B. Freeman, "Darwin in Chinese"; P. J. P. Whitehead, "Darwin in Chinese"; Xiaoxing Jin, "Translation and Transmutation"; and my forthcoming book on the emergence of modern science and ecological consciousness in Chinese and Western societies.

7. Qin Gong, "Lu Xun de ertong wenxue fanyi."
8. See Andrew F. Jones, *Developmental Fairy Tales*, 152–74; and Vasily Eroshenko, *The Narrow Cage and Other Modern Fairy Tales*. For my interpretation of Lu Xun's autobiographical stories such as "The Comedy of Ducks" (*Ya de xiju* 鴨的喜劇), "Rabbits and Cats" (*Tu he mao* 兔和貓), and "Dogs, Cats, Mice" (*Gou mao shu* 狗·貓·鼠), see my forthcoming article on Lu Xun and children's literature.
9. Qin Gong, "Lu Xun de ertong wenxue fanyi," 88–89.
10. Qin Gong, "Lu Xun de ertong wenxue fanyi," 79.
11. Qin Gong, "Wusi shiqi de ertong wenxue fanyi (xia)," 25.

invocation of animals from the vantage points of the May Fourth movement and Chinese nation building. For Qian Liqun, Lu Xun's animals are ultimately expressions of a May Fourth humanism: Qian views Lu Xun's references to nature, including its "wild beasts" and "evil birds," as literary responses to the despair and moral degeneration suffered by the human self.[12] Traditionally, short stories such as "A Madman's Diary" and "Medicine" have been read as expressions of the dehumanization that Chinese people suffered and, at times, inflicted on one another. In both stories, human cannibalism, or the reduction of human beings to mere animal flesh, was Lu Xun's shorthand for the systemic exploitation that he witnessed in Chinese society. Canine figures—such as dogs, wolves, hyenas, and foxes in "A Madman's Diary"—are often read as metaphors for the basest instincts of human beings. For Lu Xun, the forces of domination came from abroad as well. Andrew F. Jones views Lu Xun's animal imagery as emblematic of modern China's semicolonial status in the early twentieth century. In Jones's interpretation, "animal training" symbolizes the process by which colonized peoples, like animals in captivity, are "enlightened"—or essentially "trained"—by Western powers to be modern.[13] In short, Lu Xun's animal imagery validates a spectrum of interpretative frameworks ranging from Chinese nation building to anti-colonial critique.

However, such interpretations of Lu Xun's nonhuman references risk perpetuating a degree of Chinese nationalism or exceptionalism in his critique of domination. That is to say, they contribute to a portrayal of Lu Xun as deploying nonhuman metaphors to center the Western victimization of Chinese people, when his critique of domination often applied more so to Chinese actors than to Western powers. The tendency of Lu Xun to criticize Chinese authorities was a prickly thorn from the vantage points of both Nationalist and Communist leaders. Whereas KMT censors had always found Lu Xun to be a nuisance, CCP members debated Lu Xun's political posturing internally and sometimes criticized his literary theories openly.[14] Indeed, the satirical nature of Lu Xun's essays was perceived as potentially derailing the CCP's mission to shore up literature as a domain of ideological work. In the Yan'an talks of 1942, Mao Zedong explicitly warned cadres, writers, and intellectuals against mimicking Lu Xun's style of "burning satire and freezing irony" and deploying it against the CCP and its allies.[15] From the Republican period to the Cultural Revolution and beyond, Lu Xun's writings have been read, disseminated,

---

12. Qian Liqun, *Qian Liqun zhongxue jiang Lu Xun*, 77. See also Qian Liqun, *Xinling de tanxun*, 214–27.

13. Andrew Jones, *Developmental Fairy Tales*, 150.

14. See Zhou Haiying, *Lu Xun yu wo qishi nian*, 4–5; and Jon Eugene von Kowallis, "Lu Xun," 153–57.

15. Mao Zedong, "From 'Talks at the Yenan Forum on Literature and Art,'" 36.

230 Lu Xun, Nonhumans, and the Critique of Domination

and deployed to divergent political ends.[16] This chapter adds yet one more twist to the reception of Lu Xun today.

The Discourse of Animality as Sociopolitical Critique

An article published on September 27, 1936 in the children's supplement of the *Shanghai Daily* (*Shen bao* 申報) infuriated the dying Lu Xun. In "What Elementary School Students Should Know" (*Xiao xuesheng men yingyou de renshi* 小學生們應有的認識), an author by the pen name of Meng Su 夢蘇 comments on a string of murders of Japanese nationals in the cities of Chengdu, Beihai, Hankou, and Shanghai.[17] Meng Su explains that it is "twice the crime" to kill a foreign citizen than a compatriot because it could damage diplomatic relations and even cause an international scandal. He urges Chinese citizens to observe the peace and asks other nations to do the same toward Chinese nationals abroad. Lu Xun read Meng Su's article, as he was suffering from an illness that would ultimately claim his life less than a month later. His reaction was so intense that despite having a fever, he penned a scathing response the same day.[18] "From the standpoint of the Chinese people," Lu Xun writes, "one should not value the lives of fellow citizens at half of those of foreign nationals [*zhi waiqiao de yiban* 值外僑的一半]."[19] This article would be known as Lu Xun's last piece of published writing.

From his 1907 essay "The History of Humankind" to his criticism of Meng Su in 1936, Lu Xun was preoccupied with the issues of humanity and animality. In fact, the last line in his last essay is no exception. Urging others not to mislead children about imperial Japan, Lu Xun writes, "Fellow adults, we were born with human heads [*shengzhe rentou* 生著人頭], so let us continue to speak like human beings [*jiang renhua* 講人話]!"[20] The truth, as we now know, is that imperial Japan escalated its occupation of China to a full-scale invasion less than a year later.[21] Meng Su's article not only encouraged a policy of appeasement but also misrepresented the urgency of the situation. In Lu Xun's view, Meng Su had inadvertently devalued the lives of fellow Chinese people through his expression of "twice the crime" and

---

16. See Merle Goldman, "The Political Use of Lu Xun"; Sebastian Veg, "New Readings of Lu Xun"; and Gloria Davies, "Lu Xun in 1966."

17. As quoted in Lu Xun, "Li ci cunzhao [qi]," 657–58.

18. Lu Xun's article was published on October 20, 1936, the day after his death; it was later anthologized in the volume *Essays from Semi-concession Studio, Supplement*. See Lu Xun, "Li ci cunzhao [qi]."

19. Lu Xun, "Li ci cunzhao [qi]," 658.

20. Lu Xun, "Li ci cunzhao [qi]," 659.

21. Imperial Japan invaded and occupied northeastern China on September 18, 1931. A full-scale invasion began on July 7, 1937, leading to the Nanjing Massacre in December later that year.

his appeal for peaceful coexistence. On September 28, Lu Xun mailed his essay to Li Liewen 黎烈文, the editor of a literary journal. He added an insult to the accompanying note: "This author [Meng Su] is truly an animal [*ci zuozhe zhen chulei ye* 此作者真畜類也]."[22]

For Lu Xun, the critique of domination among nations and cultures often comes through in the discourse of animality. More specifically, I argue that the discourse of animality and savageness in Lu Xun's essays criticizes various forms of domination, including imperialism, colonialism, nationalism, and racism. In "Impromptu Reflections No. 42," Lu Xun satirizes Western and Chinese discourses of the "savage." In the 1919 article, he mentions hearing from friends that a doctor at an Anglican church in Hangzhou called Chinese people "natives [*turen* 土人]" in his medical textbook.[23] Trained in medicine, Lu Xun acknowledges that the term originally carries no negative connotations since it refers to people indigenous to a particular land. However, the doctor allegedly used the term to mean "savage peoples [*yeman minzu* 野蠻民族]." Lu Xun, though uncomfortable with its humiliating tone, concedes that the "facts" do support such a claim. He enumerates vices and crimes in Chinese society such as cannibalism, polygamy, and opium smoking. He further ridicules the Chinese tradition of foot-binding, calling it "first rate" compared to the indigenous practices of tattooing and body modification. Lu Xun thereby reclaims the Western doctor's epithet for Chinese people, turning it into a legitimate critique of Chinese society and traditions.

As such, Lu Xun's criticisms put Chinese exceptionalism under scrutiny. In "Impromptu Reflections No. 48," Lu Xun analyzes the link between the trope of animality and Chinese attitudes toward non-Chinese peoples. In the 1919 article published under a pen name, Lu Xun observes how Chinese people have historically treated non-Chinese peoples as either "fowl and beasts" (*qinshou* 禽獸) or "lords and saints" (*shengshang* 聖上).[24] In other words, Chinese people are either superior or inferior to others: if they are not focused on their own humiliation and pain, then they are preoccupied with their supremacy. This narcissistic attitude underwrites what Lu Xun sees as Chinese people's treatment of other peoples: "We never call them friends and say that we are the same."[25] Historically, Han Chinese viewed non-Han peoples and ethnic minorities on the borderlands as savages or

---

22. *LXQJ* 14:157.
23. Lu Xun, "Suigan lu sishi'er," 343.
24. *LXQJ* 1:352.
25. *LXQJ* 1.352. Compare to what Barmé calls the "self-approbation and self-hate" of Chinese people. See Geremie R. Barmé, "To Screw Foreigners Is Patriotic," 219–21.

nonhumans.[26] In this essay, Lu Xun reminds readers that Chinese people are not in the position to see themselves as culturally or morally superior. As C. T. Hsia puts it, Lu Xun is "most piercing as an essayist when he is needling popular assumptions of national superiority and puncturing the dormant state of mind induced by centuries of cultural insularity."[27] Here, Lu Xun explicitly rejects associating non-Chinese peoples with barbarism or animality.

The critique of domination in human society and in the animal world intersects most clearly in the following text. On October 30, 1933, Lu Xun published a column titled "How to Train Wild Animals," for the *Shanghai Daily*.[28] In the column, Lu Xun criticizes Western domination of humans and nonhumans alike. He begins by citing the arrival of Carl Hagenbeck's circus in Shanghai and a recent lecture given by Richard Sawade, manager of the circus. Sawade is quoted as saying,

> Some may think that wild animals can be handled by force or by the fist, but to oppress them is a mistake, for this is the way in which primitives used to do things, and today's training methods are altogether different. The method we use now is the power of love, with which we can gain their trust in humans, for only the power of love and a gentle disposition will move them.
>
> 有人以為野獸可以用武力拳頭去對付它，壓迫它，那便錯了，因為這是從前野蠻人對付野獸的辦法，現在訓練的方法，便不是這樣。現在我們所用的方法，是用愛的力量，獲取它們對於人的信任，用愛的力量，溫和的心情去感動它們。[29]

Lu Xun compares Sawade's approach to animal training to traditional Chinese methods of governance. Lu Xun offers two models: the "way of the tyrant" (*badao* 霸道) and the "way of the sovereign" (*wangdao* 王道). Tyrants use violence to dominate others, while sovereigns persuade subjects to follow their rule. In Lu Xun's interpretation, Sawade's approach is closer to *wangdao* since he opposes the use of physical force against nonhumans. At the same time, what Sawade calls the "power of love" (*ai de liliang* 愛的力量) is in reality a subtle form of domination and control. Lu Xun is quick to point out its irony: after gaining the nonhumans' trust, circus

---

26. In the late 1930s, the Nationalist government began to modify terms for ethnic minorities that may be regarded as discriminatory. For instance, Chinese characters for ethnic minorities often included nonhuman radicals used to describe insects, dogs, cows, horses, and sheep. Anthropologists such as Rui Yifu 芮逸夫 proposed removing the nonhuman radicals or replacing them with the human radical. See Rui Yifu, "Xinan shaoshu minzu chongshou pianpang mingming kaolüe." On Han Chinese perceptions of non-Chinese peoples historically, see William C. Cooper and Nathan Sivin, "Man as a Medicine"; Frank Dikötter, "Hairy Barbarians, Furry Primates, and Wild Men"; Yuri Pines, "Beasts or Humans"; Magnus Fiskesjö, "The Animal Other"; and Carla Nappi, "On Yeti and Being Just."

27. C. T. Hsia, *A History of Modern Chinese Fiction*, 46.

28. Lu Xun, "Yeshou xunlian fa," 384–86.

29. As quoted in Lu Xun, "Yeshou xunlian fa," 384.

trainers transform them into performers who have no choice but to live and work in captivity. For Andrew F. Jones who relates Lu Xun's text to the semicolonized status of Republican China, "animal training stands in for the process by which the backward are made 'forward,' benighted nations are enlightened, and colonial subjects are trained for modern life."[30] Lu Xun, through his critique of Sawade's animal training techniques, explains how the veneer of peaceful coexistence between humans and nonhumans, and between rulers and subjects, can conceal differentials in power and status.

Ultimately, Lu Xun's essay on animal training finds its sharpest point as an oblique critique of state domination. While Jones focuses on Lu Xun's critique of Western colonialism, I suggest that Lu Xun indicts the Chinese state as well. Lu Xun likens Sawade's "power of love" to the Chinese term *mu* 牧, meaning "to herd livestock." For Lu Xun, the domination of rulers over subjects, and of humans over nonhumans, culminates in the ironic metaphor of animal herding. In classical Chinese, the term *mu* refers not only to the herding of farm animals but also to the governing of state subjects.[31] Whereas wild animals are to be forcibly tamed, farm animals are to be managed and exploited in the most civilized way possible. To differentiate this method of governance from *badao* and *wangdao*, Lu Xun satirically proposes a third one called *weixin* 威信, or "prestige." Lu Xun considers *weixin* to be a form of "civilized" domination: one that elicits compliance through the show of force and its accompanying propaganda. For Lu Xun, this form of domination is more sinister than physical violence, since nonhuman subjects have no pretext to fight back. Unlike wild animals, farm animals do not have the agency to be "wild"—that is, to resist or disobey. Under the rule of *weixin*, domesticated creatures readily offer their milk, flesh, and labor without resistance. Lu Xun's implication is that human subjects could be managed and exploited in the same way. While Lu Xun's text criticizes the abuse of nonhumans on one level, it engages the discourse of state domination on another level. Although Lu Xun does not explicitly name the Chinese state or a Western colonial power in the text, the training of animals functions as a veiled critique of a state's domination over its human subjects.

Animal Epithets in the Polemics between Lu Xun and Liang Shiqiu

Animal epithets find their most intense and politically risky use in the polemics between Lu Xun and Liang Shiqiu from the late 1920s to 1936, the year of Lu Xun's

---

30. Andrew Jones, *Developmental Fairy Tales*, 150.
31. Lu Xun, "Yeshou xunlian fa," 386n5. As the editor's footnote indicates, the term *mu* refers to a governor's position among ancient Chinese states.

234 Lu Xun, Nonhumans, and the Critique of Domination

death. In modern Chinese literary history, Lu Xun and Liang represented opposite ends of the ideological spectrum. While Lu Xun never joined the CCP, he was widely seen as the figurehead of Chinese leftism. In contrast, Liang belonged to the Crescent School, an elite circle of Chinese authors and intellectuals educated in Europe and the United States, having himself received a doctoral degree in English from Harvard University. Liang would eventually move to Taiwan and subsequently translated Shakespeare's complete works. Lu Xun and Liang's polemics tended to revolve around three issues—namely class, humanism, and translation.[32] They debated these issues for nearly a decade, exchanging more than a hundred essays.

State domination and class ideologies were debated in a series of heated exchanges from 1929 to 1930. After the Nationalist government began to purge and assassinate writers associated with the Communist movement in 1927, literary studies became an ideological minefield. Animal epithets, especially those of the canine variety, were deployed liberally. When Liang Shiqiu questioned whether leftist writers truly promoted "classless" literature in his 1929 essay "Does Class Really Exist in Literature?" the Communist writer Feng Naichao called Liang a "capitalist's dog [*ziben jia de zougou*]." As a rejoinder, Liang penned a satirical piece titled "A Capitalist's Tired Dog" (*Ziben jia de fa zougou* 資本家的乏走狗) in which he jokes about a tired dog looking for a master who would pay in "rubles." Through this one loaded word, Liang insinuated that some Chinese leftist writers were secretly working for the Soviet Union, a serious accusation at the time that could draw the attention of Nationalist authorities. While Lu Xun initially tried to prevent the exchange from escalating, he himself joined the fray in 1930 with the essay "An Exhausted Stray Dog of the Capitalists." In the text, Lu Xun suggests that all capitalists' dogs, even those without masters, by habit serve the rich and bark rabidly [*kuangfei*] at the poor.[33] Although reiterating Feng's canine epithets, Lu Xun minimizes political escalation by emphasizing that these dogs are "without masters [*sangjia de*]." That is, none of the authors involved in the polemics are acting on the behalf of a state or party. In doing so, Lu Xun attempts to contain the political fallout of such a heated literary exchange.

Despite Lu Xun's efforts at deescalation, Liang Shiqiu followed up with another polemic, this time using a different animal epithet. In the 1930 essay "Lu Xun and Cattle" (*Lu Xun yu niu* 魯迅與牛), Liang writes, "Actually, I do not know whose grass Mr. Lu Xun is munching on or to which party he belongs. I do not know, and I do not want to know."[34] By feigning ignorance, Liang calls attention to Lu Xun's unspoken

---

32. Li Zhao, *Lu Xun Liang Shiqiu lunzhan shilu.*

33. Lu Xun invokes the term *kuang* that he uses in "A Madman's Diary." In classical Chinese, *kuang* refers to a rabid dog that barks at everyone, unable to recognize its master. Ironically, the "capitalist's dog" is able to distinguish between rich and poor people.

34. Liang Shiqiu, "Lu Xun yu niu," 161.

political stance. Liang ends the essay by noting that Lu Xun has to date refused to criticize "one particular party."[35] In short, Liang is challenging Lu Xun to declare his political affiliation. Given the Nationalists' bloody crackdown of Communists and their sympathizers at the time, Liang's accusations were not merely serious but could potentially endanger Lu Xun's life. In any case, Lu Xun continued to refrain from joining any political party officially.

While Liang Shiqiu's insinuations were perceived as recklessly courting the attention of KMT authorities, he rightly detected a degree of political ambivalence in Lu Xun's writings. In particular, Lu Xun's use of bovine imagery sheds light on his complex political orientation. In the 1926 essay "The Origin of 'The Story of Ah Q,'" Lu Xun introduces the metaphor of the "tired ox" to explain his personal and political motivations. Lu Xun outlines three conditions under which the so-called tired ox would perform labor for others: (1) that he must not work too hard (i.e., do more than he is willing to or is capable of), (2) that he must not belong to any one family (i.e., political party), and (3) that he must not sell his flesh (i.e., be a martyr for a cause).[36] If these conditions are met and the task does not cause harm to others, then the tired ox would gladly help one family or another. In other words, Lu Xun attempts to declare his independent or noncommittal position regarding politics. With a touch of off-color humor, Lu Xun even jokes that the ox is willing to pose as a dairy cow, if the "milk" produced is drinkable.[37] Otherwise, Lu Xun says, the ox would rather run away and hide in the mountains. Lu Xun's metaphor belies an uncompromising individualism. To preserve his autonomy, Lu Xun says that he would rather descend "from being profound to being superficial, from a fighter to a domesticated animal [chusheng]."[38] That is to say, Lu Xun would rather not live up to his lofty reputation than to be controlled by it.

Another reference sheds additional light on Lu Xun's bovine imagery. The term ruzi niu, or a "child's ox," is arguably the most cited animal epithet associated with Lu Xun. Its prominence stems from his 1932 poem "Laughing at My Own

---

35. Liang Shiqui, "Lu Xun yu niu," 162. It appears that Liang Shiqiu was targeting Lu Xun's posture of political ambiguity. That is to say, if Lu Xun were truly sympathetic to the CCP cause, then he should criticize the KMT more explicitly. Otherwise, if Lu Xun had no interest in joining the CCP, then he should feel free to be more critical of it. In this sense, "one particular party" could refer to either party.

36. Lu Xun, "A Q zhengzhuan de chengyin," 394–95.

37. If it helps to state the obvious, bulls produce all types of bodily fluids but milk. I was surprised to encounter what was essentially a "dirty joke" by Lu Xun. It illustrates the broad range of Lu Xun's humor and sensibilities that should be preserved rather than ignored or sanitized by literature scholars. On the techniques of mockery used by authors such as Lu Xun, Lin Yutang, and Liang Shiqiu, see Christopher Rea, The Age of Irreverence, 80–84.

38. Lu Xun, "A Q zhengzhuan de chengyin," 395.

Predicament" in which the speaker agrees to a life of service as a "child's ox." The poem's most famous couplet is as follows:

橫眉冷對千夫指　　　Frowning coldly at a thousand pointing fingers,
俯首甘為孺子牛　　　I bow my head and willingly serve as a child's ox.[39]

Mainstream interpretations have interpreted this couplet as Lu Xun's acceptance of his role as a "servant of the [Chinese] people" and his endorsement of Chinese leftism.[40] However, the circumstances were more complicated in reality. Lu Xun had been reluctant to align with Chinese leftists before 1927 and only accepted his position as the figurehead of the Chinese League of Leftist Writers in the early 1930s. Even so, some of the league's members such as Zhou Yang had openly criticized Lu Xun and continued to do so until his death. In this context, the "child's ox" signals complexity in the relationship between Lu Xun and Chinese leftism.[41] Originally, the "child's ox" is intended to signify a loving parent's willingness to appear submissive to the child. In the *Commentary of Zuo*, Duke Jing of the State of Qi is said to be playing with his son one day and lets the child ride on his back like an ox. However, the child falls off accidentally and yanks on the harness, pulling out several of the duke's teeth in the process. Not only is the duke not angry with him, but he eventually names the boy as his successor. This story, at first glance, follows the trajectory of Lu Xun's famous call to "save the children." However, given Lu Xun's troubled relationship with the Leftist League, his evocation of the "child's ox" appears to be a mixed signal.

In my view, the poem's references to bowing one's head, being pointed at, and working as a child's ox indicate more acquiescence than acceptance, more struggle than service. If one compares Lu Xun's use of bovine metaphors in his literary works and in his private life, the "child's ox" in "Laughing at My Own Predicament" becomes even more dissonant. Indeed, the use of bovine metaphors in Lu Xun's private correspondence tends to convey a degree of grievance. For instance, Lu Xun's domestic partner, Xu Guangping, recalls him saying, "I am very much like an ox. I eat grass and squeeze out [*jichu*] milk and blood."[42] Here, Lu Xun likens his creative process to an act of self-sacrifice. Moreover, Lu Xun was known to complain about the lack of respect he would receive for his sacrifices. In a December 16, 1926 letter to Xu Guangping, Lu Xun laments the criticisms directed toward him: "I used

---

39. Jon Eugene von Kowallis, *The Lyrical Lu Xun*, 202–8.
40. Jin Xinlai, *"Ren" yu "shou" de jiuge*, 21–23.
41. For a summary of Lu Xun's complicated relationship with the Leftist League and Zhou Yang, see Gloria Davies, *Lu Xun's Revolution*, 209–14. Other scholars have given various explanations as to why Lu Xun accepted his position in the Leftist League. See Leo Ou-Fan Lee, "Literature on the Eve of Revolution"; and Wang-chi Wong, *Politics and Literature in Shanghai*, 39–58.
42. Xu Guangping, *Xu Guangping wenji*, 2:3.

to feed others with my blood. Although I grew weaker, I was glad to do so. But now, they ridicule me for being thin and weak. Even those who fed on my blood laugh at me now."[43] Lu Xun's evocation of the "child's ox" should be read with the above contexts in mind. In other words, while Lu Xun accepted his status as a champion of Chinese leftism, he also acknowledged through the dissonant metaphor the costs to his autonomy and well-being. Indeed, Lu Xun's health deteriorated in the last months of his life, as he continued to spar with critics. As T. A. Hsia notes, Lu Xun's weight was barely 85 pounds when he died.[44] When Lu Xun's bovine references are analyzed in conjunction, a rather heterodox narrative of Lu Xun's life and work emerges.

Ultimately, the polemics between Lu Xun and Liang Shiqiu find a modicum of resolution in the companionship of nonhuman beings. Despite their ideological differences, both Lu Xun and Liang spoke fondly of childhood experiences with nonhuman animals. In his autobiographical essay "Dogs, Cats, Mice," Lu Xun speaks fondly of the mice that he found in his house as a ten-year-old. Like Lu Xun, Liang Shiqiu expressed a deep interest in nonhumans in his essays. Whereas the young Lu Xun enjoyed the company of mice, Liang's family kept two dogs and a monkey as companions. In "Befriending Animals" ("Yu dongwu wei you" 與動物為友), Liang discusses the deep bond between humans and nonhumans. While he recalls befriending animals as a child, Liang regrets as an adult that his nonhuman companions were locked up in a room or a cage. As in Lu Xun's essay "How to Train Wild Animals," Liang recognizes the harm of keeping nonhumans in captivity. Perhaps, on the account of nonhumans, the literary rivals could posthumously find some common ground.

Coda

Originally trained as a physician, Lu Xun showed an early interest in evolutionary theory and zoology and wrote some of his earliest works on the animal kingdom during the Qing-Republican transition. As Lu Xun's literary reputation grew in the late 1910s and 1920s, nonhumans began to appear in his poems, fables, short stories, and essays, forming new constellations of meaning in the process. Lu Xun, ever a keen observer of Chinese politics and a formidable wielder of the pen, would often employ animal references to discuss politically complex topics, sparring with critics across the political spectrum. Although Lu Xun ultimately aligned himself with Chinese leftism in the early 1930s, he resisted joining any one political party officially. As this chapter has shown, Lu Xun's writings about nonhuman animals not

---

43. *LXQJ* 11:253.
44. Tsi-an Hsia, *The Gate of Darkness*, 145.

only criticized domination across species, national, and ideological boundaries, but they also probed the conditions for coexistence between compatriots and rivals at a time when the young Chinese republic remained fragile. Today, Lu Xun is memorialized in the PRC as a cultural figurehead of Chinese Communism, but his legacy is—and ought to be—much more complex than that. This chapter has drawn on a broad range of Lu Xun's texts over the course of his career and assembled a constellation of his understudied animal references. Through the figurative language of nonhuman animals, Lu Xun's sociopolitical commentary, including his critique of domination, remains as incisive as ever.

Postface

Carlos Rojas

When Xiao Nan, the protagonist of Ng Kim Chew's 2015 short story "Benediction," enters the elaborate replica of a Lu Xun memorial museum that her stepfather, Ah Fu, has created in his home in Malaysia, the first thing she notices is the Chinese author's portrait: "On the wall was hanging Lu Xun's postmortem portrait (the one with whiskers)."[1] A wide array of postmortem images of Lu Xun entered public circulation after his death, including numerous photographs, sketches, and woodblock prints, but the story's parenthetical specification that the portrait Xiao Nan sees is "the one with whiskers" clarifies that the image in question is actually the plaster death mask created by Okuda Kyōka, which is currently on display at the Lu Xun Memorial Museum in Shanghai (Figure 15.1).[2]

Ng's story comments on the various sorts of vestigial literary and cultural connections that may link ethnic Chinese in Southeast Asia to their putative Chinese homeland, but the story's emphasis on the replica of Lu Xun's death mask underscores a more specific dimension of the author's work and its multiple afterlives. Unlike most of the other images that were produced of Lu Xun after his death, the death mask Okuda produced is one of the few such portraits that not only bears a visual resemblance to Lu Xun but also contains material traces of his bodily presence—in the form of the handful of mustache and eyebrow hairs that got stuck in the plaster mold when it was removed from his face. Whereas most of the other postmortem images are—to use the influential "icon-index-symbol" semiotic taxonomy proposed by Samuel Peirce—primarily "iconic" in nature, meaning that they are linked to their referent by their visual resemblance, the death mask produced by Okuda is a signifier that is not only iconic but also indexical, meaning that its relationship to its referent is defined by a direct causal relationship (in this case,

---

1. Ng Kim Chew, "Zhufu," 25.
2. For an overview of Lu Xun's postmortem images, including the death mask, see Yiwen Liu, "Witnessing Death."

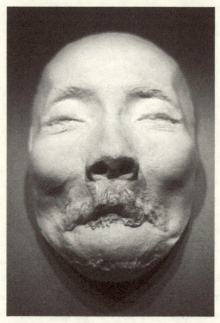

Figure 15.1: Death mask of Lu Xun, cast in plaster by Okuda Koka

the process of making a physical mold of Lu Xun's face).[3] The version of the death mask that is described in Ng's story, however, is not the original artifact that was produced on the day of Lu Xun's death, but rather it is a reproduction—meaning that it is an iconic signifier of an earlier signifier that had a simultaneously iconic and indexical relationship to its referent. Moreover, technically speaking, what appears in Ng's story is not even Ah Fu's reproduction of Okuda's original death mask, but rather it is Ng's textual description of Ah Fu's reproduction of the original death mask—meaning that Ng's reference to the mask is, in Peirce's terms, a "symbolic" signifier that is linked to the physical mask by the completely arbitrary and unmotivated sign system that is human language. What appears in Ng's story, in other words, is a symbol signifying an icon signifying a hybrid icon-index signifying Lu Xun's face—which, in turn, functions as a symbol of the author himself.

In the opening allusion to the death mask in Ng Kim Chew's story, we find a succinct allusion to a complex set of overlapping semiotic processes by which Lu Xun's life and work have entered global circulation following his death. From an almost fetishistic fascination with material relics linked directly to the author, to

---

3. Peirce developed his theory of semiotics over a span of many volumes. For an overview, see Short, *Peirce's Theory of Signs*.

a wide array of distant and highly mediated reimaginations of his works, Lu Xun's postmortem legacy is as eclectic as the author's literary oeuvre itself. If we regard Lu Xun's literary oeuvre as his public face, accordingly, then we may take inspiration from Ng's description of the Malaysian re-creation of Lu Xun's death mask and describe the postmortem global circulation of Lu Xun's legacy as his "post-face." Far from a singular and unitary phenomenon, however, the author's post-face is the result of multiple overlapping, and often divergent, processes of reproduction and transformation, as text-based, theme-based, image-based, and ideology-based lines of filiation intersect with one another in complex and unpredictable ways.

Lu Xun's son, Zhou Haiying, who was just seven at the time of his father's death, has described how when he first noticed his father's hairs stuck to the plaster mold that Okuda had made, he "felt very uncomfortable, as though the hairs had been plucked from my own body."[4] This description of the son's discomfort underscores the sort of vicarious identification that Lu Xun's legacy was capable of inspiring, not only among those who were close to him, like is son, but also putative strangers. At the same time, Zhou's description of feeling as though the hairs had been "plucked from [his] own body" recalls one of the trademark powers of Sun Wukong, the supernatural simian protagonist of the classic Ming dynasty novel *Journey to the West*, who was able to pluck hairs from his body and transform them into clones of himself or "whatever shape or substance he desired."[5] Known as his "body beyond the body technique" (身外身法), this practice refers to Sun Wukong's ability to project his identity beyond himself—with these projections ranging from exact replicas to unrecognizable transformations. Lu Xun, meanwhile, could be viewed as a modern-day Sun Wukong, with his texts being the equivalent of the monkey's hairs, and as Lu Xun's texts circulate to distant regions and future eras, they have similarly undergone a nearly endless process of translation and transformation.

Just as Sun Wukong's nominal function in *Journey to the West* is to accompany his master Tang Sanzang—who is a fictionalized version of the historical seventh-century Chinese monk Xuanzang—on his quest to the "Western Regions" (South and Central Asia) to retrieve Buddhist sutras from and bring them back to China, Lu Xun similarly remained deeply committed throughout his career to the process of introducing foreign literature into China. Conversely, just as Sun Wukong has subsequently become one of the Chinese fictional characters who has been most enthusiastically embraced in cultural productions from around world, Lu Xun is similarly one of twentieth-century China's most globally influential authors. At the same time, Sun Wukong and Lu Xun both embody a crucial paradox wherein their very identity has come to be defined by their powers of transformation, and whereas Sun

---

4. Zhou Haiying, "Chonghui Shanghai yi tongnian," 1271.
5. *Journey to the West*, trans. Anthony Yu, 1:128.

242   Postface

Wukong's identity is grounded on his powers of self-transformation, a key element of Lu Xun's postmortem popularity similarly lies in his ability to signify different things for different readers. The primary continuity in the countless filiations—or postfaces—that Lu Xun's work has spawned, accordingly, lies in their insistent and inexorable process of transformation and reinvention.

Appendix

Chinese Characters of Lu Xun's Names, Pen Names, and Work Titles Cited in This Volume

Lu Xun's Names and Pen Names

Ling Fei 令飛
Lu Xun 魯迅
Yucai 豫才
Yushan 豫山
Yuting 豫亭
Zhijiangsuoshi 之江索士
Zhijiangsuozi 之江索子
Zhou Chuo 周逴
Zhou Shuren 周樹人
Zhou Zhangshou 周樟壽

Publications (in Chronological Order by Volume)

From the Earth to the Moon (*Yuejie lüxing* 月界旅行, 1903) (translation)
Voyage to the Center of the Earth (*Dixin lüxing* 地心旅行, 1903) (translation)
Anthology of Fiction from beyond the Border (*Yuwai xiaoshuo ji* 域外小説集, 1909)
    (translation collection, with Zhou Zuoren)
Outcry (*Nahan* 吶喊) (1923)
    "Diary of a Madman" (*Kuangren riji* 狂人日記, 1918)
    "An Incident" (*Yi jian xiaoshi* 一件小事, 1919)
    "Kong Yiji" (*Kong Yiji* 孔乙己, 1919)
    "Medicine" (*Yao* 藥, 1919)
    "A Passing Storm" (*Fengbo* 風波, 1920)
    "The Story of Hair" (*Toufa de gushi* 頭髮的故事, 1920)
    "Tomorrow" (*Mingtian* 明天, 1920)
    "My Old Hometown" (*Guxiang* 故鄉, 1921)
    "Dragon Boat Festival" (*Duanwu jie* 端午節, 1922)
    "The Rabbits and the Cat" (*Tu he mao* 兔和貓, 1922)
    "The True Story of Ah Q" (*Ah Q zhengzhuan* 阿Q正傳, 1922)
    "Village Opera" (*Shexi* 社戲, 1922)
    Preface to *Outcry* (*Nahan zixu* 《吶喊》自序, 1923)

244 Appendix

A Brief History of Chinese Fiction (*Zhongguo xiaoshuoshi lüe* 中國小說史略, 1925)
Hot Wind (*Refeng* 熱風, 1925)
    "Impromptu Reflections No. 42" (*Suigan lu sishi'er* 隨感錄四十二, 1919)
    "Impromptu Reflections No. 48" (*Suigan lu sishiba* 隨感錄四十八, 1919)
    "Impromptu Reflections No. 49" (*Suigan lu sishijiu* 隨感錄四十九, 1919)
Hesitation (*Panghuang* 彷徨, 1926)
    "A Happy Family" (*Xingfu de jiating* 幸福的家庭, 1924)
    "New Year's Sacrifice" (*Zhufu* 祝福, 1924)
    "Soap" (*Feizao* 肥皂, 1924)
    "Upstairs in the Tavern" (*Zai jiuloushang* 在酒樓上, 1924)
    "The Divorce" (*Lihun* 離婚, 1925)
    "The Lamp of Eternity" (*Changming deng* 長明燈, 1925)
    "Master Gao" (*Gao laofuzi* 高老夫子, 1925)
    "The Misanthrope" (*Guduzhe* 孤獨者, 1925)
    "Regrets for the Past" (*Shangshi* 傷逝, 1925)
Inauspicious Star (*Huagai ji* 華蓋集, 1926)
Graves (*Fen* 墳, 1927)
    "The History of Humankind" (*Ren zhi lishi* 人之歷史, 1907)
    "On Imbalanced Cultural Development" (*Wenhua pian zhi lun* 文化偏至論, 1907)
    "On the Power of Mara Poetry" (*Moluo shili shuo* 摩羅詩力說, 1907)
    "What Happens after *Nuola* Leaves Home?" (*Nala zouhou zenyang* 娜拉走後怎樣,
        1923)
    Afterword to *Graves* (*Xiezai Fen houmian* 寫在墳後面, 1926)
    "On the 'Why "Fair Play" Should Be Deferred' That Should Be Slowed Down" (*Lun
        "fei'erpolai" yinggai huanxing* 論"費厄潑賴"應該緩行, 1926)
Sequel to Inauspicious Star (*Huagai ji xu bian* 華蓋集續編, 1927)
Wild Grass (*Yecao* 野草, 1927)
    "Autumn Night" (*Qiuye* 秋夜, 1924)
    "Hope" (*Xiwang* 希望, 1925)
    "The Passerby" (*Guoke* 過客, 1925)
    "Tremors on the Border of Degradation" (*Tuibai xian de chandong* 頹敗線的顫動, 1925)
Dawn Blossoms Plucked at Dusk (*Zhaohua xi shi* 朝花夕拾, 1928)
    "Ah Chang and the *Classic of Mountains and Seas*" (*Ah Chang yu Shanhaijing* 阿長與
        《山海經》, 1926)
    "Dogs, Cats, Mice" (*Gou mao shu* 狗·貓·鼠, 1926)
    "Fan Ainong" (*Fan Ainong* 范愛農, 1926)
    "Professor Fujino" (*Tengye xiansheng* 藤野先生, 1926)
And That's All (*Eryi ji* 而已集, 1928)
    "Revolutionary Era Literature" (*Geming shidai de wenxue* 革命時代的文學, 1927)
The Torrent (*Benliu* 奔流, 1928–1929) (journal coedited with Yu Dafu)
Destruction (*Huimie* 毀滅, 1931) (translation)
Three Leisures (*San xian ji* 三閑集, 1932)
    "Voiceless China" (*Wusheng de Zhongguo* 無聲的中國, 1927)

Two Hearts (*Er xin ji* 二心集, 1932)

"An Exhausted Stray Dog of the Capitalists" (*Sangjia de ziben jia de fa zougou* 「喪家的」「資本家的乏走狗」, 1930)

"Hard Translation" and the "Class Nature of Literature" (*Yingyi yu wenxue de jieji xing* 硬譯與文學的階級性, 1930)

"Thoughts on the League of Left-Wing Writers" (*Duiyu zuoyi zuojia lianmeng de yijian* 對於左翼作家聯盟的意見, 1930)

"A Glimpse at Shanghai Literature" (*Shanghai wenyi zhi yi pie* 上海文藝之一瞥, 1931)

Letters between Two Places (*Liang di shu* 兩地書, 1933)

Writings of False Freedom (*Weiziyou shu* 偽自由書, 1933)

"From Satire to Humor" (*Cong fengci dao youmo* 從諷刺到幽默, 1933)

South of the North (*Nanqiang beidiao ji* 南腔北調集, 1934)

"How I Came to Write Fiction" (*Wo zenme zuoqi xiaoshuo lai* 我怎麼做起小説來, 1933)

Dead Souls (*Si hunling* 死魂靈, 1935) (translation)

Uncollected Work (*Ji waiji* 集外集, 1935)

"Laughing at My Own Predicament" (*Zichao* 自嘲, 1932)

Old Stories Retold (*Gushi xinbian* 故事新編, 1936)

"Mending Heaven" (*Butian* 補天, 1922)

"The Flight to the Moon" (*Benyue* 奔月, 1926)

"Forging Swords" (*Zhujian* 鑄劍, 1927)

"Leaving the Pass" (*Chuguan* 出關, 1935)

Quasi-romantic Discourses (*Zhun fengyue tan* 准風月談, 1936)

"How to Train Wild Animals" (*Yeshou xunlian fa* 野獸訓練法, 1933)

"Ode to the Night" (*Ye song* 夜頌, 1933)

Essays from Semi-concession Studio (*Qiejieting zawen* 且介亭雜文, 1937)

"Amateur Talk on Literature" (*Menwai wentan* 門外文談, 1934)

"Miscellaneous Talk after Illness" (*Bing hou zatan* 病後雜談, 1934)

"Take-ism" (*Nalaizhuyi* 拿來主義, 1934)

Essays from Semi-concession Studio III (*Qiejieting zawen mobian* 且介亭雜文末編, 1937)

"'The Pass' in *Leaving the Pass*" (*Chuguan de 'guan'* 《出關》的「關」, 1936)

Essays from Semi-concession Studio, Supplement (*Qiejieting zawen fuji* 且介亭雜文附集, 1937)

"Death" (*Si* 死, 1936)

"A Document on File (7)" (*Li ci cunzhao [qi]* 立此存照 [七], 1936)

"On Our Literary Movement at Present" (*Lun xianzai women de wenxue yundong* 論現在我們的文學運動, 1936)

Outline of the Literary History of the Han (*Han wenxueshi gangyao* 漢文學史的綱要, 1938)

Addendum to Sequel to Inauspicious Star (*Huagai ji xubian bubian* 華蓋集続編補編, 1948)

"The Origin of 'The Story of Ah Q'" (*Ah Q zhengzhuan de chengyin* 《阿Q正傳》的成因, 1926)

Addendum to Additions to the Collection of the Uncollected (*Jiwai ji shiyi bubian* 集外集拾遺補編, 1952)

"Toward a Refutation of Malevolent Voices" (*Po e sheng lun* 破惡聲論, 1908)

"About the Intellectual Class" (*Guanyu zhishi jieji* 關於知識階級, 1927)

246 Appendix

Publications (in Alphabetical Order by Title)

"About the Intellectual Class" (*Guanyu zhishi jieji* 關於知識階級, 1927), in *Addendum to Additions to the Collection of the Uncollected* (*Jiwai ji shiyi bubian* 集外集拾遺補編, 1952)

Additions to the Collection of the Uncollected, 1952

Afterword to *Graves* (*Xiezai Fen houmian* 寫在墳後面, 1926), in *Graves*, 1927

"Ah Chang and the *Classic of Mountains and Seas*" (*Ah Chang yu Shanhaijing* 阿長與《山海經》, 1926), in *Dawn Blossoms Plucked at Dusk*, 1928

"Amateur Talk on Literature" (*Menwai wentan* 門外文談, 1934), in *Essays from Semi-concession Studio*, 1937

And That's All (*Eryi ji* 而已集, 1928)

Anthology of Fiction from beyond the Border (*Yuwai xiaoshuo ji* 域外小説集, 1909)

"Autumn Night" (*Qiuye* 秋夜, 1924), in *Wild Grass*, 1927

Brief History of Chinese Fiction, A (*Zhongguo xiaoshuoshi lüe* 中國小説史略, 1925)

Dawn Blossoms Plucked at Dusk (*Zhaohua xi shi* 朝花夕拾, 1928)

Dead Souls (*Si hunling* 死魂靈, 1935) (translation)

"Death" (*Si* 死, 1936), in *Essays from Semi-concession Studio, Supplement*, 1937

Destruction (*Huimie* 毀滅, 1931) (translation)

"Diary of a Madman" (*Kuangren riji* 狂人日記, 1918), in *Outcry*, 1923

"The Divorce" (*Lihun* 離婚, 1925), in *Hesitation*, 1926

"Document on File (7), A" (*Li ci cunzhao [qi]* 立此存照 [七], 1936), in *Essays from Semi-concession Studio, Supplement*, 1937

"Dogs, Cats, Mice" (*Gou mao shu* 狗·貓·鼠, 1926), in *Dawn Blossoms Plucked at Dusk*, 1928

"Dragon Boat Festival" (*Duanwu jie* 端午節, 1922), in *Outcry*, 1923

Essays from Semi-concession Studio (*Qiejieting zawen* 且介亭雜文, 1937)

Essays from Semi-concession Studio III (*Qiejieting zawen mobian* 且介亭雜文末編, 1937)

Essays from Semi-concession Studio, Supplement (*Qiejieting zawen fuji* 且介亭雜文附集, 1937)

"An Exhausted Stray Dog of the Capitalists" (*Sangjia de ziben jia de fa zougou* 「喪家的」「資本家的乏走狗」, 1930), in *Two Hearts*, 1932

"Fan Ainong" (*Fan Ainong* 范愛農, 1926), in *Dawn Blossoms Plucked at Dusk*, 1928

"The Flight to the Moon" (*Benyue* 奔月, 1926), in *Old Stories Retold*, 1936

"Forging Swords" (*Zhujian* 鑄劍, 1927), in *Old Stories Retold*, 1936

"From Satire to Humor" (*Cong fengci dao youmo* 從諷刺到幽默, 1933), in *Writings of False Freedom*, 1933

From the Earth to the Moon (*Yuejie lüxing* 月界旅行, 1903) (translation)

"A Glimpse at Shanghai Literature" (*Shanghai wenyi zhi yi pie* 上海文藝之一瞥, 1931), in *Two Hearts*, 1932

Graves (*Fen* 墳, 1927)

"A Happy Family" (*Xingfu de jiating* 幸福的家庭, 1924), in *Hesitation*, 1926

"Hard Translation" and the "Class Nature of Literature" (*Yingyi yu wenxue de jieji xing* 硬譯與文學的階級性, 1930), in *Two Hearts*, 1932

Hesitation (*Panghuang* 彷徨, 1926)

"The History of Humankind" (*Ren zhi lishi* 人之歷史, 1907), in *Graves*, 1927

"Hope" (*Xiwang* 希望, 1925), in *Wild Grass*, 1927

Hot Wind (*Refeng* 熱風, 1925)

"How I Came to Write Fiction" (*Wo zenme zuoqi xiaoshuo lai* 我怎麼做起小說來, 1933)

"How to Train Wild Animals" (*Yeshou xunlian fa* 野獸訓練法, 1933), in *Quasi-romantic Discourses*, 1936

"Impromptu Reflections No. 42" (*Suigan lu sishi'er* 隨感錄四十二, 1919), in *Hot Wind*, 1925

"Impromptu Reflections No. 48" (*Suigan lu sishiba* 隨感錄四十八, 1919), in *Hot Wind*, 1925

"Impromptu Reflections No. 49" (*Suigan lu sishijiu* 隨感錄四十九, 1919), in *Hot Wind*, 1925

Inauspicious Star (*Huagai ji* 華蓋集, 1926)

"An Incident" (*Yi jian xiaoshi* 一件小事, 1919), in *Outcry*, 1923

"Kong Yiji" (*Kong Yiji* 孔乙己, 1919), in *Outcry*, 1923

"The Lamp of Eternity" (*Changming deng* 長明燈, 1925), in *Hesitation*, 1926

"Laughing at My Own Predicament" (*Zichao* 自嘲, 1932), in *Uncollected Work*, 1935

"Leaving the Pass" (*Chuguan* 出關, 1935), in *Old Stories Retold*, 1936

Letters between Two Places (*Liang di shu* 兩地書, 1933)

"Master Gao" (*Gao laofuzi* 高老夫子, 1925), in *Hesitation*, 1926

"Medicine" (*Yao* 藥, 1919), in *Outcry*, 1923

"Mending Heaven" (*Butian* 補天, 1922), in *Old Stories Retold*, 1936

"The Misanthrope" (*Guduzhe* 孤獨者, 1925), in *Hesitation*, 1926

"Miscellaneous Talk after Illness" (*Bing hou zatan* 病後雜談, 1934), in *Essays from Semi-concession Studio*, 1937

"My Old Hometown" (*Guxiang* 故鄉, 1921), in *Outcry*, 1923

"New Year's Sacrifice" (*Zhufu* 祝福, 1924), in *Hesitation*, 1926

"Ode to the Night" (*Ye song* 夜頌), in *Quasi-romantic Discourses*, 1936

Old Stories Retold (*Gushi xinbian* 故事新編, 1936)

"On Imbalanced Cultural Development" (*Wenhua pian zhi lun* 文化偏至論), in *Graves*, 1927

"On Our Literary Movement at Present" (*Lun xianzai women de wenxue yundong* 論現在我們的文學運動, 1936), in *Essays from Semi-concession Studio, Supplement*, 1937

"On the 'Why "Fair Play" Should Be Deferred' That Should Be Slowed Down" (*Lun "fei'erpolai" yinggai huanxing* 論"費厄潑賴應該緩行, 1926), in *Graves*, 1927

"On the Power of Mara Poetry" (*Moluo shili shuo* 摩羅詩力說, 1907), in *Graves*, 1927

"The Origin of 'The Story of Ah Q'" (*Ah Q zhengzhuan de chengyin* 《阿Q正傳》的成因, 1926), in *Addendum to Sequel to* Inauspicious Star, 1948

Outcry (*Nahan* 吶喊) (1923)

Outline of the Literary History of the Han (*Han wenxueshi gangyao* 漢文學史的綱要, 1938)

"'The Pass' in *Leaving the Pass*" (*Chuguan de "guan"* 《出關》的"關", 1936), in *Essays from Semi-concession Studio III*, 1937

"The Passerby" (*Guoke* 過客, 1925), in *Wild Grass*, 1927

"A Passing Storm" (*Fengbo* 風波, 1920), in *Outcry*, 1923

Preface to *Outcry* (*Nahan zixu* 《吶喊》自序, 1923), in *Outcry*, 1923

"Professor Fujino" (*Tengye xiansheng* 藤野先生, 1926), in *Dawn Blossoms Plucked at Dusk*, 1928

"The Rabbits and the Cat" (*Tu he mao* 兔和貓, 1922), in *Outcry*, 1923

248   Appendix

"Regrets for the Past" (*Shangshi* 傷逝, 1925), in *Hesitation*, 1926

"Revolutionary Era Literature" (*Geming shidai de wenxue* 革命時代的文學, 1927), in *And That's All*, 1928

Sequel to Inauspicious Star (*Huagai ji xubian* 華蓋集續編, 1927)

"Soap" (*Feizao* 肥皂, 1924), in *Hesitation*, 1926

"The Story of Hair" (*Toufa de gushi* 頭髮的故事, 1920), in *Outcry*, 1923

"Take-ism" (*Nalaizhuyi* 拿來主義, 1934), in *Essays from Semi-concession Studio*, 1937

"Thoughts on the League of Left-Wing Writers" (*Duiyu zuoyi zuojia lianmeng de yijian* 對於左翼作家聯盟的意見, 1930), in *Two Hearts*, 1932

Three Leisures (*San xian ji* 三閑集, 1932)

"Tomorrow" (*Mingtian* 明天, 1920), in *Outcry*, 1923

The Torrent (*Benliu* 奔流, 1928–1929) (journal coedited with Yu Dafu)

"Toward a Refutation of Malevolent Voices" (*Po e sheng lun* 破惡聲論, 1908), in *Addendum to Additions to the Collection of the Uncollected*, 1952

"Tremors on the Border of Degradation" (*Tuibai xian de chandong* 頹敗線的顫動, 1925), in *Wild Grass*, 1927

"The True Story of Ah Q" (*Ah Q zhengzhuan* 阿Q正傳, 1922), in *Outcry*, 1923

Two Hearts (*Er xin ji* 二心集, 1932)

Uncollected Work (*Ji waiji* 集外集, 1935)

"Upstairs in the Tavern" (*Zai jiuloushang* 在酒樓上, 1924), in *Hesitation*, 1926

"Village Opera" (*Shexi* 社戲, 1922), in *Outcry*, 1923

"Voiceless China" (*Wusheng de Zhongguo* 無聲的中國, 1927), in *Three Leisures*, 1932

Voyage to the Center of the Earth (*Dixin lüxing* 地心旅行, 1903) (translation)

"What Happens after *Nuola* Leaves Home?" (*Nala zouhou zenyang* 娜拉走後怎樣, 1923), in *Graves*, 1927

Wild Grass (*Yecao* 野草, 1927)

Writings of False Freedom (*Weiziyou shu* 偽自由書, 1933)

Bibliography

LXQJ: *Lu Xun quanji* 鲁迅全集 [Lu Xun's complete works]. Beijing: Beijing renmin chubanshe, 2005.

Abe Auestad, Reiko. "Japanese Ibsens." In *Ibsen in Context*, edited by Narve Fulsås and Tore Rem, 239–47. Cambridge: Cambridge University Press, 2021.

Adorno, Theodor W. *Negative Dialectics*. Edited by E. B. Ashton. New York: Seabury Press, 1973.

Ah Lei 阿累. "Yimian" 一面 [One meeting]. *Zhongliu* 中流 1, no. 5 (1926): 297–99.

Aho, Juhani. *Junggesellenliebe und andere Novellen* [Bachelor love and other novellas], translated by Milli Vinkentiwna Konowalow, Halle: Otto Hendel Verlag, 1906.

Aho, Juhani. *Novellen* [Novellas], translated by Friedr. v . Känel, Leipzig: Reclam, 1897.

Anderson, Benedict. *Imagined Communities: Reflections on the Origin and Spread of Nationalism*. London: Verso, 2006.

Anderson, Marston. *The Limits of Realism: Chinese Fiction in the Revolutionary Period*. Berkeley: University of California Press, 1990.

Andreev, Leonid. "Ben-Tovit." *Sobranie Sochinenii V Shesti Tomakh – 1* [Collected works in 6 volumes – 1], 1355–62. Moscow: Khudozhestvennaia literatura, 1990.

Andreev, Leonid. "Moran" 默然 [Silence]. Translated by Liu Bannong 劉半農. *Zhonghua xiaoshuo jie* 17 (1914): 1–13.

Andreev, Leonid. "On the Day of the Crucifixion." In *The Crushed Flower*, translated by Herman Bernstein, 43–48. New York: Knopf, 1921.

Andreev, Leonid. *The Red Laugh*. Translated by Alexandra Linden. London: T. F. Unwin, 1905.

Anonymous. "An unsere Leser" [To our readers]. *Aus fremden Zungen* 24 (1903): n.p.

Apter, Emily S. *Against World Literature: On the Politics of Untranslatability*. London: Verso, 2013.

Badiou, Alain. *Théorie du sujet* [Theory of the subject]. Paris: Seuil, 1982.

Barmé, Geremie R. "To Screw Foreigners Is Patriotic: China's Avant-Garde Nationalist." *Chinese Journal* 34 (1995): 209–34.

Baroja, Pío. *La estrella del capitán Chimista* [The star of Captain Chimista]. Madrid: Rafael Caro Raggio, 1930.

Baroja, Pío. *Los pilotos de altura* [Navigators]. Madrid: Rafael Caro Raggio, 1929.

250   Bibliography

Baroja, Pío. *Yan-Si-Pao o la esvástica de oro* [Yan-Si-Pao or the golden swastika]. Madrid: Prensa Moderna, 1928.

Bassoe, Pedro Thiago Ramos. "Judging a Book by Its Cover: Natsume Sōseki, Book Design, and the Value of Art." *Review of Japanese Culture and Society* 29 (2017): 159–74.

Beauvoir, Simone de. *The Long March: An Account of Modern China*. Translated by Austryn Wainhouse. London: Phoenix, 2001.

Beebee, Thomas Oliver, ed. *German Literature as World Literature*. London: Bloomsbury, 2014.

Beijing Lu Xun bowuguan 北京鲁迅博物館 [Beijing Lu Xun Museum], ed. "Xiwen shu muci" 西文書目次 [The content of Western books]. In *Lu Xun shouji he cangshu mulu* 鲁迅手跡和藏書目錄 [The content of Lu Xun's manuscripts and book collection]. Beijing: Beijing Lu Xun bowuguan, 1959.

Beijing Lu Xun bowuguan 北京鲁迅博物館 [Beijing Lu Xun Museum]. *Lu Xun shouji he cangshu mulu* 鲁迅手跡和藏書目錄 [Lu Xun's manuscript and book collections]. Vol. 3. Beijing: Lu Xun bowuguan, 1959.

Beijing Lu Xun bowuguan Lu Xun yanjiushi 北京鲁迅博物館鲁迅研究室 [Lu Xun Research Center of Beijing Lu Xun Museum], ed. *Lu Xun cangshu yanjiu* 鲁迅藏書研究 [Reader on the book collection of Lu Xun]. Beijing: Zhongguo wenlian chuban gongsi, 1991.

Beijing Lu Xun bowuguan 北京鲁迅博物館 [Beijing Lu Xun Museum], ed. *Lu Xun yi* Si Hunling *shougao* 鲁迅譯《死魂靈》手稿 [Manuscript of Lu Xun's translation of *Dead Souls*], 5 vols. Shanghai: Shanghai kexue jishu wenxian chubanshe, 2017.

Benjamin, Walter. *The Origin of German Tragic Drama*. Edited by George Steiner and John Osborne. London: Verso, 2009.

Benjamin, Walter. "On the Concept of History," *Selected Writings*. Vol. 4. Edited by Howard Eiland and Michael W. Jennings, 389–400. Cambridge, MA: Harvard University Press, 2003.

Blasco Ibáñez, Vicente. *La vuelta al mundo de un novelista* [A novelist's trip around the world]. Valencia: Prometeo, 1924.

Boven, Henri van. *Histoire de la littérature Chinoise moderne* [History of modern Chinese literature]. Tianjing: Chihli Press, 1946.

Bowring, Richard John. *Mori Ōgai and the Modernization of Japanese Culture*. Cambridge: Cambridge University Press, 1979.

Braid, Barbara, and Hanan Muzaffar. *Bodies in Flux: Embodiments at the End of Anthropocentrism*. Leiden: Brill Rodopi, 2019.

Brandes, Georg. "World Literature (1899)." In *World Literature: A Reader*, edited by Theo D'Haen, César Domínguez, and Mads Rosendahl Thomsen, 23–27. London: Routledge, 2013.

Brière, Octave. "Un écrivain populaire: Lou Sin (1881–1936)" [A popular writer: Lu Xun (1881–1936)]. *Bulletin de l'Université L'Aurore, III*. 7, no. 1 (1946): 51–78.

Brooks, Peter. *Troubling Confessions: Speaking Guilt in Law and Literature*. Chicago: University of Chicago Press, 2000.

Butler, Judith. *Precarious Life: The Powers of Mourning and Violence*. New York: Verso, 2004.

Calichman, Richard F. Preface to *What Is Modernity? Writings of Takeuchi Yoshimi*. Translated by Richard F. Calichman, vii–xiii. New York: Columbia University Press, 2005.

Casanova, Pascale. "Literature as a World." *New Left Revjew* 31 (2005): 71–90.

Casanova, Pascale. "Literature as a World." In *World Literature: A Reader*, edited by Theo D'Haen, César Domínguez, and Mads Rosendahl Thomsen, 275–88. London: Routledge, 2013.

Casanova, Pascale. *The World Republic of Letters*. Translated by M. B. Debevoise. Cambridge, MA: Harvard University Press, 2007.

Casement, William. "William Morris on Labor and Pleasure." *Social Theory and Practice* 12, no. 3 (1986): 351–82.

Chan, Roy B. *The Edge of Knowing: Dreams, History, and Realism in Modern Chinese Literature*. Seattle: University of Washington Press, 2016.

Chang Kigŭn. "Chunggong ŭi A Q" [Ah Q of Communist China]. *Sedae* 1, no. 6 (November 1963): 179–83.

Cheah, Pheng. *What Is a World? On Postcolonial Literature as World Literature*. Durham, NC: Duke University Press, 2016.

Chen, Xiaoming. *From the May Fourth Movement to Communist Revolution: Guo Moruo and the Chinese Path to Communism*. Albany: State University of New York Press, 2007.

Cheng, Anne. "La Chine pense-t-elle? Leçon inaugurale prononcée le jeudi 11 décembre 2008" [Does China think? Inaugural speech delivered on December 11, 2008] Published online January 24, 2013. https://books.openedition.org/cdf/184.

Cheng, Eileen J. "Bordering on the Divine: Introduction to *Morning Blossoms Gathered at Dusk*." In Lu Xun, *Wild Grass* and *Morning Blossoms Gathered at Dusk*, translated by Eileen J. Cheng, edited by Theodore Huters, 7–27. Cambridge, MA: Harvard University Press, 2022.

Cheng, Eileen J. "'In Search of New Voices from Alien Lands': Lu Xun, Cultural Exchange, and the Myth of Sino-Japanese Friendship." *Journal of Asian Studies* 73, no. 3 (2014): 589–618.

Cheng, Eileen J. *Literary Remains: Death, Trauma, and Lu Xun's Refusal to Mourn*. Honolulu: University of Hawai'i Press, 2013.

Cheng, Eileen J. "Performing the Revolutionary: Lu Xun and the Meiji Discourse on Masculinity." *Modern Chinese Literature and Culture*, no. 1 (2015): 1–43.

Cheng, Eileen J. "Recycling the Scholar-Beauty Narrative: Lu Xun on Love in an Age of Mechanical Reproductions." *Modern Chinese Literature and Culture* 18, no. 2 (2006): 1–38.

Cheng, Eileen J. "Vulnerable Subjects: Introduction to *Morning Blossoms Gathered at Dusk*." In Lu Xun, *Wild Grass* and *Morning Blossoms Gathered at Dusk*, translated by Eileen J. Cheng, edited by Theodore Huters, 103–25. Cambridge, MA: Harvard University Press, 2022.

Cheng, Jing. *Lu Xun: Una vida de triunfo y tristeza* [Lu Xun: A life of victory and sadness]. Translated by Antonio Rodríguez Rodríguez and Qiu Baoqi. Madrid: Editorial Popular, 2009.

Cheng Yat-sze 鄭逸思. "*Lielaozhuan*: Renxing benlie"《烈佬傳》：人性本烈 [*Lielaozhuan*: Human nature is intense]. In *Diwujie Hongloumeng jiang pinglunji: Huang Biyun Lielaozhuan*, 第五屆紅樓夢獎評論集：黃碧雲《烈佬傳》[Collected criticisms for the Fifth Dream of the Red Chamber Award: Wong Bik-wan's *Lielaozhuan*], edited by Hong Kong Baptist University Faculty of Arts, 208–10. Hong Kong: Tiandi Chuban, 2016.

Chinnery, J. D. "The Influence of Western Literature on Lǔ Xùn's 'Diary of a Madman.'" *Bulletin of the School of Oriental and African Studies* 23, no. 2 (1960): 309–22.

Ch'oe Ch'angnŭk, and Zhao Yingqiu 趙穎秋. "Kaebyŏksa 'Chungguk tanp'yŏn sosŏlchip' pŏnyŏkcha sogo" [Inquiry into the translator of Genesis Press's 'Collected Chinese Short Stories']. *Taedong munhwa yŏn'gu* 116 (2021): 259–94.

Ch'oe Chinho. *Sangsang toen Lu Swin kwa hyŏndae Chungguk: Han'guk esŏ Lu Swin iranŭn murŭm* [Imagined Lu Xun and modern China: The question that is Lu Xun in Korea]. Seoul: Somyŏng ch'ulp'an, 2019.

Ch'oe Ŭnjŏng. "Chungguk hyŏndae sosŏl ŭi pŏnyŏk hyŏnhwang mit tokcha suyong yangsang: Ch'oegŭn 10-yŏn'gan ŭl chungsim ŭro" [Current translation status and reader reception patterns of modern Chinese fiction: With a focus on the last ten years]. *Han-Chung inmunhak yŏn'gu* 48 (2015): 103–25.

Chŏn Hyŏngjun. *Tong Asiajŏk sigak ŭro ponŭn Chungguk munhak* [Chinese literature from an East Asian perspective]. Seoul: Sŏul taehakkyo ch'ulp'anbu, 2004.

Chŏng Chonghyŏn. "Lu Swin ŭi ch'osang: 1960–1970-yŏndae naengjŏn munhwa ŭi Chungguk simsang chiri" [Portrait of Lu Xun: Imagined geography regarding China in the context of the 1960s and the 1970s Cold War culture]. *Sai* 14 (2013): 51–103.

Clifford, James. *Routes: Travel and Translation in the Late Twentieth Century.* Cambridge, MA: Harvard University Press, 1997.

Cohn, Joel R. *Studies in the Comic Spirit in Modern Japanese Fiction.* Cambridge, MA: Harvard University Press, 1998.

Conrad, Sebastian. *What Is Global History?* Princeton: Princeton University Press, 2016.

Cooper, William C., and Nathan Sivin. "Man as a Medicine: Pharmacological and Ritual Aspects of Traditional Therapy Using Drugs Derived from the Human Body." In *Chinese Science: Explorations of an Ancient Tradition*, edited by Joseph Needham, Shigeru Nakayama, and Nathan Sivin, 203–72. Cambridge, MA: MIT Press, 1973.

Couser, G. Thomas. *Memoir: An Introduction.* New York: Oxford University Press, 2012.

Cui Wendong 崔文東. "Qingnian Lu Xun yu deyu 'shijie wenxue': *Yuwai xiaoshuoji* caiyuan kao" 青年魯迅與德語"世界文學"：《域外小説集》材源考 [Lu Xun and *Weltliteratur*: On the sources of collection of foreign literature]. *Wenxue pinglun* 文學評論 [Literature review], no. 6 (2020): 191–200.

Cui, Wenjin. "'Literal Translation' and the Materiality of Language: Lu Xun as a Case." *Frontiers of Literary Studies in China* 6, no. 3 (2012): 393–409.

Cui, Wenjin. *Lu Xun's Affirmative Biopolitics: Nothingness and the Power of Self-Transcendence.* New York: Routledge, 2022.

Cui Xiongquan 崔雄權. "Jieshou yu piping: Lu Xun yu xiandai Chaoxian wenxue" 接受與批評：魯迅與現代朝鮮文學 [Reception and criticism: Lu Xun and modern Korean literature]. *Yanbian daxue xuebao* 延邊大學學報 1 (1993): 54–60.

Damrosch, David. *What Is World Literature?* Princeton: Princeton University Press, 2003.

Damrosch, David. "What Is World Literature?" In *World Literature: A Reader,* edited by Theo D'Haen, César Domínguez, and Mads Rosendahl Thomsen, 198–206. London: Routledge, 2013.

Damrosch, David. "Introduction: World Literature in Theory and Practice." In *World Literature in Theory,* 1–11. Chichester: Wiley-Blackwell, 2014.

Danly, Robert Lyons. *In the Shade of Spring Leaves: The Life of Higuchi Ichiyō with Nine of Her Best Short Stories.* New York: Norton, 1981.

Davies, Gloria. "Lu Xun in 1966: On Valuing a Maoist Icon." *Critical Inquiry* 46, no. 3 (2020): 515–35.

Davies, Gloria. *Lu Xun's Revolution: Writing in a Time of Violence.* Cambridge, MA: Harvard University Press, 2013.

Dazai Osamu 太宰治. *Atogaki* あとがき [Postscript]. In *Dazai Osamu zenshū* 太宰治全集 [A complete collection of Dazai Osamu's works], edited by Yamanouchi Shōshi 山内祥史, 7:129–30. Tokyo: Chikuma Shobō, 1989.

Dazai Osamu 太宰治. *Sekibetsu* 惜別 [Regrettable parting]. In *Dazai Osamu zenshū* 太宰治全集 [A complete collection of Dazai Osamu's works], edited by Yamanouchi Shōshi, 7:3–127. Tokyo: Chikuma Shobō, 1989.

Dazai Osamu 太宰治. " 'Sekibetsu' no ito" 「惜別」の意図 [Intentions for *Regrettable parting*]. In *Dazai Osamu zenshū* 太宰治全集 [A complete collection of Dazai Osamu's works], edited by Yamanouchi Shōshi, 10:280–82. Tokyo: Chikuma Shobō, 1989.

Deleuze, Gilles. *Difference and Repetition.* Translated by Paul Patton. New York: Columbia University Press, 1994.

Deleuze, Gilles, and Félix Guattari. *A Thousand Plateaus: Capitalism and Schizophrenia.* Translated by Brian Massumi. Minneapolis: University of Minnesota Press, 2005.

Deng Xiaolin 鄧嘯林. "Zui yaojin de shi you yibu hao zidian——zaitan Lu Xun xiansheng he cidian" 最要緊的是有一部好字典——再談魯迅先生和詞典 [The most important thing is to have a good dictionary—Another discussion about Lu Xun and dictionaries]. *Cishu yanjiu* 辭書研究, no. 6 (1989): 94–99.

Derrida, Jacques. "Marx & Sons." Translated by G. M. Goshgarian. In *Ghostly Demarcations,* edited by Michael Sprinker. London: Verso, 1999.

Derrida, Jacques. "Plato's Pharmacy." In Jacques Derrida, *Dissemination,* translated by Barbara Johnson, 63–171. Chicago: University of Chicago Press, 1981.

Dikötter, Frank. "Hairy Barbarians, Furry Primates, and Wild Men: Medical Science and Cultural Representations of Hair in China." In *Hair: Its Power and Meaning in Asian Cultures,* edited by Alf Hiltebeitel and Barbara D. Miller, 51–74. Albany: State University of New York Press, 1998.

Dole, Andrew. *Reframing the Masters of Suspicion: Marx, Nietzsche, and Freud.* London: Bloomsbury, 2018.

Doleželová-Velingerová, Milena. "Lu Xun's 'Medicine.'" In *Modern Chinese Literature in the May Fourth Era,* edited by Merle Goldman, 221–32. Cambridge, MA: Harvard University Press, 1977.

254   Bibliography

Dong Bingyue 董炳月. "Wenzhang wei meishu zhiyi—Lu Xun zaonian de meishu guan yu xiangguan wenti" 文章為美術之一——魯迅早年的美術觀與相關問題 [Literature as a form of fine arts: Early Lu Xun's understandings of fine arts]. *Wenxue pinglun* 文學評論, no. 4 (2015): 21–30.

Dooghan, Daniel M. "Old Tales, Untold: Lu Xun against World Literature." *Journal of Modern Literature in Chinese* 14, no. 1 (2017): 31–64.

Du Yong 杜庸. "Wo yelai tantan zhuangding" 我也來談談裝訂 [Let me also talk about binding]. *Kaiming* 開明 1, no. 12 (1929): 765–66.

Eagleton, Terry. *Literary Theory: An Introduction.* Minneapolis: University of Minnesota Press, 2008.

Eber, Irene. "The Reception of Lu Xun in Europe and America: The Politics of Popularization and Scholarship." In *Lu Xun and His Legacy*, edited by Leo Ou-fan Lee, 242–73. Berkeley: University of California Press, 1985.

Eroshenko, Vasily. *The Narrow Cage and Other Modern Fairy Tales.* Translated by Adam Kuplowsky. New York: Columbia University Press, 2023.

Etherington, Ben, and Jarad Zimbler. Introduction to *The Cambridge Companion to World Literature*, edited by Ben Etherington and Jarad Zimbler, 1–20. Cambridge: Cambridge University Press, 2018.

Even-Zohar, Itamar. "Polysystem Studies." *Poetics Today* 11, no. 1 (1990): 1–268.

Fan Jin 范勁. "Lu Xun yanjiu zai Deguo" 魯迅研究在德國 [Lu Xun studies in Germany]. *Wenyi yanjiu* 文藝研究, no. 1 (2018): 64–76.

Fang Chuanzong 方傳宗. "Maobian zhuangding de liyou" 毛邊裝訂的理由 [Reasons for *maobian* binding]. *Yusi* 語絲, no. 129 (1927): 179–80.

Fisk, Gloria. *Orhan Pamuk and the Good of World Literature.* New York: Columbia University Press, 2018.

Fiskesjö, Magnus. "The Animal Other: China's Barbarians and Their Renaming in the Twentieth Century." *Social Text* 29, no. 4 (2011): 57–79.

Fleissner, Jennifer L. "Obsessional Modernity: The 'Institutionalization of Doubt.'" *Critical Inquiry* 34, no. 1 (2007): 106–34.

Fluck, Winfried. "The Search for Distance: Negation and Negativity in Wolfgang Iser's Literary Theory." *New Literary History* 31, no. 1 (Winter 2000): 175–210.

Fokkema, Douwe W. "Lu Xun: The Impact of Russian Literature." In *Modern Chinese Literature in the May Fourth Era*, edited by Merle Goldman, 89–102. Cambridge, MA: Harvard University Press, 1977.

Foster, Paul B. "The Ironic Inflation of Chinese National Character: Lu Xun's International Reputation, Romain Rolland's Critique of 'The True Story of Ah Q,' and the Nobel Prize." *Modern Chinese Literature and Culture* 13, no. 1 (2001): 140–68.

Fox, Alan. "The Practice of *Huayan* Buddhism." In *Chinese Buddhism: Past, Present, and Future*, 259–86. Yilan, Taiwan: Foguang University Center for Buddhist Studies, 2015.

Freeman, R. B. "Darwin in Chinese." *Archives of Natural History* 13, no. 1 (1986): 19–24.

Fujii Shōzō 藤井省三. "Dazai Osamu no 'Sekibetsu' to Takeuchi Yoshimi no 'Rojin'" 太宰治の『惜別』と竹内好の『魯迅』 [Dazai Osamu's *Regrettable Parting* and Takeuchi

Yoshimi's *Lu Xun*]. *Kuni bungaku: Kaishaku to kyōzai no kenkyū* 國文學：解釈と教材の研究 47, no. 14 (2002): 56–65.

Fujii Shōzō 藤井省三. "Lu Xun yu Riben ji shijie wenxue" 魯迅與日本及世界文學 [Lu Xun, Japan, and world literature]. *Wenyi bao* 文藝報, October 13, 2021, Waiguo wenyi, 2006.

Fujii Shōzō 藤井省三. *Roshia no kage: Natsume Sōseki to Rojin* ロシアの影－夏目漱石と魯迅 [Russian impression: Natsume Soseki and Lu Xun]. Tokyo: Heibonsha, 1985.

Gálik, Marián. *Milestones in Sino-Western Literary Confrontation, 1898–1979.* Wiesbaden: Harrassowitz, 1986.

Gamsa, Mark. *The Chinese Translation of Russian Literature: Three Studies.* Leiden: Brill, 2008.

Gänger, Stefanie. "Circulation: Reflections on Circularity, Entity, and Liquidity in the Language of Global History." *Journal of Global History* 12, no. 3 (November 2017): 303–18.

Gao, Fang. "Idéologie et traduction: La réception des traductions de Lu Xun en France" [Ideology and translation: The reception of Lu Xun's translations in France]. *Meta: Journal des traducteurs/Meta: Translators' Journal* 59, no. 1 (2014): 47–71.

García Sanchiz, Federico. *La ciudad milagrosa (Shanghai)* [The miracle city (Shanghai)]. Madrid: V. H. Sanz Calleja, 1926.

Garshin, Vsevolod. *Rasskazy.* Leningrad: *Khudozhestvennaia literatura*, 1978.

Gaspar, Enrique. *El Anacronópete; Viaje a China; Metempsicosis* [The Anacronópete; Travel to China; Metempsychosis]. Barcelona: Daniel Cortezo y Cia., 1887.

Ge Baoquan 戈寶權. "Lu Xun zai shijie wenxue shi shang de diwei" 魯迅在世界文學史上的地位 [Lu Xun in the history of world literature]. *Renwen zazhi* 人文雜誌, no. 4 (1981): 13–15.

Goethe, Johann Wolfgang von. *Conversations with Eckermann, 1823–1832.* Translated by John Oxenford. San Francisco: North Point Press, 1984.

Goethe, Johann Wolfgang von. "Prometheus" (a bilingual version), translated by Michael Hamburger. In *Selected Poems*, edited by Christopher Middleton, 26–31. Boston: Suhrkamp/Insel, 1983.

Gogol, Nikolai. "Diary of a Madman." In *Nikolai Gogol: The Collected Tales*, translated by Richard Pevear and Larissa Volokhonsky, 273–93. New York: Knopf, 1998.

Goldman, Merle. "The Political Use of Lu Xun." *China Quarterly* 91 (1982): 446–61.

Gómez de la Serna, Ramón. *Caprichos* [Caprices]. Madrid: Cuadernos Literarios, 1925.

Gómez de la Serna, Ramón. *Los dos marineros* [The two sailors]. Madrid: Prensa Popular, 1924.

Goscilo, Helena. *Dehexing Sex: Russian Womanhood during and after Glasnost.* Ann Arbor: University of Michigan Press, 1996.

Gu Fengtian 谷鳳田. "Wo duiyu yi" 我對於憶 [My take on *Memories*]. *Hongshui* 洪水 1, no. 10 (1926): 375–76.

Gu Jun 谷君. "Yeshi guanyu maobian shu" 也是關於毛邊書 [Also about *maobian* books]. *Kaiming* 開明 112 (1929): 764–65.

Gu, Ming Dong. "Lu Xun, Jameson, and Multiple Polysemia." *Canadian Review of Comparative Literature* 28, no. 4 (2001): 434–53.

256   Bibliography

Gunn, Janet Varner. *Autobiography: Toward a Poetics of Experience*. Philadelphia: University of Pennsylvania Press, 1982.

Guo Moruo 郭沫若. *Chuangzao shinian* 創造十年 [Ten years about the Creation Society]. In *Moruo zizhuan* 沫若自傳 [Autobiography of Moruo], vol. 2. Hong Kong: Sanlian shudian, 1978.

Guo Moruo 郭沫若. "Lun shi" 論詩 [On poetry]. In *Guo Moruo yanjiu ziliao* 郭沫若研究資料 [Research materials of Guo Moruo], edited by Wang Xunzhao 王訓昭, Lu Zhengyan 盧正言, Shao Hua 邵華, Xiao Binru 肖斌如, and Lin Minghua 林明華, 111–14. Beijing: Zhishi chanquan chubanshe, 2010.

Guo Moruo 郭沫若. "Lun Zhong De wenhua shu" 論中德文化書 [On Chinese and German cultures]. In *Guo Moruo quanji* 郭沫若全集 [The complete collection of Guo Moruo's works], 15:148–58. Beijing: Renmin wenxue chubanshe, 1990.

Guo Moruo 郭沫若. "Piping yu meng" 批評與夢 [Criticism and dreams]. In *Guo Moruo yanjiu ziliao* 郭沫若研究資料 [Research materials of Guo Moruo], edited by Wang Xunzhao 王訓昭, Lu Zhengyan 盧正言, Shao Hua 邵華, Xiao Binru 肖斌如, and Lin Minghua 林明華, 128–34. Beijing: Zhishi chanquan chubanshe, 2010.

Guo Moruo 郭沫若. "Zhongguo wenhua zhi chuantong jingshen" 中國文化之傳統精神 [The traditional spirit in Chinese culture]. In *Guo Moruo yanjiu ziliao* 郭沫若研究資料 [Research materials of Guo Moruo], edited by Wang Xunzhao 王訓昭, Lu Zhengyan 盧正言, Shao Hua 邵華, Xiao Binru 肖斌如, and Lin Minghua 林明華, 135–40. Beijing: Zhishi chanquan chubanshe, 2010.

Guo Moruo 郭沫若. "Zhuxiashi ru guan" 柱下史入關 [The archivist entering the pass]. In *Guo Moruo quanji* 郭沫若全集 [The complete collection of Guo Moruo's works], 10:152–60. Beijing: Renmin wenxue chubanshe, 1985.

Han Sŏrya. "No Sin kwa Chosŏn munhak" [Lu Xun and Korean literature]. *Chosŏn munhak* 110 (October 1956): 187–94.

Hanan, Patrick. "The Technique of Lu Hsün's Fiction." *Harvard Journal of Asiatic Studies* 34 (1974): 53–96.

Han'guk Lu Swin Chŏnjip Pŏnyŏk Wiwŏnhoe [Korean Committee on Translation of Lu Xun's complete works]. "'Lu Swin chŏnjip' ŭl palgan hamyŏ" [On the occasion of publishing 'The complete works of Lu Xun']. In Lu Xun, *Lu Swin chŏnjip* [The complete works of Lu Xun], translated by Hong Sŏkp'yo and Yi Pogyŏng, 1:15–17. Seoul: Kŭrinbi ch'ulp'ansa, 2010.

Harris, Kristine. "*The New Woman* Incident: Cinema, Scandal, and Spectacle in 1935 Shanghai." In *Transnational Chinese Cinemas: Identity, Nationhood, Gender*, edited by Sheldon H. Lu, 277–302. Honolulu: University of Hawai'i Press, 1997.

Hashimoto, Satoru. *Afterlives of Letters: The Transnational Origins of Modern Literature in China, Japan, and Korea*. New York: Columbia University Press, 2023.

Hashimoto, Satoru. "Intra-Asian Reading; or, How Lu Xun Enters into a World Literature." In *The Making of Chinese-Sinophone Literatures as World Literature*, edited by Kuei-fen Chiu and Yingjin Zhang, 83–102. Hong Kong: Hong Kong University Press, 2022.

Hayot, Eric. *On Literary Worlds*. Oxford: Oxford University Press, 2016.

He, Chengzhou. "Chinese Ibsens." In *Ibsen in Context*, edited by Narve Fulsås and Tore Rem, 248–55. Cambridge: Cambridge University Press, 2021.

He Min 何旻. "Jixie fuzhi shidai de meijie nigu—Zhou shi xiongdi yu xin wenxue maobian ben de sucheng" 機械複製時代的媒介擬古——周氏兄弟與新文學毛邊本的塑成 [Media antiquarianism in the era of mechanical reproduction: The Zhou brothers and the making of *maobian* new literature]. *Zhongguo xiandai wenxue yanjiu congkan* 中國現代文學研究叢刊, no. 5 (2021): 26–39.

He Min 何旻. "Xiandai shijie wenxue huanliu zhong de 'jingmei' yu 'yuyu' zhiwu: Zhoushi xiongdi yu zuowei wenxue meijie fanyi de *Yuwai xiaoshuo ji* maobian ben" 現代世界文學環流中的"精美"與"餘裕"之物：周氏兄弟與作為文學媒介翻譯的《域外小説集》毛邊本 [The "exquisite" and "leisurely" object in the circuit of modern world literature: Zhou brothers and the *maobian* version of *Stories from overseas* as the medium of literary translation]. *Lu Xun yanjiu yuekan* 魯迅研究月刊, no. 2 (2021): 41–47.

Hegel, G. W. F. *The Phenomenology of Spirit*. Translated by Terry Pinkard. Cambridge: Cambridge University Press, 2018.

Helgesson, Stefan, and Pieter Vermeulen. "World Literature in the Making." In *Institutions of World Literature*, edited by Stefan Helgesson and Pieter Vermeulen, 1–20. New York: Routledge, 2015.

Higuchi Ichiyō 樋口一葉. *Zenshū Higuchi Ichiyō* 全集樋口一葉 [The complete works of Higuchi Ichiyō]. Tokyo: Shōgakukan, 1976.

Hill, Christopher L. *Figures of the World: The Naturalist Novel and Transnational Form*. Evanston, IL: Northwestern University Press, 2020.

Hill, Michael Gibbs. *Lin Shu, Inc.: Translation and the Making of Modern Chinese Culture*. Oxford: Oxford University Press, 2012.

Ho, Benjamin Tze Ern. *China's Political Worldview and Chinese Exceptionalism: International Order and Global Leadership*. Amsterdam: Amsterdam University Press, 2021.

Holquist, Michael. *Dostoevsky and the Novel*. Princeton: Princeton University Press, 1977.

Hong Hyomin. "Chungguk munhak kwa Chosŏn munhak" [Chinese literature and Korean literature]. *Kyŏnghyang Sinmun*, August 10, 1947.

Hong Sŏkp'yo. *Han-Chung munhak ŭi taehwa: Yi Yuksa wa Lu Swin kŭrigo Han-Chung sangho munhwa insik* [Korean-Chinese literary dialogues: Yi Yuksa, Lu Xun, and Korean-Chinese mutual cultural perception]. Seoul: Ihwa yŏja taehakkyo ch'ulp'an munhwawŏn, 2021.

Hong Sŏkp'yo. *Lu Swin kwa kŭndae Han'guk: Tong Asia kongjon ŭl wihan sangsang* [Lu Xun and early modern Korea: Imagination for the sake of East Asian coexistence]. Seoul: Ihwa yŏja taehakkyo ch'ulp'an munhwawŏn, 2017.

Hong Zicheng 洪子誠 et al., eds. *Shijian he qi: Bai nian xin shi xuan*. 時間和旗：百年新詩選 [Time and the flag: Anthology of one hundred years of new poetry]. Beijing: Sanlian shudian, 2015.

Horiba Kiyoko 堀場清子, ed. *"Seitō" jyosei kaihō ronshū* 『青鞜』女性解放論集 [Collected essays on the emancipation of women in *Bluestockings*]. Tokyo: Iwanami shoten, 1991.

Hsia, C. T. *A History of Modern Chinese Fiction*. New Haven: Yale University Press, 1971.

258   Bibliography

Hsia, Tsi-an. *The Gate of Darkness: Studies on the Leftist Literary Movement in China*. Seattle: University of Washington Press, 1968.

Hu Shi 胡適. *Hu Shi quanji* 胡適全集 [The complete works of Hu Shi]. Hefei: Anhui jiaoyu chubanshe, 2003.

Huang Ruyi 黄汝翼. "You guanyu maobian zhuangding" 又關於毛邊裝訂 [Again about maobian binding]. *Yusi* 語絲, no. 141 (1927): 20.

Hubbs, Joanna. *Mother Russia: The Feminine Myth in Russian Culture*. Bloomington: Indiana University Press, 1988.

Hughes, Glenn. *Transcendence and History: The Search for Ultimacy from Ancient Societies to Postmodernity*. Columbia: University of Missouri Press, 2003.

Hunter, Dard. *Papermaking: The History and Technique of an Ancient Craft*. New York: Dover, 1978.

Huss, Ann. "The Madman that Was Ah Q: Tradition and Modernity in Lu Xun's Fiction." In *The Columbia Companion to Modern East Asian Literature*, edited by Kirk A. Denton, 136–44. New York: Columbia University Press, 2003.

Huters, Theodore. "Blossoms in the Snow: Lu Xun and the Dilemma of Modern Chinese Literature." *Modern China* 10, no. 1 (1984): 49–77.

Huters, Theodore. *Bringing the World Home: Appropriating the West in Late Qing and Early Republican China*. Honolulu: University of Hawai'i Press, 2005.

Ibsen, Henrik. *A Doll's House and Other Plays*. Translated by Deborah Dawkin and Erik Skuggevik. London: Penguin, 2016.

Inoue Hisashi 井上ひさし. *Shanhai mūn* シャンハイムーン [Shanghai moon]. Tokyo: Shūeisha, 1991.

Itō Toramaru 伊藤虎丸. *Ro Jin to Nihonji n: Ajia no kindai to 'ko' no shisō* 魯迅と日本人－アジアの近代と「個」の思想 [Lu Xun and Japanese: Modern Asian idea of "individuals"]. Tokyo: Asahi sensho, 1983.

Jäger, Georg. "Reclams Universal-Bibliothek bis zum Ersten Weltkrieg" [Reclam's Universal Library up to World War I]. In *Reclam 125 Jahre Universal-Bibliothek 1867–1992* [Reclam 125 years of the Universal Library 1867–1992], edited by Dietrich Bode, 25–49. Stuttgart: Reclam, 1992.

Jameson, Fredric. "Third-World Literature in the Era of Multinational Capitalism." *Social Text* 15 (Fall 1986): 65–88.

Jia Yan 賈巖, and Jiang Jingkui 姜景奎. "Yijie yu chuanbo: Lu Xun de Yindu 'laisheng'" 譯介與傳播：魯迅的印度"來生 [Translation and communication: Lu Xun's Indian "Afterlife"]. *Lu Xun yanjiu yuekan* 魯迅研究月刊 (2017): 27–33.

Jin, Xiaoxing. "Translation and Transmutation: The *Origin of Species* in China." *British Journal for the History of Science* 52, no. 1 (2019): 117–41.

Jin Xinlai 靳新來. *"Ren" yu "shou" de jiuge: Lu Xun bi xia de dongwu yixiang* "人"與"獸"的糾葛：魯迅筆下的動物意象 [The entanglement of "human" and "beast": Lu Xun's animal imagery]. Shanghai: Shanghai sanlian shudian, 2010.

Jing Si 靜思. "Chuban shiye de yishu" 出版事業的藝術 [The art of publishing]. *Beixin* 北新 13 (1926): 8.

Jones, Andrew F. *Developmental Fairy Tales: Evolutionary Thinking and Modern Chinese Culture*. Cambridge, MA: Harvard University Press, 2011.

Jun Shi 鈞石 and Quan Ping 全平. "Duiyu *Yi* de gongdao hua" 對於憶的公道話 [Impartial comments on *Memories*]. *Hongshui* 洪水 2, no. 15 (1926): 128–29.

Kaldis, Nicholas. *The Chinese Prose Poem: A Study of Lu Xun's Wild Grass (Yecao)*. Amherst, NY: Cambria Press, 2014.

Kaminski, Joanness D. "Grafting German Romanticism onto the Chinese Revolution: Goethe, Guo Moruo, and the Pursuit of Self-Transcendence." In *Romantic Legacies: Transnational and Transdisciplinary Contexts*, edited by Shun-liang Chao, John Michael Corrigan, and James Engell, 270–86. New York: Routledge, 2019.

Karl, Rebecca E. *Staging the World: Chinese Nationalism at the Turn of the Twentieth Century*. Durham, NC: Duke University Press, 2002.

Kawamura Minato 川村湊. "'Sekibetsu' ron—'Daitōa no shinwa' no maboroshi" 「惜別」論—「大東亜の親和」の幻 [A study of *Regrettable Parting*: The illusion of "Pan-Asian affinity"]. *Kuni bungaku: Kaishaku to kyōzai no kenkyū* 36, no. 4 (1991): 68–75.

Keene, Donald. *Dawn to the West: Japanese Literature of the Modern Era*. New York: Holt, Rinehart, and Winston, 1984.

Kim Yangsu. "Tong Asia ŭi munhakchŏk t'ongno rosŏŭi Lu Swin: Hwang Sŏgyŏng, 'Oraedoen chŏngwŏn' kwa Gwŏ Songp'ŏn, 'Sŏlmaeng' pigyo" [Lu Xun as East Asia's literary passage: Comparison of Hwang Sŏgyŏng's "Old Garden" and Guo Songfen's "Snow Blind"]. *Chungguk munhak yŏn'gu* 80 (2020): 157–77.

King, Lynda J. "Reclam's Universal-Bibliothek: A German Success Story." *Teaching German* 28, no. 1 (1995): 1–6.

Kinna, Ruth. "William Morris: Art, Work, and Leisure." *Journal of the History of Ideas* 61, no. 3 (2000): 493–512.

Kitaoka Masako 北岡正子. *Lu Xun Jiu wang zhi meng de qu xiang* 魯迅救亡之夢的去向 [The trajectory of Lu Xun's dream of national salvation]. Translated by Li Dongmu 李東木. Beijing: Sanlian shudian, 2015.

Kitaoka Masako 北岡正子. *Moluo shi li shuo cai yuan kao* 摩羅詩力説材源考 [A study of sources of "On the power of Mara poetry"]. Translated by He Naiying何乃英. Beijing: Beijing Normal University Press, 1981.

Kitaoka Masako 北岡正子. *Ro Jin bungaku no engen wo saguru: Mara shiriki setsu zaigenkō* 魯迅文學の淵源を探る—「摩羅詩力説」材源考 [Finding Lu Xun's literary source: A textual analysis of "On the power of Mara poetry"]. Tokyo: Kyūko shoin, 2015.

Kiyama Hideo 木山英雄. *Wenxue fugu yu wenxue geming* 文學復古與文學革命 [Literary restoration and literary revolution]. Edited and translated by Zhao Jinghua 趙京華. Beijing: Beijing daxue chubanshe, 2004.

Kohn, Livia. *Daoism: A Contemporary Philosophical Investigation*. New York: Routledge, 2019.

Kowallis, John Eugene von. "Lu Xun and Gogol." *Soviet and Post-Soviet Review* 28, no. 1–2 (2002): 101–12.

Kowallis, Jon Eugene von. "Lu Xun and Terrorism: A Reading of Revenge and Violence in *Mara* and Beyond." In *Creating Chinese Modernity: Knowledge and Everyday Life, 1900–1940*, edited by Peter Zarrow, 83–98. New York: Peter Lang, 2007.

Kowallis, Jon Eugene von. "Lu Xun's Early Essays and Present-Day China." *Studia Orientalia Slovaca* 12, no. 1 (2013): 1–16.

Kowallis, Jon Eugene von. "Lu Xun: The Sexier Story." *Chinese Literature: Essays, Articles, Reviews* 27 (2005): 153–66.

Kowallis, Jon Eugene von. *The Lyrical Lu Xun: A Study of His Classical-Style Verse*. Honolulu: University of Hawai'i Press, 1996.

Kowallis, Jon Eugene von. "On Translating Lu Xun's Fiction." *Studia Orientalia Slovaca* 2, no. 2 (2012): 193–213.

Kuaiji Zhoushi xiongdi 會稽周氏兄弟 [The Zhou brothers in Kuaiji]. *Yuwai xiaoshuo ji* 域外小説集 [Anthology of fiction]. Tokyo: Kanda Publishing House, 1909.

Kürschner, Joseph. "Was wir wollen" [What we want]. *Aus fremden Zungen* 1 (1891): n.p.

Kürschner, Joseph. "Zum dritten Jahrgang" [About the third year]. *Aus fremden Zungen* 1 (1893): n.p.

Lee, Leo Ou-Fan. "Literature on the Eve of Revolution: Reflections on Lu Xun's Leftist Years, 1927–1936." *Modern China* 2, no. 3 (1976): 277–326.

Lee, Leo Ou-fan. *Voices from the Iron House: A Study of Lu Xun*. Bloomington: Indiana University Press, 1987.

Leng Yan 冷眼. "Yige yong shujia zhe de pianjian" 一個用書架者的偏見 [The prejudice of a bookshelf user]. *Kaiming* 開明 1, no. 5 (1928): 259–60.

Li Chunlin 李春林. "Liangwei 'renxing tiancai' de 'Nahan' yu 'Juejiao': Lu Xun yu Jia'erxun de bijiao yanjiu (shang)" 兩位"人性的天才"的"吶喊"與"絶叫"——魯迅與迦爾洵的比較研究（上）[The "calls to arms" and "screams" of two "geniuses of humanity": A comparative study of Lu Xun and Garshin (1) *Lu Xun lun waiguo wenxue*]. *Lu Xun yanjiu yuekan* 魯迅研究月刊 10 (2004): 46–52.

Li Dake 李大可 and Chŏn Hyŏngjun 全炯俊. "Lu Xun zai Hanguo shehui biange yundong zhong de jieshou fangshi: Yi Li Yongxi wei zhongxin" 魯迅在韓國社會變革運動中的接受方式：以李泳禧為中心 [Modes of Lu Xun reception in Korean social reform movements: With a focus on Yi Yŏnghŭi]. *Lu Xun yanjiu yuekan* 魯迅研究月刊 6 (2011): 27–35, 81.

Li Zhao 黎照. *Lu Xun Liang Shiqiu lunzhan shilu* 魯迅梁實秋論戰實錄 [The true record on the polemics between Lu Xun and Liang Shiqiu]. Beijing: Hualing chubanshe, 1997.

Liang Haijun 梁海軍. "Lu Xun zai Fayu shijie de chuanbo yu yanjiu" 魯迅在法語世界的傳播與研究 [The dissemination and study of Lu Xun in the French-speaking world]. PhD diss., Hunan Normal University, 2016.

Liang Shiqiu 梁實秋. "Lu Xun yu niu" 魯迅與牛 [Lu Xun and cattle]. In *Lu Xun yu Liang Shiqiu lunzhan wenxuan* 魯迅與梁實秋論戰文選 [Selected texts on the polemics between Lu Xun and Liang Shiqiu], edited by Bi Hua 璧華, 158–64. Hong Kong: Tiandi tushu, 1979.

Lichtensein, Gustav. "Vorwort." In Päivärinta, Pietari. *Finnische Novellen* [Finnish novellas], vol. 1. translated by Gustav Lichtensein, Leipzig: Reclam, 1890.

Lin Minjie 林敏潔 et al. *Lu Xun yu ershi shiji Zhong-wai wenhua jiaoliu* 魯迅與20世紀中外文化交流 [Lu Xun and the cultural exchanges between China and the world in the twentieth century]. Nanchang: Baihuazhou wenyi chubanshe, 2018.

Lin Yi 林翼. "Guanyu zhuangding" 關於裝訂 [About binding]. *Kaiming* 開明 1, no. 1 (1928): 45–46.

Lin Yu 林玉. "Yijian de yijian" 意見的意見 [Opinions about opinions]. *Kaiming* 開明 1, no. 4 (1928): 237–39.

Ling Yue 凌逾. "Chong gou Zhong-Xi wenhua yinshu: Cong feixugou de xugou kan wenxue dashi: Lun *Lielaozhuan*" 重構中西文化因數：從非虛構的虛構看文學大勢：論《烈佬傳》 [Reconstituting Eastern and Western cultures: Examining literary trends through nonfictional fiction with *Lielaozhuan* as example]. In *Diwujie Hongloumeng jiang pinglunji: Huang Biyun Lielaozhuan* 第五屆紅樓夢文學獎評論集：黃碧雲《烈佬傳》 [Collected criticisms for the Fifth Dream of the Red Chamber Award: Wong Bik-wan's *Lielaozhuan*], 111–28.

Lisi, Leonardo F. *Marginal Modernity: The Aesthetics of Dependence from Kierkegaard to Joyce.* New York: Fordham University Press, 2013.

Liu, Jianmei. "Guo Moruo: Radically Changing Attitudes toward Zhuangzi." In *Zhuangzi and Modern Chinese Literature*, 21–45. New York: Oxford University Press, 2016.

Liu, Lydia H. *Translingual Practice: Literature, National Culture, and Translated Modernity—China, 1900–1937.* Stanford: Stanford University Press, 1995.

Liu, Yiwen. "Witnessing Death: The Circulation of Lu Xun's Postmortem Image." *Trans Asia Photography* 9, no. 2 (2019). https://read.dukeupress.edu/trans-asia-photography/article-standard/doi/10.1215/215820251_9-2-204/312807/Witnessing-Death-The-Circulation-of-Lu-Xun-s.

Lizcano, Pablo. "Lu Sin: La honda tristeza de toda revolución" [Lu Xun: The deep sadness of all revolutions]. *El País*, August 29, 1979.

Lloyd, Vincent. *Law and Transcendence: On the Unfinished Project of Gillian Rose.* Basingstoke: Palgrave Macmillan, 2009.

Lovell, Julia. Introduction to *The Real Story of Ah-Q and Other Tales of China: The Complete Fiction of Lu Xun*, xiii–xxxix. London: Penguin, 2009.

Lu Hsun. *Diario de un loco* [Diary of a madman]. Translated by Sergio Pitol. Barcelona: Tusquets, 1971.

Lu Hsun. *Sobre la classe intel·lectual* [On the intellectual class]. Translated by Joan Francesc Mira. Valencia: Tres i Quatre, 1973.

Lu Sin. *Antiguos relatos vueltos a contar* [Old tales retold]. Beijing: Ediciones en Lenguas Extranjeras, 1972.

Lu Sin. *Grito de llamada* [Outcry]. Translated by Iñaki Preciado and Miguel Shiao. Madrid: Alfaguara, 1978.

Lu Sin. *La verdadera historia de A Q y otros cuentos* [The true story of Ah Q and other short stories]. Translated by Luis Enrique Délano. Estella: Salvat, 1971.

Lu Sin. *Novelas escogidas* [Selected novels]. Translated by Luis Enrique Délano. Beijing: Ediciones en Lenguas Extranjeras, 1960.

Lu Xun 魯迅. "210713 Zhi Zhou Zuoren" 210713致周作人 [1921 July 13: A letter to Zhou Zuoren]. *LXQJ* 11:391–96.

Lu Xun 魯迅. "210731 Zhi Zhou Zuoren" 210731致周作人 [1921 July 31: A letter to Zhou Zuoren]. *LXQJ* 11:400–403.

262 Bibliography

Lu Xun 魯迅. "210806 Zhi Zhou Zuoren" 210806致周作人 [1921 August 6: A letter to Zhou Zuoren]. *LXQJ* 11:403–6.

Lu Xun 魯迅. "270925 Zhi Tai Jingnong" 270925致台靜農 [1927 September 25: A letter to Tai Jingnong]. *LXQJ* 12:73–75.

Lu Xun 魯迅. "A Q zhengzhuan" 阿Q正傳 [The true story of Ah Q]. *LXQJ* 1:512–59.

Lu Xun 魯迅. "*A Q zhengzhuan* de chengyin" 《阿Q正傳》的成因 [The origins of *The True Story of Ah Q*]. *LXQJ* 3:394–403.

Lu Xun 魯迅. "Chu guan" 出關 [Leaving the pass]. *LXQJ* 2:454–67.

Lu Xun 魯迅. "*Chuguan* de 'guan'" 《出關》的關 [The pass in *Leaving the Pass*]. *LXQJ* 6:536–43.

Lu Xun 魯迅. "Cong 'biezi' shuokaiqu" 從"別字"說開去 [Talking around "misglossed characters"], *LXQJ* 6:289–94.

Lu Xun 魯迅. "Ewen yiben *A Q zhengzhuan* xu ji zhuzhe zixu zhuanlüe" 俄文譯本《阿Q正傳》序及著者自敘傳略 [Preface to the Russian translation of *The True Story of Ah Q* and biographical sketch of the author]. *LXQJ* 7:83–88.

Lu Xun 魯迅. *Fen* 墳 [Graves]. *LXQJ* 1:1–304.

Lu Xun 魯迅. *Guxiang* 故鄉 [Hometown]. *LXQJ* 1:344–358.

Lu Xun 魯迅. "Guduzhe" 孤獨者 [The misanthrope]. *LXQJ* 2:88–112.

Lu Xun 魯迅. *Han wenxueshi gangyao* 漢文學史綱要 [A sketch of Chinese literary history]. *LXQJ* 9:351–442.

Lu Xun 魯迅. "Huran xiangdao (er)" 忽然想到（二）[Sudden thoughts (part two)]. *Jingbao fukan* 京報副刊, no. 42 (1925): 8.

Lu Xun 魯迅. "Kou si zagan" 扣絲雜感 [Miscellaneous thoughts on the confiscation of *Yusi*]. *Yusi* 語絲, no. 154 (1927): 267–72.

Lu Xun 魯迅. "Li ci cunzhao [qi]" 立此存照 [七] [A document on File (7)]. *LXQJ* 6: 657–59.

Lu Xun 魯迅. "Lun 'fei'e polai' yinggai huanxing" 論"費厄潑賴"應該緩行 [Why "fair play" should be deferred]. *LXQJ* 1:286–97.

Lu Xun 魯迅. *Lu Xun lun waiguo wenxue* 魯迅論外國文學 [Lu Xun on foreign literatures], edited by Fujian Shifan Daxue Zhongwenxi 福建師範大學中文系. Beijing: Waiguo wenxue chubanshe, 1982.

Lu Xun 魯迅. *Lu Xun yiwen ji* 魯迅譯文集 [Collected translations of Lu Xun]. Beijing: Renmin wenxue chubanshe, 1958.

Lu Xun 魯迅. "Moluo shili shuo" 摩羅詩力說 [On the power of Mara poetry]. *LXQJ* 1:65–120.

Lu Xun 魯迅. "Nahan zixu" 《呐喊》自序 [Preface to *Outcry*]. *LXQJ* 1:437–43.

Lu Xun 魯迅. "Nalaizhuyi" 拿來主義 [Take-ism]. *LXQJ* 6:39–42.

Lu Xun 魯迅. "Po e sheng lun" 破惡聲論 [Toward a refutation of malevolent voices]. *LXQJ* 8:25–40.

Lu Xun 魯迅. "Qingnian bi du shu" 青年必讀書 [The necessary books for youth]. *LXQJ* 3:12–13.

Lu Xun 魯迅. "Ren zhi lishi" 人之歷史 [The history of humankind]. *LXQJ* 1:12–13.

Lu Xun 魯迅. "'Renxing de tiancai: Jia'erxun' yizhe houji" 《人性的天才：迦爾洵》譯者後記 ["Genius of humanity: Garshin" translator's postface]. *Chunchao* 春潮1, no. 9 (1929): 13.

Lu Xun 魯迅. "Shanghai wenyi zhi yi pie" 上海文藝之一瞥 [A glimpse at Shanghai literature]. *LXQJ* 4:298–315.

Lu Xun 魯迅. "*Shi'er ge* hou ji" 《十二個》後記 [Afterword to *The Twelve*]. In *Lu Xun zhu yi biannian quan ji* 魯迅著譯編年全集 [Complete works and translations of Lu Xun in chronological order], 7:220–23. Beijing: Renmin chubanshe, 2009.

Lu Xun 魯迅. "Shige zhi di" 詩歌之敵 [Enemies of poetry]. *LXQJ* 7:245–52.

Lu Xun 魯迅. "Si" 死 [Death]. *LXQJ* 6:631–35.

Lu Xun 魯迅. "Suigan lu sishi'er" 隨感錄四十二 [Impromptu reflections no. 42]. *LXQJ* 1:343–45.

Lu Xun 魯迅. "Suigan lu sishiba" 隨感錄四十八 [Impromptu reflections no. 48]. *LXQJ* 1:352–53.

Lu Xun 魯迅. "Tengye xiansheng" 藤野先生 [Mr. Fujino]. *LXQJ* 2:313–20.

Lu Xun 魯迅. "Tingshuo meng" 聽説夢 [Hear about dreams]. *LXQJ* 4:481–85.

Lu Xun 魯迅. "*Tuo'ersitai zhi si yu shaonian Ouluoba* yi hou ji" 《托爾斯泰之死與少年歐羅巴》譯後記 [Translator's note on "The death of Tolstoy and young Europe"]. *LXQJ* 10:337–38.

Lu Xun 魯迅. "Wenhua pian zhi lun" 文化偏至論 [On imbalanced cultural development]. *LXQJ* 1:45–64.

Lu Xun 魯迅. "Wenyi yu zhengzhi de qitu" 文藝與政治的歧途 [The divergent roads of literature and politics]. *LXQJ* 7:115–23.

Lu Xun 魯迅. "Wo zenme zuoqi xiaoshuo lai" 我怎麼做起小説來 [How I came to write fiction]. *LXQJ* 4:525–30.

Lu Xun 魯迅. "*Xiao yuehan* yinyan." 《小約翰》引言 [A prelude to *Little John*]. *LXQJ* 10:280–90.

Lu Xun 魯迅. "Xiezai *Fen* houmian" 寫在墳後面 ["Afterword" to *Graves*]. *LXQJ* 1:298.

Lu Xun 魯迅. "Yeshou xunlian fa" 野獸訓練法 [How to train wild animals]. *LXQJ* 5:384–86.

Lu Xun 魯迅. "Ye song" 夜頌 [Ode to the night]. *LXQJ* 5:203.

Lu Xun 魯迅. "Yingyi yu wenxue de jiejixing" 硬譯和文學的階級性 [Hard translation and the class nature of literature]. *LXQJ* 4:199–227/388–98.

Lu Xun 魯迅. "*Yuwai xiaoshuo ji* lüeli" 《域外小説集》略例 [Introduction to *Anthology of Fiction*]. *LXQJ* 10:171.

Lu Xun 魯迅. "*Yuwai xiaoshuo ji* xuyan" 《域外小説集》序言 [Preface to *Anthology of Fiction*]. *LXQJ* 10: 170.

Lu Xun 魯迅. "Zai xiandai Zhongguo de Kongfuzi" 在現代中國的孔夫子 [Confucius in contemporary China]. Translated from Japanese by anonymous. *LXQJ* 6:324–33.

Lu Xun 魯迅. "*Zhongguo xinwenxue daxi* xiaoshuo erji xu" 《中國新文學大系》小説二集序 [Preface to *The lineage of new Chinese literature*, fiction vol. 2). *LXQJ* 6:246–74.

Lu Xun 魯迅. "Zhufu" 祝福 [New Year's sacrifice]. *LXQJ* 2:5–21.

Lu Xun 魯迅. "Zi chao" 自嘲 [Laughing at My Own Predicament]. *LXQJ* 7:151.

264 Bibliography

Lu Xun. "Afterword to *Graves.*" Translated by Theodore Huters. In *Jottings under Lamplight*, edited by Eileen J. Cheng and Kirk A. Denton, 30–36. Cambridge, MA: Harvard University Press, 2017.

Lu Xun. "Ah Chang and the Classic of Mountains and Seas." In *Wild Grass and Morning Blossoms Gathered at Dusk*, translated by Eileen J. Cheng, edited by Theodore Huters, 141–49. Cambridge, MA: Harvard University Press, 2022.

Lu Xun. "Autumn Night." In *Wild Grass and Morning Blossoms Gathered at Dusk*, translated by Eileen J. Cheng, edited by Theodore Huters, 33–35. Cambridge, MA: Harvard University Press, 2022.

Lu Xun. *Breve historia de la novela china* [A brief history of Chinese fiction]. Translated by Rosario Blanco Facal. Barcelona: Azul, 2001.

Lu Xun. *Colección de un errante* [A wanderer's collection]. Translated by Wang Liyun and Dídac Masip. Barcelona: Lamolapress, 2021.

Lu Xun. *Contar nuevo de historias viejas* [Old tales retold]. Translated by Laureano Ramírez. Madrid: Hiperión, 2001.

Lu Xun. "Death." Translated by Eileen Cheng. In *Jottings under Lamplight*, edited by Eileen J. Cheng and Kirk A. Denton, 62–65. Cambridge, MA: Harvard University Press, 2017.

Lu Xun. *Diari d'un boig i altres relats* [Diary of a madman and other stories]. Translated by Carles Prado-Fonts. Barcelona: Edicions de 1984, 2007.

Lu Xun. *Diario de un demente y la auténtica historia de Ah Q* [Diary of a madman and the true story of Ah Q]. Translated by Néstor Cabrera and Puerto Barrutabeña. Madrid: Kailas, 2014.

Lu Xun. *Diario de un demente y otros cuentos* [Diary of a madman and other stories]. Translated by Néstor Cabrera. Madrid: Editorial Popular, 2008.

Lu Xun. "El inteligente, el tonto y el siervo" [The wise man, the fool, and the slave]. Translated by Manuel Pavón Belizón. *China traducida y por traducir*, 2020. http://china-traducida. net/traducciones/el-inteligente-el-tonto-y-el-siervo-lu-xun.

Lu Xun. "Father's Illness." In *Wild Grass and Morning Blossoms Gathered at Dusk*, translated by Eileen J. Cheng, edited by Theodore Huters, 182–89. Cambridge, MA: Harvard University Press, 2022.

Lu Xun. "A Glimpse at Shanghai Literature." Translated by Roy Chan and Yu Chih Chou. In *Jottings under Lamplight*, edited by Eileen J. Cheng and Kirk A. Denton, 225–37. Cambridge, MA: Harvard University Press, 2017.

Lu Xun. *Gritos: Diario de un loco y otros relatos* [Outcry: Diary of a madman and other stories]. Translated by Iñaki Preciado. Madrid: Miraguano, 2017.

Lu Xun. "'Hard Translation' and the 'Class Character of Literature.'" In *Selected Works of Lu Hsun*, translated by Yang Hsien-yi and Gladys Yang, 3:65–86. Beijing: Foreign Languages Press, 1960.

Lu Xun. "Hope" 希望. In *Wild Grass* [Chinese-English bilingual ed.], translated by Yang Xianyi and Gladys Yang, 32–37. Hong Kong: Chinese University of Hong Kong Press, 2003.

Lu Xun. "How I Came to Write Fiction." Translated by Jon Eugene von Kowallis. In *Jottings under Lamplight*, edited by Eileen J. Cheng and Kirk A. Denton, 54–57. Cambridge, MA: Harvard University Press, 2017.

Lu Xun. "The Illustrated Twenty-Four Filial Exemplars." In *Wild Grass and Morning Blossoms Gathered at Dusk*, translated by Eileen J. Cheng, edited by Theodore Huters, 150–58. Cambridge, MA: Harvard University Press, 2022.

Lu Xun. *Kong Yiji y otros cuentos* [Kong Yiji and other stories]. Translated by Miguel Ángel Petrecca. Santiago de Chile: LOM, 2016.

Lu Xun. *La mala hierba* [Wild grass]. Translated by Blas Piñero. Madrid: Bartleby Editores, 2013.

Lu Xun. *La verdadera historia de A Q* [The true story of Ah Q]. Buenos Aires: Centro Editor de América Latina, 1970.

Lu Xun. *La verídica historia de A Q* [The true story of Ah Q]. Translated by Ernesto Posse. Madrid: Compañía Europea de Comunicación e Información, 1991.

Lu Xun. "Leaving the Pass." In *The Real Story of Ah-Q and Other Tales of China: The Complete Fiction of Lu Xun*, translated by Julia Lovell, 372–81. New York: Penguin, 2009.

Lu Xun. *Mala herba* [Wild grass]. Translated by Seán Golden and Marisa Presas. Barcelona: Edicions 62, 1994.

Lu Xun. "On the Power of Mara Poetry." Translated by Shu-ying Tsau and Donald Holoch. In *Modern Chinese Literary Thought, 1893–1945*, edited by Kirk A. Denton, 96–109. Stanford: Stanford University Press, 1996.

Lu Xun. "A Preface to Bai Mang's *The Children's Pagoda*." In *Selected Works of Lu Hsun*, translated by Yang Hsien-yi and Gladys Yang, 4:261–62. Beijing: Foreign Languages Press, 1960.

Lu Xun. "Preface to *Cheering from the Sideline*." In *Diary of a Madman and Other Stories*, translated by William A. Lyell, 21–28. Honolulu: University of Hawai'i Press, 1990.

Lu Xun. "Preface to *Na Han* [Outcry]." In *The Real Story of Ah-Q and Other Tales of China: The Complete Fiction of Lu Xun*, translated by Julia Lovell, 15–20. London: Penguin, 2009.

Lu Xun. "Preface to *Old Tales Retold*." In *Lu Xun, The Real Story of Ah-Q and Other Tales of China: The Complete Fiction of Lu Xun*, translated by Julia Lovell, 295–97. London: Penguin, 2009.

Lu Xun. *The Real Story of Ah-Q and Other Tales of China: The Complete Fiction of Lu Xun*. Translated by Julia Lovell. London: Penguin, 2009.

Lu Xun. "Take-ism." Translated by Kirk Denton. In *Jottings under Lamplight*, edited by Eileen J. Cheng and Kirk A. Denton, 281–83. Cambridge, MA: Harvard University Press, 2017.

Lu Xun. "Tremors on the Border of Degradation." In *Wild Grass and Morning Blossoms Gathered at Dusk*, translated by Eileen J. Cheng, edited by Theodore Huters, 75–78. Cambridge, MA: Harvard University Press, 2022.

Lu Xun. "The True Story of Ah Q." In *Lu Xun: Selected Works, Volume One*, translated by Yang Xianyi and Gladys Yang. Beijing: Foreign Language Press.

Lu Xun. "Why 'Fair Play' Should Be Deferred." Translated by Andrew F. Jones. In *Jottings under Lamplight*, edited by Eileen J. Cheng and Kirk A. Denton, 156–64. Cambridge, MA: Harvard University Press, 2017.

Lu Xun et al. *Antología del cuento chino maravilloso* [Anthology of magical Chinese fiction]. Edited by Rolando Sánchez-Mejías. Barcelona: Océano, 2003.

Lu Xun et al. *Flores e leña* [Flowers and firewood]. Edited and translated by Fernando Pérez-Barreiro Nolla. Vigo: Edicións Xerais de Galicia, 1982.

Lunacharsky, Anatoly. *Marukusu Shugi Geijutsuron* マルクス主義藝術論 [Marxist theory of art]. Translated by Nobori Shomu 昇曙夢. Tokyo: Shakai Shobô, 1947.

Lunacharsky, Anatoly. *Yishu lun* 藝術論 [On art]. Translated by Lu Xun. In *Lu Xun yiwen quanji* 魯迅譯文全集 [Complete translation works of Lu Xun], 4:189–280. Fuzhou: Fujian jiaoyu, 2008.

Ma Feng 馬峰. "Lu Xun zai Yinni de chuanbo yu yingxiang" 魯迅在印尼的傳播與影響 [The dissemination and influence of Lu Xun in Indonesia]. In *Nanyang Lu Xun: Jieshou yu yingxiang* 南洋魯迅：接受與影響 [South Seas Lu Xun: Acceptance and influence], edited by Sixiang bianji weiyuanhui 思想編輯委員會, 219–45. Taipei: Lianjing chubanshe, 2020.

Ma, Sen. "Lu Xun, iniciador de la literatura china moderna" [Lu Xun, initiator of modern Chinese literature]. Translated by Luz Del Amo. *Estudios Orientales* 3, no. 3 (8) (1968): 255–74.

Ma, Xiaolu. "The Missing Link: Japan as an Intermediary in the Transculturation of the Diary of a Madman." *Frontiers of Literary Studies in China* 2 (2014): 331–46.

Ma, Xiaolu. "Transculturation of Madness: The Double Origin of Lu Xun's 'Diary of a Madman.'" *Literature and Medicine* 33, no. 2 (Fall 2015): 348–67.

Magagnin, Paolo. "Agents of May Fourth: Jing Yinyu, Xu Zhongnian, and the Early Introduction of Modern Chinese Literature in France." *Translating Wor(l)ds*, no. 4 (2020): 55–73.

Mani, Venkat. *Recoding World Literature: Libraries, Print Culture, and Germany's Pact with Books*. New York: Fordham University Press, 2016.

Mao Zedong. "From 'Talks at the Yenan Forum on Literature and Art.'" In *Literature of the People's Republic of China*, edited by Kai-yu Hsu, 29–36. Bloomington: Indiana University Press, 1980.

Mao Zedong. "On Lu Xun." October 10, 1937. https://www.marxistphilosophy.org/maozedong/mx2/018.htm.

Marín-Lacarta, Maialen. "La recepción de traducciones literarias por su valor documental: El caso de la literatura china moderna y contemporánea en España" [The reception of literary translations based on their documentary value: The case of modern and contemporary Chinese literature in Spain]. In *Caleidoscopio de traducción literaria* [Kaleidoscope of literary translation], edited by Pilar Martino Alba and Salud M. Jarilla, 45–56. Madrid: Dykinson, 2012.

Marín-Lacarta, Maialen. "Mediación, recepción y marginalidad: Las traducciones de literatura china moderna y contemporánea en España [Mediation, reception, and marginality: The translations of modern and contemporary Chinese literature in Spain]." Institut

National des Langues et Civilisations Orientales (Paris) and Universitat Autònoma de Barcelona, 2012.

Maruyama Noboru 丸山昇. *Lu Xun, geming, lishi* 鲁迅·革命·歷史 [Lu Xun, revolution, history]. Translated by Wang Junwen 王俊文. Beijing: Beijing daxue chubanshe, 2005.

Mas, Sinibaldo de. *L'Angleterre et le Céleste Empire* [England and the celestial empire]. Paris: Henri Plon, 1857.

Mas, Sinibaldo de. *L'Angleterre, la Chine et l'Inde* [England, China, and India]. Paris: Jules Tardieu, 1858.

Mas, Sinibaldo de. *La Chine et les puissances chrétiennes* [China and the Christian powers]. Paris: Louise Hachette et Cie, 1861.

Merhautová, Lucie. "Česká literární moderna v časopise Aus fremden Zungen—čtyři příklady prostředkování" [Czech literary modernity in the journal *Aus fremden Zungen*—four examples of mediation]. *Slovo a smysl* 12, no. 24 (2015): 93–125.

Mignolo, Walter D., and Catherine E. Walsh. *On Decoloniality: Concepts, Analytics, Praxis*. Durham, NC: Duke University Press, 2018.

Moore, Bryan L. *Ecological Literature and the Critique of Anthropocentrism*. Cham: Springer, 2017.

Moore, Robert. "Paris by Way of the Moon: Translations of Popular French Fiction in Late-Qing China." PhD diss., University of Oregon, 2021.

Moretti, Franco. "Conjectures on World Literature." *New Left Review* 1, no. 1 (2000): 54–68.

Moretti, Franco. *Modern Epic: The World-System from Goethe to García Márquez*. London: Verso, 1996.

Mori Ōgai 森鷗外. *Ōgai zenshū* 鷗外全集 [The complete works of Mori Ōgai]. Tokyo: Iwanami shoten, 1971–1975.

Moslund, Sten Pultz, Marlene Karlsson Marcussen, and Martin Karlsson Pedersen. *How Literature Comes to Matter: Post-Anthropocentric Approaches to Fiction*. Edinburgh: Edinburgh University Press, 2022.

Müller, Sabine Lenore, and Tina-Karen Pusse. *From Ego to Eco: Mapping Shifts from Anthropocentrism to Ecocentrism*. Leiden: Brill Rodopi, 2018.

Nagahori Yuzo 長堀祐造. *Lu Xun yu Tuoluociji: "Wenxue yu geming" zai Zhongguo* 鲁迅與托洛茨基：《文學與革命》在中國 [Lu Xun and Trotsky: Literature and revolution in China]. Translated by Wang Junwen 王俊文. Taipei: Renjian chubanshe, 2015.

Nagashima, Yōichi. "From 'Literary Translation' to 'Cultural Translation': Mori Ōgai and the Plays of Henrik Ibsen." *Japan Review* 24 (2012): 85–104.

Nakamura Toshiko 中村都市子. *Nihon no Ipusen genshō* 日本のイプセン現象: *1906–1916* [The Ibsen phenomenon in Japan, 1906–1916]. Fukuoka: Kyūshū daigaku shuppankai, 1997.

Nappi, Carla. "On Yeti and Being Just: Carving the Borders of Humanity in Early Modern China." In *Animals and the Human Imagination: A Companion to Animal Studies*, edited by Aaron Gross and Anne Vallely, 55–78. New York: Columbia University Press, 2012.

Natsume Kinnosuke 夏目金之助. *Sōseki zenshū* 漱石全集 [Complete works of Sōseki] 28 vols. Tokyo: Iwanami Shōten, 2019.

Ng Kim Chew 黃錦樹. "Buyi" 補遺 [Supplement]. In Ng Kim Chew 黃錦樹, *Youdao zhidao* 由島至島 [From island to island], 267–90. Taipei: Rye Field Publishing, 2001.

Ng Kim Chew 黃錦樹. "M de shizong" M的失蹤 [The disappearance of M]. In Ng Kim Chew, *Meng yu zhu yu liming* 夢與豬與黎明 [Dream and swine and aurora], 10–42. Taipei: Jiuge, 1994.

Ng Kim Chew 黃錦樹. "Si zai nanfang" 死在南方 [Death in the south]. In Ng Kim Chew, *Meng yu zhu yu liming* 夢與豬與黎明 [Dream and swine and aurora], 182–210. Taipei: Jiuge, 1994.

Ng Kim Chew 黃錦樹. "Ta shuo ta jianguo Lu Xun" 他說他見過魯迅 [He says he saw Lu Xun]. In Ng Kim Chew, *Minguo de manchuan* 民國的慢船 [Slow boat to the Republic of China], 89–110. Taipei: Monsoon Zone Publishing, 2019.

Ng Kim Chew 黃錦樹. "Zhufu" 祝福 [Benediction]. In Ng Kim Chew, *Yu* 魚 [Fish], 15–39. Taipei: Ink, 2015.

Ng Kim Chew. "Death in the South." In Ng Kim Chew, *Slow Boat to China and Other Stories*, translated and edited by Carlos Rojas, 47–68. New York: Columbia University Press, 2016.

Ng Kim Chew. "The Disappearance of M." In Ng Kim Chew, *Slow Boat to China and Other Stories*, translated and edited by Carlos Rojas, 1–24. New York: Columbia University Press, 2016.

Ng Kim Chew. "Supplement." In Ng Kim Chew, *Slow Boat to China and Other Stories*, translated and edited by Carlos Rojas, 209–36. New York: Columbia University Press, 2016.

Ollé, Manel. "Mala herba" [Wild grass]. *La Vanguardia*, October 14, 1994.

Ollé, Manel. "Supervivències" [Survivals]. *El País*, September 6, 2007.

Onchi Kōshirō 恩地孝四郎. *Sōhon no shimei: Onchi Kōshirō sōtei bijutsu ronshū* 裝本の使命：恩地孝四郎裝幀美術論集 [The mission of book design: Onchi Kōshirō's works on the art of typography]. Tokyo: Abe shuppan, 1992.

Ōnuki Shinju 大貫伸樹. *Seihon tansaku* 製本探索 [Exploration of bookbinding]. Tokyo: Insatsu gakkai shuppanbu, 2005.

Ortells-Nicolau, Xavier, and David Martínez-Robles. "Publicaciones históricas" [Historical publications]. *Archivo China-España* [Archive China-Spain]. Accessed March 31, 2022. http://ace.uoc.edu/publicaciones-historicas.

Oteyza, Luis de. *El diablo blanco* [The white devil]. Madrid: Pueyo, 1928.

Ozaki Hotsuki 尾崎秀樹. *Ro Jin to no taiwa* 魯迅との対話 [A dialogue with Lu Xun]. Tokyo: Keisō Shobō, 1969.

Päivärinta, Pietari. *Finnische Novellen* [Finnish novellas], vol. 1. Translated by Gustav Lichtensein. Leipzig: Reclam, 1890.

Päivärinta, Pietari. *Finnische Novellen* [Finnish novellas], vol. 2. Translated by Gustav Lichtensein. Leipzig: Reclam, 1892.

Pak Chaeu 朴宰雨. *Hanguo de Zhongguo xiandai wenxue yanjiu tonglun* 韓國的中國現代文學研究統論 [Survey of modern Chinese literature studies in Korea]. Seoul: Ach'im, 2008.

Pak Chaeu 朴宰雨. "21 shiji Dongya yujing li de Lu Xun jiazhi" 21世紀東亞語境裡的魯迅價值 [Value of Lu Xun in the context of twenty-first century East Asia]. In *You Han-Zhong Lu Xun yanjiu duihua zouxiang Dongya Lu Xun xue* 由韓中魯迅研究對話走向東亞魯迅

學 [From Korean-Chinese dialogues in Lu Xun studies toward East Asian Luxunology], edited by Pak Chaeu 朴宰雨, 230–33. Seoul: Ach'im, 2008.

Pak Chaeu 朴宰雨. "Qi, bashi niandai Hanguo de biange yundong yu Lu Xun: Yi Li Yongxi, Ren Xuanyong liang wei yundongjia wei zhongxin" 七、八十年代韓國的變革運動與魯迅：以李泳禧、任軒永兩位運動家為中心 [Korean reform movements in the 1970s and the 1980s and Lu Xun: With a focus on two activists Yi Yŏnghŭi and Im Hŏnyŏng]. *Lu Xun yanjiu yuekan* 魯迅研究月刊 1 (2001): 39–44.

Pak Chaeu 朴宰雨. "Shoudao Lu Xun yingxiang de Dongya zhishifenzi de leixing fenxi: Yi Hanguo zhishifenzi de leixing wei zhongxin" 受到魯迅影響的東亞知識分子的類型分析：以韓國知識分子的類型為中心 [Analyzing types of East Asian intellectuals who received Lu Xun's influence: With a focus on types of Korean intellectuals]. *Xindi wenxue* 新地文學 34 (December 2015): 111–28.

Pak Chaeu 朴宰雨. "Xuyan. Lu Xun zai Hanguo: jieshou mailuo yu shehui yingxiang" 序言. 魯迅在韓國：接受脈絡與社會影響 [Preface. Lu Xun in Korea: Reception trajectories and social influence]. In *Hanguo Lu Xun yanjiu jingxuanji* 韓國魯迅研究精選集 [A selection of Korean Lu Xun studies], edited by Pak Chaeu (Piao Zaiyu) 朴宰雨, translated by Jin Yingming 金英明 et al., 1–21. Beijing: Zhongyang bianyi chubanshe, 2016.

Pak Kyŏngni. *Q ssi ege: Pak Kyŏngni sanmunjip* [To Mr. Q: Collected prose of Pak Kyŏngni]. Reprint. Seoul: Sol, 1993.

Peniche de Lugo, Francisco. "China y Europa" [China and Europe]. *La España moderna*, July 1900, xx.

Peterson, William S. 1991. *The Kelmscott Press: A History of William Morris's Typographical Adventure*. Berkeley: University of California Press, 1991.

Pines, Yuri. "Beasts or Humans: Pre-Imperial Origins of the 'Sino-Barbarian' Dichotomy." In *Mongols, Turks, and Others: Eurasian Nomads and the Sedentary World*, edited by Reuven Amitai and Michal Biran, 59–102. Leiden: Brill, 2005.

Pippin, Robert M. *Modernism as a Philosophical Problem: On the Dissatisfactions of European High Culture*. Cambridge, MA: Blackwell, 1991.

Pizer, John. *The Idea of World Literature: History and Pedagogical Practice*. Baton Rouge: Louisiana State University Press, 2006.

Porcel, Baltasar. "Canton (2): Las hormigas azules" [Canton (2): The blue ants]. *Destino*, July 14, 1973, 6–8.

Porcel, Baltasar. "China: La mujer y el amor" [China: Women and love]. *Destino*, July 21, 1973, 24–27.

Porcel, Baltasar. *China, una revolución en pie* [China, a revolution on its feet]. Barcelona: Destino, 1974.

Porcel, Baltasar. "Del doctor Sun al general Chiang" [From Doctor Sun to General Chiang]. September 15, 1973, 16–19.

Porcel, Baltasar. "El frente cultural" [The cultural front]. *Destino*, October 20, 1973, 35–39.

Porcel, Baltasar. "Shanghai (y 2): Industrias y obreros" [Shanghai (and 2): Industries and workers]. *Destino*, September 1, 1973, 6–9.

270 Bibliography

Prado-Fonts, Carles. "Del xinès al català, traduccions per generació espontània" [From Chinese into Catalan, translations by spontaneous generation]. *Quaderns: Revista de traduccio*, no. 6 (2001): 107–17.

Prado-Fonts, Carles. "Orientalismo a su pesar: Gao Xingjian y las paradojas del sistema literario global" [Orientalism despite itself: Gao Xingjian and the paradoxes of the global literary system]. *Inter Asia Papers*, no. 4 (2008): 1–25.

Prado-Fonts, Carles. *Secondhand China: Spain, the East, and the Politics of Translation.* Evanston, IL: Northwestern University Press, 2022.

Pusey, James Reeve. *China and Charles Darwin*. Cambridge, MA: Council on East Asian Studies at Harvard University, 1983.

Qi Guang 齊光. "Maobian shu yu zazhi" 毛邊書與雜誌 [*Maobian* books and magazines]. *Taosheng* 濤聲, no. 4 (1931): 4.

Qian, Kun. *Imperial-Time-Order: Literature, Intellectual History, and China's Road to Empire.* Leiden: Brill, 2016.

Qian Liqun 錢理群. "Lu Xun yu Zhongguo xiandai sixiang wenhua" 魯迅與中國現代思想文化 [Lu Xun and modern Chinese thought and culture]. In *Aisixang wang* 愛思想網. 2012. http://www.aisixang.com/data/57341.html.

Qian Liqun 錢理群. *Qian Liqun zhongxue jiang Lu Xun* 錢理群中學講魯迅 [Qian Liqun discusses Lu Xun with high school students]. Beijing: Sanlian shudian, 2011.

Qian Liqun 錢理群. *Xinling de tanxun* 心靈的探尋 [Spirit's search]. Shijiazhuang: Hebei jiaoyu chubanshe, 2002.

Qin Gong 秦弓. "Lu Xun de ertong wenxue fanyi" 魯迅的兒童文學翻譯 [Lu Xun's translation of children's literature]. *Shandong shehui kexue* 山東社會科學, no. 4 (2013): 86–87.

Qin Gong 秦弓. "Wusi shiqi de ertong wenxue fanyi (xia)" 五四時期的兒童文學翻譯 (下) [Translating children's literature in the May Fourth period (sequel)]. *Xuzhou shifan daxue xuebao* 徐州師範大學學報 30, no. 6 (2004): 22–27.

Qiu Yunduo 邱運鐸, 1936. "'Haiyan' duhou ji" 《海燕》讀後記 [After-thoughts on "Seagull"]. In *1913–1983 Lu Xun yanjiu xueshu ziliao huibian* 魯迅研究學術資料匯編 [Research materials of Lu Xun studies, 1913–1983], 1:1349–50. Beijing: Zhongguo wenlian chuban gongsi, 1985.

Rancière, Jacques. *The Politics of Literature*. Translated by Julie Rose. Cambridge, MA: Polity, 2011.

Rea, Christopher. *The Age of Irreverence: A New History of Laughter in China*. Berkeley: University of California Press, 2015.

Ricoeur, Paul. *The Conflict of Interpretations*. Translated by D. Ihde. Evanston, IL: Northwestern University Press, 1969.

Ricoeur, Paul. *Freud and Philosophy: An Essay on Interpretation*. Translated by Denis Savage. New Haven: Yale University Press, 1970.

Riedl, Frederick. 1906. *A History of Hungarian Literature*. New York: Appleton, 1906.

Robins, Christopher. "Japanese Visions of Lu Xun in the Light of the Magic Lantern Incident." *Asia-Pacific Journal: Japan Focus* 5, no. 2 (2007): 1–24.

Rolland, Romain. *Tolstoy*. London: Adelphi Terrace, 1911. https://www.gutenberg.org/files/49435/49435-h/49435-h.htm.

Rolland, Romain. *Vie de Tolstoy* [The life of Tolstoy]. Project Gutenberg, 2011. https://www.gutenberg.org/files/37951/37951-h/37951-h.htm.

Rose, Gillian. *The Broken Middle: Out of Our Ancient Society*. Oxford: Blackwell, 1992.

Rose, Gillian. *Hegel contra Sociology*. London: Athlone, 1981.

Rose, Gillian. *Love's Work: A Reckoning with Life*. New York: New York Review of Books, 1995.

Rose, Gillian. *Mourning Becomes the Law: Philosophy and Representation*. Cambridge: Cambridge University Press, 1996.

Rui Yifu 芮逸夫. "Xinan shaoshu minzu chongshou pianpang mingming kaolüe" 西南少數民族蟲獸偏旁命名考略 [Investigations into the use of insect and animal names for ethnic minorities in the southwest]. In *Zhonghua minzu ji qi wenhua lungao (shangce)* 中國民族及其文化論稿（上冊）[A manuscript on Chinese ethnicities and their cultures (vol. 1 of 2)], 73–117. Taipei: Yiwen yinshuguan, 1972.

Said, Edward. "Traveling Theory." In *The World, the Text, and the Critic*, 31–53. Cambridge, MA: Harvard University Press, 1983.

Schick, Kate. *Gillian Rose: A Good Enough Justice*. Edinburgh: Edinburgh University Press, 2012.

Schmid, Andre. *Korea between Empires, 1895–1919*. New York: Columbia University Press, 2002.

Scott-Baumann, Alison. *Ricoeur and the Hermeneutics of Suspicion*. London: Bloomsbury, 2012.

Shen Baojun 沈寶鈞. "Duiyu zhuangding yu paiyin zhi guanjian" 對於裝訂與排印之管見 [Humble opinions on bookbinding and design]. *Kaiming* 開明 1, no. 12 (1929): 763–64.

Shen Min 沈珉. *Xiandai xing de lingyifu miankong: Wanqing zhi minguo de shukan xingtai yanjiu* 現代性的另一副面孔：晚清至民國的書刊形態研究 [Another face of modernity: Books and periodicals in late Qing and Republican China]. Beijing: Zhongguo shuji chubanshe, 2015.

Shibata Shōkyoku 柴田宵曲. *Shibata Shōkyoku bunshū* 柴田宵曲文集 [Collection of Shibata Shōkyoku's essays]. Tokyo: Ozawa shoten, 1991.

Shih, Shu-mei. "Global Literature and the Technologies of Recognition." *PMLA/Publications of the Modern Language Association of America* 119, no. 1 (2004): 16–30.

Shih, Shu-mei. *The Lure of the Modern: Writing Modernism in Semicolonial China, 1917–1937*. Berkeley: University of California Press, 2001.

Shōji Sensui 庄司浅水. *Insatsu bunka shi* 印刷文化史 [History of print culture]. Tokyo: Insatsu gakkai shuppanbu, 1957.

Short, T. L. *Peirce's Theory of Signs*. Cambridge: Cambridge University Press, 2007.

Shuichi Nakayama. "The Impact of William Morris in Japan, 1904 to the Present." *Journal of Design History* 9, no. 4 (1996): 273–83.

Shuixian 水仙. "Tan kaiben (shang)" 談開本（上）[On format (part 1)]. *Kaiming* 開明, no. 28 (1930): 1–2.

Shuixian 水仙. "Tan kaiben (xia)" 談開本（下）[On format (part 1)]. *Kaiming* 開明, no. 29 (1931): 1–2.

272   Bibliography

Silverstein, Michael. "Translation, Transduction, Transformation: Skating 'Glossando' on Thin Semiotic Ice." In *Translating Cultures: Perspectives on Translation and Anthropology*, edited by Paula G. Ruben and Abraham Rosman, 75–108. Oxford: Berg, 2003.

Sin Chŏngho. "Pukhan ŭi Chungguk munhak yŏn'gu (1949–2000)" [Study of Chinese literature in North Korea (1949–2000)]. *Chungguk hakpo* 49 (2004): 339–58.

Sin Ŏnjun. "Chungguk ŭi taemunho No Sin pangmun'gi" [Visiting Lu Xun, the literary giant of China]. *Sin Tonga*, April 1934, 150–52.

Slaughter, Joseph R. *Human Rights, Inc.: The World Novel, Narrative Form, and International Law*. New York: Fordham University Press, 2007.

Sŏ Ŭnsuk. "Han'guk tokcha ŭi Chungguk munhak pŏnyŏngmul e taehan insik kwa p'yŏngga yŏn'gu: 2008-yŏndo ch'ulgan Chungguk sosŏl pŏnyŏngmul ŭl chungsim ŭro" [Study of Korean readers' perception and evaluation of translations of Chinese literature: With a focus on translations of Chinese novels published in 2008]. *Chunggukhak yŏn'gu* 50 (2009): 519–38.

Son Chibong. "21-segi Chung-Han munhak pŏnyŏk ŭi hyŏnhwang kwa chŏnmang" [The present state and prospect of twenty-first-century Sino-Korean literary translation]. *Han-Chung inmunhak yŏn'gu* 48 (2015): 63–85.

Song Binghui 宋炳輝. "Cong Zhong'E wenxue jiaowang kan Lu Xun 'Kuangren riji' de xiandai yiyi—jian yu Guogeli tongming xiaoshuo bijiao" 從中俄文學交往看魯迅《狂人日記》的現代意義：兼與果戈理同名小説比較 [Looking at the modern meaning of Lu Xun's "Diary of a madman" from the angle of Sino-Russian literary interactions—and comparison with Gogol's story of the same name]. *Zhongguo bijiao wenxue* 中國比較文學, no. 4 (2014): 133–40.

Spitta, Sylvia. *Between Two Waters: Narratives of Transculturation in Latin America*. Houston: Rice University Press, 1995.

Spivak, Gayatri Chakravorty. "Three Women's Texts and a Critique of Imperialism." *Critical Inquiry* 12, no. 1 (1985): 243–61.

Starre, Alexander. "The Pleasures of Paper: Tethering Literature to Obsolete Material Forms." In *Cultures of Obsolescence: History, Materiality, and the Digital Age*, 127–44. New York: Palgrave Macmillan, 2015.

Sun Fuyuan 孫伏園. *Lu Xun xiansheng er san shi* 魯迅先生二三事 [Two or three stories about Mr. Lu Xun]. 2nd ed. Shanghai: Zuojia shuwu, 1944.

Sun Qilin 孫啟林. "Lu Xun he ta de Chaoxian duzhe" 魯迅和他的朝鮮讀者 [Lu Xun and his Korean readers]. In *Lu Xun yanjiu ziliao* 魯迅研究資料 [Lu Xun studies sourcebook], edited by Beijing Lu Xun bowuguan Lu Xun yanjiushi 北京魯迅博物館魯迅研究室 [Lu Xun Research Center, Beijing Lu Xun Museum], 11:433–42. Tianjin: Tianjin renmin chubanshe, 1983.

Sun Fuxi 孫福熙. "Chuban shiye de yishu" 出版事業的藝術 [The art of publishing]. *Shenbao* 申報, September 15, 1926, 25.

Sun Yu 孫郁. *Lu Xun yu Eguo* 魯迅與俄國 [Lu Xun and Russia]. Beijing: Renmin wenxue chubanshe, 2015.

Suzuki Keiko. "Kindai nihon shuppan gyō kakuritsu ki ni okeru Ōkura Shōten" 近代日本出版業確立期における大倉書店 [Okurashoten during the formative period of modern Japanese publishing]. *Eigaku shi kenkyū*, no. 18 (1986): 101–13.

Takeuchi Yoshimi 竹内好. *Ro Jin* 魯迅 [Lu Xun]. Tokyo: Miraisha, 1961.

Takeuchi Yoshimi. *What Is Modernity? Writings of Takeuchi Yoshimi*. Translated by Richard F. Calichman. New York: Columbia University Press, 2005.

Talens, Jenaro. "Revolució de la literatura I literatura de la revolució" [Literature's revolution and revolution's literature]. In *Sobre la classe intel·lectual* by Lu Hsun [Lu Xun], translated by Joan Francesc Mira, 9–42. Valencia. Tres i Quatre, 1973.

Tam, Kwok-kan. *Chinese Ibsenism: Reinventions of Women, Class, and Nation*. Singapore: Springer, 2019.

Tan Zhenxiang 譚鎮詳. "Guanyu zhuangding" 關於裝訂 [About binding]. *Kaiming* 開明 1, no. 1 (1928): 46.

Thornber, Karen. *Empire of Texts in Motion: Chinese, Korean, and Taiwanese Transculturations of Japanese Literature*. Cambridge, MA: Harvard University Asia Center, 2009.

Toda, Eduard. *La vida en el Celeste Imperio* [Life in the Celestial Empire]. Madrid: El Progreso Editorial 1887.

Tolstoy, L. N. *"Bethink Yourselves." Tolstoy's Letter on the Russo-Japanese War*. Boston: American Peace Society, 1904.

Trotsky, Leon. *Literature and Revolution*. Edited by William Keach. Translated by Rose Strunsky. Chicago: Haymarket Books, 2005.

Trouillot, Michel-Rolph. *Silencing the Past: Power and the Production of History*. Boston: Beacon, 2015.

Valera, Luis. *Sombras chinescas: Recuerdos de un viaje al celeste imperio* [Chinese shadows: Memories of a trip to the celestial empire]. Madrid: La Viuda é Hijos de Tello, 1902.

Veblen, Thorstein. *The Theory of Leisure Class*. Oxford: Oxford University Press, 2009.

Veg, Sebastian. "Democratic Modernism: Rethinking the Politics of Early Twentieth-Century Fiction in China and Europe." *boundary 2* 38, no. 3 (2011): 27–65.

Veg, Sebastian, "New Readings of Lu Xun: Critic of Modernity and Re-inventor of Heterodoxy." *China Perspectives* 3 (2014): 49–56.

Vinyes, Ramon. "Xina" [China]. *Meridià*, no. 31 (1938): 5.

Wang, Baorong. "George Kin Leung's English Translation of Lu Xun's *A Q Zhengzhuan*." *Archiv orientální* 85, no. 2 (2017): 253–53.

Wang, David Der-wei. "Introduction: Worlding Literary China." In *A New Literary History of Modern China*, 1–28. Cambridge, MA: Harvard University Press, 2018.

Wang, David Der-wei. *The Monster that Is History:History, Violence, and Fictional Writing in Twentieth-Century China*. Berkeley: University of California Press, 2004.

Wang Fen 王墳. "Duzhe de yijian" 讀者的意見 [Reader's opinions]. *Kaiming* 開明 1, no. 2 (1928): 93–94.

Wang Furen 王富仁. *Lu Xun qianqi xiaoshuo yu Eluosi wenxue* 魯迅前期小説與俄羅斯文學 [Lu Xun's early fiction and Russian literature]. Tianjin: Tianjin jiaoyu chubanshe, 2008.

274 Bibliography

Wang Hui 汪暉. *Shiji de dansheng: Zhongguo geming yu zhengzhi de luoji* 世紀的誕生：中國革命與政治的邏輯 [The birth of the century: The Chinese revolution and the logic of politics]. Beijing: Sanlian shudian 2020.

Wang Hui. "Depoliticized Politics, from East to West." *New Left Review* 41 (September/October 2006): 29–45.

Wang Jiaping 王家平. "Lu Xun fanyi wenxue yanjiu de xiangdu yu chuangxin" 魯迅翻譯文學研究的向度與創新 [The direction and innovation of the study of Lu Xun's literature translation]. *Guangming ribao* 光明日報. 2016. http://www.nopss.gov.cn/BIG5/n1/2016/1208/c373410-28934260.html.

Wang, Pu. "Poetics, Politics, and Ursprung/Yuan: On Lu Xun's Conception of Mara Poetry." *Modern Chinese Literature and Culture* 23, no. 2 (2011): 34–63.

Wang, Pu. "The Promethean Translator and Cannibalistic Pains: Lu Xun's 'Hard Translation' as a Political Allegory." *Translation Studies* 6, no. 3 (2012): 324–38.

Wang, Pu. *The Translatability of Revolution, Guo Moruo and Twentieth-Century Chinese Culture*. Cambridge, MA: Harvard East Asian Monographs, 2018.

Wang Xiangyuan 王向遠. "'Yaxiya zhuyi' 'Dadongya zhuyi' jiqi yuyong wenxue" "亞細亞主義" "大東亞主義" 及其御用文學 ["Asianism," "greater East Asianism" and their imperial literature]. *Mingzuo xinshang* 名作欣賞 25 (2015): 53–61.

Wang Xirong 王錫榮. "Lu Xun de 'shijieren' gainian he shijie de 'ren' gainian" 魯迅的"世界人" 概念和世界的 "人" 概念 [Lu Xun's concept of "global humans" and the concept of "man" in the world]. 2013. http://www.chinawriter.com.cn/bk/2013-09-11/72238.html.

Wang Yanting 王燕亭. "Guojia tushuguan baocun benshuku minguo maobian shu diaoyan" 國家圖書館保存本書庫民國毛邊書調研 [Investigation of the National Library collection of Republican-era *maobian* books]. *Tushuguan lilun yu shijian* 圖書館理論與實踐, no. 6 (2013): 51–52.

Wang Yougui 王友貴. *Fanyijia Lu Xun* 翻譯家魯迅 [Lu Xun, the translator]. Tianjin: Nankai daxue chubanshe, 2005.

Wellek, René. *A History of Modern Criticism 1750–1950*. Vol. 2. New Haven: Yale University Press, 1955.

Whitehead, P. J. P. "Darwin in Chinese: Some Additions." *Archives of Natural History* 15, no. 1 (1988): 61–62.

Williams, Raymond. *Marxism and Literature*. Oxford: Oxford University Press, 1977.

Wittgenstein, Ludwig. *Philosophical Investigations*. 4th ed. Translated by G. E. M. Anscombe, P. M. S. Hacker, and Joachim Schulte. Chichester: Wiley-Blackwell, 2009.

Wong Bik-wan 黃碧雲. *Lielaozhuan* 烈佬傳 [Biography of a lad]. Hong Kong: Tiandi chuban, 2012.

Wong Bik-wan 黃碧雲. "Moxiang shenghuo, wenxue yu shijie" 默想生活，文學與世界 [Vita contemplativa, literature and the world]. July 20, 2014, Hong Kong Book Fair, speech.

Wong Bik-wan 黃碧雲. "Yiwang zhi biyao, lixing zhi biran, weixiao zhi bixu—Lishi yu xiaoshuo de kuanrong" 遺忘之必要、理性之必然、微笑之必須—歷史與小說的寬容 [The necessity of forgetfulness, the ineluctability of reason, the indispensability of smiles—on history and novelistic tolerance]. In *Diwujie Hongloumeng jiang pinglunji:*

Huang Biyun Lielaozhuan 第五屆紅樓夢獎評論集：黃碧雲《烈佬傳》[Collected criticisms for the Fifth Dream of the Red Chamber Award: Wong Bik-wan's *Lielaozhuan*], 22–40. Hong Kong: Tiandi tushu, 2016.

Wong Bik-wan 黃碧雲. 2016. "Yuyan wuyong, chenmo keshang: Hongloumengjiang dejiang ganyan" 言語無用，沉默可傷：紅樓夢獎得獎感言 [Speech is futile, silence is hurtful: Dream of the Red Chamber Award acceptance speech]. In *Diwujie Hongloumeng jiang pinglunji: Huang Biyun Lielaozhuan* 第五屆紅樓夢獎評論集：黃碧雲《烈佬傳》 [Collected criticisms for the Fifth Dream of the Red Chamber Award: Wong Bik-wan's *Lielaozhuan*], 13–20. Hong Kong: Tiandi tushu, 2016.

Wong, Lawrence Wang-chi. "The Beginning of the Importation of New Literature from Exotic Countries into China: Zhou Zuoren and *Yuwai xiaoshuoji*." *Asia Pacific Translation and Intercultural Studies* 1, no. 3 (2014): 175–91.

Wong, Wang-chi. *Politics and Literature in Shanghai: The Chinese League of Left-Wing Writers, 1930–1936*. Manchester: Manchester University Press, 1991.

Xian Liqiang 咸立強. *Xunzhao guisu de liulangzhe: Chuangzao she yanjiu* 尋找歸宿的流浪者：創造社研究 [Wanderers looking for destiny: Research on the Creation Society]. Shanghai: Dongfang chuban zhongxin, 2006.

Xiao Chun 肖純. "Guanyu shukan kaiben" 關於書刊開本 [On the format of books and periodicals]. *Keji yu chuban* 科技與出版, no. 11 (2010): 39.

Xie, Haiyan. "'Grabbism' and Untranslatability: Reinterpreting Lu Xun's Position as a Translator." *Comparative Literature Studies* 57, no. 1 (2020): 126–47.

Xie Miao 謝淼. "'Shijie wenxue' zhong de 'A Q zhengzhuan' zaoqi yijie" "世界文學"中的《阿Q正傳》早期譯介 [The early translations and introductions of *The Real Story of Ah Q* in world literature]. *Zhongguo wenxue yanjiu* 中國文學研究 4 (2020): 174–80.

Xiong Ying 熊鷹. "Lu Xun dewen cangshu zhong de 'shijie wenxue' kongjian" 魯迅德文藏書中的"世界文學"空間 [The "World Literature" space in Lu Xun's German book collections]. *Wenyi yanjiu* 文藝研究, no. 5 (2017): 38–46.

Xu Beichen 徐北辰. "Ping 'Haiyan'" 評 '海燕' [On "Seagull"]. *LXQJ* 6: 541.

Xu Bochun 徐伯純. "Guanyu zhuangding" 關於裝訂 [On book binding]. *Kaiming* 開明 1, no. 1 (1928): 46.

Xu Guangping 許廣平. *Xu Guangping wenji* 許廣平文集 [The collected works of Xu Guangping]. Nanjing: Jiangsu wenyi chubanshe, 1998.

Xu Jiu'an 許久庵. "Wo de yijian zhi pianpian de buchong" 我的意見之片片的補充 [Addition to the fragments of my opinions]. *Kaiming* 開明 2, no. 2 (1929): 87.

Xu Rong 徐榮. "Tan kaiben ji kaiben zhulu" 談開本及開本著錄 [On format and documentation]. *Tushuguan zazhi* 圖書館雜誌, no. 4 (1982): 31–32.

Yang Bin 楊斌. "Lu Xun yu Yu Dafu: Teshu de youyi" 魯迅與郁達夫：特殊的友誼 [Lu Xun and Yu Dafu: A special friendship]. *Geren tushuguan* 個人圖書館, July 25, 2019. http://www.360doc.com/content/19/0725/11/7442640_850907953.shtml.

Yi Kwangsu. "Chŏnjaenggi ŭi chakkajŏk t'aedo" [Stance of wartime writers]. *Chosŏn Ilbo*, January 6, 1936.

Yi Kwangsu. "What Is Literature?" [Munhak iran hao]. Translated by Jooyeon Rhee. *Azalea: Journal of Korean Literature & Culture* 4 (2011): 293–313.

276 Bibliography

Yi Kwangsu. *Yi Kwangsu chŏnjip* [Complete works of Yi Kwangsu]. Vol. 8. Seoul: Usinsa, 1979.

Yi Kyehong. "Chungguk munhak chakp'um chal p'allinda" [Chinese literary works sell well]. *Tonga Ilbo*, June 3, 1991.

Yi Myŏngsŏn. *Yi Myŏngsŏn chŏnjip* [Complete works of Yi Myŏngsŏn]. Vol. 2. Edited by Kim Chunhyŏng. Seoul: Pogosa, 2007.

Yi Ren 以仁, and Quan Ping 全平. "Guanyu 'Yi': Tongxin liangze" 關於憶：通信兩則 [On *Memories*: Two letters]. *Hongshui* 洪水 2, no. 13 (1926): 36–39.

Yi Ugyŏn. *Lu Swin ingnŭn pam, na rŭl ingnŭn sigan* [Nights reading Lu Xun, hours reading myself]. Seoul: Hyumŏnisŭt'ŭ, 2020. Google Play E-book.

Yi Yŏnghŭi. *Chayuin, chayuin: Yi Yŏnghŭi kyosu ŭi segye insik* [Free man, free man: Professor Yi Yŏnghŭi's perception of the world]. Seoul: Pŏmusa, 1990.

Yi Yŏnghŭi. "Lu Swin egesŏ palgyŏn hanŭn onŭl ŭi uri" [Ourselves today discovered in Lu Xun]. In L*Ach'im kkoch'ŭl chŏnyŏge chupta: Lu Swin sanmunjip* [Morning flowers collected in the evening: Collected prose of Lu Xun], 2nd ed., translated and edited by Yi Ugyŏn, 5–9. Seoul: Yemun, 2003.

Yi Yuksa. *Yi Yuksa chŏnjip* [Complete works of Yi Yuksa]. Edited by Kim Yongjik and Son Pyŏnghŭi. Seoul: Kipŭn saem, 2004.

Yin Huai 陰槐. "Wo de yijian zhi pianpian" 我的意見之片片 [Fragments of my opinions]. *Kaiming* 開明 1, no. 11 (1929): 655.

Yiu, Angela. "Delivering Lu Xun to the Empire: The Afterlife of Lu Xun in the Works of Takeuchi Yoshimi, Dazai Osamu, and Inoue Hisashi." In *The Affect of Difference: Representations of Race in East Asian Empire*, edited by Christopher P. Hanscom and Dennis Washburn, 328–46. Honolulu: University of Hawai'i Press, 2016.

Yu, Anthony, trans. *Journey to the West*. Vol. 1. Chicago: University of Chicago Press, 2012.

Yu Dafu 郁達夫. "Jige wenti" 幾個問題 [A few questions]. *Sin Chew Jit Pao* 星洲日報, January 18, 1939.

Yu Gong 愚公. "Wo yelai gongxian yidian yijian" 我也來貢獻一點意見 [Let me also contribute some thoughts]. *Kaiming* 開明 2, no. 4 (1929): 243.

Yu Ta-Fu, Lao Sheh, Lu Sin, and Mao Tun. *Diez grandes cuentos chinos* [Ten great Chinese short stories]. Translated by Poli Délano and Luis Enrique Délano. Santiago de Chile: Quimantú, 1971.

Yuan Shimin 原石民. "Maobian zhuangding yulun" 毛邊裝訂餘論 [Supplementary thoughts on *maobian* binding]. *Yusi* 語絲, no. 149 (1927): 179–80.

Yue, Gang. *The Mouth that Begs: Hunger, Cannibalism, and the Politics of Eating in Modern China*. Durham, NC: Duke University Press, 1999.

Yuen Siu-cheung 袁兆昌. "Huang Biyun: Wanzi Lielao youhua shuo" 黃碧雲：灣仔烈佬有話說 [Wong Bik-wan: Wanchai *lielao* has things to say]. In *Diwujie Hongloumeng jiang pinglunji: Huang Biyun Lielaozhuan* 第五屆紅樓夢獎評論集：黃碧雲《烈佬傳》 [Collected criticisms for the Fifth Dream of the Red Chamber Award: Wong Bik-wan's *Lielaozhuan*]. Hong Kong: Tiandi tushu, 2016, 172.

Zhang Chuntian 張春田. "Cong Nuola chuzou dao Zhongguo gaizao: Jianji Lu Xun yu 'qimeng' huayu zhi guanxi" 從娜拉出走到中國改造——兼及魯迅與'啟蒙'話語之關係

[From Nora's departure to China's reforms: With an additional discussion on the relationship between Lu Xun and the discourse of "Enlightenment"]. *Wenyi lilun yu piping* 文藝理論與批評, no. 2 (2008): 38–42.

Zhang Chuntian 張春田. *Sixiangshi shiye zhong de "Nuola": Wusi qianhou de nüxing jiefang huayu* 思想史視野中的"娜拉"：五四前後的女性解放話語 [Nora in intellectual history: The discourse of the emancipation of women around the May Fourth]. Taipei: Xinrui wenchuang, 2013.

Zhang, Huiwen. "Lu Xun contra Georg Brandes: Resisting the Temptation of World Literature." *EU-topías (Interculturality, Communication, and European Studies)* 14 (2017): 135–45.

Zhang Kangwen 張康文. "'Mahua Lu Xun' yu 'Dongya Lu Xun'—duihua de keneng yu bukeneng" "馬華魯迅"與"東亞魯迅"——對話的可能與不可能 [The possibility and impossibility of dialogue between "Malaysian Chinese Lu Xun" and "East Asian Lu Xun"]. In *Nanyang Lu Xun: Jieshou yu yingxiang* 南洋魯迅：接受與影響 [South Seas Lu Xun: Acceptance and influence], edited by Sixiang bianji weiyuanhui 思想編輯委員會, 187–200. Taipei: Lianjing chubanshe, 2020.

Zhang Lihua 張麗華. "'Yiwen' yu chuangzao: Lu Xun 'Yao' zhong 'hongbai de hua' yu 'wuya' de youlai" '譯文'與創造：魯迅'藥'中'紅白的花'與'烏鴉'的由來 ["Mistranslation" and creation: The origin of the "red and white flowers" and the "crow" in Lu Xun's "Medicine"]. *Zhongguo xiandai wenxue yanjiu congkan* 中國現代文學研究叢刊1 (2016): 64–78.

Zhang Longxi. *From Comparison to World Literature*. New York: State University of New York Press, 2015.

Zhang Songjian 張松建. *Wenxin de yitong: Xinma huawen wenxue yu Zhongguo xiandai wenxue lunji* 文心的異同：新馬華文文學與中國現代文學論集 [The similarities and differences in the heart of literature: Essays on new Malaysian Chinese literature and modern Chinese literature]. Beijing: Zhongguo shehui kexue chubanshe, 2013.

Zhang Taiyan 章太炎. *Zhuzi xue lüeshuo* 諸子學略說 [Discursive comments on pre-Qin thinkers]. In *Zhang Taiyan zhenglun xuanji* 章太炎政論選集 [A collection of Zhang Taiyan's political essays], edited by Tang Zhijun 湯志鈞, 1:285–306. Beijing: Zhonghua shuju, 1977.

Zhang, Yingjin. "Mapping Chinese Literature as World Literature." *CLCWeb* 17, no. 1 (March 2015): 1–10.

Zhang, Yue. "Evolución de las imágenes chinas en la poesía de Lorca" [The evolution of Chinese images in Lorca's poetry]. *Círculo de Lingüística Aplicada a la Comunicación*, no. 74 (2018): 133–46.

Zhang Zhuyun 張竹筠. "Wuxiang yu xiangzheng: Lu Xun de 'Changming deng' he Jiaerxun de 'Hong hua' zhi bijiao" 物象與象征——魯迅的《長明燈》和迦爾洵的《紅花》之比較 [Image and symbol: A comparison of Lu Xun's "Lamp of Eternity" and Garshin's "Red Flower"]. *Hebei shifan daxue xuebao* 河北師範大學學報 8 (1991): 49–51.

Zhou Haiying 周海嬰. "Chonghui Shanghai yi tongnian" 重回上海憶童年 [Returning to Shanghai and recalling my childhood]. In *Lu Xun huiyilu* 魯迅回憶錄 [Memories of Lu Xun], 3:1237–72. Beijing: Beijing chubanshe, 1999.

Zhou Haiying 周海嬰. *Lu Xun yu wo qishi nian* 魯迅與我七十年 [Lu Xun and I for seventy years]. Haikou: Nanhai chuban gongsi, 2001.

Zhou Zuoren 周作人. "Guanyu Lu Xun zhi'er" 關於魯迅之二 [About Lu Xun, Part 2]. In *Guadou ji* 瓜豆集 [The collection of melons and beans], 161–69. Shijiazhuang: Hebei jiaoyu chubanshe, 2002.

Zhou Zuoren 周作人. *Lu Xun de gujia* 魯迅的故家 [Lu Xun's family]. Shijiazhuang: Hebei jiaoyu chubanshe, 2002.

Zhou Zuoren 周作人. *Lu Xun xiaoshuo li de renwu* 魯迅小説裡的人物 [The characters in Lu Xun's fiction]. Shanghai: Shanghai chuban gongsi, 1954.

Zhou Zuoren 周作人. "Qi Ming an" 啟明案 [Qi Ming's remarks]. *Yusi* 語絲, no. 149 (1927): 20.

Zhou Zuoren 周作人. "Zai shi Dongjing (Lu Xun de qingnian shidai shi'er)" 再是東京（魯迅的青年時代十二）[Another account on Tokyo (Lu Xun's Youth 12)]. In *Zhou Zuoren sanwen quanji* 周作人散文全集 [Complete collection of prose by Zhou Zuoren], edited by Zhong Shuhe, 12:614–18. Guangxi: Guangxi shifan daxue chubanshe 2009.

Zhou Zuoren 周作人, trans. "Yueren yangke" 樂人揚珂 [Janko Muzykant]. In *Yuwai xiaoshuo ji* 域外小説集, 1–10. Tokyo: Kanda insatsujo, 1909.

Zhu Yongfang 朱永芳. "A Lei sanwen 'yimian' xiugai pingxi" 阿累散文"一面"修改評析 [Analysis of the revision of Ah Lei's essay "One Meeting"]. *Yuwen yuekan* 語文月刊, no. 4 (2011): 21.

Zhu Yuhong 祝宇紅. *Gushi ruhe xinbian: Lun Zhongguo xiandai chongxie xing xiaoshuo* 故事如何新編：論中國現代重寫型小説 [How old tales were retold: On modern Chinese fiction of rewriting old tales]. Beijing: Peking University Press, 2010.

Zhuang Huaxing 莊華興. "Lu Xun zai lengzhan qianqi de Malaiya yu Xinjiapo" 魯迅在冷戰前期的馬來亞與新加坡 [Lu Xun in Malaya and Singapore in the early Cold War period]. In *Nanyang Lu Xun: jieshou yu yingxiang* 南洋魯迅：接受與影響 [South Seas Lu Xun: Acceptance and influence], edited by Sixiang bianji weiyuanhui 思想編輯委員會, 201–17. Taipei: Lianjing chubanshe, 2020.

Index

Page numbers in *italics* refer to figures and tables.

absolute, the, 223–25. *See also* universality in world literature
Adorno, Theodor, 2, 181
aesthetic irony, 213, 214
"Ah Chang and the *Classic of Mountains and Seas*," 206–8
Ah Fu, 167–70, *171*, 239
Aho, Juhani, 3, 47
"Alexander Blok," 29–30
allegory, recuperating subaltern occlusions, 149–55
"Amateur Talk on Literature" (Lu Xun), 65–66
Anderson, Benedict, 156
Anderson, Marston, 151, 158, 196
Andreev, Leonid, 54–58, 63
Angela Yiu, 140–42
animal training, essay on, 232–33
animality in Lu Xun's works, 16, 221; "child's ox," 235–37; critique of domination, 227–30; "Dogs, Cats, Mice," 237; polemics between Lu Xun and Liang Shiqiu, 233–37; references to animals, 226–27, 237–38; as sociopolitical critique, 230–33
Anthology of Fiction from beyond the Border (Lu Xun and Zhou Zuoren), 12–13; compilation approach, 34; deckleedges, 89–91; dissemination in Japan, 7; front cover, 40, *41* fig 2.2 and 2.3, 89 fig 5.2; German works, 43, *44* table

2.1; inspiration from "Red Flower" (Garshin), 58–59; modernity critique, 87–91; origins, 38–40; works from minor languages, 43
Aoki Masaru, 103
Apter, Emily, 11
Arts and Crafts Movement, 84, 85
Asnyk, Adam, 3
Aus fremden Zungen, 34, 35–40, *41* fig 2.1, 43
authorship, 212
autobiographical memoir, 198–200

Badiou, Alain, 26, 27, 29
Bassoe, Pedro, 91
Bastman, Ida, 8
Baudelaire, Charles, 24–25
Beauvoir, Simone de, 9
Beijing Lu Xun Museum, 43
Belizón, Manuel Pavón, 127
"Benediction" (Ng Kim Chew), 167, 169–71, 174, 239
"Ben-Tovit" (Andreev), 54–58
"Bethink Yourselves" appeal (Tolstoy), 135
Bildung, 219
Blanco Facal, Rosario, 125
Blok, Alexander, 29–31
body, philosophy of, 186–89
Brandes, Georg, 20, 22
Brehm, Alfred, 228
Brière, Octave, 8

280   Index

British Arts and Crafts Movement, 85
Brooks, Peter, 133
Buch, Hans Christoph, 9, 10
Buck, Pearl, 120, 121
"Buyi" (Ng Kim Chew), 166
Byron, George Gordon (Lord Byron), 132

Camus, Albert, 162
Caragiale, Luca Ion, 3
Casanova, Pascale, 21–22, 162
Catalan translations, 125, 126
causality in transnational interactions, 117, 129
Chang Kigŭn, 108
Cheah, Pheng, 11, 23–24, 161
Chekhov, Anton, 9, 124
Cheng, Anne, 112–13
Cheng, Eileen, 4, 74–75, 132
Chetyre (Garshin), 58–59
Chiang Kai-shek, 108, 109
children's literature, 228
"child's ox," 235–37
China: 1911 revolution (first Chinese
    Revolution), 26; Cultural Revolution,
    109–10, 122, 123, 153, 168; economic
    development and modernization,
    179; Japanese colonial rule, 103–5;
    May Fourth era (loosely 1917–1925),
    24–29, 69, 74–77; May Fourth
    Movement, 103, 163, 166
Chinese Communist Party (CCP), 229,
    234, 235
Chinese exceptionalism, 179, 231–32
Chinese League of Leftist Writers, 141–42,
    236
Chinese literature: government-sponsored
    translation, 10; interaction with world
    literature, 11–12
Chinese national character/Chineseness,
    133; Confucian values, 153–54; post-
    imperial identity of China, 155–61
Chinese woodcut movement, 111
Chon Hyŏngjun, 111

Chow Mei-nan, 158
Chuanzong, Fang, 83–84, 93
circulation as a metaphor, 117–18
Cissarz, Johann Vincenz, 37
Clifford, James, 175
Cold War, 107–9, 112
Collected Short Stories of Lu Xun, 105–6
confession, as theme as Lu Xun's writing,
    132–33
Confucian values, 150–51, 152–54, 190–93
Conrad, Sebastian, 117, 129
cosmopolitanism, 39–40
Creation Society, 182, 188, 219, 222
Crescent School, 234
Cultural Revolution, 109–10, 122, 123,
    153, 168

Damrosch, David, 1–2, 5, 68, 115, 131
Daodejing, 15
Daoism, 15, 180–82, 187–88, 191
Davies, Gloria, 1
Dazai Osamu, 14, 133, 137–41
de Staël, Germaine, 39
death: Graves (Lu Xun), 202–3; of Lu Xun,
    104, 163, 225, 237; Lu Xun's death
    mask, 239–41, 240 fig. 15.1; portrayed
    in Wild Grass, 200–202
deckle-edged books: Anthology of Fiction
    from beyond the Border, 89–91; conten-
    tion about in early twentieth-century
    China, 83–84; as modernity critique,
    84–87; the paradox of revolution,
    95–98; and social class, 95–96,
    97–98
Deleuze, Gilles, 115–16
democracy, 155–61
Derrida, Jacques, 172
Destino magazine, 122–23
"Diary of a Madman" (Lu Xun): compari-
    son to Garshin's "Red Flower," 62, 63;
    Dazai's work based on, 139; dehu-
    manization in, 229; self-introspection,
    198–99; translations, 123; use of

techniques from Gogol's Diary, 51–54, 63; writing intention, 196

distortions (*qubi*), 51, 52, 57, 58–59, 197

"Dogs, Cats, Mice" (Lu Xun), 237

Dole, Andrew, 191

Doll's House, A (Ibsen), 13, 68, 69, 77–81

East Germany, 8–9

Eastern European literature, 5, 34

Eckermann, Johann Peter, 1

economic development of China, 179

Elements of the Philosophy of Right and his Aesthetics (Hegel), 213

English translations of Lu Xun's works, 7, 8, 56

Enlightenment, 193

Etherington, Ben, 11

ethnic groups in China, 231–32

European literature: Lu Xun's collection, 5, 43–47; naturalist school, 77; North–South divide, 39, 45

European-Romantic poetic works, 21

Ewald, Carl, 228

exchange students, 7

Fabre, Jean-Henri, 228

Fadeyev, Alexander, 97–98

"fair play," 215–16

fairy tales, 228

"family resemblances," 81–82

Feng Naichao, 234

filiation, 172–73

"fin-de-siècle" style, 37

Finnish literature: Päivärinta, 45–47; Runeberg, 46–47

Finnish translations, 8, 9–10

Foreign Languages Press, 10

forgiveness, 143

"French binding," 96. *See also* deckle-edged books

French literature, 36–37, 39

French translations, 7

Freud, Sigmund, 184–85

Gänger, Stefanie, 117–18

Gao Xingjian, 125, 127

Garshin, Vsevolod, 58–62, 63

gender: female oppression, 205–6; feminist literature, 73; women's rights, 69–70, 74, 79–81

German works: in *Anthology of Fiction*, 34–35, 43; Lu Xun's access to, 3–4

German, as intermediary language, 4, 50

Germany: *Anthology of Fiction from beyond the Border*, 38–40, 43; book series of world literature, 40–47; magazines of world literature, 35–40; politics in dissemination, 8–9; *Weltliteratur*, 1–2, 10–11, 33–35

ghostwriting: recuperating subaltern occlusions in national allegory, 149–55; as term, 149

Gjalski, Ksaver Šandor, 3

"Glimpse at Shanghai Literature, A" (Lu Xun), 217–22

Goethe, Johann Wolfgang von, 1–2, 35, 181

Gogol, Nikolai, 51–54, 63

Golden, Seán, 125

Goyo, Hashiguchi, 86

grabbism, 4–5, 49–50, 63, 183

Graves (Lu Xun), 202–3, 202 fig 12.3

Great East Asia Joint Manifesto (Dazai), 138–39

guangbian, 93–94

Guattari, Félix, 115–16

guilt, as theme as Lu Xun's writing, 132–33

Gunn, Janet Varner, 200

Guo Moruo, 15, 179–94

Hakuson, Kuriyagawa, 25

Han Chinese, 231–32

Han Sŏrya, 107

Hanan, Patrick, 45

hard translation approach, 4–5, 31

Hashimoto, Satoru, 102, 115

Hayot, Eric, 21

Hegel, G. W. F., 212, 213–15, 220–21, 224

282   Index

Heidegger, Martin, 11
hermeneutics of suspicion, 180, 185
Hisashi, Inoue, 14, 133, 141–45
"Hometown" (Lu Xun), 104–5
Hong Hyomin, 106–7
Hong Sokp'yo, 113
"Hope" (Lu Xun), 24–29
Horkheimer, Max, 181
Hsia, C. T., 181
Hsu, Sung-nien (also known as Xu
    Songnian), 7
Hu Shi, 70–71, 103
Hughes, Glen, 193
Hungarian Revolution, 27–28
Hwang Sogyong, 111

I Am a Cat (Soseki), 86–88, *86* fig 5.1, 91,
    96–97
Ibsen, Henrik, 13, 68, 69–81. See also *A
    Doll's House*
Ichiyo, Higuchi, 71–81
The Illustrated Twenty-Four Exemplars (Lu
    Xun), 199
Im Hŏnyŏng, 111, 110
immigrants, role in circulating Lu Xun's
    works, 7
"In the Wilderness" (Päivärinta), 46–47
"Inauspicious Star" (Lu Xun), 208
Inoue Hisashi, 14, 133, 141–45
intellectuals, relationship to the masses,
    49
international circulation of Lu Xun's works,
    5–8. *See also* world literature
intertextual engagement: Russian literature,
    49–50, 51, 54, 58, 63; subaltern alter-
    ity, 147–48
"Intra-Asian Reading; or, How Lu Xun
    Enters into a World Literature"
    (Hashimoto), 115
Italian translations, 124

Japan: Japanese-style modernity, 139; Lu
    Xun's career in, 3–4; physical form of

the book, 87; Russo-Japanese War,
    134–35; Sino-Japanese War, 134
Japanese: "Alexander Blok" translation,
    29–30; high score of Lu Xun in
    Japanese exam, 133–34; as inter-
    mediary language, 4, 50
Japanese literature: feminist writers, 73; Lu
    Xun as part of, 133, 137–45
"Jige wenti" (Yu Dafu), 163
Jones, Andrew F., 233
kai system, 94–95
Kaminski, Joannes D., 181
Kelmscott Press, 85, 97
Kierkegaard, Søren, 212
Kim Chunyŏp, 107
Kim Il Sung, 111–12
Kim Kwanggyun, 106
Kim Kwangju, 105–6, 108
Kim T'aejun, 104, 106
Kim Young Sam, 112
"Kong Yiji" (Lu Xun), 7, 148, 161–62
Korea: 1990s onwards, 112–16; Cold War
    rivalries, 107–9; first mention of Lu
    Xun, 103; liberation space, 105–7;
    perceptions about Japanese colonial
    rule of China, 103–5; reception and
    translation of Lu Xun's works in,
    13–14, 101–3, 113–16; social move-
    ments, 109–12
Korean War (1950–1953), 107
Kowallis, Jon Eugene von, 20
Krasnyi tzvetok (Garshin), 58–62
Kürschner, Joseph, 37–38
Kyn, Jean Baptiste Yn-Yu, 7

"Lamp of Eternity" (Lu Xun), 58, 59–62, 63
Laozi legend, 15, 179–84, 185–93
law: ethics of revolution, 217–22; "immod-
    est jurisprudence," 213; Lu Xun's
    approach to, 210–11, 223–25
Le spleen de Paris (Baudelaire), 24–25
League of Left-Wing Writers, 141–42, 236
leftism. *See* political left

Lee, Leo Ou-fan, 136
"leisure," 96
Leung, George Kin, 7
Leys, Simon, 128
Li Liewen, 231
Liang Shiqiu, 227, 233–37
Lichtensein, Gustav, 45–46
Lielaozhuan (Wong Bik-wan), 14, 146–55
Lin Yutang, 215–16, 226–27
Ling Fei (pen name), 19
Liu Bannong, 56–57
Lizcano, Pablo, 124–25
Lloyd, Vincent, 213
Loa Ho, 6
loneliness, as literary theme, 25, 26
Lovell, Julia, 5
Lu Xun: canonization as father of modern
    Chinese literature, 197–200; circula-
    tion of works outside of China, 5–8;
    death, 104, 163, 225, 237; death mask,
    239–41, *240* fig. 15.1; high score in
    Japanese exam, 133–34; last piece of
    published writing, 230–31; names
    and pen names, 243; Nobel Prize
    nomination, 6; ongoing popularity
    of, 5, 241–42; politics in dissemina-
    tion, 8–10; publications list, 243–48;
    reading of and engagement with world
    literature, 3–5; son (Zhou Haiying),
    172, 241; supporting younger writers/
    virtual children, 171–75; works as part
    of world literature, 1–2, 5–6, 10–12;
    writing intentions and trajectories,
    195–97
"Lu Xun and I" (Yi Yonghui), 109
"Lu Xun fever," 163–64
"Lu Xun" (Kim Kwanggyun), 106
Lunacharsky, Anatoly, 31–32
"Luxunology," 2

"M de shizong" (Ng Kim Chew), 164–65
Ma, Xiaolu, 118
magazines of world literature, 35–40

Malraux, André, 120
Mani, Venkat, 35
Mao Zedong: cult of, 9; "On Lu Xun,"
    197–98; "On New Democracy,"
    107–8; Spanish interest in, 122; "Talks
    at the Yan'an Forum on Literature and
    Art," 174–75; use of Mao's poetry in
    Ng Kim Chew's "Benediction," 168;
    Yan'an talks, 174, 229; in Yi Yonghui's
    writings, 109–10
maobian: contention about in early
    twentieth-century China, 83–84,
    93–94; as modernity critique, 84–87;
    the paradox of revolution, 95–98; and
    social class, 95–96, 97–98
Mara poetry, 19, 20–24, 38, 132–33
Marín-Lacarta, Maialen, 123–24
Marxism: mixing with Chinese thinking,
    193–94; political and intellectual
    legacy, 172; relay translation, 31
Masako, Kitaoka, 20, 22, 28
May Fourth humanism, 229
May Fourth Movement, 103, 163, 166
May Fourth nationalism, 158, 161
May Fourth period, 24–29, 69, 74–77
"Medicine" (Lu Xun), 54–58, 63, 229
Meng Su, article in *Shanghai Daily*, 230–31
Mills, Harriet, 9
Mira, Joan Francesc, 124
"The Misanthrope" (Lu Xun), 226
missionaries, 7–8
Mo Yan, 127
modernity: critique in *Anthology of Fiction
    from beyond the Border*, 87–93;
    Japanese vs Western, 139; in Lu Xun's
    works, 212–13; *maobian*, 84–87
Moretti, Franco, 21
Morning Blossoms (Lu Xun), 15; aesthetic
    and philosophic direction, 197;
    autobiographical nature, 198–200;
    effacement, 197–208; front cover, *198*
    fig 12.1; representation, 208–9; shared
    existence, 203–204

"Morning Flowers Collected in the Evening: Collected Prose of Lu Xun" (Yi Ugyon), 112
Morris, William, 85–87, 97
multispecies approach to world literature, 16
"My Old Hometown" (Lu Xun), 7, 170, 174

Naedong, Chong, 104
Nagahori Yuzo, 31
Nanyang (South Seas) region, 163
"nation of human beings," 5, 132
national allegory, 65–66, 149–55
National Revolution (1925–1927), 24
nationalism, 39–40
Nationalist government, 234–35
"native peoples," 231–32
native soil literature, 50–51
naturalist school, 77
New Culture Movement, 60, 163, 196–97
"new voices from alien lands," 4, 5, 31, 45
"New Year's Sacrifice" (Lu Xun), 168–69, 170
Ng Kim Chew, 14–15, 164–66, 167, 169–72, 173, 239–41
Nietzsche, Friedrich, 132, 184–85
nihilism, 180–81
Noboru, Maruyama, 26
Nolla, Fernando Perez-Barreiro, 125
nonhuman animals, 16, 221. See animality in Lu Xun's works; "child's ox," 235–37; critique of domination, 227–30; "Dogs, Cats, Mice," 237; polemics between Lu Xun and Liang Shiqiu, 233–37; references to animals, 226–27, 237–38; as sociopolitical critique, 230–33
nonresistance theory, 138, 142
norm: ethics of revolution, 217–22; Lu Xun's approach to, 210–11, 223–25; "Why 'Fair Play' Should Be Deferred" (Lu Xun), 215–17
normativity, 24

Novelas escogidas (Foreign Language Press), 121

Ogai, Mori, 71–72
Okuda Koka, 239, 240 fig. 15.1
Old Tales Retold (Lu Xun), 125–26
Ollé, Manel, 126
"On Lu Xun" (Mao Zedong), 197–98
"On New Democracy" (Mao Zedong), 107–8
Onjun, Sin, 104
Outcry (Lu Xun), 69–70, 136, 155, 195–96

Paekhwa, Yang, 103–4
page size, 94–95
Päivärinta, Pietari, 45–47
Pak Chaeu, 111, 114
Pak Honggyu, 113
Pak Hŭngbyŏng, 111
Pak Kyŏngni, 108–9
Park Chung Hee, 109, 110
Peirce, Samuel, 239
periodization, 24–25, 26, 28–29
Petőfi, Sandor, 19, 20, 22, 25, 27–29
Philipp, Anton, 42
phonocentrism, 155
Pitol, Sergio, 123–24
poetry, 12; Mara poetry, 19, 20–24, 38, 132–33; and revolution, 29–32
polemics, between Lu Xun and Liang Shiqiu, 233–37
political left, 6, 234; animality in Lu Xun's works, 230–33, 237–38; empire, nation, and democracy, 155–61; Korea, 112; League of Left-Wing Writers, 141–42; Lu Xun as figurehead, 9–10, 234; Western suspicion, 9
politics in dissemination, 8–10
Porcel, Baltasar, 122–23, 128
postimperial identity of China, 155–61
postmodernism, 223–24
Preciado, Iñaki, 124

pre-Qin, 180–81
Presas, Marisa, 125
private property, 217
Prometheus myth, 31–32
property rights, 217
prose poems, 24–29
Pusey, James, 227

Qi Shoushan, 228
Qian Liqun, 229
Qian Xingcun, 104
qubi (distortions), 51, 52, 57, 58–59, 197

Ramírez, Laureano, 125–26
Reclam Verlag (Reclam Publisher), 40–42
"Red Flower" (Garshin), 58–62
Red Laugh (Andreev), 57
"Regrets for the Past" (Lu Xun), 73–77
Regrettable Parting (Osamu), 137, 138
rehabilitation, as theme as Lu Xun's writing, 132–33
relationality, 203–6
relay translation, 29–32, 110–111, 124
repentance, as theme as Lu Xun's writing, 132–33, 134
Republican Revolution, 23, 67, 103
resistance, nationalist mythology, 223
revolution: of 1911 (first Chinese Revolution), 26; Cultural Revolution, 109–10, 122, 123, 153, 168; laws and norms, 217–22; paradox of, 95–98; poetry of Lu Xun, 23, 26, 29–32
Ricoeur, Paul, 180, 183–84, 185
Riedl, Frederick, 27–28
Robins, Christopher, 142
Rolland, Romain, 131–32
Rose, Gillian, 211–15, 217–22, 223–24
Routes (Clifford), 175
Runeberg, Johan Ludvig, 46–47
Russian literature, 13; *Aus fremden Zungen*, 36–37; "Ben-Tovit" (Andreev), 54–58; *Krasnyi tzvetok* (Garshin), 58–62; Lu Xun's engagement with, 49–51, 62–64;

Zapiski sumasshedshego (Gogol), 51–54
Russo-Japanese War, 134–35

Said, Edward, 175
Sala-Sanahuja, Joaquim, 128
Salvat Editores, 122, 123–24
Saryang, Kim, 102
"savage peoples," 231–32
Sawade, Richard, 232–33
Schmid, Andre, 101
"scholar-hooligan," 218–21
scientific literature, 227–28
Selected Works of Lu Xun (Korean National Press), 107
self-awakening, 197–200
self-transcendence, 180
Sendai Medical Academy, Japan, 133–34
"severe style," 213–15
sexual violation dream, 173–74
Shanghai Daily, 230–31, 232
"Shanghai Literature" (Lu Xun), 217–22
Shanghai, "Lu Xun fever," 163–64
Shanghai Moon (Hisashi), 141–42
Shelley, Percy Bysshe, 132
Shiao, Miguel, 124
Shih, Shu-mei, 6
Shiji (Sima Qian), 181–82
Shinju, Oneki, 96
Shuixian (pen name), 94–95
"Si zai nanfang" (Ng Kim Chew), 165–66
"Silence" (Andreev), 56–57
Sima Qian, 181–82
Sin Chŏngho, 111
Sinervo, Elvi, 9–10
singularity, 203–6
Sino-Japanese War (1894–1895), 134
Sinocentrism, 114
Slaughter, Joseph, 210–11
slave mentality, 159
Slavic literature, 5
social class: "Lamp of Eternity" (Lu Xun), 61; *maobian* debate, 95–96, 97–98;

286 Index

polemics between Lu Xun and Liang Shiqiu, 234

Society of Jesus, 8

Soseki, Natsume, 85–87, 91, 92, 96–97

South Korean Liberation Front, 110

South Seas region, 163

Southeast Asia, Lu Xun's works transported to, 163, 164

space, temporality of reading, 93–95. *See also* physical form of the book

Spain: China in Spain before Lu Xun, 119–21; reception and translation of Lu Xun's works in, 14, 118, 121–27; Spanish language context, 118–19, 129–30; translation of Chinese literature in wider context, 127–30

Specters of Marx (Derrida), 172

spectral filiation, 172–73

speculative experience, 212–13

Spitta, Sylvia, 102

Spivak, Gayatri Chakravorty, 161

Sun Fuxi, 96–97

Sun Wukong, 241–42

Sun Yu, 138

"suspended temporality," 180, 193–94

suspicion, spirit of, 182–85

"take-ism," 223

Takeuchi Yoshimi, 110–11, 211

Talens, Jenaro, 124, 128

"Talks at the Yan'an Forum on Literature and Art" (Mao Zedong), 174–75, 229

temporality of reading, 93–95

"The Thirteenth Night" (Ichiyo), 77–81

Thornber, Karen, 102

Tolstoy, Leo, 134–37, 140, 142

Tolstoyan figure, Lu Xun as, 137–38

To Chongil, 112–13

transculturation: Lu Xun in Korea, 101–3, 105–9, 114–16; as term, 102

translations: *Anthology of Fiction from beyond the Border*, 12–13; enriching Chinese literature, 90; hard translation

approach, 4–5, 31; Lu Xun's career in translation, 3–5; of Lu Xun's works, 65; relay translation, 29–32, 110–11, 124

translations of Lu Xun's works: into Catalan, 125, 126; Chinese government-sponsored translations, 10; into Czech, 65; into English, 7, 8, 56; into Esperanto, 65; into Finnish, 8; into French, 8, 65; into German, 10, 65; into Japanese, 7, 65; into Korean, 65, 101–2, 103–4, 105, 113–16; into more than seventy languages, 5–7, 118; into Russian, 65, 67–68; into Spanish, 118, 120, 121–27

Trotsky, Leon, 29–31

Trouillot, Michel-Rolph, 150–51

"The True Story of Ah Q" (Lu Xun): authorial design, 66–67; conception of world literature, 68; Confucian values, 150–51; estrangement, 66; illustrating China's society and culture, 128; in Korea, 103–4, 108–9; national allegory, 65–66; rereading through Wong Bik-wan's *Lielaozhuan*, 146–55, 160–61; in Spain, 122; status as literature, 67–68; worlding, 161–62

Tusquets, 123–24

"The Twelve" (Blok), 29–30

uncut books. *See* deckle-edged books

"The Unfinished Works of Lu Xun" (Yi Myongson), 106

Universal-Bibliothek, 40–43

universality in world literature, 15–16, 210–11, 217, 223–25

utilitarianism, 96

van Eeden, Frederik, 228

Vazov, Ivan, 3

Vinyes, Ramon, 120–21

"voice of the heart," 5

"Voiceless China" (Lu Xun), 65–66

Wang, Chi-chen, 9

Wang, David Der-wei, 11–12, 51–52, 136–37

Wang Hui, 23

Wang Lan, 108

"We Are All Lu Xun's Children," 171–75

weixin, 233

Weltliteratur, 1–2, 10–11, 33–35

West Germany, 8–9

Western modernity, 139

What Is Global History? (Conrad), 117

"Why 'Fair Play' Should Be Deferred" (Lu Xun), 143, 215–17

Wild Grass (Lu Xun), 15, 200–202; aesthetic and philosophic direction, 197; effacement, 197–208; front cover, *201* fig 12.2; "Hope" included in, 24; relationality and singularity, 204–6; representation, 208–9; surrender to the other, 206–8

Wilde, Oscar, 199

Williams, Raymond, 130

Wittgenstein, Ludwig, 68, 81–82

"The Wizard" (Päivärinta), 46, 47

women's rights, 69–70, 74, 79–81

Wong Bik-wan, 14, 146–49; ghostwriting, 149–55; rereading "The True Story of Ah Q" through Wong's *Lielaozhuan*, 146–55, 160–61; reverse influence on Lu Xun, 148–49

world literature: definition, 5, 10–11; era of (*Weltliteratur*), 1–2, 10–11; global flows, 117–18; Lu Xun's reading of and engagement with, 3–5; Lu Xun's works as part of, 5–6, 10–12, 68; Mara essay, 20–22. *See also* international circulation of Lu Xun's works

world making, 15

world poetry, 12

worlding: as concept, 11–12, 15; suspended temporality and the worlding of nontranscendence, 193–94; "The True Story of Ah Q" (Lu Xun), 161–62

Xinsheng (planned but never published journal), 38

Xu Guangping, 227, 236–37

Xu Songnian (also known as Sung-nien Hsu), 7

Xu Su, 108

Yang, Gladys, 10

Yang Paekhwa, 103

Yang Xianyi, 10

Ye Lingfeng, 219

Yeroshenko, Vasyl, 228

Yi Kawŏn, 108

Yi Kwangsu, 101–2

Yi Kyuhae, 111

Yi Myŏngsŏn, 106, 108

Yi Pyŏngju, 109

Yi Ugyon, 114, 115

Yi Yonggyu, 105–6, 108

Yi Yonghui, 109–10

Yi Yuksa, 104–5, 115

Yoshimi, Takeuchi, 135–36

youth, as literary theme, 26–27

Yu Dafu: compositions after disappearance, 164–67; "Lu Xun fever," 163–64

Yu Kisok, 103

Zapiski sumasshedshego (Gogol), 51–54

Zhang Lihua, 56–57

Zhang, Yingjin, 11

Zhou Haiying (son of Lu Xun), 172, 241

Zhou Yang, 236

Zhou Zuoren: *Aus fremden Zungen*, 37–38; bibliographic revolution, 84; compiling the *Anthology of Fiction Beyond the Border*, 34; German works, 3–4; Japanese translation of "Kong Yiji," 7; *maobian* debate, 95; Russian literature, 58–59; valorization of translation, 90; works from minor languages, 40–42. See also *Anthology of Fiction from beyond the Border*

zhuan, 66

"Zhufu" [Benediction] (Ng Kim Chew),
167, 169–71
Zimbler, Jarad, 11
Zola, Émile, 37